MCP Mathematics

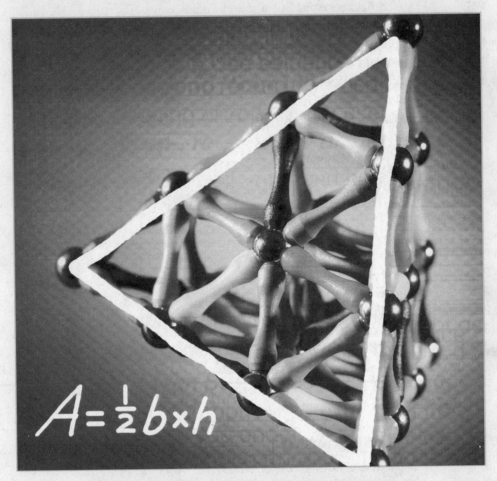

$$A = \tfrac{1}{2}\,b \times h$$

Richard Monnard • Royce Hargrove

ISBN 0-7652-6064-6
Printed in the United States of America
1   19

Project Staff

Art & Design:	Robert Dobaczewski, Kathleen Ellison, Senja Lauderdale, David Mager, Jim O'Shea, Angel Weyant
Editorial:	Stephanie P. Cahill, Gina Dalessio, Phyllis Dunsay, Mary Ellen Gilbert, Dena Kennedy, Theresa McCarthy, Marilyn Sarch
Marketing:	Doug Falk, Clare Harrison
Production/ Manufacturing:	Irene Belinsky, Lawrence Berkowitz, Louis Campos, Diane Fristachi, Pamela Gallo, Leslie Greenberg, Suellen Leavy, Ruth Leine, Karyn Mueller, Michele Uhl
Publishing Operations:	Carolyn Coyle, Richetta Lobban

Dale
Seymour
Publications
Pearson Learning Group

1-800-321-3106
www.pearsonlearning.

Contents

Contents

Chapter (8) Add and Subtract Fractions

Chapter (9) Multiply and Divide Fractions

Chapter (10) Add and Subtract Decimals

Contents

Chapter ⑮ Graphs, Statistics, and Probability

Chapter ⑯ Equations, Integers, and Graphs

CHAPTER 1

Name Ava Joy W.

Numbers and Place Value

Addition and Subtraction Facts

It's Algebra!

The fifth-grade class has entered 13 animals in the school pet show. Write two addition and two subtraction equations using the numbers of puppies, kittens, and pets.

We are looking for the two addition and two subtraction facts that make a **fact family**.

We know the sum or total number of pets in the show is ___13___.

There are ___7___ puppies and ___6___ kittens entered.

To write the addition facts, we add the **addends**, ___7___ and ___6___.

$$8 + 5 = \underline{13}$$
puppies kittens pets

$$8 + 5 = \underline{13}$$
addends sum

To write the subtraction facts, we subtract ___8___ and ___5___ from the total number of pets.

subtrahend ↓

$$13 - 5 = \underline{8}$$
pets kittens puppies

$$13 - 5 = \underline{8}$$
minuend difference

The fact family for 5, 8, and 13 is made of two ___Addition___ facts and two ___Subtraction___ facts.

$$\begin{array}{r} 8 \\ +5 \\ \hline 13 \end{array} \qquad \begin{array}{r} 5 \\ +8 \\ \hline 13 \end{array} \qquad \begin{array}{r} 13 \\ -5 \\ \hline 8 \end{array} \qquad \begin{array}{r} 13 \\ -8 \\ \hline 5 \end{array}$$

Getting Started

Write the fact family for each set of numbers.

1. 2, 4, 6

2+4=6   6-4=2
4+2=6   6-2=4

2. 7, 15, 8

8+7=15   15-8=7
7+8=15   15-7=8

Add or subtract.

3. 16 − 9 = ___7___

4.
$$\begin{array}{r} 7 \\ +3 \\ \hline 10 \end{array}$$

Practice

Write the fact family for each set of numbers.

1. 3, 4, 7
   - 3+4=7
   - 4+3=7
   - 7-4=3
   - 7-3=4

2. 2, 9, 7
   - 7+2=9
   - 2+7=9
   - 9-7=2
   - 9-2=7

3. 6, 7, 13
   - 6+7=13
   - 7+6=13
   - 13-7=6
   - 13-6=7

4. 8, 0, 8
   - 8+0=8
   - 0+8=8
   - 8-8=0
   - 8-0=8

5. 12, 5, 7
   - 5+7=12
   - 7+5=12
   - 12-5=7
   - 12-7=5

6. 9, 17, 8
   - 9+8=17
   - 8+9=17
   - 17-9=8
   - 17-8=9

7. 7, 1, 8
   - 7+1=8
   - 1+7=8
   - 8-7=1
   - 8-1=7

8. 11, 6, 5
   - 6+5=11
   - 5+6=11
   - 11-6=5
   - 11-5=6

Add or subtract.

9. $7 + 2 = \underline{9}$

10. $3 + 1 = \underline{4}$

11. $11 - 5 = \underline{6}$

12. $14 - 7 = \underline{7}$

13. $7 + 6 = \underline{13}$

14. $8 - 5 = \underline{3}$

15. $8 + 0 = \underline{8}$

16. $10 - 8 = \underline{2}$

17. $15 - 8 = \underline{7}$

18. $9 + 6 = \underline{15}$

19. $5 + 9 = \underline{14}$

20. $16 - 8 = \underline{8}$

21. $\begin{array}{r} 11 \\ -\ 8 \\ \hline 3 \end{array}$

22. $\begin{array}{r} 8 \\ +\ 7 \\ \hline 15 \end{array}$

23. $\begin{array}{r} 10 \\ -\ 4 \\ \hline 6 \end{array}$

24. $\begin{array}{r} 9 \\ -\ 0 \\ \hline 9 \end{array}$

25. $\begin{array}{r} 10 \\ -\ 7 \\ \hline 3 \end{array}$

26. $\begin{array}{r} 1 \\ +\ 5 \\ \hline 6 \end{array}$

27. $\begin{array}{r} 6 \\ +\ 6 \\ \hline 12 \end{array}$

28. $\begin{array}{r} 9 \\ -\ 3 \\ \hline 6 \end{array}$

29. $\begin{array}{r} 10 \\ -\ 7 \\ \hline 3 \end{array}$

30. $\begin{array}{r} 15 \\ -\ 6 \\ \hline 9 \end{array}$

31. $\begin{array}{r} 8 \\ +\ 9 \\ \hline 17 \end{array}$

32. $\begin{array}{r} 8 \\ +\ 4 \\ \hline 12 \end{array}$

33. $\begin{array}{r} 6 \\ +\ 9 \\ \hline 15 \end{array}$

34. $\begin{array}{r} 6 \\ -\ 1 \\ \hline 5 \end{array}$

35. $\begin{array}{r} 12 \\ -\ 6 \\ \hline 6 \end{array}$

36. $\begin{array}{r} 7 \\ +\ 5 \\ \hline 12 \end{array}$

37. $\begin{array}{r} 9 \\ +\ 9 \\ \hline 18 \end{array}$

38. $\begin{array}{r} 2 \\ +\ 6 \\ \hline 8 \end{array}$

39. $\begin{array}{r} 4 \\ +\ 9 \\ \hline 13 \end{array}$

40. $\begin{array}{r} 9 \\ -\ 1 \\ \hline 8 \end{array}$

41. $\begin{array}{r} 7 \\ +\ 3 \\ \hline 10 \end{array}$

42. $\begin{array}{r} 8 \\ -\ 8 \\ \hline 0 \end{array}$

43. $\begin{array}{r} 11 \\ -\ 4 \\ \hline 7 \end{array}$

44. $\begin{array}{r} 6 \\ +\ 5 \\ \hline 11 \end{array}$

45. $\begin{array}{r} 1 \\ +\ 0 \\ \hline 1 \end{array}$

46. $\begin{array}{r} 14 \\ -\ 5 \\ \hline 9 \end{array}$

47. $\begin{array}{r} 5 \\ +\ 7 \\ \hline 12 \end{array}$

48. $\begin{array}{r} 3 \\ -\ 2 \\ \hline 1 \end{array}$

49. $\begin{array}{r} 10 \\ -\ 1 \\ \hline 9 \end{array}$

50. $\begin{array}{r} 7 \\ +\ 8 \\ \hline 15 \end{array}$

Lesson 1-1 • Addition and Subtraction Facts

Addition Properties

Addition properties are like special tools.
They make it easier to work with numbers.

Commutative Property

You can add in any order.

$5 + 2 = 7$ $\qquad$ $2 + 5 = 7$

$3 + 6 + 7 =$ __16__ $\qquad$ $7 + 3 + 6 =$ __16__

Associative Property

You can change the grouping.
REMEMBER Add the numbers in parentheses first.

$(6 + 3) + 5 = 14$ $\qquad$ $6 + (3 + 5) = 14$

$(8 + 2) + 4 =$ __14__ $\qquad$ $8 + (2 + 4) =$ __14__

Identity Property

Adding zero does not change a number.

$5 + 0 = 5$ $\qquad$ $0 + 7 = 7$ $\qquad$ $0 + 1 =$ __1__ $\qquad$ $8 + 0 =$ __8__

Here are some other useful things to know about zero.
- Subtracting zero does not change a number. $\qquad$ $9 - 0 = 9$ $\qquad$ $7 - 0 =$ __7__
- Subtracting a number from itself leaves zero. $\qquad$ $8 - 8 = 0$ $\qquad$ $3 - 3 =$ __0__

Adding and subtracting are **inverse operations**.
You can subtract to check addition.

$15 - 9 = 6$ because $6 + 9 = 15$ $\qquad$ $12 - 7 =$ __5__ because __5__ + __7__ = __12__

REMEMBER Solving for n is finding the value for n in an equation.

Getting Started

Solve for n.

1. $0 + 0 = n$

$\qquad$ $n =$ __0__

2. $0 + 6 = n$

$\qquad$ $n =$ __6__

Subtract. Check by adding.

3.	15	**4.**	12	**5.**	18
	$-\ 9$		$-\ 7$		$-\ 9$
	6		5		9

Add. Check by grouping the addends another way.

6.	5	**7.**	2	**8.**	6
	3		6		3
	$+\ 4$		$+\ 3$		$+\ 4$
	12		11		13

9. $(5 + 2) + 6 = n$

$\qquad$ $n =$ __13__

10. $(5 + 1) + 6 = n$

$\qquad$ $n =$ __12__

Practice

Solve for n.

1. $5 + 0 = n$

   $n = \underline{5}$

2. $6 - 0 = n$

   $n = \underline{6}$

3. $0 - 0 = n$

   $n = \underline{0}$

4. $9 - 9 = n$

   $n = \underline{0}$

5. $5 + 8 = n$

   $n = \underline{13}$

6. $8 + 5 = n$

   $n = \underline{13}$

7. $9 + 7 = n$

   $n = \underline{16}$

8. $9 + n = 16$

   $n = \underline{7}$

Subtract. Check by adding.

9. $\begin{array}{r} 11 \\ -\ 6 \\ \hline 5 \end{array}$

10. $\begin{array}{r} 15 \\ -\ 7 \\ \hline 8 \end{array}$

11. $\begin{array}{r} 14 \\ -\ 5 \\ \hline 9 \end{array}$

12. $\begin{array}{r} 16 \\ -\ 8 \\ \hline 8 \end{array}$

13. $\begin{array}{r} 14 \\ -\ 7 \\ \hline 7 \end{array}$

14. $\begin{array}{r} 6 \\ -\ 6 \\ \hline 0 \end{array}$

15. $\begin{array}{r} 17 \\ -\ 8 \\ \hline 9 \end{array}$

16. $\begin{array}{r} 12 \\ -\ 5 \\ \hline 7 \end{array}$

17. $\begin{array}{r} 13 \\ -\ 6 \\ \hline 7 \end{array}$

18. $\begin{array}{r} 15 \\ -\ 6 \\ \hline 9 \end{array}$

19. $\begin{array}{r} 11 \\ -\ 8 \\ \hline 3 \end{array}$

20. $\begin{array}{r} 14 \\ -\ 9 \\ \hline 5 \end{array}$

Add. Check by grouping the addends another way.

21. $\begin{array}{r} 4 \\ 3 \\ +\ 2 \\ \hline 9 \end{array}$

22. $\begin{array}{r} 7 \\ 2 \\ +\ 6 \\ \hline 15 \end{array}$

23. $\begin{array}{r} 8 \\ 1 \\ +\ 4 \\ \hline 13 \end{array}$

24. $\begin{array}{r} 4 \\ 3 \\ +\ 5 \\ \hline 12 \end{array}$

25. $\begin{array}{r} 5 \\ 2 \\ +\ 6 \\ \hline 13 \end{array}$

26. $\begin{array}{r} 7 \\ 1 \\ +\ 7 \\ \hline 15 \end{array}$

27. $(8 + 0) + 6 = n$

    $n = \underline{14}$

28. $2 + (4 + 5) = n$

    $n = \underline{11}$

29. $(4 + 4) + 5 = n$

    $n = \underline{13}$

30. $6 + (2 + 3) = n$

    $n = \underline{11}$

31. $(1 + 6) + 3 = n$

    $n = \underline{10}$

32. $7 + (3 + 5) = n$

    $n = \underline{15}$

Now Try This!

Arrange the numbers 1 through 10 into 5 pairs of numbers so that the paired numbers have the sums of 6, 7, 9, 16, and 17.

$\underline{3} + \underline{3} = 6$ $\underline{3} + \underline{4} = 7$ $\underline{5} + \underline{4} = 9$

$\underline{8} + \underline{8} = 16$ $\underline{8} + \underline{9} = 17$

Lesson 1-2 • Addition Properties

Name _____

Practice Addition and Subtraction Facts

✓

Add.

1.
$\begin{array}{r} 2 \\ +1 \\ \hline 3 \end{array}$
$\begin{array}{r} 7 \\ +2 \\ \hline 9 \end{array}$
$\begin{array}{r} 7 \\ +4 \\ \hline 11 \end{array}$
$\begin{array}{r} 1 \\ +3 \\ \hline 4 \end{array}$
$\begin{array}{r} 1 \\ +8 \\ \hline 9 \end{array}$
$\begin{array}{r} 2 \\ +3 \\ \hline 5 \end{array}$
$\begin{array}{r} 3 \\ +2 \\ \hline 5 \end{array}$
$\begin{array}{r} 7 \\ +9 \\ \hline \end{array}$
$\begin{array}{r} 1 \\ +4 \\ \hline 5 \end{array}$

2.
$\begin{array}{r} 3 \\ +0 \\ \hline 3 \end{array}$
$\begin{array}{r} 5 \\ +5 \\ \hline \end{array}$
$\begin{array}{r} 8 \\ +6 \\ \hline 14 \end{array}$
$\begin{array}{r} 6 \\ +0 \\ \hline 6 \end{array}$
$\begin{array}{r} 0 \\ +6 \\ \hline 6 \end{array}$
$\begin{array}{r} 2 \\ +9 \\ \hline 11 \end{array}$
$\begin{array}{r} 3 \\ +1 \\ \hline 4 \end{array}$
$\begin{array}{r} 6 \\ +3 \\ \hline 9 \end{array}$
$\begin{array}{r} 6 \\ +5 \\ \hline 11 \end{array}$

3.
$\begin{array}{r} 9 \\ +1 \\ \hline 10 \end{array}$
$\begin{array}{r} 7 \\ +0 \\ \hline 7 \end{array}$
$\begin{array}{r} 5 \\ +2 \\ \hline 7 \end{array}$
$\begin{array}{r} 2 \\ +2 \\ \hline 4 \end{array}$
$\begin{array}{r} 1 \\ +2 \\ \hline 3 \end{array}$
$\begin{array}{r} 2 \\ +6 \\ \hline 8 \end{array}$
$\begin{array}{r} 9 \\ +4 \\ \hline 13 \end{array}$
$\begin{array}{r} 5 \\ +3 \\ \hline 8 \end{array}$
$\begin{array}{r} 7 \\ +3 \\ \hline 10 \end{array}$

4.
$\begin{array}{r} 0 \\ +9 \\ \hline 9 \end{array}$
$\begin{array}{r} 9 \\ +9 \\ \hline 18 \end{array}$
$\begin{array}{r} 3 \\ +3 \\ \hline 6 \end{array}$
$\begin{array}{r} 1 \\ +6 \\ \hline 7 \end{array}$
$\begin{array}{r} 9 \\ +0 \\ \hline 9 \end{array}$
$\begin{array}{r} 0 \\ +2 \\ \hline 2 \end{array}$
$\begin{array}{r} 7 \\ +7 \\ \hline 14 \end{array}$
$\begin{array}{r} 0 \\ +3 \\ \hline 3 \end{array}$
$\begin{array}{r} 4 \\ +7 \\ \hline 11 \end{array}$

5.
$\begin{array}{r} 7 \\ +8 \\ \hline \end{array}$
$\begin{array}{r} 5 \\ +6 \\ \hline 11 \end{array}$
$\begin{array}{r} 1 \\ +1 \\ \hline 2 \end{array}$
$\begin{array}{r} 2 \\ +4 \\ \hline 6 \end{array}$
$\begin{array}{r} 5 \\ +9 \\ \hline \end{array}$
$\begin{array}{r} 2 \\ +5 \\ \hline 7 \end{array}$
$\begin{array}{r} 5 \\ +4 \\ \hline 9 \end{array}$
$\begin{array}{r} 1 \\ +0 \\ \hline 1 \end{array}$
$\begin{array}{r} 7 \\ +1 \\ \hline 8 \end{array}$

6.
$\begin{array}{r} 8 \\ +8 \\ \hline 16 \end{array}$
$\begin{array}{r} 9 \\ +2 \\ \hline 11 \end{array}$
$\begin{array}{r} 5 \\ +7 \\ \hline 12 \end{array}$
$\begin{array}{r} 1 \\ +7 \\ \hline 8 \end{array}$
$\begin{array}{r} 5 \\ +8 \\ \hline 13 \end{array}$
$\begin{array}{r} 0 \\ +4 \\ \hline 4 \end{array}$
$\begin{array}{r} 6 \\ +9 \\ \hline 15 \end{array}$
$\begin{array}{r} 6 \\ +7 \\ \hline 13 \end{array}$
$\begin{array}{r} 4 \\ +9 \\ \hline 13 \end{array}$

7.
$\begin{array}{r} 9 \\ +6 \\ \hline 15 \end{array}$
$\begin{array}{r} 5 \\ +1 \\ \hline 6 \end{array}$
$\begin{array}{r} 4 \\ +3 \\ \hline 7 \end{array}$
$\begin{array}{r} 6 \\ +1 \\ \hline 7 \end{array}$
$\begin{array}{r} 8 \\ +1 \\ \hline 9 \end{array}$
$\begin{array}{r} 2 \\ +0 \\ \hline 2 \end{array}$
$\begin{array}{r} 8 \\ +2 \\ \hline 10 \end{array}$
$\begin{array}{r} 3 \\ +8 \\ \hline 11 \end{array}$
$\begin{array}{r} 6 \\ +2 \\ \hline 8 \end{array}$

8.
$\begin{array}{r} 6 \\ +4 \\ \hline 10 \end{array}$
$\begin{array}{r} 4 \\ +0 \\ \hline 4 \end{array}$
$\begin{array}{r} 9 \\ +5 \\ \hline 14 \end{array}$
$\begin{array}{r} 0 \\ +7 \\ \hline 7 \end{array}$
$\begin{array}{r} 3 \\ +4 \\ \hline 7 \end{array}$
$\begin{array}{r} 4 \\ +1 \\ \hline 5 \end{array}$
$\begin{array}{r} 8 \\ +9 \\ \hline 17 \end{array}$
$\begin{array}{r} 4 \\ +8 \\ \hline 12 \end{array}$
$\begin{array}{r} 0 \\ +1 \\ \hline 1 \end{array}$

9.
$\begin{array}{r} 8 \\ +7 \\ \hline 15 \end{array}$
$\begin{array}{r} 1 \\ +5 \\ \hline 6 \end{array}$
$\begin{array}{r} 6 \\ +6 \\ \hline 12 \end{array}$
$\begin{array}{r} 3 \\ +9 \\ \hline 12 \end{array}$
$\begin{array}{r} 8 \\ +4 \\ \hline 12 \end{array}$
$\begin{array}{r} 4 \\ +2 \\ \hline 6 \end{array}$
$\begin{array}{r} 3 \\ +6 \\ \hline 9 \end{array}$
$\begin{array}{r} 8 \\ +3 \\ \hline 11 \end{array}$
$\begin{array}{r} 5 \\ +0 \\ \hline 5 \end{array}$

10.
$\begin{array}{r} 1 \\ +9 \\ \hline 10 \end{array}$
$\begin{array}{r} 0 \\ +8 \\ \hline 8 \end{array}$
$\begin{array}{r} 8 \\ +0 \\ \hline 8 \end{array}$
$\begin{array}{r} 0 \\ +0 \\ \hline 0 \end{array}$
$\begin{array}{r} 2 \\ +7 \\ \hline 9 \end{array}$
$\begin{array}{r} 4 \\ +5 \\ \hline 9 \end{array}$
$\begin{array}{r} 9 \\ +7 \\ \hline 16 \end{array}$
$\begin{array}{r} 9 \\ +8 \\ \hline 17 \end{array}$
$\begin{array}{r} 4 \\ +6 \\ \hline 10 \end{array}$

Subtract.

1. $3 - 1 = 2$ $1 - 0 = 1$ ✓ $12 - 4 = 8$ $9 - 4 = 5$ $10 - 7 = 3$ $7 - 7 = 0$ $8 - 1 = 7$ $14 - 5 = 9$ $6 - 0 = 6$

2. $15 - 9 = 6$ $8 - 7 = 1$ $10 - 8 = 2$ $18 - 9 = 9$ $8 - 0 = 8$ $13 - 4 = 9$ $7 - 0 = 7$ $3 - 2 = 1$ $12 - 5 = 7$

3. $8 - 4 = 4$ $11 - 3 = 8$ $8 - 6 = 2$ $4 - 0 = 4$ $9 - 0 = 9$ $10 - 4 = 6$ $11 - 4 = 7$ $5 - 3 = 2$ $1 - 1 = 0$

4. $8 - 2 = 6$ $6 - 3 = 3$ $6 - 2 = 4$ $4 - 1 = 3$ $7 - 3 = 4$ $3 - 3 = 0$ $11 - 8 = 3$ $2 - 1 = 1$ $10 - 1 = 9$

5. $9 - 2 = 7$ $7 - 1 = 6$ $5 - 5 = 0$ $5 - 0 = 5$ $15 - 8 = 7$ $4 - 3 = 1$ $13 - 5 = 8$ $10 - 3 = 7$ $5 - 1 = 4$

6. $6 - 5 = 1$ $13 - 9 = 4$ $9 - 6 = 3$ $12 - 8 = 4$ $11 - 2 = 9$ $9 - 1 = 8$ $2 - 2 = 0$ $10 - 6 = 4$ $7 - 6 = 1$

7. $16 - 9 = 7$ $15 - 7 = 8$ $7 - 5 = 2$ $14 - 9 = 5$ $17 - 8 = 9$ $12 - 6 = 6$ $8 - 5 = 3$ $12 - 7 = 5$ $5 - 4 = 1$

8. $6 - 4 = 2$ $9 - 9 = 0$ $12 - 9 = 3$ $16 - 8 = 8$ $9 - 5 = 4$ $6 - 1 = 5$ $8 - 8 = 0$ $16 - 7 = 9$ $9 - 7 = 2$

9. $11 - 9 = 2$ $11 - 7 = 4$ $4 - 2 = 2$ $11 - 6 = 5$ $11 - 5 = 6$ $15 - 6 = 9$ $7 - 4 = 3$ $2 - 0 = 2$ $14 - 6 = 8$

10. $6 - 6 = 0$ $13 - 8 = 5$ $10 - 5 = 5$ $3 - 0 = 3$ $14 - 7 = 7$ $9 - 3 = 6$ $0 - 0 = 0$ $7 - 2 = 5$ $13 - 7 = 6$

Lesson 1-3 • Practice Addition and Subtraction Facts

Place Value Through Thousands

The government space agency plans to sell used moon buggies to the highest bidders. What did Charley pay for the one he bought?

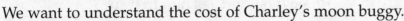

100%

We want to understand the cost of Charley's moon buggy.

Charley paid exactly _____. To understand how much money this is, we will look at the place value of each digit in the price.

REMEMBER The numbers 0, 1, 2, 3, 4, 5, 6, 7, 8, and 9 are called digits. The position of the digit decides its place value.

thousands	hundreds	tens	ones
_____	_____	_____	_____

In 7,425, the digit 4 represents hundreds, and the

digit 7 represents _____.

Numbers can be written in **standard** or **expanded form**.

Standard Form	Expanded Form
7,425	**7,000 + 400 + 20 + 5**

We say Charley paid seven thousand, four hundred

twenty-five dollars. We write _____.

Getting Started

Write in standard form.

1. five thousand, six hundred fifty-eight 5,658 ✓   2. 3,000 + 50 + 8 3,058 ✓

Write in words.

3. 6,497 ✓   4. 823 ✓   5. 9,045 ✓

Six thousand, four hu-   eight hundred, twenty-   nine thousand, fourty-

ndred, Nintey-Seven   three   five

Write the place value of each green digit.

6. 3,948   7. 9,603   8. 7,529   9. $5,370

Tens   thousands   hundreds   ones

Practice

Write in standard form.

1. eight hundred fifty-three

   853 ✓

2. six thousand, two hundred twenty-five

   6,225 ✓

3. four thousand, nine hundred

   4,900 ✓

4. three thousand, six hundred six

   3,606 ✓

5. seven thousand, twenty

   7,020 ✓

6. nine thousand, four hundred seventeen

   9,417 ✓

7. six hundred sixty-two

   662 ✓

8. three thousand, thirty-eight

   3,038 ✓

9. 7,000 + 300 + 30 + 9 = 7,339 ✓

10. 4,000 + 60 + 2 = 4,062 ✓

11. 500 + 6 = 506 ✓

12. 2,000 + 700 + 8 = 2,708 ✓

Write in words.

13. 6,257 Six thousand, two hundred fifty-seven

14. 3,209 three thousand, two hundred, nine

15. 765 Seven hundred sixty-five

16. 8,050 eight thousand, fifty

17. 89 eighty-nine

18. 4,961 four thousand, nine hundred, sixty-one

19. 2,006 two thousand, six

20. 8,863 eight thousand, eight hundred, sixty-three

21. 7,210 seven thousand two hundred, ten

22. 9,176 nine thousand, one hundred seventy-six

23. 1,311 one thousand, three hundred, eleven

24. 5,320 five thousand, three hundred, twenty

Write the place value of each green digit.

25. 9,650 ✓

    hundreds

26. 8,639 ✓

    thousands

27. 136 ✓

    tens

28. $4,257 ✓

    hundreds

29. 97

    ones ✓

30. 7,348 ✓

    tens

31. 5,090 ✓

    hundreds

32. 3,748 ✓

    thousands

33. 7,516 ✓

    ones

34. $3,259 ✓

    hundreds

35. 831 ✓

    hundreds

36. 6,547 ✓

    ones

Comparing and Ordering Numbers

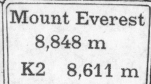

It's Algebra!

The two highest mountains on Earth are Mount Everest and K2. Which mountain ranks first as the highest point on Earth?

> **Mount Everest**
> **8,848 m**
> **K2   8,611 m**

We want to know which mountain is higher.

Mt. Everest is __8,848__ meters high, while K2 is __8,611__ meters in height.

To know which is higher, we compare the heights of the two mountains. We compare __8848__ and __8,611__.

96.8

We align the two numbers by place value and, starting at the left, compare the digits.

8,848	8,848
8,611	8,611
8 = 8	8 > 6

We say 8,848 **is greater than** 8,611 or 8,611 **is less than** 8,848.

We write 8,848 > 8,611 or 8,611 < 8,848.

__Mount Everest__ is the highest mountain on Earth.

Getting Started

Write < or > in the circle.

1. 73 ⊙< 76   2. 246 ⊙< 426   3. 3,287 ⊙> 3,247

4. 5,275 ⊙< 6,796   5. 4,572 ⊙> 4,562   6. 9,205 ⊙< 9,215

Write the numbers in order from least to greatest.

7. 5,246   4,375   6,295   8. 6,203   6,245   6,196   9. 3,058   3,028   3,167

4,375 5,246 6,295   6,196 6,203 6,245   3,028 3,058 3,167

Practice

Write < or > in the circle.

1. 67 ⬭> 63
2. 92 ⬭< 95
3. 126 ⬭> 123
4. 562 ⬭< 652
5. 309 ⬭> 299
6. 417 ⬭< 471
7. 3,644 ⬭< 4,564
8. 5,947 ⬭< 5,949
9. 3,699 ⬭> 3,000
10. 7,243 ⬭> 7,234
11. 1,006 ⬭< 1,008
12. 9,450 ⬭> 9,350
13. 6,225 ⬭> 6,224
14. 8,500 ⬭< 8,600
15. 4,060 ⬭> 4,059

Write the numbers from least to greatest.

16. 349 285 351

    255 349 351

17. 603 596 728

    596 603 728

18. 400 399 401

    399 400 401

19. 2,659 2,650 2,670

    2650 2,659 2,670

20. 7,810 7,920 7,890

    7810 7,890 7920

21. 5,236 4,868 4,976

    4,868 4,976 5,236

22. 3,965 3,695 3,569

    3,569 3,695 3,965

23. 8,196 8,194 8,190

    8,190 8,191 8,196

24. 4,210 4,021 4,110

    4,210 4,021 4,110

Problem Solving

Use the chart to answer questions 25 through 30.

25. Which mountain is the highest?
    Elbert

26. Which mountain is the lowest?
    Blanca

27. Which mountain is the fourth
    highest? LaPlata

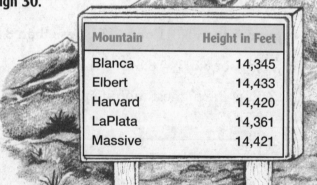

Mountain	Height in Feet
Blanca	14,345
Elbert	14,433
Harvard	14,420
LaPlata	14,361
Massive	14,421

28. How many mountains are higher than Harvard? 2

29. How many mountains are less than 14,350 feet high? 1

30. List the mountains from highest to lowest.
    Elbert, Massive, Harvard, LaPlata, Blanca

Lesson 1-5 • Comparing and Ordering Numbers

Name _____

Place Value Through Hundred Billions

95.8

India is the second most populated country in the world. How does its population compare with that of China?

We want to compare the population of India with that of China.

To understand large numbers, we need to extend the place value chart to include the billions and millions periods.

To compare these two numbers, we begin at the left and compare each pair of digits in the same place value.

Population	
India	1,049,700,000
China	1,286,975,000

The first digit of each number is the same.

billions			millions			thousands			ones		
hundreds	tens	ones	hundreds	tens	ones	hundreds	tens	ones	hundreds	tens	ones
		1	0	4	9	7	0	0	0	0	0
		1	2	8	6	9	7	5	0	0	0

In the hundred millions place, the 2 is greater than the 0.

We say 1,286,975,000 is _____ than 1,049,700,000.

We write 1,286,975,000 _____ 1,049,700,000.

We say the population of India is **one billion, forty-nine million, seven hundred thousand,** and that of China is **one billion, two hundred eighty-six million, nine hundred seventy-five thousand.**

Getting Started

1. Write in standard form: thirty-six billion, eighty-five million, two hundred fifty-three thousand, seven hundred nine. __36,085,253,709__

2. Write in words: 209,326,250,086 __Two hundred nine billion, Three hundred twenty Six million, Two hundred fifty thousand, eighty-six__

Write the place value of each green digit.

3. 6**3**9,276,439,140   4. 49,**6**57,394

   __Hundred billions__   __hundred thousand__

Write < or > in each circle.

5. 6,968,215 6,944,318

6. 13,276,493 13,726,493

Practice

Write in standard form.

1. six billion, two hundred fifteen million, three hundred thousand, twenty-nine

   6,215,300,029 ✓

2. three hundred twelve billion, six hundred twenty-seven million, fifty-five thousand

   312,627,055,000 ✓

3. ninety-six million, seven hundred forty-five thousand, eight hundred twenty-six

   96,000,745,826

4. eleven billion, four hundred eleven million, sixty-three   11,411,000,063

Write in words.

5. 5,002,939   five million, two thousand, nine hundred thirty-nine

6. 49,000,153,007   fourty nine billion, one hundred fifty three thousand, seven

7. 13,819,000,506   thirteen billion, eight hundred nineteen, five hundred six

8. 100,300,016   One hundred million, three hundred thousand, sixteen

Write the place value of each green digit.

9. 94,679,250

   millions

10. 1,236,946,000

   billions

11. 47,392,165

   ten millions

12. 126,739,475,321

   millions

13. 113,196,256

   hundred millions

14. 87,209,000,000

   ten billions

15. 326,437,792

   ten thousands

16. 675,964,286,000

   hundred billions

17. 127,096,358

   millions

18. 39,475,139,471

   billions

19. 59,736,285

   ten millions

20. 425,000,000,000

   ten billions

Write < or > in each circle.

21. 37,349,246 ⊙< 37,459,680

22. 196,475,857,216 ⊙< 196,547,857,216

23. 39,758,427,511 ⊙> 39,758,427

24. 715,426,823,976 ⊙< 751,798,156,392

Name _____

96.4%

Rounding Numbers

Soccer has become one of the world's most popular sports. Matches often attract huge crowds of people. About how many people attended this soccer match?

WEMBLEY STADIUM
CUP FINAL
TOTAL ATTENDANCE
104,647

We want to estimate the number of people who attended the soccer match.

The exact attendance was _____.

To estimate the number of people, we can round the attendance number to the nearest thousand.

> To round a number to a particular place value, locate the digit to be rounded.

If the digit to the right is 0, 1, 2, 3, or 4, the digit we are rounding stays the same. All the digits to the right are replaced by zeros.

Rounded to the nearest hundred, 104,647 is _____.

If the digit to the right is 5, 6, 7, 8, or 9, the digit we are rounding is increased by 1. All digits to the right are replaced by zeros.

Rounded to the nearest thousand, 104,647 is _____.

Rounded to the nearest thousand, there were _____ people at the soccer match.

Getting Started

Round to the nearest hundred.

1. 864   2. 15,143   3. 609,056   4. 12,450

   900   15,100   100   12,500

Round to the nearest thousand.

5. 37,295   6. 126,529   7. 53,816   8. 756,500

   3,7200   127,000   54,000   757,000

Practice

Round to the nearest hundred.

1. 926
   900

2. 3,426
   3,400

3. 5,638
   5,600

4. 6,509
   6,500

5. 11,450
   11,500

6. 16,049
   16,000

7. 48,195
   48,200

8. 23,428
   23,400

9. 216,815
   216,800

10. 139,350
    139,400

11. 786,230
    786,200

12. 526,999
    527,000

Round to the nearest thousand.

13. 6,795
    7,000

14. 4,271
    4,000

15. 3,500
    4,000

16. 8,012
    8,000

17. 15,392
    15,000

18. 86,475
    86,000

19. 11,111
    11,000

20. 74,950
    75,000

21. 423,275
    423,000

22. 638,725
    639,000

23. 819,500
    820,000

24. 324,009
    324,000

25. 751,475
    751,000

26. 279,856
    280,000

27. 380,076
    380,000

28. 437,539
    438,000

Now Try This!

Box 1

| a | b |
| c | D |

One letter is drawn from Box 1 and one number is drawn from Box 2.

One possible outcome is (a, 2). List the others.

(2a) (4a) (2b) (4b) (2c) (4c) (6a) (6b) (6c) (6d) (2d) (4d)

Box 2

| 2 | 4 |
| 6 | |

How many different outcomes are possible? ___6___

Add a letter to Box 1 and a number to Box 2.

Now how many possible outcomes are there? ___12___

Name _____

Problem Solving: Use a Four-Step Plan

Kathleen's goal is to solve six sets of Honor Problems. There are eight problems in a set. If it takes Kathleen about one and one-half hours to solve 12 problems, how many hours will it take her to solve all the problems?

100%

★ **SEE**

We want to know how long it will take Kathleen to solve all of the problems.

There are __6__ sets of problems. There are __8__ problems in each set.

It takes Kathleen one and one-half hours, or __90__ minutes, to complete __12__ problems.

★ **PLAN**

To find the total number of problems Kathleen will solve, we multiply the number of sets by the number of problems in each. We multiply __6__ by __8__. To find how many groups of 12 problems there are, we divide the total number of problems by the number she can work in the given time. We divide __48__ by __12__. To find the number of minutes it will take to solve all the problems, we multiply the number of groups of six by the number of minutes in an hour and a half.

We multiply __4__ by __90__. To rename minutes as hours, we divide the number of minutes by 60.

We divide __360__ by __60__.

★ **DO**

$$
\begin{array}{r} 6 \\ \times\ 8 \\ \hline 48 \end{array}
\text{ total problems}
$$

$$
12\overline{)48} \quad \text{groups of 12}
$$
4

$$
\begin{array}{r} 4 \\ \times\ 90 \\ \hline 360 \end{array}
\text{ minutes}
$$

$$
\begin{array}{r} 6 \\ 60\overline{)360} \\ -360 \\ \hline 0 \end{array}
\text{ hours}
$$

It will take __6__ hours to solve all of the problems.

★ **CHECK**

We can check our work by reworking our computation and asking ourselves if each answer seems reasonable.

Apply

1. Jennifer has saved $18 and Carl has saved $5. If each saves $2 a month, how many more months will it take Jennifer to have exactly twice as much as Carl? *It took 4 months.*

2. A phone call costs 50 cents for the first three minutes and 10 cents for each additional minute. If the total cost of the call was $3.50, how many minutes long was it? *It took 33 minutes.*

7. Read Problem 2 again. What if the cost of the call were $4.00 instead of $3.50? Now how many minutes long would the phone call have been? *38 minutes*

3. Design a plan showing how it would be possible to plant 10 trees in 5 rows, and have 4 trees in each row.

8. When can an eight-digit number with a 9 in the millions place be less than an eight-digit number with an 8 in the millions place? *OK*

4. A letter costs 37 cents to mail and a post card costs 23 cents. Jason sent mail to eight friends and the cost was $2.68. How many letters did Jason send? *He sent 6 letters.*

9. Manny Moneybucks won one million dollars in a contest. The prize would be paid at the rate of one thousand dollars a month. How many months would it take for Manny to get all of his prize money? *It would take 1,000 months.*

5. I have some jelly beans. When I divide them into equal groups of five, I have three left over, but when I divide them into equal groups of seven, there are six left over. I have fewer than 50 beans. How many jelly beans do I have? *he/her has 48. jelly beans.*

10. Suppose you win a contest. You have a choice of two ways to be paid the prize: $10,000 a year for the rest of your life or $1,000 a month for 1,000 months. Which way would you choose and why? *10,000 will be more because it is more money*

6. Darlene had some marbles before she won an additional 17 from Joe. Darlene then lost one-third of her marbles to her brother. If Darlene now has 34 marbles, how many did she have when she started? *She had 34 when she started.*

Name _____

Calculator: The Basic Keys

A calculator can make many operations easier. Numbers and operations are entered by pressing the keys on the keyboard. We use a calculator code to show the order in which to press the keys. Turn your calculator on, enter the codes below, and write the results on the empty screens.

5 [+] 8 [=] | 13 |

16 [−] 9 [=] | 7 |

Sometimes a key is pressed by mistake. The clear key [C] clears all entries in the calculator and returns the screen to 0. The clear-entry key [CE] cancels only the most recent entry.

Complete each code.

1. 9 [+] 8 [+] 6 [C] [=] | 0 |

3. 9 [+] 8 [+] 6 [CE] [=] | 17 |

5. 15 [−] 3 [CE] [+] 6 [=] | 21 |

2. 12 [−] 6 [−] 2 [C] [=] | 0 |

4. 12 [−] 6 [−] 2 [CE] [=] | 6 |

6. 27 [÷] 9 [C] [+] 3 [=] | 3 |

The equals key [=] is also called the constant key. It repeats the last operation and number entered.

Complete each code.

7. 3 [+] 3 [=] [=] [=] [=] | 15 |

9. 7 [+] 7 [=] [=] [=] [=] [=] | 42 |

11. 8 [+] 8 [=] [=] [=] [=] | 40 |

13. 21 [−] 7 [=] [=] [=] | 0 |

8. 12 [−] 4 [=] [=] [=] | 0 |

10. 25 [−] 5 [=] [=] [=] [=] | 5 |

12. 6 [+] 8 [=] [=] [=] [=] [=] | 46 |

14. 36 [−] 6 [=] [=] [=] [=] [=] | 6 |

Practice

Complete each code. Write each result on the screen.

1. 7 (+) 6 (=) [13]

2. 17 (−) 8 (=) [9]

3. 8 (+) 7 (=) [15]

4. 8 (−) 6 (=) [2]

5. 3 (+) 8 (+) 4 (=) [15]

6. 15 (−) 9 (+) 4 (=) [10]

7. 8 (+) 6 (+) 7 (=) [21]

8. 21 (−) 7 (−) 6 (=) [8]

9. 17 (−) 9 (+) 6 (=) [14]

10. 8 (−) 5 (+) 9 (=) [12]

11. 14 (−) 3 (+) (C) (=) [0]

12. 9 (+) 4 (−) 5 (+) 7 (C) (=) [0]

13. 13 (+) 7 (−) 7 (+) 5 (CE) (=) [13]

14. 9 (+) 6 (−) 4 (CE) (−) 7 (=) [8]

Problem Solving

Use your calculator to solve each problem.

15. Tom rode his bike 9 miles on Monday, 6 miles on Wednesday and 7 miles on Friday. How far did Tom ride his bike? 22 miles

16. Ann tried 25 free throws and made 13. Rhonda tried 20 free throws, and made 5 more than Ann. How many free throws did Rhonda make?
18 more

(Now Try This!)

Use your calculator to find the missing number in each number path.

1.
Start	Add	Subtract	Subtract	Add	Add	Finish
9	5	7	3	5	8	17

2.
Start	Add	Add	Subtract	Add	Subtract	Finish
0	7	6	8	4	9	0

3.
Start	Subtract	Add	Subtract	Add	Subtract	Finish
8	0	5	9	7	6	5

Lesson 1-9 • Calculator: The Basic Keys

Name **Ava Joy W.**

Add or subtract.

1. 5 + 9 = **14**
2. 7 + 8 = **15**
3. 15 − 6 = **9**
4. 7 − 7 = **0**

5. 4
　 +7
　 11

6. 16
　 − 9
　 7

7. 14
　 − 8
　 6

8. 9
　 − 0
　 9

9. 7
　 + 0
　 7

10. 6
　　2
　 + 3
　 11

Write the place value of each green digit.

11. 17,291
Hundreds Place

12. 603,201
Hundredthousands Place

13. 35,916
ones Place

14. 815,960,000
hundredmillions Place

Write < or > in the circle.

15. 86 **<** 96

16. 357,251,211,010 **>** 351,252,100,701

17. 67,040 **<** 76,400

18. 3,954 **>** 3,594

19. 86,751 **>** 68,975

20. 275,386 **>** 275,097

Write in standard form.

21. sixteen million, four hundred fifty-seven thousand, nine hundred four

16,457,904

22. two hundred billion, sixty-four million, seven thousand, thirty-seven

200,064,007,037

Write in words.

23. 31,405,000 **Thirty one million, four hundred five thousand.**

24. 16,008,000,000 **Sixteen billion, eight million.**

Round to the nearest hundred.

25. 3,265
3,300

26. 6,500
6,500

Round to the nearest thousand.

27. 15,638
16,000

28. 75,475
75,000

Circle the letter of the correct answer.

1 $7 + 8$

  a. 14
  b. 15
  c. 16
  d. NG

2 $16 - 7$

  a. 7
  b. 8
  c. 9
  d. NG

3
    6
    2
  + 7

  a. 8
  b. 9
  c. 17
  d. NG

4 $n + 3 = 9$
  $n = ?$

  a. 3
  b. 6
  c. 12
  d. NG

5 $4 + n = 4$
  $n = ?$

  a. 0
  b. 4
  c. 8
  d. NG

6 What is the place value of the digit 6 in 4,639 ?

  a. ones
  b. tens
  c. hundreds
  d. NG

7 What is the place value of the digit 7 in 37,186?

  a. ones
  b. tens
  c. hundreds
  d. NG

8 What is the place value of the digit 0 in 208,596?

  a. thousands
  b. ten thousands
  c. hundred thousands
  d. NG

9 379 ◯ 397

  a. <
  b. >
  c. =

10 7,929 ◯ 7,992

  a. <
  b. >
  c. =

11 1,673,291,790 ◯ 1,672,391,709

  a. <
  b. >
  c. =

12 Round 13,743 to the nearest hundred.

  a. 13,000
  b. 13,700
  c. 13,800
  d. NG

13 Round 46,257 to the nearest thousand.

  a. 46,000
  b. 46,200
  c. 47,000
  d. NG

14 Round 259,500 to the nearest thousand.

  a. 259,000
  b. 260,000
  c. 261,000
  d. NG

92.9 **score**

STOP

Add and Subtract Whole Numbers

Adding 2- and 3-Digit Numbers

The Wright brothers made the world's first airplane flights on December 17, 1903, at Kitty Hawk, North Carolina. Orville made the first flight but Wilbur made the longest. How far did the Wright brothers fly on those two flights?

We need to find the total distance the Wright brothers flew.

Orville flew _____ feet and Wilbur flew _____ feet.

To find the total distance, we add _____ and _____.

Orville   120 feet
Wilbur   852 feet

Add the ones.	Add the tens.	Add the hundreds.
$\begin{array}{r}120\\+852\\\hline2\end{array}$ $0 + 2 = 2$	$\begin{array}{r}120\\+852\\\hline72\end{array}$ $2 + 5 = 7$	$\begin{array}{r}120\\+852\\\hline972\end{array}$ $1 + 8 = 9$

The Wright brothers flew a total of _____ feet in their first two flights.

Getting Started

Add.

1. $\begin{array}{r}56\\+48\\\hline104\end{array}$

2. $\begin{array}{r}18\\+74\\\hline92\end{array}$

3. $\begin{array}{r}32\\+49\\\hline81\end{array}$

4. $\begin{array}{r}56\\+83\\\hline139\end{array}$

5. $\begin{array}{r}134\\+57\\\hline191\end{array}$

6. $\begin{array}{r}24\\+269\\\hline293\end{array}$

7. $\begin{array}{r}284\\+53\\\hline337\end{array}$

8. $\begin{array}{r}896\\+73\\\hline969\end{array}$

Copy and add.

9. $117 + 359$

$\begin{array}{r}359\\+117\\\hline476\end{array}$

10. $636 + 338$

$\begin{array}{r}636\\+338\\\hline974\end{array}$

11. $485 + 394$

$\begin{array}{r}485\\+394\\\hline879\end{array}$

Practice

Add.

1. 63
   + 29
   ___
    92

2. 51
   + 26
   ___
    77

3. 37
   + 19
   ___
    56

4. 68
   + 81
   ___
   149

5. 54
   + 73
   ___
   127

6. 215
   + 83
   ___
    298

7.   68
   + 471
   ___
    539

8. 537
   + 49
   ___
    586

9. 617
   + 62
   ___
    679

10. 694
   + 84
   ___
    778

11. 215
   + 326
   ___
    541

12. 409
   + 376
   ___
    785

13. 632
   + 185
   ___
    817

14. 328
   + 467
   ___
    795

15. 515
   + 284
   ___
    799

Copy and add.

16. 611 + 243
611 + 243 = 854

17. 319 + 432
432 + 319 = 751

18. 708 + 248
708 + 248 = 956

19. 573 + 284
573 + 284 = 857

20. 79 + 80
80 + 79 = 159

21. 326 + 47
326 + 47 = 373

22. 58 + 306
306 + 58 = 864

23. 212 + 448
212 + 448 = 660

24. 327 + 192
327 + 192 = 519

25. 76 + 517
517 + 76 = 593

26. 843 + 195
843 + 195 = 1,038

27. 754 + 236
754 + 236 = 990

Problem Solving

Solve each problem.

28. On Tuesday, 143 fifth graders visited the air museum. On Wednesday, 218 sixth graders toured the art museum. How many students went on the field trips to the two museums?

218
+ 143
___
361

361 Students

29. One hundred twelve fifth graders took bag lunches on their field trip. Ninety-six sixth graders carried their lunches on their tour. How many students took their lunches to the museums?

112 208 Students took lunches.
96
___
208

30. How many bottle caps between them did two boys collect? One saved 65 and the other saved 349.

284

65 + 349 = 414

31. Is the sum of 852 and 475 greater or less than the sum of 799 and 499?

Greater

Lesson 2-1 • Adding 2- and 3-Digit Numbers

Column Addition

The state of Maine is larger than Vermont, New Hampshire, and Massachusetts put together. What is the total area of these three smaller states?

100 %

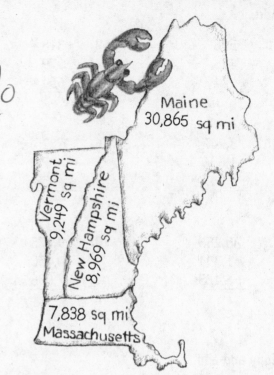

Maine 30,865 sq mi

Vermont 9,249 sq mi

New Hampshire 8,969 sq mi

7,838 sq mi Massachusetts

We need to find the total area of Vermont, New Hampshire, and Massachusetts.

Vermont is __9,249__ square miles,

New Hampshire is __8,969__ square miles,

and Massachusetts is __7,838__ square miles.

To find the total area, we add the areas of all three

states. We add __9,249__, __8,969__, and __7,838__.

Add the ones.	Add the tens.	Add the hundreds.	Add the thousands.
² 9,249 8,969 + 7,838 6	¹² 9,249 8,969 + 7,838 56	²¹ 9,249 8,969 + 7,838 056	² 9,249 8,969 + 7,838 26,056

The total area of Vermont, New Hampshire, and

Massachusetts is __26,056__ square miles.

Getting Started

Add.

1. ¹¹
    736
    458
    + 695
    ‾‾‾‾
    1,889

2. ¹¹
    498
    76
    + 625
    ‾‾‾‾
    11,99

3. ¹¹¹
    8,216
    987
    +   43
    ‾‾‾‾
    9,296

4. ²¹²
    1,917
    6,212
    3,965
    + 2,468
    ‾‾‾‾
    14,562

Copy and add.

5. 896 + 3,248 + 652

    ¹¹
    +¹896
    3,248
    652
    ‾‾‾‾
    4,796

6. 96 + 2,795 + 865

    ¹
    1+2 96
    2,795
    865
    ‾‾‾‾
    3,756

7. 8,485 + 6,458 + 5,216

    ¹¹
    8,485
    + 6,458
    5,216
    ‾‾‾‾
    20,159

Practice

Add.

1. $\begin{array}{r} \overset{1\ 1}{596} \\ 428 \\ +\ 74 \\ \hline 1{,}098 \end{array}$

2. $\begin{array}{r} \overset{1\ 2}{318} \\ 79 \\ +\ 654 \\ \hline 1{,}051 \end{array}$

3. $\begin{array}{r} \overset{1\ 1}{483} \\ 727 \\ +\ 851 \\ \hline 2{,}061 \end{array}$

4. $\begin{array}{r} \overset{1\ 2}{547} \\ 685 \\ +\ 219 \\ \hline 1{,}451 \end{array}$

5. $\begin{array}{r} \overset{1\ 1\ 2}{3{,}247} \\ 1{,}656 \\ +\ 947 \\ \hline 5{,}850 \end{array}$

6. $\begin{array}{r} \overset{1\ 1\ 1}{7{,}225} \\ 74 \\ +\ 858 \\ \hline 8{,}157 \end{array}$

7. $\begin{array}{r} \overset{1}{412} \\ 3{,}639 \\ +\ 4{,}725 \\ \hline 8{,}776 \end{array}$

8. $\begin{array}{r} \overset{1}{59} \\ 753 \\ +\ 6{,}257 \\ \hline 7{,}069 \end{array}$

9. $\begin{array}{r} \overset{1\ 2\ 1}{5{,}286} \\ 1{,}394 \\ +\ 6{,}475 \\ \hline 13{,}155 \end{array}$

10. $\begin{array}{r} \overset{2\ 1}{9{,}275} \\ 6{,}450 \\ +\ 7{,}096 \\ \hline 22{,}821 \end{array}$

11. $\begin{array}{r} \overset{2\ 2\ 1}{6{,}352} \\ 874 \\ 628 \\ +\ 5{,}395 \\ \hline 13{,}249 \end{array}$

12. $\begin{array}{r} \overset{2\ 1\ 2}{8{,}216} \\ 4{,}728 \\ 3{,}219 \\ +\ 6{,}853 \\ \hline 24{,}016 \end{array}$

Copy and add.

13. $1{,}475 + 9{,}654 + 3{,}617$
14,746

14. $3{,}872 + 6{,}593 + 76$
10,541

15. $4{,}232 + 7{,}912 + 825$
12,969

16. $396 + 975 + 856$
2,217

17. $3{,}279 + 85 + 7{,}293$
10,657

18. $654 + 96 + 8{,}455$
9,205

19. $8{,}273 + 4{,}176 + 6{,}228$
18,677

20. $7{,}593 + 2{,}483 + 5{,}312$
15,388

21. $8{,}948 + 7{,}316 + 9{,}286$
25,550

Problem Solving

Use the chart to solve each problem.

Gallons of Water Used	
Monday	3,794
Tuesday	4,316
Wednesday	4,615
Thursday	5,212
Friday	4,475

22. How much water was used on Monday, Wednesday, and Friday?
12,884

23. How much water was used on Tuesday, Wednesday, and Thursday?
14,143

24. How much water was used in the five days?
21,412

Estimating Sums

Larry is a flight attendant for a major airline. He keeps track of the number of miles he flies each month. Estimate the distance Larry has flown since September.

Log Book	
September	8,465 miles
October	11,878 miles

We want to estimate the number of miles Larry has flown.

To estimate the distance, we round each monthly distance to the nearest thousand and add.

Notice that the numbers are both rounded to the thousands place because that is the greatest place value they both have in common.

8,465 is rounded to ___8,000___.

11,878 is rounded to ___12,000___.

The estimated sum is ___20,000___.

Larry has flown about ___20,000___ miles.

,3

91%

Another way to estimate a sum is to use front-end estimation. Adjust your answer to get a closer estimate.

$$\begin{array}{r} 279 \\ + 605 \\ \hline 800 \end{array}$$

79 + 5 is close to 100.
So 279 + 605 is about 900.

Getting Started

Estimate each sum by rounding the addends to the greatest common place value.

1. $\begin{array}{r} 687 \\ + 793 \\ \hline \end{array}$
    1,500

2. $\begin{array}{r} 16,350 \\ + 7,275 \\ \hline \end{array}$
    23,000

3. $\begin{array}{r} 37,852 \\ + 6,275 \\ \hline \end{array}$
    44,000

4. $\begin{array}{r} \$758.16 \\ + 186.50 \\ \hline \end{array}$
    $1,000.00

5. $\begin{array}{r} \$3,742.38 \\ + 6,849.26 \\ \hline \end{array}$
    $11,000.00

6. $\begin{array}{r} \$38,215.39 \\ + 7,812.06 \\ \hline \end{array}$
    $46,000.00

Copy and estimate each sum by using front-end estimation and adjusting.

7. 557 + 678
    557 + 678 = 1,100

8. 4,329 + 3,592
    4,329 + 3,592 = 7,000

9. $47,615 + $75,589
    $47,615 + $75,589 = $11,000

Practice

Estimate each sum by rounding the addends to the greatest common place value.

1. 736
    + 435
    ‾‾‾‾‾
    1,100

2. $3,694
    + 587
    ‾‾‾‾‾
    $4,600   4,300

3. 8,439
    + 6,650
    ‾‾‾‾‾
    15,000

4. 9,245
    + 8,273
    ‾‾‾‾‾
    17,000

5. 3,865
    + 7,256
    ‾‾‾‾‾
    11,000

6. 13,475
    + 9,150
    ‾‾‾‾‾
    22,000

7. $162.45
    + 73.95
    ‾‾‾‾‾
    $230.00

8. 49,725
    + 75,212
    ‾‾‾‾‾
    130,000

9. 127,247
    + 438,500
    ‾‾‾‾‾
    600,000   500,000

10. 38,725
    + 73,689
    ‾‾‾‾‾
    110,000

11. $217.75
    + 468.52
    ‾‾‾‾‾
    $700.00

12. $3,275.16
    + 789.50
    ‾‾‾‾‾
    $3,800.00   4,100

13. 745,925
    + 627,215
    ‾‾‾‾‾
    1,300,000

14. $13,795.92
    + 8,227.75
    ‾‾‾‾‾
    $22,000.00

15. 136,795
    + 8,500
    ‾‾‾‾‾
    146,000

Copy and estimate each sum by using front-end estimation and adjusting.

16. 478 + 569
    478 + 569 = 900

17. $3,942 + $687 $3,900
                     + $600
                     ‾‾‾‾‾
                     $4,500

18. 9,645 + 4,509
    9,645 + 4,509 = 1,300

19. 6,973 + 4,768
    10,000

20. 39,046 + 55,389
    94,000

21. 209,349 + 567,499
    209,349 + 567,499 = 700,000

22. 35,462 + 7,096
    42,000

23. 16,494 + 6,095
    22,000

24. $55,599 + $6,285
    $55,599 + $6,285 = 66,000

[Now Try This!]

Sometimes you can use clustering to estimate the sum of three or more numbers that are close to the same number.

Look at this sum. 98 + 93 + 102 + 99

Notice that all the numbers are close to 100.

This means 98 + 93 + 102 + 99 is close to 4 × 100, or 400.

Estimate each sum.

1. 8 + 7 + 12 + 11

2. 22 + 26 + 24 + 25

3. 49 + 44 + 52

Name _____

Adding 6-Digit Numbers

92%

The Dakota Territory was first opened for homesteading in 1863. How many people lived in the states of North and South Dakota in the year 2000?

The Year 2000

North Dakota
642,199

South Dakota
754,844

We want to find the population (pop.) of North and South Dakota in the year 2000.

The population of North Dakota was _642,199_,

and that of South Dakota was _754,844_.

To find the total population, we add _____ and _____.

Start adding the ones, and continue adding each column to the left.

```
   642,199
 + 754,844
  1,397,043
```

There were _1,397,043_ people living in North and South Dakota in the year 2000.

REMEMBER When adding any numbers, including money, align the place values carefully. In the case of money, be sure to include the dollar sign and decimal point in the sum.

Getting Started _____

Add.

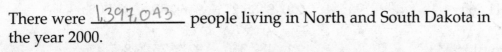

1. 67,294
  + 38,615
   105,909 ✓

2. $6,243.15
  +   756.28
   $6,999.43 ✓

3. 267,395
  + 538,246
   795,641 ✓

Copy and add.

4. $11,275.85 + $16,984.36

5. 984,247 + 651,426

6. 327,128 + 49,765 + 4,386

Practice

Add.

1. 34,739
    + 6,726
    41,465

2. 4,757
    + 75,839
    80,596

3. 57,265
    + 18,491
    75,756

4. 112,536
    + 455,392
    567,928

5. 648,257
    + 316,826
    965,083

6. $2,169.85
    + 795.37
    $2,965.22

7. $4,256.48
    + 3,817.52
    $8,074.00

8. 196,275
    + 827,385
    1,023,660

9. 453,750
    + 936,248
    1,389,998

10. $16,375.37
    + 9,683.82
    $26,059.19

11. 756,385
    + 836,298
    1,592,683

12. $47,384.36
    + 26,428.75
    $73,813.11

Copy and add.

13. 13,751 + 8,475
    22,226

14. $9,275.16 + $3,186.36
    12,461.52

15. 16,750 + 11,240 + 9,126
    37,116

16. 32,756 + 9,748 + 14,755
    57,259

17. $4,725.50 + $876.39 + $2,175.29
    7,777.18

18. 136,795 + 56,726
    193,521

19. 212,750 + 3,968 + 11,265
    227,993

20. $485.27 + $16,295 + $3,705.83
    $14,853.53

21. 326,758 + 246,720 + 613,953
    1,187,431

22. 487,350 + 927,375 + 867,426
    2,282,151

Problem Solving

Use the map to solve each problem.

23. How many people live in the cities of San Francisco and Oakland?
    1,203,800

24. What is the total population of Oakland, Fremont, and San Jose?
    1,546,200

25. How many people live in all four cities on the map?
    2,327,800

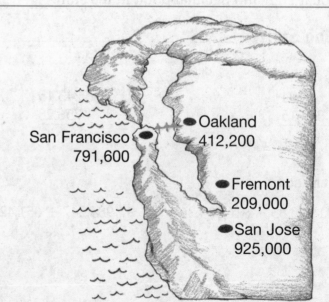

San Francisco 791,600

Oakland 412,200

Fremont 209,000

San Jose 925,000

Subtracting 2- and 3-Digit Numbers

The North and South Platte Rivers join to form the Platte River in Nebraska. The North Platte was part of the famous Oregon Trail. How much longer is the North Platte River than the South Platte River?

8570
-5

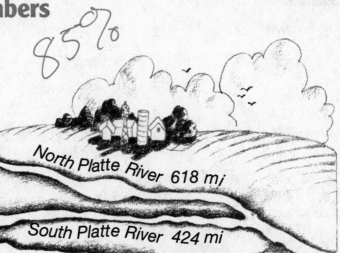

North Platte River 618 mi

South Platte River 424 mi

We need to find the difference in the lengths of the two Platte Rivers.

The North Platte is __618__ miles long while the

South Platte is __424__ miles long.

To find the differences, we subtract __424__ from __618__.

Subtract the ones.	6 hundreds and 1 ten =	Subtract the hundreds.
8 − 4 = 4	5 hundreds and 11 tens	5 − 4 = 1
	Subtract the tens.	

$$\begin{array}{r} 618 \\ -424 \\ \hline 4 \end{array} \qquad \begin{array}{r} {\scriptstyle 5\,11} \\ 618 \\ -424 \\ \hline 94 \end{array} \quad (11-2=9) \qquad \begin{array}{r} {\scriptstyle 5} \\ 618 \\ -424 \\ \hline 194 \end{array}$$

The North Platte is __194__ miles longer than the South Platte.

Getting Started

Subtract.

1.
$$\begin{array}{r} {\scriptstyle 8\,14} \\ 94 \\ -48 \\ \hline 46 \end{array}$$

2.
$$\begin{array}{r} 76 \\ -43 \\ \hline 33 \end{array}$$

3.
$$\begin{array}{r} {\scriptstyle 3\,11} \\ 416 \\ -52 \\ \hline 364 \end{array}$$

4.
$$\begin{array}{r} {\scriptstyle 7\,13} \\ 683 \\ -47 \\ \hline 636 \end{array}$$

5.
$$\begin{array}{r} {\scriptstyle 8\,11} \\ 916 \\ -324 \\ \hline 592 \end{array}$$

6.
$$\begin{array}{r} {\scriptstyle 7\,13} \\ 483 \\ -165 \\ \hline 318 \end{array}$$

7.
$$\begin{array}{r} {\scriptstyle 10\,15} \\ 715 \\ -286 \\ \hline 429 \end{array}$$

8.
$$\begin{array}{r} {\scriptstyle 7\,11\,17} \\ \$8.27 \\ -4.88 \\ \hline \$3.39 \end{array}$$

Copy and subtract.

9. 862 − 591 = 271

10. $7.93 − $2.81 = $5.12

11. 553 − 196 = 357

Practice

Subtract.

1. 76
   − 42
   34

2. 88
   − 79
   9

3. 327
   − 83
   244

4. 723
   − 18
   705

5. 474
   − 281
   193

6. 717
   − 225
   492

7. $8.83
   − 5.37
   $3.46

8. 945
   − 219
   726

9. 653
   − 486
   167

10. $5.18
    − 3.99
    19

11. 924
    − 687
    237

12. 457
    − 378
    79

13. 721
    − 389
    332

14. 684
    − 399
    885

15. 832
    − 496
    336

16. $5.15
    − 3.49
    $1.66

Copy and subtract.

17. 89 − 16 = 73
18. 92 − 27 = 65
19. 138 − 57 = 81
20. 148 − 63 = 75

21. 214 − 59 = 155
22. 675 − 281 = 394
23. $9.71 − $6.28 = 3.53
24. 487 − 273 = 214

25. 721 − 583 = 138
26. $825 − $196 = 6.29
27. 532 − 476 = 56
28. 894 − 249 = 645

29. $4.28 − $1.75 = 2.53
30. 672 − 496 = 176
31. 816 − 197 = 619
32. $3.19 − $1.79 = 140

Problem Solving

Use the chart to solve each problem.

33. How much more coastline does Texas have than Oregon?

34. What is the sum of the combined coastlines of New York, Oregon, and Texas?

35. Texas has how much less coastline than the combined coastlines of New York and Oregon?

United States Coastlines	
New York	127 miles
Oregon	296 miles
Texas	367 miles

Subtracting From Zeros

In 1699, Louisiana became a royal colony of France. How many years later did Louisiana become a territory of the United States?

We need to find how long it took Louisiana to become a part of the United States.

Louisiana became a colony of France in _____.

It became a territory of the United States when

it was purchased in _____.

To find the number of years between its becoming a French colony and its becoming a part of the United States, we subtract the earlier date from

the more recent one. We subtract _____ from _____.

Subtract the ones.	Subtract the tens.	Subtract the hundreds.	Subtract the thousands.
800 = 7 hundreds and 10 tens 10 tens = 9 tens and 10 ones	9 tens − 9 tens = 0 tens	7 hundreds − 6 hundreds = 1 hundred	1 thousand − 1 thousand = 0 thousands

$$\begin{array}{r} {\scriptstyle 9} \\ {\scriptstyle 7\ 10\ 13} \\ 1803 \\ -\ 1699 \\ \hline 4 \end{array}$$

$$\begin{array}{r} {\scriptstyle 7\ 9} \\ 1\cancel{8}03 \\ -\ 1699 \\ \hline 04 \end{array}$$

$$\begin{array}{r} {\scriptstyle 7} \\ 1\cancel{8}03 \\ -\ 1699 \\ \hline 104 \end{array}$$

$$\begin{array}{r} 1803 \\ -\ 1699 \\ \hline 104 \end{array}$$

Louisiana became part of the United States _____ years after it became a French colony.

Getting Started

Subtract.

1. $\begin{array}{r} 870 \\ -\ 496 \\ \hline 374 \end{array}$

2. $\begin{array}{r} \$4.08 \\ -\ 3.59 \\ \hline \$\ .49 \end{array}$

3. $\begin{array}{r} 3,056 \\ -\ 2,684 \\ \hline 327 \end{array}$

4. $\begin{array}{r} 9,308 \\ -\ 4,675 \\ \hline 4,623 \end{array}$

5. $\begin{array}{r} \$40.05 \\ -\ 16.87 \\ \hline \$23.18 \end{array}$

6. $\begin{array}{r} 9,302 \\ -\ 1,875 \\ \hline 7,427 \end{array}$

7. $\begin{array}{r} 8,001 \\ -\ 3,975 \\ \hline 4,026 \end{array}$

8. $\begin{array}{r} \$60.00 \\ -\ 9.75 \\ \hline 50.25 \end{array}$

Copy and subtract.

9. $70.65 − $24.79
   $45.86

10. 4,703 − 4,656
    47

11. 9,030 − 4,798
    4,232

Practice

Subtract.

1. 3,905
− 2,659
_1,246_

2. 8,063
− 2,785
_5,278_

3. 6,247
− 3,968
_2,279_

4. 5,710
− 2,396
_3,314_

5. 6,070
− 2,985
_3,085_

6. $37.08
− 29.89
_7.19_

7. 7,006
− 2,589
_4,417_

8. $40.37
− 9.56
_$30.81_

Copy and subtract.

9. 8,704 − 3,596
_5,108_

10. $70.09 − $32.58
_$37.51_

11. 6,000 − 852
_5,148_

12. 4,398 − 4,029
_369_

13. $58.08 − $29.59
_$28.49_

14. 8,757 − 6,458
_2,299_

15. 3,050 − 1,976
_1,074_

16. $80.08 − $37.85
_$42.23_

17. 4,082 − 2,697
_1,385_

18. $70.00 − $29.56
_$40.44_

19. 8,104 − 3,976
_4,128_

20. 9,054 − 6,780
_2,274_

Problem Solving

Use the chart to solve each problem.

21. How much longer than the Illinois River is the Ohio/Allegheny River?
1,335 kilometers

22. How much longer than the Arkansas River is the Missouri River?
1,378 kilometers

23. What is the combined length of the Illinois River and the Missouri River?
4,493 kilometers

24. What is the total length of these four tributaries of the Mississippi River?
8,943 kilometers

Major Tributaries of the Mississippi River	
Arkansas	2,348 kilometers
Illinois	767 kilometers
Missouri	3,726 kilometers
Ohio/Allegheny	2,102 kilometers

[Now Try This!]

You have a yellow, a blue, an orange, and a green shoelace.
Make as many different sets of two shoelaces as you can.

Yellow and blue, Orange and blue, green and blue, orange and yellow, green and yellow, and orange and green.

Name _Ava Joy Washington ♡_

Estimating Differences

The Moon travels in an oval-shaped
orbit around Earth every $29\frac{1}{2}$ days.
Estimate, to the nearest thousand miles,
the difference between the Moon's
closest and farthest points from Earth.

93%

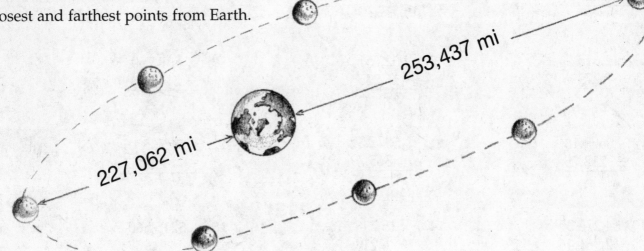

253,437 mi

227,062 mi

We want to estimate the difference between the two
distances, to the nearest thousand miles.

To estimate a difference, we round the minuend and
subtrahend and subtract.

253,437 rounded to the nearest thousand is _253,000_.

227,062 rounded to the nearest thousand is _227,000_.

The estimated difference is _26,000_.

There are about 26,000 miles between the closest
and farthest points of the Moon's orbit.

Getting Started

**Estimate each difference by rounding to the greatest
common place value.**

1.	926	2.	15,650	3.	46,750
	− 275		− 9,427		− 7,210
	600		7,000		40,000

4.	$475.39	5.	$4,294.86	6.	$9,285.17
	− 126.15		− 847.58		− 1,721.15
	$400.00		$3,400.00		$ 7,000.00

Practice

Estimate the difference by rounding to the greatest common place value.

1. 962
   − 315
   700

2. 836
   − 297
   500

3. 850
   − 335
   600

4. 4,325
   − 2,686
   1,000

5. 9,720
   − 3,819
   6,000

6. 6,075
   − 1,750
   4,000

7. 12,615
   − 7,279
   6,000

8. 52,651
   − 16,235
   30,000   *50,000*
              − 20,000
              30,000

9. 839,750
   − 214,210
   600,000

10. $679.18
    − 213.75
    $500.00

11. $872.39
    − 365.79
    $500.00

12. $4,765.16
    − 426.52
    $4,400.00

13. $4,275.35   *$4,000.00*
    − 2,961.46   *− 3,000.00*
    $1,000.00 *$1,000.00*

14. $15,748.57   *$16,000.00*
    − 6,214.12   *− 6,000.00*
    $10,000.00 *10,000.00*

15. $215,560   *$216,000*
    − 6,957   *− 7,000*
    $209,000 *$209,000*

16. $5,675.49
    − 3,899.42

17. $10,648
    − 7,493

18. $416,698
    − 32,455

Now Try This!

You can also use front-end estimation to estimate a difference.
Adjust your answer to get a closer estimate.

   41,231
   − 32,807   1,231 is less than 2,807.
   10,000   So 41,231 − 32,807 is less than 10,000.

Estimate each difference.

1. 972
   − 570

2. 72,963
   − 48,991

3. $338.01
   − 122.47

4. $5,423
   − 2,599

5. 1,937
   − 1,740

6. 99,667
   − 68,915

Subtract 6-Digit Numbers

In 1953, Auguste Piccard and his son
Jacques set a record, by exploring the
Mediterranean Sea in a bathyscaph
lowered to about 10,299 feet. Seven
years later, Jacques Piccard and Don
Walsh descended just over 35,798 feet
in the Pacific Ocean to set a new record.
By how many feet was the record extended?

We want to know the difference between the depths
of the 1953 and the 1960 dives.

Jacques and his father dove __10,299__ feet.

Jacques and Don dove __35,798__ feet.

To find the number of feet the record was extended,
we subtract the old record from the new one. We subtract

__10,299__ from __35,798__.

Subtract the ones first and continue subtracting each place
value to the left, renaming when necessary.

$$
\begin{array}{r}
6\,'8 \\
35,\!798 \\
-\ 10,\!299 \\
\hline
25,\!499
\end{array}
$$

The Piccard-Walsh team bettered the record by __25,499__ feet.

Getting Started

Subtract.

1. $\begin{array}{r} 73,246 \\ -\ 9,563 \\ \hline 63,683 \end{array}$

2. $\begin{array}{r} 127,086 \\ -\ 56,796 \\ \hline 70,290 \end{array}$

3. $\begin{array}{r} \$8,752.38 \\ -\ 4,615.19 \\ \hline \$4,137.19 \end{array}$

Copy and subtract.

4. 612,672 − 572,375   40,297
    40,297

5. $4,075.08 − $1,796.29
    $2,278.79

Practice

Subtract.

1. 17,459
    − 9,675
    ___
    7,784

2. 86,247
    − 39,186
    ___
    47,061

3. 72,054
    − 19,680
    ___
    52,194

4. 139,650
    − 46,776
    ___
    92,874

5. 425,000
    − 86,293
    ___
    338,707

6. $6,385.36
    − 597.48
    ___
    $5,787.88

7. 370,746
    − 186,929
    ___
    183,187

8. 623,005
    − 217,638
    ___
    405,637

9. 825,647
    − 195,267
    ___
    630,380

10. $5,000.00
    − 1,666.67

11. 998,258
    − 439,475

12. 608,250
    − 129,186

Copy and subtract.

13. 14,320 − 9,750

14. $376.51 − $129.75
    $246.76

15. 16,209 − 12,326

16. 80,085 − 47,492

17. 126,359 − 75,278

18. 905,709 − 506,575

19. 820,575 − 297,739

20. 629,585 − 230,789

21. $3,250.26 − $1,786.75

22. $7,500.00 − $697.79
    $6,802.21

Problem Solving

Use the chart to solve each problem.

23. How much deeper is the Atlantic Ocean than the Indian Ocean?

24. What is the difference between the deepest points in the Pacific and Arctic Oceans?

Greatest Ocean Depths	
Arctic	18,456 feet
Atlantic	30,246 feet
Indian	24,460 feet
Pacific	35,820 feet

Name _____

Problem Solving: Act It Out

Frank bought a pair of ski boots from Patty for $60.
Two weeks later he sold them to his friend Scott for $70.
At the end of the ski season Frank bought the boots
back for $80. The next fall he sold the boots to Ronnie for
$90. How much money did Frank make or lose in buying
and selling the ski boots?

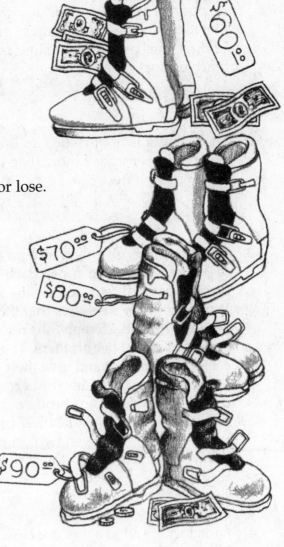

⭐ SEE

We want to know the amount of money Frank will make or lose.

Frank originally bought the ski boots for __$60__.

He sold the boots to Scott for __$70__.

He bought the boots back for __$80__.

He sold the boots to Ronnie for __$90__.

⭐ PLAN

Keeping track of the money spent and earned is difficult
to do. We can make it simpler by acting the problem out.
We will need four students to act the parts of Frank,
Patty, Scott, and Ronnie. Each actor will need to start
with $100 in play money.

⭐ DO

Follow the actions of the problem as the actors play
their roles. Frank starts with $100.

He buys the boots from Patty for __$60__. Frank sells the boots to Scott for __$70__.

He buys the boots back for __$80__. He sells the boots to Ronnie for __$90__.

Have Frank count his money. He now has _____. Since he started with $100, he _____.

⭐ CHECK

After Frank buys the ski boots for $60, he has _____ left.

He sells the boots for $70. He then has _____.

He buys the boots back for $80. He has _____.

He sells the ski boots for $90. He has _____.

Apply

Solve each problem.

1. Tony has less than 30 marbles. When he puts them in groups of five, he has one left. When he puts them in groups of three, he has none left. How many marbles does he have?

   Tony has 18 left

2. Show that it is not practical to fold a sheet of paper in half more than eight consecutive times.

3. Three brothers give their sister a total of 30 cents to buy an apple. Each brother pays 10 cents for his share. When the sister discovers that the apple only costs 25 cents, she returns the five cents to her brothers. They each take one cent and give their sister the remaining two cents for her trouble. Therefore each brother only paid nine cents for a total of 27 cents, and the sister was given two cents. What happened to the other penny?

   The Sister had them

4. Nine lockers all in a row are closed. Nine students line up and perform the following actions: The first student goes to every locker and opens each door. The second student then goes to every second locker, opens it if it is closed, and closes it if it is open. The third student goes to every third locker, opens it if it is closed, and closes it if it is open. If this continues for all nine students, what lockers are open at the conclusion of the ninth student's trip?

   1, 4, and 9

5. Use a ruler, yardstick, or meter stick to determine the thickness of one sheet of paper.

   1 cm

6. The hour hand and minute hand of a clock cross at noon. How many times will the hands cross between noon and midnight? Do not count noon, but do count midnight.

   12:00

7. What is the greatest whole number and what is the least whole number that would be represented by 6,400 if rounded to the nearest hundred?

   6,500   6,300

8. What is the greatest and what is the least dollar amount of money that would be represented by $3,000 if rounded to the nearest thousand dollars?

   4,000

   2,000

9. Ten flowers grow in a circle. A butterfly gathers nectar from one, and then continues to visit every third flower around the circle. Tell whether the butterfly visits all 10 flowers and prove your answer.

10. Suppose Don Noe has some dimes, nickels, and pennies. He has exactly 12 coins worth exactly 25¢. What coins does Don have? Explain how you got your answer.

    1 dime
    1 nickle
    10 pennies

Name Eat Biscut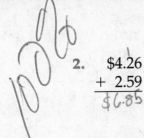

Add.

1. $\begin{array}{r} \overset{1\,1}{126} \\ +\ 85 \\ \hline 211 \end{array}$

2. $\begin{array}{r} \overset{1}{\$4.26} \\ +\ 2.59 \\ \hline \$6.85 \end{array}$

3. $\begin{array}{r} \overset{1\ 1\ 1}{1{,}965} \\ +\ 8{,}246 \\ \hline 10{,}211 \end{array}$

4. $\begin{array}{r} \overset{1\ 1\ 12}{18{,}279} \\ 38{,}657 \\ +\ 92{,}158 \\ \hline 149{,}094 \end{array}$

Estimate each sum by using front-end estimation and adjusting.

5. $\begin{array}{r} 386 \\ +\ 148 \\ \hline 400 \end{array}$

6. $\begin{array}{r} 6{,}736 \\ +\ 2{,}651 \\ \hline 8{,}000 \end{array}$

7. $\begin{array}{r} 15{,}974 \\ +\ 7{,}338 \\ \hline 22{,}000 \end{array}$

8. $\begin{array}{r} 49{,}150 \\ +\ 21{,}896 \\ \hline 60{,}000 \end{array}$

Add.

9. $\begin{array}{r} \overset{1\ 1}{489} \\ +\ 652 \\ \hline 1{,}141 \end{array}$

10. $\begin{array}{r} \overset{1\ 1\ 1}{39{,}095} \\ +\ 5{,}758 \\ \hline 44{,}843 \end{array}$

11. $\begin{array}{r} \overset{1\ 1}{87{,}502} \\ +\ 56{,}298 \\ \hline 1{,}43{,}800 \end{array}$

12. $\begin{array}{r} \overset{1\ 1}{748{,}493} \\ +\ 636{,}094 \\ \hline 1{,}384{,}587 \end{array}$

Subtract.

13. $\begin{array}{r} \overset{6}{7}49 \\ -\ 51 \\ \hline 698 \end{array}$

14. $\begin{array}{r} 16{,}750 \\ -\ 8{,}974 \\ \hline 7{,}776 \end{array}$

15. $\begin{array}{r} \$120.08 \\ -\ 96.79 \\ \hline \$23.29 \end{array}$

16. $\begin{array}{r} 413{,}696 \\ -\ 49{,}739 \\ \hline 363{,}957 \end{array}$

Estimate each difference by rounding to the greatest common place value.

17. $\begin{array}{r} 832 \\ -\ 279 \\ \hline 500 \end{array}$

18. $\begin{array}{r} 7{,}540 \\ -\ 2{,}659 \\ \hline 5{,}000 \end{array}$

19. $\begin{array}{r} 15{,}270 \\ -\ 8{,}312 \\ \hline 7{,}000 \end{array}$

20. $\begin{array}{r} 88{,}659 \\ -\ 61{,}236 \\ \hline 30{,}000 \end{array}$

Subtract.

21. $\begin{array}{r} 751 \\ -\ 479 \\ \hline 272 \end{array}$

22. $\begin{array}{r} 4{,}659 \\ -\ 2{,}388 \\ \hline 2{,}271 \end{array}$

23. $\begin{array}{r} 86{,}454 \\ -\ 7{,}652 \\ \hline 78{,}802 \end{array}$

24. $\begin{array}{r} 49{,}602 \\ -\ 27{,}499 \\ \hline 22{,}103 \end{array}$

25. $\begin{array}{r} 685 \\ -\ 397 \\ \hline 288 \end{array}$

26. $\begin{array}{r} 7{,}647 \\ -\ 4{,}892 \\ \hline 2{,}755 \end{array}$

27. $\begin{array}{r} 93{,}247 \\ -\ 61{,}983 \\ \hline 31{,}264 \end{array}$

28. $\begin{array}{r} 69{,}458 \\ -\ 3{,}901 \\ \hline 65{,}557 \end{array}$

Circle the letter of the correct answer.

1 $9 + 6$

a. 13
b. 14
c. 15
d. NG

2 $17 - 8$

a. 7
b. 8
c. 9
d. NG

3 $n + 5 = 5$
$n = ?$

a. 0
b. 5
c. 10
d. NG

OK

4 What is the place value of the digit 3 in 963,214?

a. ones
b. tens
c. hundreds
d. NG

5 What is the place value of the digit 9 in 392,065?

a. hundred thousands
b. ten thousands
c. thousands
d. NG

6 426 ◯ 624

a. <
b. >
c. =

7 32,593 ◯ 32,586

a. <
b. >
c. =

8
$4.39
$+ 5.27

a. $9.66
b. $966
c. 966
d. NG

9
36,784
+ 14,261

a. 40,945
b. 41,045
c. 51,045
d. NG

10 Estimate the sum by using front-end digits and adjusting.

369
+ 245

a. 500
b. 600
c. 700
d. NG

11 Estimate the sum by rounding.

6,924
+ 15,165

a. 21,000
b. 22,000
c. 23,000
d. NG

12
608
− 239

a. 369
b. 379
c. 431
d. NG

13
$296.15
− 87.59

a. $116.56
b. $211.14
c. $216.56
d. NG

score

STOP

Multiply Whole Numbers

Multiplication Facts and Properties

100%

It's Algebra!

Jogging is a great form of aerobic exercise. On Saturday, Jewel plans to jog 4 miles, at the same rate of speed she is jogging today. How long will it take Jewel to jog the 4 miles?

One Mile Jog		
Runner	StartTime	Finish Time
Jewel	9:00	9:09

We want to find the total time it will take Jewel to jog 4 miles.

We know she jogged 1 mile in _____ minutes.

She is going to jog _____ miles on Saturday. To find the time it will take Jewel to jog the total distance, we multiply _____ × _____.

factor   factor   product

↓   ↓   ↓

9   ×   4   =   _____

$\begin{array}{r} 9 \\ \times 4 \\ \hline \end{array}$

It will take Jewel 36 minutes to jog 4 miles. Multiplication has several basic properties.

Commutative Property

Factors can be multiplied in any order.

$6 \times 4 = 24$ $5 \times 7 = \underline{35}$

$4 \times 6 = 24$ $7 \times 5 = \underline{35}$

Associative Property

Factors can be grouped in any way.

$(4 \times 2) \times 3 = 24$ $(5 \times 1) \times 6 = \underline{30}$

$4 \times (2 \times 3) = 24$ $5 \times (1 \times 6) = \underline{30}$

Zero Property

If one factor is 0, the product is 0.

$4 \times 0 = 0$ $8 \times 0 = \underline{0}$

$0 \times 4 = 0$ $0 \times 8 = \underline{0}$

Identity Property

If one factor is 1, the product is the same as the other factor.

$7 \times 1 = 7$ $5 \times 1 = \underline{5}$

$1 \times 9 = 9$ $1 \times 3 = \underline{3}$

Getting Started

Multiply.

1. $\begin{array}{r} 0 \\ \times 8 \\ \hline 0 \end{array}$

2. $\begin{array}{r} 1 \\ \times 3 \\ \hline 3 \end{array}$

3. $9 \times 6 = \underline{54}$

4. $(4 \times 2) \times 7 = \underline{56}$

Practice

Multiply.

1.
  $\begin{array}{r} 1 \\ \times 1 \\ \hline 1 \end{array}$
  $\begin{array}{r} 2 \\ \times 5 \\ \hline 10 \end{array}$
  $\begin{array}{r} 8 \\ \times 1 \\ \hline 8 \end{array}$
  $\begin{array}{r} 1 \\ \times 6 \\ \hline 6 \end{array}$
  $\begin{array}{r} 3 \\ \times 6 \\ \hline 18 \end{array}$
  $\begin{array}{r} 9 \\ \times 3 \\ \hline 27 \end{array}$
  $\begin{array}{r} 1 \\ \times 7 \\ \hline 7 \end{array}$
  $\begin{array}{r} 3 \\ \times 2 \\ \hline 6 \end{array}$

2.
  $\begin{array}{r} 4 \\ \times 2 \\ \hline 8 \end{array}$
  $\begin{array}{r} 1 \\ \times 9 \\ \hline 9 \end{array}$
  $\begin{array}{r} 1 \\ \times 4 \\ \hline 4 \end{array}$
  $\begin{array}{r} 0 \\ \times 1 \\ \hline 0 \end{array}$
  $\begin{array}{r} 7 \\ \times 1 \\ \hline 7 \end{array}$
  $\begin{array}{r} 4 \\ \times 4 \\ \hline 16 \end{array}$
  $\begin{array}{r} 1 \\ \times 2 \\ \hline 2 \end{array}$
  $\begin{array}{r} 0 \\ \times 0 \\ \hline 0 \end{array}$

3.
  $\begin{array}{r} 3 \\ \times 0 \\ \hline 0 \end{array}$
  $\begin{array}{r} 7 \\ \times 4 \\ \hline 28 \end{array}$
  $\begin{array}{r} 7 \\ \times 0 \\ \hline 0 \end{array}$
  $\begin{array}{r} 2 \\ \times 2 \\ \hline 4 \end{array}$
  $\begin{array}{r} 3 \\ \times 3 \\ \hline 9 \end{array}$
  $\begin{array}{r} 3 \\ \times 1 \\ \hline 3 \end{array}$
  $\begin{array}{r} 8 \\ \times 8 \\ \hline 64 \end{array}$
  $\begin{array}{r} 5 \\ \times 4 \\ \hline 20 \end{array}$

4.
  $\begin{array}{r} 4 \\ \times 8 \\ \hline 32 \end{array}$
  $\begin{array}{r} 9 \\ \times 7 \\ \hline 63 \end{array}$
  $\begin{array}{r} 5 \\ \times 9 \\ \hline 45 \end{array}$
  $\begin{array}{r} 8 \\ \times 2 \\ \hline 16 \end{array}$
  $\begin{array}{r} 2 \\ \times 3 \\ \hline 6 \end{array}$
  $\begin{array}{r} 0 \\ \times 2 \\ \hline 0 \end{array}$
  $\begin{array}{r} 6 \\ \times 9 \\ \hline 54 \end{array}$
  $\begin{array}{r} 5 \\ \times 6 \\ \hline 30 \end{array}$

5.
  $\begin{array}{r} 5 \\ \times 8 \\ \hline 40 \end{array}$
  $\begin{array}{r} 5 \\ \times 5 \\ \hline 25 \end{array}$
  $\begin{array}{r} 7 \\ \times 8 \\ \hline 56 \end{array}$
  $\begin{array}{r} 4 \\ \times 0 \\ \hline 0 \end{array}$
  $\begin{array}{r} 2 \\ \times 6 \\ \hline 12 \end{array}$
  $\begin{array}{r} 1 \\ \times 5 \\ \hline 5 \end{array}$
  $\begin{array}{r} 6 \\ \times 6 \\ \hline 36 \end{array}$
  $\begin{array}{r} 6 \\ \times 7 \\ \hline 42 \end{array}$

6.
  $\begin{array}{r} 3 \\ \times 8 \\ \hline 24 \end{array}$
  $\begin{array}{r} 1 \\ \times 0 \\ \hline 0 \end{array}$
  $\begin{array}{r} 4 \\ \times 1 \\ \hline 4 \end{array}$
  $\begin{array}{r} 9 \\ \times 8 \\ \hline 72 \end{array}$
  $\begin{array}{r} 7 \\ \times 9 \\ \hline 63 \end{array}$
  $\begin{array}{r} 3 \\ \times 5 \\ \hline 15 \end{array}$
  $\begin{array}{r} 6 \\ \times 2 \\ \hline 12 \end{array}$
  $\begin{array}{r} 9 \\ \times 9 \\ \hline 81 \end{array}$

7.
  $\begin{array}{r} 4 \\ \times 7 \\ \hline 28 \end{array}$
  $\begin{array}{r} 3 \\ \times 9 \\ \hline 27 \end{array}$
  $\begin{array}{r} 6 \\ \times 3 \\ \hline 18 \end{array}$
  $\begin{array}{r} 6 \\ \times 8 \\ \hline 48 \end{array}$
  $\begin{array}{r} 7 \\ \times 7 \\ \hline 49 \end{array}$
  $\begin{array}{r} 7 \\ \times 2 \\ \hline 14 \end{array}$
  $\begin{array}{r} 9 \\ \times 5 \\ \hline 45 \end{array}$
  $\begin{array}{r} 9 \\ \times 2 \\ \hline 18 \end{array}$

[Now Try This!]

The Distributive Property can help you multiply.
Think of one factor as the sum of two addends.
Multiply the other factor by each addend. Then add the products.

$$4 \times 18 = 4 \times (10 + 8)$$
$$= (4 \times 10) + (4 \times 8)$$
$$= 40 + 32$$
$$= 72$$

Use the Distributive Property to find each product.

1. 6×21
   126   BW

2. 7×34
   238   BW

3. 5×17
   85   BW

4. 8×29
   232

5. 9×16
   144

6. 3×49
   147

Name _____

Multiples and Common Multiples

The fifth graders are comparing lists of **nonzero multiples**. The first six nonzero multiples of 2 shown on the board are 2, 4, 6, 8, 10, and 12. The three dots indicate that the list of multiples of 2 does not end. The students compare this list with the set of multiples of 5. What will be the least common multiple of 2 and 5?

Number	Multiples
2	0, 2, 4, 6, 8, 10, 12, …
3	0, 3, 6, 9, 12, 15, 18, …
4	0, 4, 8, 12, 16, 20, 24, …
5	0, 5, 10, 15, 20, 25, 30, …

We are looking for the least common multiple of 2 and 5.

The **least common multiple (LCM)** of two or more numbers is the smallest number that can be evenly divided by those numbers.

We know the multiples of 2 are 2, __4__, __6__, __8__, __10__, __12__, …

The multiples of 5 are __5__, __10__, __15__, __20__, __25__, __30__, …

The multiples of 2, and the number 0, are also called even numbers. The other whole numbers are called odd numbers.

Notice that although the first multiple of any number is zero, it is not listed here. Zero would never be a least common multiple.

The common multiples of 2 and 5 are __10__, __20__, __30__, …

The least common multiple of 2 and 5 is __10__.

Getting Started

1. Write the first 8 multiples of 6.

__6__, __12__, __18__, __24__, __30__, __36__, __42__, __48__

2. Write the first 8 multiples of 9.

__9__, __18__, __27__, __36__, __45__, __54__, __63__, __72__

3. Write the common multiples of 6 and 9 that you listed.

__18__, __36__

4. Write the least common multiple of 6 and 9

__18__

Write the least common multiple.

5. 2, 6 __6__

6. 5, 7 __35__

Write even or odd for each number.

7. 3 __odd__

8. 0 __even__

Practice

1. Write the first 8 multiples of 4.
   _4_, _8_, _12_, _16_,
   _20_, _24_, _28_, _32_

2. Write the first 8 multiples of 8.
   _8_, _16_, _24_, _32_,
   _40_, _48_, _56_, _64_

3. Write the common multiples of 4 and 8 that you listed.
   _8_, _16_, _24_, _32_

4. Write the least common multiple of 4 and 8.
   _8_

Write the least common multiple.

5. 2, 3 _6_

6. 2, 4 _4_

7. 3, 9 _9_

8. 4, 5 _20_

9. 3, 5 _15_

10. 5, 6 _30_

11. 7, 8 _56_

12. 4, 6 _12_

13. 4, 10 _20_

14. 9, 12 _36_

15. 10, 15 _30_

16. 8, 12 _24_

Write even or odd for each number.

17. 7 _odd_ 18. 10 _even_ 19. 15 _odd_ 20. 35 _odd_ 21. 28 _even_ 22. 83 _odd_

Now Try This!

A number is **even** if it has 2 as one of its factors.
A number is **odd** if 2 is *not* one of its factors.

Write the largest possible set of factors for each multiplication problem.
Write the product. Then identify each product as odd or even.

$7 \times 6 = 7 \times (3 \times 2) = 42$ **even**   2 is a factor of 42.

1. $5 \times 14 =$ _5 × (7×2)_ = _70_ _even_

2. $6 \times 18 =$ _6 × (3×2) × (9×2)_ = ___ ___

3. $15 \times 21 =$ ___ = ___ ___

Decide if the product of these numbers would be even or odd.

4. even × odd = _____

5. odd × odd = _____

6. even × even = _____

44   Lesson 3-2 • Multiples and Common Multiples

Name _____

Multiples of 10, 100, 1,000, and 10,000

Computer printers work very fast. How many
characters can this one print in 6 minutes of steady use?

5,000
characters
per minute

We want to find the total number of characters the
printer can print in 6 minutes.

The printer prints __5,000__ characters per minute.

The printer is used for __6__ minutes.

To find the total number of characters printed,

we multiply __6__ by __5,000__.

Study the pattern in these multiplication equations.

$6 \times 1 = 6$	$6 \times 5 = 30$
$6 \times 10 = 60$	$6 \times 50 = 300$
$6 \times 100 = 600$	$6 \times 500 = 3,000$
$6 \times 1,000 = 6,000$	
$6 \times 10,000 = 60,000$	$6 \times 5,000 = $ _____

The printer can print __30,000__ characters in 6 minutes.

REMEMBER To multiply by multiples of 10, 100, and 1,000 mentally,
we find the product of the nonzero digits. Write that product followed
by the same number of zeros as in the multiple.

$5 \times 1 = $ _____ $5 \times 10 = $ _____ $5 \times 100 = $ _____

$5 \times 6 = $ _____ $5 \times 60 = $ _____ $5 \times 600 = $ _____

$5 \times 1,000 = $ _____ $5 \times 10,000 = $ _____

$5 \times 6,000 = $ _____ $5 \times 60,000 = $ _____

Getting Started

Multiply. Use mental math.

1. $7 \times 800 = $ __5,600__

2. $3,000 \times 9 = $ __27,000__

3. $40 \times 6 = $ __240__

4. $4 \times 7,000 = $ __28,000__

5. $900 \times 8 = $ __7,200__

6. $5 \times 30 = $ __150__

7. $60 \times 3 = $ __180__

8. $4 \times 300 = $ __1,200__

9. $3,000 \times 3 = $ __9,000__

10. $6 \times 6,000 = $ __36,000__

11. $700 \times 9 = $ __6,300__

12. $5 \times 70 = $ __350__

Practice

Multiply. Use mental math.

1. $5 \times 300 =$ 1500

2. $20 \times 9 =$ 180

3. $100 \times 6 =$ 600

4. $1{,}000 \times 7 =$ 7,000

5. $6 \times 5{,}000 =$ 30,000

6. $60 \times 3 =$ 180

7. $8 \times 40{,}000 =$ 320,000

8. $3 \times 2{,}000 =$ 6,000

9. $3{,}000 \times 7 =$ 21,000

10. $600 \times 6 =$ 3,600

11. $8 \times 40 =$ 320

12. $10{,}000 \times 9 =$ 90,000

13. $90{,}000 \times 7 =$ 630,000

14. $3 \times 300 =$ 900

15. $5{,}000 \times 8 =$ 40,000

16. $6{,}000 \times 2 =$ 12,000

17. $4 \times 40{,}000 =$ 160,000

18. $700 \times 5 =$ 3,500

19. $6 \times 50 =$ 300

20. $900 \times 3 =$ 2,700

21. $20{,}000 \times 8 =$ 160,000

22. $3{,}000 \times 4 =$ 12,000

23. $60{,}000 \times 6 =$ 360,000

24. $4 \times 8{,}000 =$ 32,000

25. $2 \times 70{,}000 =$ 140,000

26. $4 \times 500 =$ 2,000

27. $60 \times 9 =$ 540

28. $9 \times 90{,}000 =$ 810,000

29. $3 \times 700 =$ 2,100

30. $7 \times 60{,}000 =$ 420,000

31. $5{,}000 \times 2 =$ 10,000

32. $90 \times 3 =$ 270

33. $2{,}000 \times 9 =$ 18,000

34. $4 \times 80{,}000 =$ 320,000

35. $3 \times 4{,}000 =$ 12,000

36. $9 \times 80{,}000 =$ 720,000

Problem Solving

Solve each problem.

37. Name tags for the sales convention come in boxes of 500. How many name tags are there in 7 boxes?

    $500 \times 7 = 3{,}500$ name tags

38. The convention manager put 40 chairs in each of the meeting rooms. How many chairs are there in 9 meeting rooms?

    $40 \times 9 = 360$ chairs

39. A sales person for a computer company flies 5,000 miles each month. How far does he fly in 6 months?

    $5{,}000 \times 6 = 30{,}000$ miles

40. Company cars for each sales team cost $30,000. How much will company cars for 8 sales teams cost?

    $\$30{,}000 \times 8 = \$240{,}000$

Name _____

Estimating Products

A water pipe broke in Simon's grocery store, and 23 boxes of soap were completely soaked. About how many grams of soap were ruined?

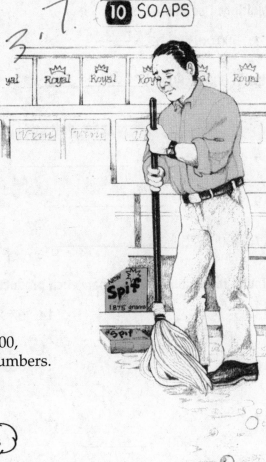

We want to estimate the total amount of soap that was ruined.

We know each box contained

_____ grams of soap.

There were _____ boxes damaged by water. To estimate, we round each factor and multiply.

1,875 rounded to the nearest 1,000 is _____.

23 rounded to the nearest 10 is _____.

REMEMBER To multiply two multiples of 10, 100, 1,000, or 10,000, we mentally multiply the nonzero whole numbers. The product will have as many zeros as there are in both factors together.

$2 \times 2 = 4$ $3 \text{ zeros} + 1 \text{ zero} = 4 \text{ zeros}$

$2,000 \times 20 = 40,000$

To estimate a product, we round each factor to its greatest place value and multiply.

About _____ grams of soap were ruined.

Getting Started

Multiply. Use mental math.

1. $8,000 \times 200 =$ _1,600,000_

2. $40 \times 10,000 =$ _400,000_

3. $6,000 \times 3,000 =$ _18,000,000_

4. $500 \times 3,000 =$ _1,500,000_

Round the factors and estimate each product.

5. $9 \times 63 =$ _600_

6. 38×72 _2,800_

7. 43×165 _8,000_

8. 425×688 _280,000_

9. $1,526 \times 65$ _140,000_

10. $4,321 \times 788$ _3,200,000_

Practice

Multiply. Use mental math.

1. 500 × 30 = _15,000_
2. 70 × 800 = _56,000_
3. 3,000 × 80 = _240,000_
4. 60 × 6,000 = _360,000_
5. 10,000 × 50 = _500,000_
6. 900 × 7,000 = _6,300,000_
7. 4,000 × 2,000 = _8,000,000_
8. 9,000 × 800 = _7,200,000_
9. 50 × 90 = _4,500_
10. 300 × 3,000 = _9,000,000_
11. 400 × 200 = _80,000_
12. 500 × 6,000 = _3,000,000_

Round the factors and estimate each product.

13. 56 × 43 2,400
14. 67 × 16 1,400
15. 9 × 439 4,000
16. 237 × 15 4,000
17. 623 × 32 18,000
18. 87 × 482 45,000
19. 128 × 256 30,000
20. 389 × 721 28,000
21. 796 × 593 48,000
22. 3,258 × 6 30,000
23. 2,847 × 9 30,000
24. 43 × 3,159 120,000
25. 8,225 × 33 240,000
26. 6,215 × 215 1,200,000
27. 387 × 465 200,000
28. 7,096 × 583 42,000,000
29. 289 × 5,653 1,800,000
30. 7,850 × 68 560,000
31. 175 × 8 2,000
32. 785 × 302 240,000
33. 9 × 5,276 50,000
34. 57 × 48 3,000
35. 4,796 × 78 400,000
36. 3,475 × 2,758 9,000,000

Problem Solving

Solve each problem.

37. The Speedy Bike Company orders bolts in barrels that hold 4,260 bolts each. About how many bolts will they receive if they order 9 barrels?

38. A TV center is charged $589 for each television it stocks. It has 53 sets in stock to sell. About how much did the store pay for its current TV inventory?

Multiplying With Regrouping

Pierre has saved exactly enough money to buy 2 pairs of running shoes at the annual shoe sale. How much has Pierre saved?

93.6

ONCE - A - YEAR

SHOE SALE!

RUNNING SHOES $39.97
TENNIS SHOES $19.97
BASKETBALL SHOES $24.49

We are looking for the total amount of money Pierre has saved.

We know a pair of running shoes costs _____.

Pierre has saved enough to buy _____ pairs.

To find the amount of money Pierre has saved, we multiply the cost of one pair of shoes by the number of pairs he will buy.

We multiply _____ by _____.

REMEMBER To multiply money, we multiply as we do whole numbers and place the decimal point between the second and the third digits from the right.

Multiply the ones.	Multiply the tens.	Multiply the hundreds.	Multiply the thousands. Place the decimal point and write the dollar sign.
$\begin{array}{r} 1 \\ \$39.97 \\ \times \quad 2 \\ \hline 4 \end{array}$	$\begin{array}{r} 1\ 1 \\ \$39.97 \\ \times \quad 2 \\ \hline 94 \end{array}$	$\begin{array}{r} 1\ 1 \\ \$39.97 \\ \times \quad 2 \\ \hline 994 \end{array}$	$\begin{array}{r} 1 \\ \$39.97 \\ \times \quad 2 \\ \hline \$79.94 \end{array}$

Pierre has saved _____.

Getting Started

Multiply. Check by estimation.

1. $\begin{array}{r} 2\ 4 \\ 257 \\ \times \quad 7 \\ \hline 1,799 \end{array}$

2. $\begin{array}{r} 4\ 3 \\ \$3.96 \\ \times \quad 5 \\ \hline \$19.80 \end{array}$

3. $\begin{array}{r} 1\ 2 \\ 6,247 \\ \times \quad 3 \\ \hline 18,741 \end{array}$

4. $\begin{array}{r} 4\ 2\ 4 \\ \$27.48 \\ \times \quad 6 \\ \hline \$22488 \end{array}$

Copy and multiply.

5. $12,426 \times 4$
    49,704

6. $\$315.07 \times 8$
    $2520.56

7. $615,210 \times 2$
    1,230,420

8. $\$1,512.38 \times 9$
    $13,611.42

Practice

Multiply. Check by estimation.

1. 96
    × 5
    480

2. $63
    × 7
    441

3. $89
    × 6
    $534

4. 57
    × 9
    513

5. 859
    × 4
    3,436

6. 937
    × 7
    6,559

7. $3.47
    × 8
    $27.76

8. $7.28
    × 2
    $14.56

9. 1,276
    × 3
    3,828

? OK 10. $32.67
    × 6
    $196.02

11. 4,758
    × 4
    19,032

12. $75.45
    × 5
    $377.25

13. 17,246
    × 9
    155,214

14. $215.37
    × 2
    $430.74

15. 36,256
    × 5
    181,280

16. $409.27
    × 7
    $2,864.89

Copy and multiply.

17. $3,036.58 × 3
    9,109.74

18. $8,174.58 × 6
    $49,017.48

19. 212,639 × 7
    1,488,473

20. 857,916 × 8
    6,863,328

21. 796 × 5
    3,980.

22. 4 × 3,275
    13,100

23. 9 × $12.07
    $108.63

24. 8,712 × 2
    17,424

25. 5 × $15.75
    $78.75

26. 32,751 × 8
    262,008

27. $165.81 × 3
    $500.43

28. 6 × 217,816
    1,306,896

Problem Solving

Solve each problem.

29. There are 1,760 yards in 1 mile. How many yards are there in 6 miles?
    10,560

30. A truck holds 2,475 gallons of milk. How many gallons will 3 trucks hold?
    7,425

31. Tennis shoes cost $59.95 and basketball shoes are $24.49. How much more do the tennis shoes cost?
    $35.46

32. The paint and supplies needed to paint 1 house cost $529.35. How much will it cost to paint 5 houses?

33. The space shuttle can carry 11,456 pounds of equipment in one trip. How many pounds can the space shuttle carry in 8 trips?

34. The library purchased 7 copies of a popular book. The book costs $23.95. How much did the library spend on the books?

Multiplying by Multiples of 10

Opal is using a computer to write her article for
the school newspaper. Her editor limited her to
14,000 characters for the entire article. She set the
margins to allow for a line width of 80 characters.
So far she has typed 146 lines. Is her article too long?

100%

We want to find the total number of characters
in Opal's article.

We know each line has _____ characters.

Opal has typed _____ lines.

To find the total number of characters in
Opal's article, we multiply the number of
lines by the number of characters in each line.

We multiply _____ by _____.

Multiply by the digit in the ones place.		Multiply by the digit in the tens place.

$$\begin{array}{r} 146 \\ \times\ \ 80 \\ \hline 0 \end{array}$$ $0 \times 146 = 0$

$$\begin{array}{r} 146 \\ \times\ \ \ \ 80 \\ \hline 11{,}680 \end{array}$$ $8 \times 146 = 1{,}168$

Opal's article has _____ characters. It is _____
than the limit of 14,000 characters.

Getting Started

Multiply. Check by estimation.

1.	52	2.	38	3.	$145	4.	186
	× 20		× 60		× 30		× 70
	1,040		2,280		$4,350		13,020

Copy and multiply.

5. $2{,}365 \times 40$

6. $\$6{,}886 \times 50$

7. $21{,}725 \times 90$

8. $85{,}648 \times 80$

94,600 $39,430   1,955,250   6,851,890

Practice

Multiply. Check by estimation.

1. 67
   × 50
   _3,350_

2. 98
   × 30
   _2,940_

3. 67
   × 80
   _5,360_

4. 32
   × 20
   _640_

5. 615
   × 90
   _55,350_

6. 723
   × 70
   _50,610_

7. $903
   × 40
   _$36,120_

8. 363
   × 60
   _21,780_

9. $3,625
   × 40
   _$145,000_

10. 8,275
    × 60
    _496,500_

11. 5,926
    × 90
    _533,340_

12. 2,658
    × 20
    _53,160_

Copy and multiply

13. 13,258 × 30
    _397,740_

14. $51,275 × 50
    _$2,563,750_

15. 24,023 × 70
    _1,681,610_

16. 85,658 × 80
    _6,852,640_

17. 48 × 80
    _3,840_

18. 70 × 385
    _26,950_

19. 20 × $1,297
    _$25,940_

20. 3,968 × 60
    _238,080_

21. 5,796 × 20
    _115,920_

22. $62,349 × 90
    _$5,611,410_

23. 16,350 × 50
    _817,500_

24. 72,056 × 40
    _2,882,240_

Problem Solving

Solve each problem.

25. How many minutes are there in one day?
    1,440 Minutes

26. How many seconds are there in one half-hour?
    1,800 Seconds

27. Nancy uses her computer 20 times each month. How many times does Nancy use her computer in one year?
    240 times

28. A can contains 80 pounds of cleaning compound. Bill used 46 pounds. How much compound is left in the can?
    34 Pounds

Now Try This!

Powers of 10 can be written using exponents.

$$10,000 = 10 \times 10 \times 10 \times 10 = 10^4.$$

Numbers can be written using powers of 10 to represent each place value.

$$35,877 = (3 \times 10^4) + (5 \times 10^3) + (8 \times 10^2) + (7 \times 10^1) + (7 \times 10^0)$$

$$721,064 = (7 \times 10^5) + (2 \times 10^4) + (1 \times 10^3) + (6 \times 10^1) + (4 \times 10^0)$$

Use exponents to write each number in expanded notation.

1. 6,831

2. 55,810

3. 459,261

Multiplying by a 2-Digit Factor

In June 1965, Ed White was the first American astronaut to walk in space. His *Gemini* space capsule made a complete trip around the globe every 89 minutes. How many minutes altogether did Ed White's ship spend orbiting the Earth?

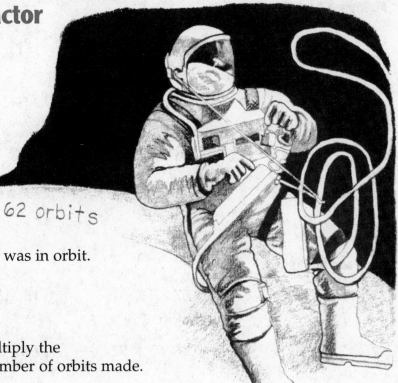

62 orbits

We want to find the total time *Gemini* was in orbit.

We know *Gemini* made _____ orbits.

Each orbit took _____ minutes.

To find the total time in orbit, we multiply the length of time for one orbit by the number of orbits made.

We multiply _____ by _____.

Multiply by the digit in the ones place.	Multiply by the digit in the tens place.	Add the products.
$\begin{array}{r} {\scriptstyle 1} \\ 62 \\ \times\ 89 \\ \hline 558 \end{array}$ ←9 × 62	$\begin{array}{r} {\scriptstyle 1} \\ {\scriptstyle 1} \\ 62 \\ \times\ 89 \\ \hline 558 \\ 4{,}960 \end{array}$ ←80 × 62	$\begin{array}{r} 62 \\ \times\ 89 \\ \hline 558 \\ 4{,}960 \\ \hline 5{,}518 \end{array}$ ←9 × 62 ←80 × 62 ←89 × 62

Gemini was in orbit for __5,518__ minutes.

Getting Started

Multiply. Check by estimation.

1. $\begin{array}{r} 45 \\ \times\ 17 \\ \hline 765 \end{array}$

2. $\begin{array}{r} 38 \\ \times\ 45 \\ \hline 1{,}710 \end{array}$

3. $\begin{array}{r} \$65.89 \\ \times\ \ \ 74 \\ \hline \$4{,}875.86 \end{array}$

Copy and multiply.

4. $7.86 × 37

$290.82

5. 2,056 × 53

108,968

6. 475 × 28

13,300

Practice

Multiply. Check by estimation.

1. 34
   × 27
   _918_

2. 18
   × 56
   _1,008_

3. 97
   × 86
   _8,342_

4. 47
   × 39
   _1,833_

5. 167
   × 43
   _7,181_

6. $8.15
   × 52
   _$423.80_

7. $23.18
   × 54
   _$1251.72_

8. 3,795
   × 76
   _288,120_

9. $86.24
   × 28

10. 4,708
    × 52

11. $20.08
    × 35

12. 9,870
    × 49

Copy and multiply.

13. 32 × 58

14. 67 × 88

15. 139 × 47

16. $3.85 × 15

17. 3,228 × 39

18. $67.75 × 72

19. 36 × 8,476

20. $30.19 × 68

21. $6.46 × 75

22. 9,465 × 39

23. 85 × 74

24. 538 × 69

25. 49 × 87

26. 33 × 4,096

27. $53.42 × 54

28. 8,328 × 58

Problem Solving

Solve each problem.

29. In one week a shoe store sold 67 pairs of running shoes. Each pair cost $25.99. How much did customers spend that week on running shoes?

30. An electrician on a construction job earns $24.83 per hour. How much does the electrician earn in one week, working 38 hours?

31. There were 27 meeting rooms reserved for a seminar. Each room contained 134 chairs. How many chairs were in use for the seminar?

32. Mrs. Davis works 35 hours each week. She gets 3 weeks vacation annually. How many hours does Mrs. Davis work each year?

33. Lucia works 3 hours after school walking dogs. She earns $2.68 an hour. She worked 21 days in February and 22 days in March. How much did Lucia earn?

34. The distance around the globe at the equator is 24,900 miles. How much farther is that distance than the 2,825-mile distance between Los Angeles and New York City?

Name _____

Multiplying by a 3-Digit Factor

Mrs. Mayer delivers meat for the Angus Meat Company. She must travel on the toll road for part of her daily route. She enters the turnpike at Exit 10 and leaves at Exit 8. On the return trip she reverses the route. If Mrs. Mayer worked 234 days last year, how many turnpike miles did she drive?

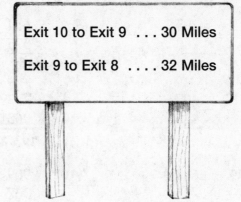

Exit 10 to Exit 9 . . . 30 Miles

Exit 9 to Exit 8 . . . . 32 Miles

We want to find the total number of turnpike miles Mrs. Mayer drove on her route last year.

We know she drove _____ turnpike miles one way. We need to double that distance to get her total daily mileage.

We multiply _____ by _____.

To find the total turnpike miles, we multiply the number of miles driven in one day by the number of days this route was taken.

We multiply _____ by _____.

Multiply by ones.	Multiply by tens.	Multiply by hundreds.	Add the products.

124	124	124	124
× 234	× 234	× 234	× 234
496	496	496	496 ← 4 × 124
↑	3 720	3 720	3 720 ← 30 × 124
4 × 124	↑	24 800	24 800 ← 200 × 124
	30 × 124	↑	29,016 ← 234 × 124
		200 × 124	

Mrs. Mayer drove _____ turnpike miles last year.

Getting Started

Multiply. Check by estimation.

1.   587
   × 265

2. $709
   × 826

   $585,634

3.   648
   × 354

Copy and multiply.

4. 783 × 612

5. 891 × 323

6. $5.18 × 427

   $2,211.86

Practice

Multiply. Check by estimation.

1. 795
    × 243

2. 654
    × 575
    376,050

3. $818
    × 375

4. 518
    × 221
    114,478

5. 407
    × 476

6. $5.39
    × 681
    $3670.59

7. 438
    × 159

8. 713
    × 390
    278,070

9. 683
    × 725

10. 909
    × 367
    333,603

11. $816
    × 793

12. 666
    × 635
    422,910

Copy and multiply.

13. 527 × 382

14. $7.82 × 356

15. 428 × 847

16. 120 × 789

17. 923 × $4.85

18. 615 × 238

19. 916 × 746

20. 306 × 473

21. 226 × 739

22. 656 × 531

23. $7.62 × 489

24. 199 × 886

Problem Solving

Solve each problem.

25. The school cafeteria serves 326 meals each day. If there are 182 school days, how many meals are served in one school year?

26. Today, the cafeteria paid $163 for milk and $40.95 for fruit. How much did the cafeteria spend on milk and fruit altogether?

27. Six cafeteria helpers each work 12 hours a week. If each helper earns $4.87 per hour, what is the payroll for cafeteria helpers each week?

28. On Tuesday, the cafeteria took in $891.50. If 285 hot meals were served for $1.15 each, how much money was earned from cold meal sales?

29. Eleanor works in the cafeteria making sandwiches. Each day she makes 154 sandwiches. If she works 145 days in one year, how many sandwiches does she make?

30. Which product is greater, 205 × 320 or 175 × 390? How can you use what you know about estimating products to answer this question without finding the product?

Zeros in a Factor

The Lincoln School Drama Club uses the proceeds from its plays to fund future productions. The latest play was attended by 79 students and 307 adults. How much did the drama club earn from the adult sales?

100%

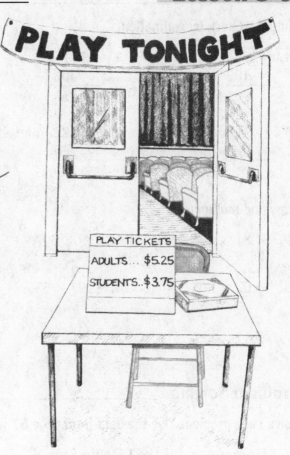

We are looking for the amount of money collected from adult ticket sales.

We know an adult ticket costs _____.

The play was attended by _____ adults.

To find the total amount collected from the adult tickets, we multiply the cost of one ticket by the number of adult tickets sold.

We multiply _____ by _____.

Multiply by ones.	Multiply by tens.	Multiply by hundreds.	Add the products. Place the dollar sign and decimal point.

$$\begin{array}{r} \$5.25 \\ \times\ 307 \\ \hline 3675 \end{array}$$

↑
7 × 525

$$\begin{array}{r} \$5.25 \\ \times\ 307 \\ \hline 36\,75 \\ 00 \end{array}$$

↑
0 × 525

$$\begin{array}{r} \$5.25 \\ \times\ 307 \\ \hline 3675 \\ 157500 \end{array}$$

↑
300 × 525

$$\begin{array}{r} \$5.25 \\ \times\ 307 \\ \hline 3675 \\ 157500 \\ \hline \$1,611.75 \end{array}$$
← 7 × 525
← 300 × 525
← 307 × 525

The drama club earned _____ from adult ticket sales.

Getting Started

Multiply. Check by estimation.

1. $\begin{array}{r} 756 \\ \times\ 408 \\ \hline \end{array}$ *308,448*

2. $\begin{array}{r} \$4.85 \\ \times\ 609 \\ \hline \end{array}$

3. $\begin{array}{r} \$807 \\ \times\ 501 \\ \hline \end{array}$ *$404,307*

Copy and multiply.

4. 567 × 703

5. $9.46 × 506 *$978,6.76*

6. 148 × 209

Practice

Multiply. Check by estimation.

1. $736
    × 103

2. $9.76
    × 406
    $3,962.56

3. $1.08
    × 504

4. 479
    × 210
    100590

5. 653
    × 356

6. $5.22
    × 720
    $375,840   100%.

7. 378
    × 902

8. 123
    × 818
    100,614

Copy and multiply.

9. $4.81 × 206

10. 759 × 307
    233,013

11. 509 × 824

12. 285 × 616
    175,560

13. $3.07 × 805

14. $297 × 536
    $159,192

15. 905 × 483

16. 610 × 199
    121,390

17. 507 × 658

18. 489 × 409
    200,001

19. $4.06 × 405

20. 708 × 509
    360,372

Problem Solving

Solve each problem. Use the data from page 57 when necessary.

21. How much did the Lincoln School Drama Club make from the sale of student tickets?

22. What was the total amount of money collected by the drama club for the school pay?

23. This year, the make-up crew used 103 grease pencils, costing $1.98 each, and 19 cans of hair spray, costing $1.09 each. How much did the crew spend on pencils alone?

    $215.38

24. Satin costume fabric costs $4.63 a yard, and cotton costs $2.89 a yard. The costume crew needs 210 yards of fabric. How much money would be saved by making the costumes out of cotton rather than satin?

Now Try This!

Imagine placing three colored balls (one red, one green, and one blue) into three colored boxes (one red, one green, and one blue) so that no ball is in a box of the same color. If the blue ball is not in the red box, which ball is in the green box?   blue

Name _____

Problem Solving: Restate the Problem

As I was going to St. Ives I was joined by a group of
seven wives. Every wife had seven sacks; every sack
had seven cats; every cat had seven kits. Kits, cats, sacks,
and wives; how many were going to St. Ives?

 SEE

We want to know the total number of kits, cats, sacks,
and wives that were going to St. Ives.

There were _____ wives with _____ sacks.

Every sack had _____ cats.

Every cat had _____ kits.

 PLAN

Since the wording of this rhyme is confusing, we restate
the problem in our own words. We also start to count the
number of each as we reword the problem.

DO

There were _____ wives. Each had _____ sacks.

(There were _____ sacks altogether.)

Each sack contained _____ cats.

(There were _____ × 7, or _____ cats.)

Each cat had _____ kittens.

(There were _____ × 7, or _____ kittens.)

To find the total number of wives, sacks, cats, and kits, we
add the number of each.

_____ + _____ + _____ + _____ = _____

There were a total of 2,800 wives, sacks, cats, and
kits going to St. Ives.

 CHECK

2,401 ÷ 7 = _____ cats   _____ ÷ 7 = _____ sacks   _____ ÷ 7 = _____ wives

Apply

Solve each problem.

1. A student had $10.00 and spent all but $2.00. How much money did the student have left?

   $2.00

2. Harvey says, "I am thinking of two numbers. Their product is 0 and their sum is 15. What are the two numbers?" Answer Harvey's question and explain why your answer is correct.

   15 and 0

3. Five snips cost 5 million snipes, three snaps cost 300 snipes, and two snops cost 20 thousand snipes. What would it cost to purchase one snip, two snaps and three snops?

   1,030,200

4. The combined cost of a baseball card and bubble gum is $1.05. The card costs 5 cents more than the gum. How much does each item cost?

   50 and 55

5. Ivan purchased several items whose total cost was $1.96. All the items were the same price. As many items were bought as the number of total cents in the cost of each item. How many items were bought?

   14

6. Five and one half million dollars worth of diamonds were lost in a lake. $200,000 worth were recovered. What is the value of the diamonds still to be recovered?

   5,300,000

7. Read Exercise 4 again. What if the card cost 15¢ more than the gum? Now how much does each cost?

   40 and 65

8. Eeny, Meeny, and Moe each multiply the same 3-digit number by a 2-digit number. Eeny gets a 7-digit answer, Meeny gets a 2-digit answer, and Moe gets a 5-digit answer. Whose answers are incorrect and how do you know?

9. Old MacDonald had some chicks. At the auction he bought twice as many chicks as he had originally. Now he has 27 chicks. How many chicks did he have originally?

10. Read Exercise 9 again. Rewrite the problem so that the correct answer is 3 chicks.

Multiply. Check Exercises 15–22 by estimation.

1. $\begin{array}{r} 7 \\ \times\,3 \\ \hline 21 \end{array}$	2. $\begin{array}{r} 9 \\ \times\,6 \\ \hline 54 \end{array}$	3. $\begin{array}{r} 5 \\ \times\,0 \\ \hline 0 \end{array}$	4. $\begin{array}{r} 8 \\ \times\,7 \\ \hline 56 \end{array}$	5. $\begin{array}{r} 9 \\ \times\,7 \\ \hline 63 \end{array}$	6. $\begin{array}{r} 6 \\ \times\,4 \\ \hline 24 \end{array}$

7. $\begin{array}{r} 37 \\ \times\,6 \\ \hline 222 \end{array}$	8. $\begin{array}{r} 259 \\ \times\,7 \\ \hline 1{,}813 \end{array}$	9. $\begin{array}{r} 1{,}384 \\ \times\,4 \\ \hline 5{,}536 \end{array}$	10. $\begin{array}{r} \$16.97 \\ \times\,8 \\ \hline \$135.76 \end{array}$

11. $\begin{array}{r} 62 \\ \times\,25 \\ \hline 1{,}550 \end{array}$	12. $\begin{array}{r} 40 \\ \times\,80 \\ \hline 3{,}200 \end{array}$	13. $\begin{array}{r} 57 \\ \times\,29 \\ \hline 1{,}653 \end{array}$	14. $\begin{array}{r} 87 \\ \times\,36 \\ \hline 3{,}132 \end{array}$

15. $\begin{array}{r} 186 \\ \times\,72 \\ \hline 13{,}398 \end{array}$	16. $\begin{array}{r} 1{,}309 \\ \times\,84 \\ \hline 109{,}956 \end{array}$	17. $\begin{array}{r} \$39.65 \\ \times\,90 \\ \hline \$3{,}568.50 \end{array}$	18. $\begin{array}{r} 2{,}431 \\ \times\,56 \\ \hline 136{,}136 \end{array}$

19. $\begin{array}{r} 628 \\ \times\,247 \\ \hline 155{,}116 \end{array}$	20. $\begin{array}{r} 825 \\ \times\,409 \\ \hline 337{,}425 \end{array}$	21. $\begin{array}{r} \$7.15 \\ \times\,326 \\ \hline \$2{,}330.90 \end{array}$	22. $\begin{array}{r} 618 \\ \times\,510 \\ \hline 315{,}180 \end{array}$

Write the least common multiple of each pair of numbers.

23. 6 and 8 __24__   24. 12 and 15 __60__   25. 2 and 9 __18__

26. 7 and 14 __28__   27. 4 and 9 __36__   28. 5 and 7 __35__

29. 6 and 9 __18__   30. 14 and 21 __42__   31. 15 and 16 __240__

Write even or odd for each number.

32. 27 __odd__   33. 34 __even__   34. 158 __even__

35. 167 __odd__   36. 900 __even__   37. 702 __even__

38. 758 __even__   39. 489 __odd__   40. 205 __odd__

Circle the letter of the correct answer.

1 What is the place value of the digit 6 in 427,165?
a. ones
b. tens
c. hundreds
d. NG

2 What is the place value of the digit 9 in 493,274?
a. thousands
b. ten thousands
c. hundred thousands
d. NG

3 709 ◯ 790
a. <
b. >
c. =

4 12,739 ◯ 12,740
a. <
b. >
c. =

5 $6.75
  + 3.19
a. $9.84
b. $9.94
c. $10.94
d. NG

6 27,096
  + 14,375
a. 31,361
b. 31,371
c. 41,371
d. NG

7 Estimate the sum to the nearest thousand.
  3,621
  + 975
a. 4,600
b. 5,000
c. 6,000
d. NG

8 $9.27 − $4.88
a. $4.39
b. $5.39
c. $5.61
d. NG

9 80,096
  − 24,798
a. 55,298
b. 56,298
c. 64,702
d. NG

10 Estimate the difference.
  67,963
  − 13,750
a. 60,000
b. 70,000
c. 80,000
d. NG

11 27 × 5
a. 105
b. 135
c. 1,035
d. NG

12 1,429
  ×   9
a. 12,816
b. 11,861
c. 12,861
d. NG

13 23
  × 48
a. 1,004
b. 1,104
c. 1,204
d. NG

/00 **score**

STOP

Divide by 1-Digit Numbers

It's Algebra!

Facts and Properties

The **quotient** in a division fact is the same as a missing factor in the related multiplication fact. If you remember the multiplication facts and how to make **fact families**, you will know the division facts.

Since we know $9 \times 4 = 36$, we also know $36 \div 4 = 9$.

$9 \times n = 36$

$n = ?$

$n \times 4 = 36$

$n = ?$

We can write two multiplication and two division equations for the numbers 4, 9, and 36.

$9 \times 4 = \underline{36}$ $\qquad$ $36 \div 4 = \underline{9}$

$\underline{4} \times 9 = 36$ $\qquad$ $36 \div 9 = \underline{4}$

The four equations form a **fact family**. The fact family for 4, 9, and 36 can also be written in vertical form.

$$\begin{array}{r} 9 \\ \times 4 \\ \hline \end{array} \qquad \begin{array}{r} 4 \\ \times 9 \\ \hline \end{array} \qquad 9)\overline{36} \qquad 4)\overline{36}$$

Division has several basic properties that can help you remember some division facts.

If the **divisor** is 1, the quotient is the same as the **dividend**.

$1)\overline{5}$ with 5

$9 \div 1 = \underline{9}$

If the divisor and the dividend are the same number, the quotient is 1.

$8)\overline{8}$ with 1

$6 \div 6 = \underline{1}$

If the dividend is zero, the quotient is zero.

$2)\overline{0}$ with 0

$0 \div 7 = \underline{0}$

NEVER divide by zero.

Getting Started

Divide.

1. $12 \div 6 = \underline{6}$

2. $0 \div 12 = \underline{0}$

3. $15 \div 15 = \underline{1}$

4. $7)\overline{49}$ with 7

5. $1)\overline{9}$ with 9

6. $6)\overline{54}$ with 9

7. $3)\overline{0}$ with 0

8. $8)\overline{32}$ with 4

9. $5)\overline{5}$ with 1

Practice

Divide.

1. $4\overline{)4}$ $7\overline{)63}$ $1\overline{)8}$ $0\overline{)0}$ $9\overline{)45}$ $0\overline{)0}$ $1\overline{)9}$ $6\overline{)48}$

2. $2\overline{)16}$ $0\overline{)0}$ $6\overline{)30}$ $2\overline{)18}$ $0\overline{)0}$ $7\overline{)7}$ $1\overline{)1}$ $4\overline{)12}$

3. $3\overline{)12}$ $2\overline{)14}$ $8\overline{)24}$ $3\overline{)3}$ $7\overline{)14}$ $6\overline{)18}$ $5\overline{)5}$ $5\overline{)45}$

4. $2\overline{)6}$ $9\overline{)72}$ $5\overline{)15}$ $8\overline{)40}$ $4\overline{)36}$ $3\overline{)27}$ $2\overline{)4}$ $0\overline{)0}$

5. $7\overline{)28}$ $2\overline{)2}$ $9\overline{)18}$ $5\overline{)20}$ $6\overline{)36}$ $5\overline{)10}$ $8\overline{)72}$ $6\overline{)42}$

6. $1\overline{)7}$ $7\overline{)21}$ $2\overline{)8}$ $1\overline{)4}$ $2\overline{)10}$ $5\overline{)40}$ $4\overline{)16}$ $3\overline{)9}$

7. $8\overline{)16}$ $4\overline{)20}$ $0\overline{)0}$ $7\overline{)35}$ $8\overline{)56}$ $9\overline{)36}$ $6\overline{)24}$ $1\overline{)6}$

8. $4\overline{)28}$ $0\overline{)0}$ $4\overline{)32}$ $6\overline{)54}$ $9\overline{)9}$ $8\overline{)48}$ $0\overline{)0}$ $2\overline{)12}$

9. $3\overline{)21}$ $8\overline{)8}$ $0\overline{)0}$ $5\overline{)25}$ $9\overline{)54}$ $8\overline{)64}$ $4\overline{)24}$ $6\overline{)30}$

10. $1\overline{)3}$ $3\overline{)15}$ $7\overline{)56}$ $9\overline{)81}$ $6\overline{)12}$ $8\overline{)32}$ $3\overline{)24}$ $7\overline{)49}$

11. $1\overline{)5}$ $7\overline{)42}$ $3\overline{)6}$ $3\overline{)18}$ $9\overline{)63}$ $5\overline{)35}$ $6\overline{)6}$ $9\overline{)27}$

Lesson 4-1 • Facts and Properties

Order of Operations

Did you know that it is possible to get two different answers to a problem by doing the calculations in a different order each time? Len and Toni both tried to simplify the expression $8 + 32 \div 4 \times 2$.

Which answer is correct?

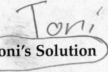

$8 + 32 \div 4 \times 2$
$40 \div 4 \times 2$

$8 + 32 \div 4 \times 2$
$8 + 8 \times 2$

Len's Solution	**Toni's Solution**
$8 + 32 \div 4 \times 2$	$8 + 32 \div 4 \times 2$
$40 \div 4 \times 2$	$8 + 8 \times 2$
10×2	$8 + 16$
20	24

The **Order of Operations** is a set of rules that tell you the order in which operations must be done.

- First, do the operations inside parentheses.

    There are no parentheses in $8 + 32 \div 4 \times 2$.

- Then, multiply and divide in order from *left* to *right*. $32 \div 4 =$ _____

    _____ $\times 2 =$ _____

- Last, add and subtract in order from *left* to *right*. $8 +$ _____ $=$ _____

The correct answer is _____ .

Getting Started

Use the order of operations to simplify each expression.

1. $8 + 4 \times 10$ 48

2. $(8 + 4) \times 10$ 120

3. $16 - (8 \div 2)$ 12

4. $25 - 6 \times 2 + 5$ 18

5. $(12 + 6) \div 3 + 12$ 18

6. $128 - 32 \times 4 + 15$ 15

Practice

Use the order of operations to simplify each expression.

1. $16 + 9 \times 2$

   34

2. $42 + 40 \div 10$

3. $(24 - 17) \times 8$

   56

4. $5 \times 6 + 2$

5. $12 + 4 \times 8$

   44

6. $(12 + 4) \times 8$

7. $15 - 3 \times (18 \div 6)$

   6

8. $4 \times 7 \div 2 + 9$

9. $6 + (9 - 4) \times 8$

   46

10. $7 + 5 - 4 \times 3$

11. $(21 \div 3) \times 2 + 6$

    20

12. $13 + 4 \times (48 \div 6)$

13. $12 + (10 - 4) \div 2$

    15

14. $8 \times (3 + 7) \div 10$

15. $9 \times 4 + (17 - 5)$

    48

Copy and simplify each expression.

16. $16 + 8 \div 2$

17. $4 + (21 - 7) \times 4$

    60

18. $36 \div 9 + 3 \times 4$

19. $(24 - 8) \div 4 + 12$

    16

20. $5 + (11 - 4) \times 5$

21. $3 + 6 - 10 \div 2$

    4

Problem Solving

Solve each problem.

22. Sam used parentheses to change the expression $5 + 8 - 3 \times 2$ so that it had the value 15. Use parentheses to show how he did it.

23. Which expression has the greater value, $(18 \div 6) \times 2 + 16$ or $15 + (18 - 3) \times 10$?

Name _____

Greatest Common Factor

Every number has at least two factors: 1 and the number itself. Numbers such as 18 and 24 have several factors in common. What is their **greatest common factor**?

We are looking for the **greatest common factor** of 18 and 24.

We need to list all the factors of each number, from the least to the greatest.

The factors of 18 are _____, _____, _____, _____, _____, and _____.

The factors of 24 are _____, _____, _____, _____, _____, _____, _____, and _____.

The factors that are common to both 18 and 24 are _____, _____, _____, and _____.

Their greatest common factor is _____.

REMEMBER The letters GCF are often used for the term greatest common factor:

The GCF of 18 and 24 is _____.

Factors:

$3 \times 6 = 18$
$2 \times 9 = 18$
$1 \times 18 = 18$

$4 \times 6 = 24$
$3 \times 8 = 24$
$2 \times 12 = 24$
$1 \times 24 = 24$

Getting Started

Write the factors for each number.

1. 6
   1, 2, 3, 6

2. 8
   1, 2, 4, 8

3. 10
   1, 2, 5, 10

4. 16
   1, 2, 4, 8   16 $-1/4$

5. 18
   1, 2, 3, 6, 9   18 $-1/4$

6. 9
   1, 3, 9

Write the common factors for each pair of numbers and circle the GCF.

7. 6 and 8
   1, ②

8. 8 and 16
   1, 2, 4, ⑧

9. 10 and 18
   1, ②

10. 8 and 36
    1, 2, ④

11. 20 and 35
    ⑤

12. 21 and 49
    1, ⑦

13. 18 and 12
    1, 2, 3, ⑥

14. 2 and 6
    1, ②

Practice

Write the factors for each number.

1. 9

1, 3, 9

2. 12

1, 2, 3, 4, 6, 12

3. 15

1, 3, 5, 15

4. 25

1, 5, 25

5. 14

1, 2, 7, 14

6. 20

1, 2, 4, 5, 10, 20

7. 24

1, 2, 3, 4, 6, 8, 12, 24

8. 22

1, 2, 11, 22

9. 49

1, 7, 49

Write the common factors for each pair of numbers and circle the GCF.

10. 6 and 9

1, ③

11. 9 and 12

1, ③

12. 15 and 25

1 ⑤

13. 28 and 49

1, ⑦

14. 32 and 40

1, 2, 4 ⑧

15. 18 and 22

1 ②

16. 32 and 72

1, 2 ⑧ 4

17. 9 and 81

1, ⑨, 3

18. 6 and 12

_____

19. 15 and 30

_____

20. 7 and 11

_____

21. 20 and 50

_____

Now Try This!

Another method for finding the GCF is to use the divisibility rules. A number is **divisible** by another number when the remainder is 0 after dividing. 18 is divisible by 1, 2, 3, 6, 9, and 18. Each of these numbers is also a factor of 18. You can use the divisibility rules to find factors of a number.

Divisibility Rules
A number is divisible by
2 if the last digit is 0, 2, 4, 6, or 8.
3 if the sum of the digits is divisible by 3.
4 if the number formed by the last two digits is divisible by 4.
5 if the last digit is 5 or 0.
6 if the number is divisible by both 2 and 3.
9 if the sum of the digits is divisible by 9.
10 if the last digit is 0.

Use the divisibility rules to find the GCF of each pair of numbers.

1. 4 and 12

GCF = _____

2. 22 and 55

GCF = _____

3. 12 and 16

GCF = _____

4. 42 and 12

GCF = _____

Factoring for Primes

A **prime** is any whole number that has exactly two factors: itself and 1. Primes can be multiplied together to make **composite numbers**. What set of prime numbers, when multiplied, equals 64?

Prime Numbers: 1 through 40

$2 = 1 \times 2$ $11 = 1 \times 11$ $23 = 1 \times 23$

$3 = 1 \times 3$ $13 = 1 \times 13$ $29 = 1 \times 29$

$5 = 1 \times 5$ $17 = 1 \times 17$ $31 = 1 \times 31$

$7 = 1 \times 7$ $19 = 1 \times 19$ $37 = 1 \times 37$

We are looking for the prime numbers that can be multiplied to equal the composite number 64.

To find the **prime factors**, we use a **factor tree**.

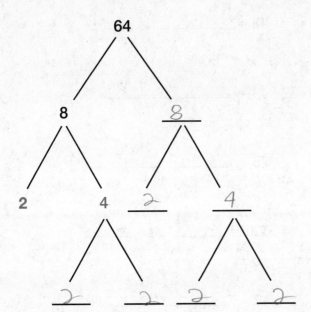

Two factors of 64 are 8×8.

The factors for each 8 are 2×4. Two branches end at the **prime number**, 2.

The factors for each 4 are 2×2. All the branches of the factor tree end in **primes**.

The branches of the factor tree end with the primes

_____, _____, _____, _____, _____, and _____.

REMEMBER We call the set of prime factors for a composite number the **product of primes**.

The product of primes for 64 is

$\underline{2} \times \underline{2} \times \underline{2} \times \underline{2} \times \underline{2} \times \underline{2}$.

Getting Started

Use a factor tree to find the product of primes for each composite number.

1. $28 = \underline{2 \times 2 \times 7}$

2. $36 = \underline{2 \times 2 \times 3 \times 3}$

3. $33 = \underline{11 \times 3}$

4. $35 = \underline{7 \times 5}$

5. $69 = \underline{23 \times 3}$

6. $75 = \underline{3 \times 5 \times 5}$

Practice

Use a factor tree to find the product of primes for each composite number.

1. 16 = 2×2×2×2

2. 24 = 2×2×2×3

3. 30 = 2×3×5

4. 32 = 2×2×2×2×2

5. 45 = 3×3×5

6. 48 = 2×2×2×2×3

7. 60 = 2×2×3×5

8. 72 = 2×2×2×3×3×4

9. 6 = 3×2

10. 18 = 2×3×3

Write the product of primes for each pair of numbers.
Circle the common prime factors. Find the GCF.

11. 20 = (2×2)×5 and 48 = (2×2)×2×2×3

GCF = 2×2 = 4

12. 54 = (2×3)×3×3 and 48 = 2×2×2×(2×3)

GCF = 3×2 = 6

13. 45 = 3×(3×5) and 75 = (3×5)×5

GCF = 5×3 = 15

14. 72 = (2×2×2)×3×3 and 120 = (2×2×2)×3×5

GCF = 2×2×2×3 = 24

15. 28 = (2)×2×(7) and 42 = (2)×3×(7)

GCF = 2×7 = 14

[Now Try This!]

You can use exponents to write the product of primes when factors are the same number. An exponent is a number that tells how many times another number is used as a factor. The exponent below tells you that the number 2 is used as a factor 3 times.

exponent
$$2^3 = 2 \times 2 \times 2$$

Find the product of primes for each number. Then, write the product using exponents.

1. 54 = _____ = _____

2. 20 = _____ = _____

3. 56 = _____ = _____

Lesson 4-4 • Factoring for Primes

Name _____

1-Digit Quotients With Remainders

Quan had trouble setting up enough chairs for the school play, because of a large post in the middle of the room. He finally arranged the chairs in 9 equal rows and 1 shorter row. How many chairs were in the equal rows? How many were in the shorter row?

We want to find the number of chairs in each of the equal rows.

We also want to know how many chairs were in the shorter row.

We know Quan used _____ chairs.

There were _____ equal rows.

To find out the number of chairs in each equal row, we divide the total number of chairs by the number of equal rows.

We divide _____ by _____.

The remainder will tell us how many chairs are in the shorter row.

quotient   remainder

$$
\begin{array}{r}
8 \text{ R3} \\
\text{divisor} \rightarrow 9\overline{)75} \leftarrow \text{dividend} \\
-72 \quad \leftarrow 9 \times 8 = 72 \\
\hline
3 \quad \leftarrow \text{Subtract. The}
\end{array}
$$
remainder must be less than the divisor.

We check division problems using multiplication and addition if necessary.

$(9 \times 8) + 3 =$ _____

Quan set up _____ chairs in each of the equal rows,

and _____ chairs in the shorter row.

Getting Started

Divide and check.

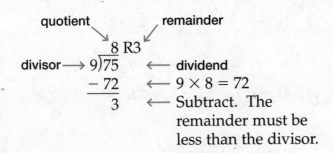

1. $4\overline{)26}$ — 6 r 2

2. $2\overline{)19}$ — 9 r 1

3. $3\overline{)18}$ — 6

4. $5\overline{)27}$ — 5 r 2

Copy and divide.

5. $85 \div 9$ — 9 r 4

6. $56 \div 7$ — 8

7. $63 \div 8$ — 7 r 7

8. $55 \div 6$ — 9 r 1

Practice

Divide.

1. $7\overline{)37}$ 5r2
2. $5\overline{)45}$ 9
3. $2\overline{)15}$ 7r1
4. $3\overline{)22}$ 7r1

5. $9\overline{)82}$ 9r1
6. $6\overline{)57}$ 9r3
7. $8\overline{)26}$ 3r2
8. $4\overline{)30}$ 7r2

9. $6\overline{)14}$ 2r2
10. $7\overline{)27}$ 3r6
11. $3\overline{)18}$ 6
12. $5\overline{)28}$ 5r3

13. $9\overline{)70}$ 7r7
14. $8\overline{)36}$ 4r4
15. $7\overline{)58}$ 8r2
16. $4\overline{)18}$ 4r2

Copy and divide.

17. $48 \div 7$ 6r6
18. $40 \div 8$ 5
19. $19 \div 3$ 6r1
20. $18 \div 4$ 4r2

21. $45 \div 6$ 7r3
22. $39 \div 9$ 4r3
23. $11 \div 5$ 2r1
24. $27 \div 7$ 3r6

25. $25 \div 3$ 8r1
26. $50 \div 7$ 7r1
27. $41 \div 6$ 6r5
28. $80 \div 9$ 8r8

Problem Solving

Solve each problem.

29. The drama teacher invited 21 students to a cast party. If all the students come in cars that carry 6 passengers, how many cars will be needed?

   4 cars

30. Each act in the play was cast with 5 different actors. There were 3 acts. How many actors were in the play?

   15 actors

31. The Jones family attended the play. They spent $24 for tickets. If each ticket costs $4, how many people in the Jones family attended the play?

   6 people

32. Altogether 75 people attended the play. There were 26 children in the audience. How many adults attended?

   49 adults

Interpreting Remainders

On Earth Day, 26 fifth graders have
volunteered to help clean up a local
beach. They will travel to the beach in
vans. Each van holds seven passengers.
How many vans will they need?

We know there are _____ fifth graders.

Each van can hold _____ fifth graders.

To find how many vans they need we

divide _____ by _____.

$$\begin{array}{r} 3 \text{ R}5 \\ 7\overline{)26} \\ -\ 21 \\ \hline 5 \end{array}$$

REMEMBER Sometimes we need to decide how to interpret the
remainder so that the answer makes sense. We may need to **use the
remainder**, to **drop the remainder**, or to **increase the quotient to the
next whole number**.

The quotient 3 R5 means there are _____ vans and _____ students left

over. Since 5 students will be in the last van, we need to round the

quotient to the next whole number.

They will need _____ vans.

Getting Started

Solve. Write *use the remainder, drop the remainder,* or *round the
quotient to the next whole number.* **Explain.**

1. There are 4 people on each team. If 29
people want to play, how many teams
can be formed?

   7 teams

2. Emily made 38 hamburgers for a
picnic. Rolls come in packages of 8.
How many packages did she buy to
have enough rolls for the hamburgers
she made?

   5 Packages

Practice

Solve each problem. Write *use the remainder*, *drop the remainder*, or *round the quotient to the next whole number*. Explain.

1. Marcus works 7 hours a day. So far this week he has worked 31 hours. How many full days has he worked?

   4 days

2. Stacy picked 26 pounds of apples. She put 3 pounds of apples in each basket. How many pounds of apples did she have left over?

   2 Pounds

3. There are 33 students in Darren's class. How many groups of 4 can the teacher make?

   8 groups

4. Melissa has 18 photos to put in an album. She puts 4 photos on each page. How many pages will she need?

   5 Pages

5. There are 70 people waiting on line for boat rides. Each boat holds 9 people. How many boats are needed for all the people who are waiting?

   8 boats

6. Steve buys a book of 20 stamps. He mails 6 letters a week. For how many weeks can he mail letters before he has to buy a new book of stamps?

   3 Weeks

Problem Solving

Use the chart to solve each problem.

7. Amy bought a large package of balloons to make balloon animals. It takes 5 balloons to make each animal. How many animals can she make?

   6 animals

8. If Amy buys a large and a small package of balloons how many balloon animals can she make?

   9 animals

9. How many extra hats will there be if Soo buys packages with enough hats for 28 people?

   2 hats

10. Forty-one people are coming to Depak's party. How many tables should he order? Would it be better if he ordered tables that seat 6 or 8? Explain.

    He should order 7 tables with 6

Party Planner

Item	Number Ordered
Tables:	
Seats 8	☐
Seats 6	☐
Balloons:	
Package of 16	☐
Package of 32	☐
Party hats:	
Package of 6	☐

Name _____

2-Digit Quotients

Mr. Porter is getting his science classroom ready for the new quarter. His largest class will have 54 students. How many tables will he need for his classroom?

We want to find the number of tables needed in Mr. Porter's classroom.

We know there will be _____ students in his largest class.

Each table seats only _____ students. To find the number of tables needed, we divide the total number of students by the number of seats available at each table.

We divide _____ by _____.

Divide the tens. $5 \div 4 = n$ Guess the closest fact that is not too large. Multiply.	Subtract and compare.	Bring down the ones.

$$\begin{array}{r} 1 \\ 4\overline{)54} \\ -4 \end{array}$$ $4 \times 1 = 4$

$$\begin{array}{r} 1 \\ 4\overline{)54} \\ -4 \\ \hline 1 \end{array}$$ $5 - 4 = 1$ $1 < 4$

$$\begin{array}{r} 1 \\ 4\overline{)54} \\ -4 \\ \hline 14 \end{array}$$

Divide the ones. $14 \div 4 = n$ Guess the closest fact that is not too large. Multiply.	Subtract and compare.	Write the remainder.

$$\begin{array}{r} 13 \\ 4\overline{)54} \\ -4 \\ \hline 14 \\ -12 \end{array}$$ $4 \times 3 = 12$

$$\begin{array}{r} 13 \\ 4\overline{)54} \\ -4 \\ \hline 14 \\ -12 \\ \hline 2 \end{array}$$ $14 - 12 = 2$ $2 < 4$

$$\begin{array}{r} 13\ \text{R}2 \\ 4\overline{)54} \\ -4 \\ \hline 14 \\ -12 \\ \hline 2 \end{array}$$

There are _____ tables needed.

Only _____ students will sit at one of the tables.

Getting Started

Divide and check.

1. $4\overline{)53}$ $31\ r1$

2. $6\overline{)66}$ 11

Copy and divide.

3. $24 \div 2$ 12

4. $81 \div 7$ $12\ r3$

Practice

Divide and check.

1. 4)63 ✓ 15 r3
2. 2)90 ✓ 45
3. 6)75 ✓ 12 r3
4. 3)86 ✓ 28 r2

5. 5)75 ✓ 15
6. 7)84 ✓ 12
7. 9)95 ✓ 10 r5
8. 8)97 ✓ 12 r1

9. 3)64 ✓ 21 r1
10. 2)57 ✓ 28 r1
11. 5)55 ✓ 11
12. 7)93 ✓ 13 r2

Copy and divide.

13. 59 ÷ 3
    19 r2
14. 36 ÷ 2
    18
15. 83 ÷ 5
    16 r3
16. 92 ÷ 7
    13 r1

17. 27 ÷ 4
    6 r3
18. 73 ÷ 6
    12 r1
19. 99 ÷ 9
    11
20. 94 ÷ 8
    11 r6

21. 36 ÷ 5
    7 r1
22. 57 ÷ 3
    19
23. 47 ÷ 4
    11 r3
24. 32 ÷ 2
    16

25. 45 ÷ 2
    22 r1
26. 79 ÷ 6
    13 r1
27. 87 ÷ 3
    29
28. 90 ÷ 4
    22 r2

Problem Solving

Solve each problem.

29. Nona is filling 5 beakers with the same amount of water, to observe evaporation. She has 75 ounces of water. How many ounces should Nona put into each beaker?

    15 ounces

30. Each of the 54 science students bought a notebook that cost $1.53. How much did the whole class pay for notebooks?

    $82.62

31. There are 4 groups of science students experimenting with batteries and bulbs. The materials for this activity cost the lab $64. What was the supply cost per group?

    $2.56

32. Only 44 of the science students signed up to go on a field trip. Each chaperone for the trip will be in charge of 3 students. How many chaperones are needed?

    15 chaperones

3-Digit Quotients

At the end of each month the Mighty Mowers divide their profits. The leftover profit is added to the next month's income. In June, the Mighty Mowers earned $370. How much did each person receive? How much profit was left to start July?

We want to find out how much money each person received in June, and how much was left over for July.

We know the Mighty Mowers earned _____ in June.

The money was divided evenly among _____ people. To find their individual earnings, we divide the group's June income by the number of workers in their group.

We divide _____ by _____.

Divide the hundreds.	**Divide the tens.**	**Divide the ones.**

$$
\begin{array}{r} 1 \\ 3\overline{)370} \\ -3\downarrow \\ \hline 07 \end{array}
\qquad
\begin{array}{r} 12 \\ 3\overline{)370} \\ -3\downarrow \\ \hline 07 \\ -6\downarrow \\ \hline 10 \end{array}
\qquad
\begin{array}{r} 123\ R1 \\ 3\overline{)370} \\ -3 \\ \hline 07 \\ -6 \\ \hline 10 \\ -9 \\ \hline 1 \end{array}
$$

Divide. $\quad 3\overline{)3}^{\,1}$
Multiply. $\quad 3 \times 1 = 3$
Subtract and $\quad 3 - 3 = 0$
compare. $\quad 0 < 3$
Bring down the tens.

Divide. $\quad 3\overline{)7}^{\,2}$
Multiply. $\quad 3 \times 2 = 6$
Subtract and $\quad 7 - 6 = 1$
compare. $\quad 1 < 3$
Bring down the ones.

Divide. $\quad 3\overline{)10}^{\,3}$
Multiply. $\quad 3 \times 3 = 9$
Subtract and $\quad 10 - 9 = 1$
compare. $\quad 1 < 3$
Write the remainder.

Each worker received _____.

There was _____ left over for July.

Getting Started

Divide and check.

1. $5\overline{)635}$ ^127^

2. $4\overline{)729}$ ^182r1^

Copy and divide.

3. $850 \div 7$ ^121r3^

4. $423 \div 6$ ^70r3^

Practice

Divide.

1. 6)725   *120 r 5*

2. 8)944   *118*

3. 3)756   *252*

4. 4)639   *159 r 3*

5. 7)826   *118*

6. 9)996   *110 r 6*

7. 5)785   *157*

8. 2)837   *418 r 1*

9. 4)956   *239*

10. 8)890   *111 r 2*

11. 2)509   *254 r 1*

12. 5)623   *124 r 3*

13. 9)999   *111*

14. 7)853   *121 r 6*

15. 3)727   *242 r 1*

16. 6)815   *135 r 5*

Copy and divide

17. 654 ÷ 3   *218*

18. 945 ÷ 2   *472 r 1*

19. 715 ÷ 6   *119 r 1*

20. 858 ÷ 7   *122 r 4*

21. 856 ÷ 5   *171 r 1*

22. 848 ÷ 4   *212*

23. 991 ÷ 9   *110 r 1*

24. 975 ÷ 8   *121 r 7*

Problem Solving

Solve each problem. Use the information on page 77 if needed.

25. The Mighty Mowers, together, worked 462 hours in one summer. If they all worked the same number of hours, how much did each person work?   *154*

26. Pablo earned $52 in two weeks. How much money did he have left after he spent $38 on clothes?

27. Anita and Larry each mowed lawns 6 hours on Saturday. How much did they earn for the Mighty Mowers?

28. The Mighty Mowers earned $347 in August. How much did each person receive? How much money was left over?

Deciding Where to Start Dividing

The human body continues to burn calories 24 hours a day, no matter how inactive a person is. How many calories are used by someone sleeping for 1 hour?

Activity	Calories Used
Walk 1 hour	about 250
Sit 4 hours	about 340
Sleep 8 hours	about 520

We are looking for the number of calories used while sleeping for 1 hour.

A person sleeping for 8 hours uses about _____ calories. To find the hourly rate of calories used while sleeping, we divide the total calories burned by the number of hours slept.

We divide _____ by _____.

Decide where to start. 8 < 5 There are not enough hundreds. Rename the hundreds as tens and start with 52 tens.

Divide the tens.	Divide the ones.
$$\begin{array}{r} 6 \\ 8\overline{)520} \\ -48 \\ \hline 40 \end{array}$$	$$\begin{array}{r} 65 \\ 8\overline{)520} \\ -48 \\ \hline 40 \\ -40 \\ \hline 0 \end{array}$$

A human being burns about _____ calories while sleeping for 1 hour.

Getting Started

Divide and check.

1. $\overset{58}{6\overline{)348}}$

2. $\overset{54}{4\overline{)216}}$

3. $\overset{35r3}{7\overline{)248}}$

4. $\overset{69r3}{9\overline{)624}}$

Copy and divide.

5. $435 \div 5$
   87

6. $343 \div 7$
   49

7. $856 \div 9$
   95r1

8. $183 \div 2$
   91r1

Practice

Divide and check.

1. 6)674 $112 r2$
2. 8)129 $16 r1$
3. 4)396 99
4. 3)698 $232 r2$

5. 7)394 $56 r2$
6. 6)504 84
7. 2)736 368
8. 9)427 $47 r4$

9. 8)468 $58 r4$
10. 4)153 $38 r1$
11. 5)835 167
12. 3)109 $36 r1$

Copy and divide.

13. 268 ÷ 4 67
14. 371 ÷ 9 $41 r2$
15. 814 ÷ 3 $271 r1$
16. 917 ÷ 7 131

17. 427 ÷ 8 $53 r3$
18. 812 ÷ 5 $162 r2$
19. 906 ÷ 7 $129 r3$
20. 159 ÷ 2 $79 r1$

21. 613 ÷ 5 $122 r3$
22. 875 ÷ 9 $97 r2$
23. 675 ÷ 3 225
24. 428 ÷ 8 $53 r4$

Problem Solving

Solve each problem. Use the chart on page 79 as needed.

25. Willie swam 285 meters in 3 minutes. How far did he swim in 1 minute?

    95 meters

26. Alicia walked 4,560 meters in the marathon. Wanda walked 2,315 meters farther than Alicia. How far did Wanda walk?

    6,875 meters

27. The team of 5 archers shot 250 arrows in 2 rounds each. How many arrows were shot by each archer in each round?

    25 arrows

28. Each student competed in the spring physical fitness test. Rob did 325 sit-ups in 5 minutes. How many did he do in 2 minutes?

    130 sit-ups

29. How many calories are used by a person sitting for 1 hour?

    85 Calories

30. How many calories does a person burn by walking for 3 hours?

Name _____

Zeros in the Quotient

Nadia and 3 friends spent Saturday afternoon sightseeing. They had lunch and decided to split the bill evenly. What was each person's share of the restaurant check?

$28.36

We want to find what each person owed for lunch.

The total bill was _____.

There were _____ people. To determine the amount each person paid for lunch, we divide the total bill by the number of people splitting the cost.

We divide _____ by _____.

Divide the dollars.

$$\begin{array}{r} 7 \\ 4\overline{)\$28.36} \\ -28 \\ \hline 0 \end{array}$$

Divide the dimes.

$$\begin{array}{r} 7\,0 \\ 4\overline{)\$28.36} \\ -28 \\ \hline 3 \end{array}$$

Bring down the pennies and divide. Place the dollar sign and decimal point.

$$\begin{array}{r} \$7.09 \\ 4\overline{)\$28.36} \\ -28 \\ \hline 36 \\ -36 \\ \hline 0 \end{array}$$

3 < 4. There are not enough dimes to divide. Put a zero in the quotient.

Each person owed _____ for lunch.

Getting Started

Divide and check.

1. 7)$7.14
2. 2)960
3. 4)800
4. 8)843

Copy and divide.

5. 920 ÷ 9
6. 530 ÷ 5
7. $9.15 ÷ 3
8. 654 ÷ 6

Practice

Divide and check.

1. 8)816
   102

2. 9)$9.45 — $1.05

3. 3)921 — 307

4. 6)600 — 100

5. 5)450 — 90

6. 2)$8.06 — $4.03

7. 4)820 — 205

8. 7)756 — 108

9. 4)915 — 228 r3

10. 8)839 — 109 r7

11. 9)$9.90 — $1.10

12. 6)651 — 108 r3

13. 3)617 — 205 r2

14. 7)735 — 105

15. 5)137 — 27 r2

16. 2)$6.14 — $3.07

Copy and divide.

17. $8.08 ÷ 8
   $1.01

18. 437 ÷ 2
   218 r1

19. 529 ÷ 5
   105 r4

20. 613 ÷ 6
   102 r1

21. 903 ÷ 9
   100 r3

22. $9.27 ÷ 3
   $3.09

23. 821 ÷ 4
   205 r1

24. 767 ÷ 7
   109 r4

Problem Solving

Solve each problem.

25. Marge ordered a hamburger for $1.46, French fries for $0.75, and orange juice for $1.15. How much was her bill?

26. Earle spent $15.24 when he took his two brothers out for lunch. They all ordered the same thing. How much was each lunch?

27. Gene paid $12.36 for 6 gallons of milk. How much did each gallon cost?

28. Betty's lunch cost $3.87 and Juan's lunch cost $4.15. How much change did Betty get from a $10 bill, if she bought both lunches?

Lesson 4-10 • Zeros in the Quotient

Name _____

Dividing the Short Way

Roosevelt High School is proud of its basketball team. Every home game this year was a sellout. The total season attendance for these games was 10,950. How many fans came to each game?

Roosevelt High School Home Games	
Macon	December 30
Fairfield	January 3
Roberts	January 10
Pittsfield	January 17
Lincoln	January 24
Danville	January 31

We are looking for the attendance at each home game.

The total season attendance for the year was _____.

Roosevelt played _____ home games.

To find the number of fans who attended each home game, we divide the season attendance by the number of home games.

We divide _____ by _____.

We can use a shortcut method.

Divide the thousands. Rename the remainder as hundreds.	Divide the hundreds. Rename the remainder as tens.	Divide the tens. Rename the remainder as ones.	Divide the ones. Write the remainder if there is one.
$\frac{1}{6 \overline{)10,950}}$	$\frac{1\ 8}{6 \overline{)10,950}}$	$\frac{1\ 82}{6 \overline{)10,950}}$	$\frac{1,825}{6 \overline{)10,950}}$

The attendance for each home game was _____.

Getting Started

Divide and check.

1. 6)5,732   *935 r2*

2. 9)$32.76   *$3.64*

3. 4)15,384   *3,896*

4. 7)75,286   *10,755 r1*

Copy and divide.

5. $623.84 ÷ 2   *$311.92*

6. 139,257 ÷ 8   *17,907 r1*

7. 457,382 ÷ 3   *152,460 r2*

8. 926,034 ÷ 5

Practice

Divide and check.

1. $3\overline{)5{,}472}$

   1,824

2. $7\overline{)8{,}216}$

   1,173 r5

3. $5\overline{)\$62.95}$

   $12.59

4. $9\overline{)12{,}438}$

   1,382

5. $6\overline{)75{,}214}$

   12,535 r4

6. $8\overline{)72{,}064}$

   9,008

7. $2\overline{)19{,}735}$

   9,867 r1

8. $4\overline{)\$139.48}$

   $34.87

9. $7\overline{)50{,}096}$

   7,156 r9

10. $8\overline{)112{,}715}$

    14,089 r3

11. $6\overline{)255{,}000}$

    42,500

12. $3\overline{)\$315.24}$

    $105.08

[Now Try This!]

Go on a treasure hunt for prime numbers.

- Write the numbers from 1 to 200, in rows of ten numbers each.
- Cross out the 1.
- Circle the 2 and cross out all the multiples of 2.
- Circle the 3 and cross out all the multiples of 3.
- Repeat this step for 5, 7, 11, 13, and 17.
- Circle all the remaining numbers.

You have discovered all the prime numbers less than 200.

List them: _____

_____

_____

Lesson 4-11 • **Dividing the Short Way**

Name **Ava I guess**

Finding the Average

Robin is a new member of the bowling league, and her
teammates are very happy with her last three bowling
scores. What is Robin's average score?

We want to find Robin's average bowling score.

We know Robin bowled _____ games.

The scores of her games were _____, _____, and _____.

To find her **average**, we add the scores and divide the
sum by the number of addends.

Add the numbers.	Divide the sum by the number of addends.
154 136 + 148 438	146 3)438

Robin's average score for the three games is _____.

Notice the sum of the average scores is the same as
the sum of the real scores.

Real Scores	Average Scores
154 136 + 148 438	146 146 + 146 438

Getting Started

Find the average for each set of numbers.

1. 627 512 310 751	2. 2,347 968 1,701	3. 95 38 21 49 77
550	1,672	56

Practice

Find the average for each set of numbers.

1. 67, 85

76

2. 34, 26, 58, 17, 28, 35

33

3. 138, 249, 435

271

4. 651, 486, 715, 811, 912

715

5. 3,248; 6,914; 4,124

4,762

6. 838, 472, 596, 850

689

Problem Solving

Solve each problem.

7. Rex paid $5.55 to bowl 3 games. What was the average amount he paid for each game?

$1.85

8. If the bowling alley snack bar sold 918 bags of pretzels in 6 months, how many bags of pretzels should the owner expect to sell this month?

153 bags

9. After two weeks on the bowling team, Tavia's scores were 129, 186, 147, and 150. What was her bowling average?

153

10. Art bought a bowling shirt for $11.89 in one store, one for $17.55 in another store, and one for $8.21 in a third store. What was the average cost of his shirts?

$12.55

11. Mr. Hope drives the team car pool for bowling. His car can travel 432 miles on 12 gallons of gas. What is his average gas mileage?

36 mpg.

12. Mr. Hope had to wait for the team an average of 25 minutes, each day they bowled. If the team bowled twice a week, how many minutes did Mr. Hope spend waiting each week?

50 min.

Use the graph to complete problems 13–15.

13. What was the average number of spares made by team members in the Bowlathon?

20 Spares

14. Which bowlers scored higher than the average? *Tavia and Rex*

15. What is the average number of spares made by the three top spare makers?

22 Spares

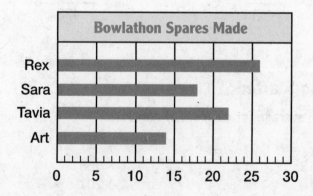

Bowlathon Spares Made

Rex
Sara
Tavia
Art

0   5   10   15   20   25   30

Name _____

Problem Solving: Look for a Pattern

The staircase shown here is made of blocks and has five steps. How many blocks are needed to build a staircase with ten steps?

 SEE

We want to know the number of blocks we would need for a staircase with ten steps.

It takes __15__ blocks to build a staircase with 5 steps.

 PLAN

Since the blocks in the picture appear to form a pattern, it is likely that a pattern with numbers will help us to solve this problem.

Making a table and recording information will be helpful in finding the pattern.

 DO

How many blocks are in a 1-step staircase? _____

2-step staircase? _____

3-step staircase? _____

Number of Steps	1	2	3	4	5	6	7	8	9	10
Number of Blocks	1	3	6	10	15	21	28	36	45	55

+2 +3 +4 +5 +6 +7 +8 +9 +10

It takes __55__ blocks to build a ten-step staircase.

 CHECK

We can check our solution by drawing a ten-step staircase and adding the number of blocks used for each step.

$1 + 2 + 3 + 4 + 5 + 6 + 7 + 8 + 9 + 10 =$ __55__

Apply

Look for a pattern to help solve each problem.

1. Study this pattern carefully. Draw a sketch of the rectangle in the twelfth position and in the thirty-seventh position.

2. A brick wall is constructed using only full bricks and half bricks. How many bricks are needed to complete the wall?

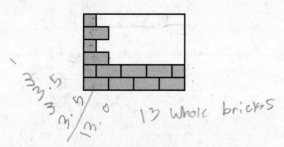

13 whole bricks

3. Bacteria double in number every hour. Study the following table:

Hours	1	2	3	4	5
Bacteria	2	4	8	16	32

How many bacteria will there be during the tenth hour?

1,024 bactiria

4. Study the pattern below and construct a possible next figure.

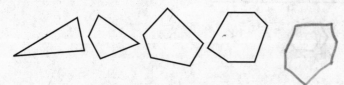

5. A patio, in the general shape of the picture, is to be made from square tiles. If the middle row will contain 15 tiles, how many tiles are needed to complete this patio?

6. Four-sided polygons have two possible diagonals, and five-sided polygons have 5 possible diagonals. How many possible diagonals are in a seven-sided polygon? 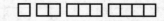 14 diagnals

7. Read Exercise 2 again. What if the wall requires 5 bricks for the bottom row? How many bricks are needed now?

8. Read Exercise 2 again. Draw another picture and rewrite the problem so that the answer is 24 bricks.

9. A pattern is started below.

☐ ☐☐ ☐☐☐ ☐☐☐☐

Write two different questions about the pattern for your classmates to answer.

10. At a math-club party, Eric Matick said, "I will give a free prize to anyone who can tell me the greatest quotient possible, with no remainder, when you divide a 4-digit number by a 2-digit number." How can you win the prize?

Divide and check.

1. $7\overline{)7}$ $\frac{1}{}$

2. $3\overline{)12}$ 4

3. $7\overline{)56}$ 8

4. $8\overline{)0}$ 0

5. $1\overline{)6}$ 6

6. $7\overline{)91}$ 13

7. $2\overline{)85}$ $42r1$

8. $8\overline{)256}$ 32

9. $6\overline{)\$7.38}$ $\$1.23$

10. $4\overline{)426}$ $106r2$

11. $7\overline{)3,496}$ $499r3$

12. $8\overline{)12,075}$ $1,500r5$

13. $6\overline{)90,168}$ $15,028$

14. $3\overline{)618}$ 206

15. $5\overline{)\$85.25}$ $\$17.05$

16. $2\overline{)10,603}$ $5,301r1$

17. $4\overline{)9,898}$ $2,474r2$

Use the order of operations to simplify each expression.

18. $5 + 9 \times 4 \div 6$

28

19. $(12 - 8) + 7 \times 6$

46

20. $18 + 12 \div (11 - 7)$

21

Write the product of primes for each composite number.

21. $27 = $ _9 × 3_

22. $60 = $ _10 × 6_

Write the greatest common factor for each pair of numbers.

23. 6 and 15

3

24. 36 and 50

2

Find the average for each set of numbers.

25. 86, 58

72

26. 127, 249, 311

229

27. 9, 6, 18, 12, 25

14

Circle the letter of the correct answer.

1. What is the place value of the 3 in 503,291?
   - a. tens
   - b. hundreds
   - c. thousands
   - d. NG

2. 8,235 ◯ 8,325
   - a. <
   - b. >
   - c. =

3. 529
   + 487
   - a. 906
   - b. 916
   - c. 1,016
   - d. NG

4. $124.95
   + 93.27
   - a. $218.22
   - b. $227.22
   - c. $228.22
   - d. NG

5. Estimate the sum.
   6,753
   + 5,215
   - a. 10,000
   - b. 11,000
   - c. 12,000
   - d. NG

6. 7,096
   − 4,398
   - a. 3,402
   - b. 3,798
   - c. 3,708
   - d. NG

7. $547.83
   − 78.49
   - a. $468.34
   - b. $469.34
   - c. $531.46
   - d. NG

8. Estimate the difference.
   8,643
   − 7,500
   - a. 1,400
   - b. 1,500
   - c. 1,600
   - d. NG

9. 38 × 7
   - a. 264
   - b. 266
   - c. 2,156
   - d. NG

10. 3,209
    ×   4
    - a. 12,836
    - b. 12,876
    - c. 128,036
    - d. NG

11. 37
    × 54
    - a. 323
    - b. 1,798
    - c. 1,898
    - d. NG

12. 5)83
    - a. 16
    - b. 16 R3
    - c. 17
    - d. NG

13. 4)4,204
    - a. 151
    - b. 1,051
    - c. 1,501
    - d. NG

score

Divide by 2-Digit Numbers

Dividing by Multiples of 10

Fran is recording the results of her timed science experiment. How many minutes and seconds did her experiment take?

We want to find the number of minutes and seconds Fran's experiment took.

We know Fran's experiment took _____ seconds.

There are _____ seconds in 1 minute. To find the minutes spent on her experiment, we divide the total seconds by the number of seconds in 1 minute. The remainder will represent the number of seconds.

We divide _____ by _____.

> **Decide where to start.**

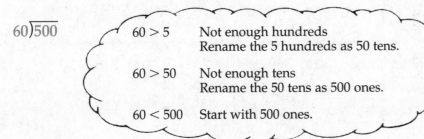

$60\overline{)500}$

60 > 5	Not enough hundreds Rename the 5 hundreds as 50 tens.
60 > 50	Not enough tens Rename the 50 tens as 500 ones.
60 < 500	Start with 500 ones.

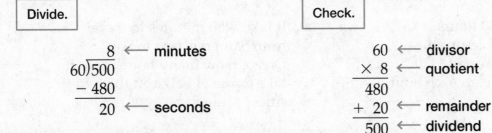

> **Divide.**

$$\begin{array}{r} 8 \leftarrow \textbf{minutes} \\ 60\overline{)500} \\ -480 \\ \hline 20 \leftarrow \textbf{seconds} \end{array}$$

> **Check.**

$$\begin{array}{r} 60 \leftarrow \textbf{divisor} \\ \times\ 8 \leftarrow \textbf{quotient} \\ \hline 480 \\ +\ 20 \leftarrow \textbf{remainder} \\ \hline 500 \leftarrow \textbf{dividend} \end{array}$$

The experiment took _____ minutes and _____ seconds.

Getting Started

Divide and check.

1. $30\overline{)120}$

2. $20\overline{)45}$

Copy and divide.

3. $421 \div 50$

4. $86 \div 70$

Practice

Divide and check.

1. $70\overline{)420}$

2. $80\overline{)560}$

3. $30\overline{)180}$

4. $50\overline{)400}$

5. $60\overline{)425}$

6. $90\overline{)634}$

7. $40\overline{)212}$

8. $20\overline{)142}$

9. $30\overline{)212}$

10. $50\overline{)\$150}$

11. $80\overline{)719}$

12. $70\overline{)650}$

13. $20\overline{)105}$

14. $90\overline{)736}$

15. $40\overline{)45}$

16. $60\overline{)490}$

Copy and divide.

17. $536 \div 60$

18. $248 \div 50$

19. $177 \div 20$

20. $735 \div 90$

21. $109 \div 40$

22. $\$560 \div 70$

23. $136 \div 30$

24. $700 \div 80$

25. $512 \div 60$

26. $126 \div 90$

27. $360 \div 60$

28. $216 \div 70$

Problem Solving

Solve each problem.

29. In April, Dino spent 30 hours delivering 500 directories for the phone company. He earned $120. How much did Dino earn each hour he worked?

30. It takes 480 minutes to travel from San Francisco to San Diego. How many hours does it take to travel between the two cities?

31. Mrs. Gomez bought a car that averages 30 miles to each gallon of gas. She drove 270 miles. How many gallons of gas did she use?

32. If a tablet of writing paper contains 80 sheets and costs $1.15, what would you expect to pay for a total of 560 sheets of paper?

1-Digit Quotients With Remainders

Kwan wants to use the store's credit plan to buy a television that costs $289. About how much will he have to pay each week?

We want to find Kwan's approximate weekly payment.

The television costs $ _____.

Kwan has _____ weeks to pay.

To determine Kwan's weekly payment, we divide the total cost by the number of weeks in the store's payment plan.

We divide _____ by _____.

Decide where to start.

$32\overline{)\$289}$

> 32 > 2   Not enough hundreds; rename as tens.
> 32 > 28   Not enough tens; rename as ones.
> 32 < 289   Start with 289 ones.

Divide.

> Round the divisor to the nearest ten. Estimate how many 30s are in 289.

$$\begin{array}{r} \$9\ R1 \\ 32\overline{)\$289} \\ -288 \\ \hline 1 \end{array}$$

Check.

$$\begin{array}{rl} 32 & \leftarrow \text{divisor} \\ \times\ 9 & \leftarrow \text{quotient} \\ \hline 288 & \\ +\ 1 & \leftarrow \text{remainder} \\ \hline 289 & \leftarrow \text{dividend} \end{array}$$

Kwan will pay about _____ each week.

Getting Started

Divide and check.

1. $13\overline{)96}$ 2. $22\overline{)176}$ 3. $49\overline{)114}$ 4. $54\overline{)170}$

Copy and divide.

5. $260 \div 27$ 6. $208 \div 45$ 7. $242 \div 29$ 8. $465 \div 78$

Practice

Divide and check.

1. $43\overline{)348}$
2. $32\overline{)198}$
3. $46\overline{)140}$
4. $49\overline{)294}$

5. $53\overline{)442}$
6. $87\overline{)437}$
7. $51\overline{)103}$
8. $73\overline{)658}$

9. $88\overline{)565}$
10. $46\overline{)\$322}$
11. $92\overline{)846}$
12. $67\overline{)575}$

Copy and divide.

13. $232 \div 43$
14. $516 \div 94$
15. $\$128 \div 32$
16. $210 \div 48$

17. $616 \div 83$
18. $561 \div 58$
19. $438 \div 72$
20. $534 \div 62$

21. $752 \div 91$
22. $682 \div 75$
23. $432 \div 64$
24. $\$165 \div 15$

Problem Solving

Solve each problem.

25. It took Megan 54 weeks to save $275 toward her airfare to Hawaii. About how much did Megan save each week?

26. Mr. Rinoldi made car payments for 39 months. If each payment was $226, how much did Mr. Rinoldi pay for his car?

[Now Try This!]

Twin primes are any two prime numbers that differ by 2. For example, 11 and 13 are twin primes because 13 − 11 = 2. Write three sets of twin primes less than 100.

Lesson 5-2 • 1-Digit Quotients With Remainders

Name _____

Estimating Quotients

Mark worked the division problem
176 ÷ 24 at the board. Mark's
classmates disagreed with his
answer. What did Mark do wrong?

We are looking for the correct quotient for the problem
176 ÷ 24.

When Mark rounded 24 to _____ and estimated the
quotient, he got _____. He estimated there are _____
24s in 176. But when he tried _____, his product was
larger than 176. He must try a smaller quotient.

Sometimes, the first quotient we try gives a product
larger than the dividend. Then a _____
number must be tried.

How many 24s in 176?

$$\begin{array}{r} 8 \\ 24\overline{)176} \\ -192 \end{array}$$

Try 8.

Too big

Try again!

$$\begin{array}{r} 7 \text{ R8} \\ 24\overline{)176} \\ -168 \\ \hline 8 \end{array}$$

Try 7.

It works.

The correct quotient for the problem 176 ÷ 24 is _____.

Getting Started

Divide and check.

1. 38)228

2. 59)435

3. 17)99

4. 48)346

5. 39)238

6. 23)138

Copy and divide.

7. 232 ÷ 25

8. 265 ÷ 37

9. 814 ÷ 95

10. 217 ÷ 35

11. 547 ÷ 61

12. 483 ÷ 53

Practice

Divide and check.

1. $52\overline{)436}$ 2. $38\overline{)216}$ 3. $58\overline{)412}$

4. $16\overline{)\$144}$ 5. $64\overline{)486}$ 6. $85\overline{)396}$

7. $39\overline{)106}$ 8. $73\overline{)680}$ 9. $94\overline{)658}$

10. $23\overline{)112}$ 11. $48\overline{)288}$ 12. $62\overline{)509}$

Copy and divide.

13. $86 \div 12$ 14. $247 \div 34$ 15. $315 \div 76$ 16. $612 \div 89$

17. $295 \div 43$ 18. $\$416 \div 52$ 19. $185 \div 96$ 20. $150 \div 27$

Problem Solving

Solve each problem.

21. In July, Wally's Campground supplied 527 gallons of drinking water to its campers from a tank that can hold 85 gallons. How many times was the tank filled that month?

22. The Brittingham College alumni band concert is a popular fundraiser. This year, 846 concert tickets were sold for $12 each. How much money was collected for the benefit of the college?

23. One tree produced 175 avocados. The avocados are packaged in boxes of 24. How many boxes are needed?

24. Rose bought a schnauzer for $250. Her parents agreed to pay the down payment of $42. Rose paid the rest in equal payments for 26 weeks. What did Rose pay each week?

Lesson 5-3 • Estimating Quotients

Name _____

2-Digit Quotients

Roberta Chen kept track of the gasoline used and miles driven on her family's vacation. Her family drove 1,512 miles. How many miles to the gallon did they average?

We need to find the average miles per gallon.

The Chen family drove _____ miles.

They used _____ gallons of gas.

To find the average, we divide the total miles driven by the number of gallons used on the trip.

We divide _____ by _____.

Decide where to start.	Divide by tens. How many 50s in 151? Try 3.	Try again! Try 2.

$$54\overline{)1,512}$$

54 > 1 Not enough thousands
54 > 15 Not enough hundreds
Start with 151 tens.

$$\begin{array}{r} 3 \\ 54\overline{)1,512} \\ -1\,62 \end{array}$$

3 × 54 = 162.
3 is too big.

$$\begin{array}{r} 28 \\ 54\overline{)1,512} \\ -1\,08 \\ \hline 432 \\ -432 \\ \hline 0 \end{array}$$

2 × 54 = 108.
2 works. Subtract and bring down the ones. Continue dividing.

The Chen family averaged _____ miles per gallon.

Getting Started

Divide and check.

1. $13\overline{)371}$

2. $28\overline{)1,988}$

3. $37\overline{)1,752}$

Copy and divide.

4. 3,278 ÷ 36

5. 3,273 ÷ 52

6. 6,412 ÷ 75

Practice

Divide and check.

1. $12\overline{)348}$

2. $64\overline{)2,432}$

3. $38\overline{)2,095}$

4. $51\overline{)3,425}$

5. $72\overline{)3,721}$

6. $24\overline{)1,468}$

7. $39\overline{)2,408}$

8. $93\overline{)9,225}$

9. $86\overline{)3,250}$

Copy and divide.

10. $4,247 \div 45$

11. $5,219 \div 63$

12. $2,176 \div 37$

13. $1,290 \div 21$

14. $7,056 \div 75$

15. $4,238 \div 58$

16. $6,453 \div 84$

17. $1,916 \div 28$

18. $7,391 \div 93$

19. $1,270 \div 67$

20. $7,052 \div 82$

21. $3,591 \div 63$

Problem Solving

Solve each problem.

22. How many days are in 864 hours?

23. Winona's car gets 32 miles to a gallon of gas. If gas costs $0.96 per gallon, how much does it cost her to drive 1,504 miles?

24. Mr. Murray paid $1,274 for a stereo system. He paid for the system in equal installments over 26 weeks. What were Mr. Murray's weekly payments?

25. Ken has collected 336 colored eggs for the Jaycees' annual Easter egg hunt. He will put them in one-dozen cartons to prevent breakage. How many cartons does Ken need?

3-Digit Quotients

Lime Delight is a popular new soft
drink bottled by The Natural Soda
Company. It is shipped to market in
wooden cases of 24 each. How many
cases are filled each day?

> ⊛ Lime Delight
> PRODUCTION:
> 19,752 bottles
> a day

We need to find the number of cases filled each day.

The Natural Soda Company bottles _____ sodas
each day.

There are _____ bottles in each case.

To find the number of cases, we divide the daily
production by the number of bottles in each case.

We divide _____ by _____.

Decide where to start.

$24\overline{)19{,}752}$

> 24 > 1   Not enough ten thousands.
> 24 > 19   Not enough thousands.
>   Start with 197 hundreds.

Divide.

$$\begin{array}{r} 823 \\ 24\overline{)19{,}752} \\ -\underline{19\ 2} \\ 55 \\ -\underline{48} \\ 72 \\ -\underline{72} \\ 0 \end{array}$$

Check.

$$\begin{array}{r} 823 \leftarrow \textbf{quotient} \\ \times\ \ 24 \leftarrow \textbf{divisor} \\ \hline 3\ 292 \\ 16\ 460 \\ \hline 19{,}752 \leftarrow \textbf{dividend} \end{array}$$

The Natural Soda Company fills _____ cases of Lime Delight each day.

Getting Started

Divide and check.

1. $16\overline{)4{,}096}$

2. $37\overline{)10{,}138}$

3. $58\overline{)36{,}440}$

Copy and divide.

4. $12{,}740 \div 79$

5. $23{,}098 \div 44$

6. $78{,}813 \div 81$

Practice

Divide and check.

1. $21\overline{)6{,}615}$

2. $67\overline{)10{,}318}$

3. $48\overline{)29{,}376}$

4. $68\overline{)37{,}148}$

5. $82\overline{)50{,}456}$

6. $93\overline{)76{,}680}$

Copy and divide.

7. $45{,}752 \div 93$

8. $56{,}443 \div 67$

9. $49{,}747 \div 84$

10. $4{,}370 \div 38$

11. $14{,}504 \div 56$

12. $33{,}396 \div 46$

13. $31{,}683 \div 65$

14. $29{,}658 \div 36$

15. $54{,}069 \div 84$

16. $62{,}700 \div 76$

17. $47{,}571 \div 57$

18. $44{,}431 \div 92$

19. $37{,}596 \div 43$

20. $68{,}316 \div 86$

21. $67{,}861 \div 79$

Problem Solving

Solve these problems.

22. The Holden Novelty Company produces 17,010 drinking straws each day. The straws are packaged in boxes of 54. How many boxes are packaged each day?

23. The Bee Clean Solvents Company sells $1,706 worth of its product each day. The cost of doing business is $1,238 each day. How much is left over for profit?

24. The Fast File Company files 567 cards each 8-hour day. How many cards can the Fast File Company file in 3 days?

25. The Yellow Pencil Company sells pencils in cases of 36 for $1.75 per case. If 32,256 pencils are sold daily, how much money does the Yellow Pencil Company make each day?

Zeros in the Quotient

Richard has been saving all
the money he earned doing
his paper route for a year.
How much savings did
Richard average each week?

We are asked to find Richard's average
weekly savings.

Richard has saved _____ in one year.

There are _____ weeks in one year.

To find Richard's weekly savings, we divide the
total he saved by the number of weeks in a year.

We divide _____ by _____.

Decide where to start.

$$
\begin{array}{r}
6 \\
52\overline{)\$315.64} \\
-312\downarrow \\
\hline
3\,6
\end{array}
$$

52 > 3
52 > 31
52 < 315
Start with 315 ones.
Divide, multiply, subtract,
and bring down.

$$
\begin{array}{r}
6\,0 \\
52\overline{)\$315.64} \\
-312 \\
\hline
3\,6
\end{array}
$$

552 > 36
36 ÷ 52 = 0
Put 0 in the
quotient.

$$
\begin{array}{r}
\$6.07 \\
52\overline{)\$315.64} \\
-312\downarrow \\
\hline
3\,64 \\
-3\,64 \\
\hline
0
\end{array}
$$

Bring down the next digit.
Divide again.
Place the dollar sign
and decimal point in
the quotient.

Check.

$$
\begin{array}{r}
\$6.07 \\
\times\quad 52 \\
\hline
12\,14 \\
303\,50 \\
\hline
\$315.64
\end{array}
$$

Richard's average weekly savings were _____.

Getting Started

Divide and check.

1. 26)$53.56   2. 46)$220.80   3. 83)33,895

Copy and divide.

4. 45,000 ÷ 64   5. 26,609 ÷ 38   6. 65,088 ÷ 92

Practice

Divide and check.

1. $15)\overline{\$15.90}$

2. $29)\overline{\$117.74}$

3. $65)\overline{26,390}$

4. $58)\overline{26,686}$

5. $72)\overline{\$508.32}$

6. $86)\overline{77,875}$

Copy and divide.

7. $24,146 \div 59$

8. $\$800.40 \div 87$

9. $48,058 \div 68$

10. $4,715 \div 23$

11. $\$216.77 \div 53$

12. $23,829 \div 47$

13. $38,955 \div 64$

14. $52,490 \div 87$

15. $\$608.00 \div 76$

16. $33,615 \div 48$

17. $\$391.68 \div 96$

18. $22,563 \div 28$

19. $\$553.88 \div 61$

20. $27,265 \div 58$

21. $\$713.78 \div 89$

Problem Solving

Solve each problem.

22. Courtney subscribes to a weekly sports magazine for $108.16 a year. How much is she paying for each single copy?

23. Ryan's new bike costs $146.88. If Ryan pays for the bike in 36 weeks, what are his weekly payments?

[Now Try This!]

Try this number puzzle and see why it is called Double Vision. Write down any three-digit number and multiply it by 11. Then multiply that product by 91. What do you notice about the answer? Try it again with a new number. Can you figure out why this happens?

Name _____

Problem Solving: Try, Check, and Revise

Complete the division example by replacing the
question marks with digits that will make the
problem work.

 SEE

We need to find the missing digits in this
division problem.

We know: $2 \times 2? = 54$.

The 4 in the hundreds place was brought down.

When a number was subtracted from 4, the

result was _____.

The 3 in the _____ place was brought down.

The remainder is _____.

 PLAN

Using our knowledge of the division process, we make an
educated guess to decide which digits are missing. As we
replace each question mark, we use the information we get to
help us decide the next digit.

 DO

$$
\begin{array}{r}
24\_\_ \\
27\overline{)65\_\_\_} \\
-\,54 \\
\hline
114 \\
-\,108 \\
\hline
6\_ \\
-\,\_\_ \\
\hline
\_3 \\
-\,\_\_ \\
\hline
1\,9
\end{array}
$$

- For the missing digit in the divisor, find $2 \times 2? = 54$. $2 \times 27 = 54$
- For the subtraction, find $?4 - ? = 6$. $14 - 8 = 6$
- For the next digit in the quotient, find $27 \times ?$ that ends in an 8. $27 \times 4 = 108$
- For the next subtraction, work backward to find $?14 - 108 = 6$. $6 + 108 = 114$
- For the first two digits in the dividend, work backward to find $?? - 54 = 11$. $11 + 54 = 65$
- For the third digit in the dividend, bring *up* the 4.
- Continue to find clues to complete the problem.

⭐ **CHECK**

To check division we can use multiplication and addition.

2_____ × _____ = _____ + _____ = _____

Apply

1. In a collection of quarters and nickels, there are two more nickels than quarters. How many nickels are there if the collection is worth $3.40?

2. Fill in each blank with a single digit to make this equation true.

$$\underline{\ }\ \underline{\ }\ \underline{\ },4\ \underline{\ }\ \underline{\ } \times 7 = 6{,}743,\ \underline{\ }\ 56$$

3. 2, 4, 6 is a set of three consecutive even numbers. 11, 13, 15 is a set of three consecutive odd numbers. Find a set of three consecutive even numbers. whose sum is 216. Find a set of four consecutive odd numbers whose sum is 216.

4. Solve this cryptarithm. Each letter stands for a unique digit.

$$\begin{array}{r} HOCUS \\ + POCUS \\ \hline PRESTO \end{array}$$

5. What whole number between 10 and 100 is twice the product of its digits?

6. The same two numbers are added and subtracted. Each letter represents a different digit. Find all the digits.

$$\begin{array}{r} XYZ \\ + \quad AB \\ \hline CDEF \end{array} \qquad \begin{array}{r} XYZ \\ - \quad AB \\ \hline BGA \end{array}$$

7. Using exactly four 4s, addition, subtraction, multiplication, division, and parentheses, write an equation to equal each of the numbers from 0 to 9.

8. Find each missing digit if the remainder is the greatest possible remainder, and explain how you did it.

$$\Box\ \Box \overline{)161} \quad \Box\ R26$$

9. When you divide a 5-digit number by a 2-digit number, what is the greatest number of digits possible in the whole number part of the quotient?

10. Write a problem that can be solved using Try, Check, and Revise. Choose two numbers. Give the sum and the product of the numbers to your classmates and ask them to find the numbers.

Lesson 5-7 • Problem Solving: Try, Check, and Revise

Divide.

1. $60\overline{)300}$

2. $40\overline{)264}$

3. $12\overline{)98}$

4. $18\overline{)73}$

5. $38\overline{)308}$

6. $34\overline{)275}$

7. $63\overline{)489}$

8. $79\overline{)700}$

9. $23\overline{)966}$

10. $36\overline{)1,728}$

11. $35\overline{)1,680}$

12. $28\overline{)1,876}$

13. $68\overline{)1,632}$

14. $42\overline{)3,250}$

15. $82\overline{)7,298}$

16. $56\overline{)5,568}$

17. $14\overline{)4,872}$

18. $26\overline{)\$110.50}$

19. $56\overline{)6,048}$

20. $58\overline{)27,190}$

21. $96\overline{)77,595}$

22. $65\overline{)\$589.55}$

23. $27\overline{)11,029}$

24. $67\overline{)\$573.52}$

25. $58\overline{)36,482}$

Circle the letter of the correct answer.

1 What is the place value of the 0 in 402,568?

- **a.** hundred thousands
- **b.** ten thousands
- **c.** thousands
- **d.** NG

2 4,309 ◯ 4,039

- **a.** <
- **b.** >
- **c.** =

3 676
+ 528

- **a.** 1,194
- **b.** 1,104
- **c.** 1,294
- **d.** NG

4 $309.56
+ 651.76

- **a.** $950.32
- **b.** $961.32
- **c.** $1,061.32
- **d.** NG

5 8,005
− 6,309

- **a.** 706
- **b.** 1,696
- **c.** 2,304
- **d.** NG

6 $915.38
− 274.59

- **a.** $640.79
- **b.** $641.79
- **c.** $761.21
- **d.** NG

7 43 × 8

- **a.** 324
- **b.** 344
- **c.** 3,224
- **d.** NG

8 5,307
× 5

- **a.** 16, 535
- **b.** 26,535
- **c.** 265,035
- **d.** NG

9 28
× 36

- **a.** 252
- **b.** 768
- **c.** 1,208
- **d.** NG

10 6,006 ÷ 6

- **a.** 11
- **b.** 101
- **c.** 1,001
- **d.** NG

11 3)21,709

- **a.** 7,236
- **b.** 7,236 R1
- **c.** 7,237
- **d.** NG

12 Find the average.
22, 16, 23, 15

- **a.** 16
- **b.** 19
- **c.** 23
- **d.** NG

13 56)450

- **a.** 11
- **b.** 8 R2
- **c.** 9
- **d.** NG

☐ score

STOP

Measurement

Units of Time

Thirty days have September, April, June, and
November. All others have 31 days except February,
which has 28 (29 in a leap year). How many minutes
were in February during the leap year of 2004?

We are looking for the number of minutes in
February 2004.

There were _____ days in February, 2004.

There are _____ hours in a day and
_____ minutes in an hour.

To find the number of minutes in this month,
we multiply the number of days in February
by the number of hours in a day and by the
number of minutes in an hour.

We multiply _____ by _____ by _____.

Time
1 minute = 60 seconds
1 hour = 60 minutes
1 day = 24 hours
1 week = 7 days
1 year = 52 weeks
1 year = 12 months
1 year = 365 days
1 leap year = 366 days
1 century = 100 years

$$
\begin{array}{r}
29 \\
\times\,24 \\
\hline
116 \\
+\,580 \\
\hline
696
\end{array}
$$

29 Days in February 2004
× 24 Hours in one day
696 Hours in February 2004

$$
\begin{array}{r}
696 \\
\times\,60 \\
\end{array}
$$

696 Hours in February 2004
× 60 Minutes in one hour
Minutes in February 2004

There were _____ minutes in February 2004.

REMEMBER To rename larger units as smaller units, we multiply.

To rename smaller units as larger units, we divide.

Getting Started

Use the table of time equivalents to complete each statement.

1. 5 weeks = __35__ days

2. 5 hours 15 minutes = __315__ minutes

Complete each sentence.

3. To change hours to minutes,

   __Multiply__ by 60.

4. To change hours to days,

   __Divide__ by 24.

Practice

Use the table of time equivalents to complete each statement.

1. 6 years = _312_ weeks

2. 4 minutes = _240_ seconds

3. 133 days = _19_ weeks

4. 144 months = _12_ years

5. 1 day = _364,000_ seconds

6. 6 days 4 hours = _148_ hours

7. 15 minutes 10 seconds = _910_ seconds

8. 100 hours = _4_ days _4_ hours

9. 5 years 3 months = _63_ months

10. 24 hours = _1,440_ minutes

11. 950 seconds = _15_ minutes _50_ seconds

12. 2,000 days = _285_ weeks _5_ days

13. 4 hours 15 minutes = _255_ minutes

14. 107 weeks = _2_ years _3_ weeks

15. 4 days = _345,600_ seconds

16. 200 years = _2_ centuries

Complete each sentence.

17. To change minutes to seconds, multiply by _60_.

18. To change weeks to years, divide by _52_.

19. To change months to years, _divide_ by 12.

20. To change minutes to hours, _divide_ by 60.

Problem Solving

Solve each problem.

21. Daphne was 12 years old on January 1, 1990. How old was she in years and days on July 1, 1992?

22. How many days are in the last 4 months of this year?

23. Miss Lopez edits 4 maps each hour at the Travel Atlas Company. She works 6 hours each day for 5 days a week. How many maps can she edit in 1 year?

24. Morris works at the Freedom Book Store from 9:00 A.M. to 3:00 P.M., Monday through Thursday. If Morris makes $4.25 per hour, what is his weekly pay?

Name _I hate this Lesson!!! ☹_

Elapsed Time

Mari works every Saturday. The time card shows the time she arrives at work and the time she leaves work. She takes a half-hour lunch. How long does Mari work on Saturday? Write the answer in hours(h) and minutes(min).

We want to find the **elapsed time**

between _____ A.M. and _____ P.M.

First, find the elapsed time from

_____ A.M. to _____ noon.

Change the time to hours and minutes, and subtract.

Next, subtract the half-hour for lunch.

```
  11  60
 1̶2̶ h 0̶0̶ min
- 10 h 30 min
   1 h 30 min
-       30 min
   1 h
```

Mari worked __1__ hour in the morning.

Now, add the time Mari works in the afternoon.

```
  1 h 00 min
+ 5 h 45 min
  6 h 45 min
```

Mari works __6__ hours __45__ minutes every Saturday.

Mari	
Saturday	
Begin Work : 10:30 AM.	
End Work : 5:45 P.M.	

Getting Started

Regroup the hours and minutes.

1. 1 h = __60__ min

2. 3 h 15 min = 2 h __75__ min

3. 2 h 30 min = 1 h __90__ min

4. 6 h 50 min = 5 h __110__ min

Subtract.

5.
```
  10 h 05 min
-  5 h 30 min
```
__4 h 35 min__

6.
```
  11 h
-  7 h 45 min
```
__3 h 15 min__

7.
```
  11 h 45 min
-  6 h 50 min
```
__4 h 55 min__

8.
```
  12 h 15 min
-  8 h 30 min
```
__3 h 45 min__

Find the elapsed time.

9. between 7:45 A.M. and 11:30 A.M. __3:45__

10. from 9:15 A.M. to 4:30 P.M. with a half-hour lunch
__6 h 45__

Practice

Regroup the hours and minutes.

1. 4 h = 3 h _6 0_ min   2. 2 h 40 min = 1 h _100_ min

3. 5 h 35 min = 4 h _95_ min   4. 3 h 18 min = 2 h _78_ min

Subtract.

5.   8 h 10 min   6.   10 h   7.   11 h 15 min   8.   9 h 12 min
  − 3 h 50 min   − 6 h 35 min   − 4 h 35 min   − 7 h 30 min
  4h 20min   3h25min   6h 40min   1h 42min

9.   5 h 25 min   10.   12 h   11.   7 h 30 min   12.   2 h 05 min
  − 4 h 50 min   − 10 h 15 min   − 5 h 35 min   − 1 h 20 min
  35min   1h 45min   1h 55min   45min

Find the elapsed time.

13. between 8:35 P.M. and 12 midnight

14. between 10:45 P.M. and 11 A.M.

15. from 5:00 P.M. to 2:30 A.M. with a 45 minute dinner break

Problem Solving

Use the time card on the right to solve each problem.

16. Aaron took half an hour for lunch on Monday. How many hours did he work that day?

17. Daniel took half an hour for lunch and forty-five minutes for dinner on Monday. How many hours did he work that day?

18. Joseph took half an hour for lunch on Monday. How much more time did Daniel spend working than Joseph on that day?

Hale's Electric Co.	Begin	End
Aaron	9:15 A.M.	5:45 P.M.
Joseph	8:30 A.M.	4:15 P.M.
Daniel	8:45 A.M.	6:30 P.M.

Name _____

Celsius and Fahrenheit Temperature

It's Algebra!

To measure temperature, you can use a Celsius scale or a Fahrenheit scale.

At what temperature does water boil on the Fahrenheit (°F) scale? _____

On the Celsius (°C) scale? _____

On Monday, Eiji recorded the high and low temperature for the day. The high temperature was 8°C. The low temperature was ⁻6°C. What was the change in temperature?

You can use the thermometer like a number line.

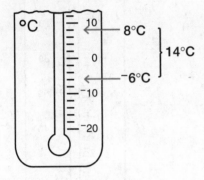

There was a _____ change in temperature on the Celsius scale.

Getting Started

Use the picture at the top of the page to answer each question.

1. At what temperature does water freeze on the Fahrenheit scale?

2. What is room temperature on the Celsius scale?

3. You are wearing a winter coat. Is the temperature 35°C or 35°F?

4. Find the change in temperature from 12°C to ⁻5°C.

5. Find the change in temperature from 45°F to 39°F.

Practice

Write each temperature in Celsius or Fahrenheit.

1.

_____

2.

_____

3.

_____

4.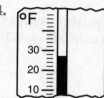

_____

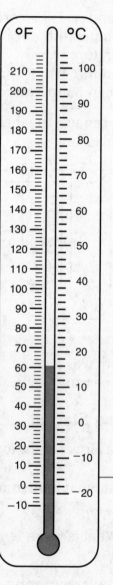

Use the picture on the right to answer each question.

5. What is the temperature on the Celsius scale?

6. What is the temperature on the Fahrenheit scale?

7. Is 10°C warmer or colder than 10°F?

8. You are going swimming. Is the temperature 30°C or 30°F?

9. You are wearing a sweater. Is the temperature 50°C or 50°F?

10. At what temperature does water boil on the Celsius scale?

Find each change in temperature.

11. 20°C to 35°C

12. 5°C to ⁻15°C

13. 67°F to 49°F

14. 23°F to 35°F

Problem Solving

Solve each problem.

15. The temperature in Fairbanks, Alaska, was ⁻10°F one day in January. On that same day, the temperature in Honolulu, Hawaii, was 73°F. What was the difference in temperature between these two cities?

16. One day in July, the high temperature for Phoenix, Arizona, was 106°. Was this temperature reading measured in degrees Celsius or degrees Fahrenheit?

Measuring Length in Inches

Jayne is learning how to make keys. She has to measure each in inches, the customary unit of length. What is the length of this key to the nearest inch? To the nearest half-inch? to the nearest quarter-inch? To the nearest eighth-inch?

We want to find the measurement of the key.

To approximate measurements, we look at the small lines between the inches.

If a measure is less than halfway between the lines, we round _____. If the measure is exactly or more than halfway between the lines, we round _____. The length of the key is _____ inches to the nearest inch, or

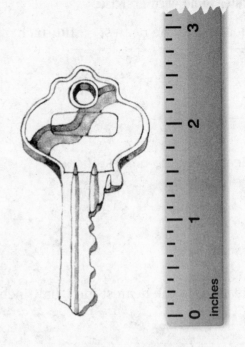

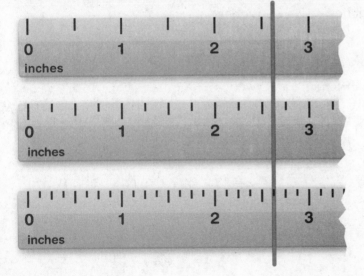

$2\frac{1}{2}$ inches to the nearest half-inch,

$2\frac{3}{4}$ inches to the nearest quarter-inch,

$2\frac{5}{8}$ inches to the nearest eighth-inch.

Getting Started

Use a ruler to do each exercise.

1. Measure the width of this page to the nearest half-inch, quarter-inch, and eighth-inch.

   _____ inches   _____ inches   _____ inches

2. Draw a pencil $5\frac{3}{4}$ inches long.

3. Draw a pen $4\frac{1}{8}$ inches long.

Practice _____

Use a ruler to do each exercise.

1. Measure to the nearest eighth-inch.

_____ inches

2. Measure to the nearest half-inch.

_____ inches

3. Measure to the nearest inch.

_____ inches

4. Measure to the nearest quarter-inch.

_____ inches

5. Measure to the nearest inch, half-inch, quarter-inch and eighth-inch.

_____ inches _____ inches _____ inches _____ inches

6. Draw a pencil $3\frac{1}{4}$ inches long.

7. Draw a string $4\frac{7}{8}$ inches long.

8. Draw a ribbon 5 inches long.

Now Try This!

A gumball machine contains a total of 2 red, 10 white and 12 orange gumballs. Mrs. Brown's four children want gum, but they all want the same color. If each gumball costs 1¢, what is the most that Mrs. Brown would have to pay to get four balls of the same color? _____ What is the most she would have to pay to have all the gumballs orange? _____

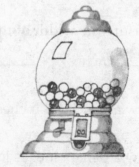

Adding and Subtracting Customary Units

It's Algebra!

During Parent-student Activity Day, customary units of length were used to measure. Mr. Herzog and Tammy both competed in the long-jump event. How much farther did Mr. Herzog jump?

Length
1 foot (ft) = 12 inches (in.)
1 yard (yd) = 3 feet
1 mile (mi) = 1,760 yards

We want to find how much farther Mr. Herzog jumped than his daughter.

Mr. Herzog jumped _____ feet _____ inches.

Tammy jumped _____ feet _____ inches.

To find the difference, we subtract the length of Tammy's jump from the length of her father's jump.

We subtract _____ from _____ .

Rename the minuend.

$$\begin{array}{r} 6 \text{ ft } 4 \text{ in.} \\ -\ 4 \text{ ft } 9 \text{ in.} \\ \hline \end{array}$$

1 ft = _____ in.

12 in. + 4 in. = _____ in.

Subtract.

$$\begin{array}{r} 5 \text{ ft } 16 \text{ in.} \\ -\ 4 \text{ ft } \ \ 9 \text{ in.} \\ \hline 1 \text{ ft } \ \ 7 \text{ in.} \end{array}$$

Change the difference to inches. 1 ft 7 in. = (1 × 12 in.) + 7 in. = _____

Mr. Herzog jumped _____ foot _____ inches or _____ inches farther than Tammy.

REMEMBER When adding or subtracting customary units, simplify the sum or difference by renaming, if necessary.
11 ft 13 in. = 12 ft 1 in. and 14 ft = 4 yds 2 ft.

Getting Started

Rename each measurement.

1. 1 yd = _____ in.

2. 6 ft 8 in. = _____ in.

3. 500 ft = _____ yd _____ ft

4. 1 mi = _____ ft

Add or subtract.

5. $\begin{array}{r} 8 \text{ ft } \ \ 3 \text{ in.} \\ +\ 4 \text{ ft } 11 \text{ in.} \\ \hline \end{array}$

6. $\begin{array}{r} 6 \text{ yd } 1 \text{ ft} \\ -\ 4 \text{ yd } 2 \text{ ft} \\ \hline \end{array}$

7. $\begin{array}{r} 9 \text{ ft} \\ -\ 6 \text{ ft } 6 \text{ in.} \\ \hline \end{array}$

8. $\begin{array}{r} 4 \text{ yd } 2 \text{ ft } 9 \text{ in.} \\ +\ 5 \text{ yd } 1 \text{ ft } 5 \text{ in.} \\ \hline \end{array}$

Copy and add or subtract.

9. 5 ft 4 in. + 6 ft 9 in.

10. 7 yd 16 in. − 2 ft 11 in.

Practice

Rename each measurement.

1. 49 in. = _____ ft _____ in.

2. 10 ft 7 in. = _____ in.

3. 3 mi = _____ ft

4. 84 in. = _____ ft

5. 16 yd = _____ in.

6. 6 mi 660 yd = _____ yd

7. 144 in. = _____ yd

8. 8 yd 1 ft = _____ in.

9. 2 mi 220 yd = _____ ft

10. 5 yd 2 ft 5 in. = _____ in.

Add or subtract.

11.   5 ft 6 in.
    + 2 ft 3 in.

12.   8 ft 6 in.
    − 5 ft 2 in.

13.   11 ft 9 in.
    − 6 ft 10 in.

14.   5 yd 2 ft
    + 4 yd 2 ft

Copy, add or subtract.

15. 5 yd 2 ft − 3 yd 2 ft

16. 9 ft 6 in. − 8 ft 8 in.

17. 2 yd 2 ft 8 in. + 3 yd 1 ft 2 in.

18. 5 yd 2 ft − 3 yd 9 in.

19. 3 yd 1 ft 5 in. + 2 ft 8 in.

20. 3 ft 9 in. + 2 ft 8 in. + 7 ft 11 in.

Circle the best estimate.

21. the height of a classroom

    3 ft   8 ft   20 ft

22. the width of this page

    5 in.   12 in. $7\frac{1}{2}$ in.

Problem Solving

Solve each problem.

23. The school record for sailing a paper airplane is 30 feet 9 inches. Paul sailed his airplane 7 yards 2 feet 6 inches. How far short of the record was his flight?

24. Mr. Cook needs some jump rope for gym class. Rope costs $1.89 for each foot. How much does a rope 4 yards 2 feet long cost?

Perimeter

The **perimeter** of a figure is the distance around the figure. The city recreation department is preparing to accept bids for a new fence around the tennis court. What is the perimeter of the tennis court?

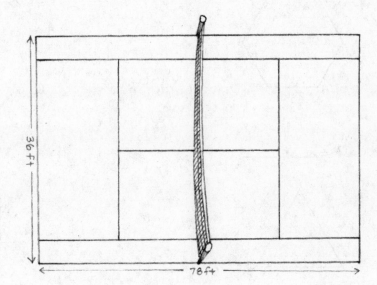

36 ft

78 ft

We need to find the total distance around the tennis court.

The tennis court has _____ sides.

The lengths are _____, _____,

_____, and _____ feet.

To find the perimeter, we add the lengths of the

sides. We add _____, _____, _____, and _____.

$$\begin{array}{r} 78 \\ 78 \\ 36 \\ + 36 \\ \hline \end{array}$$

The perimeter of the tennis court is _____ feet.

Getting Started

Find the perimeter of each figure.

1.

15 yd

8 yd   8 yd

15 yd

P = _____

2.

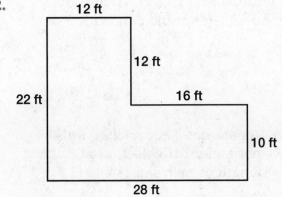

12 ft

12 ft

22 ft   16 ft

10 ft

28 ft

P = _____

Practice

Find the perimeter of each figure.

1.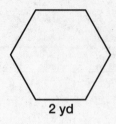

   2 yd

   P = _____

2.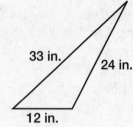

   33 in.   24 in.

   12 in.

   P = _____

3.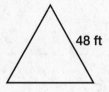

   48 ft

   P = _____

4.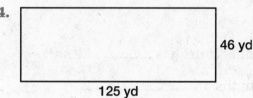

   46 yd

   125 yd

   P = _____

5.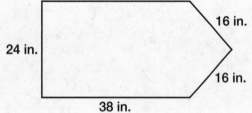

   24 in.   16 in.

   16 in.

   38 in.

   P = _____

6.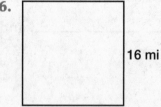

   16 mi

   P = _____

Problem Solving

Draw a picture and solve each problem.

7. A parking lot has 4 sides, each measuring 75 feet. What is the perimeter of the parking lot?

8. A yard has 2 sides 80 feet long and 2 sides 115 feet long. If fencing cost $8.55 for each foot, how much will it cost to fence in the yard?

9. A park has 3 equal sides. If its perimeter is 189 feet, what is the length of each side?

10. The length of a picture frame is 6 inches. The width is twice as long. What is the perimeter of the picture frame?

Area of Rectangles

The **area** of a figure is the number of square units it takes to cover it. Sandy is crocheting a blanket using a granny square design. What is the area of Sandy's blanket?

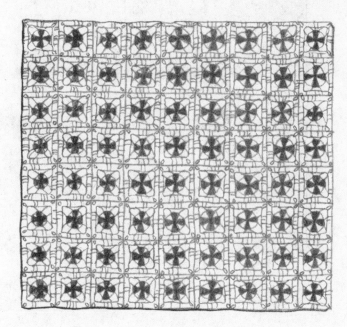

We want to find the area of Sandy's blanket in square units.

The blanket is _____ units wide and _____ units long.

We can find the number of square units by using a formula.

There are _____ rows of squares.

There are _____ squares in each row.

To find the total number of squares, we multiply the number of rows by the number of squares in each.

_____ × _____ = _____ squares

REMEMBER If we multiply the length of a rectangle by its width, we will get its area in square units.

The formula is: $A = l \times w$.

There are _____ square units in Sandy's blanket.

Getting Started

Find the area of each figure.

1.
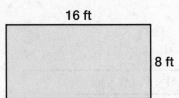
16 ft
8 ft

$A =$ _____

2.
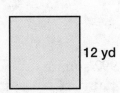
12 yd

$A =$ _____

3.
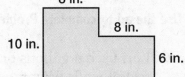
8 in.
8 in.
10 in.
6 in.

$A =$ _____

4. A rectangle has a length of 146 feet and a width of 89 feet.

$A =$ _____

5. A rectangle has a length of 245 inches and a width of 136 inches.

$A =$ _____

6. A square is 85 yards on each side.

$A =$ _____

Practice

Find the area of figure.

1.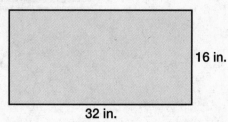
16 in.
32 in.

   A = _____

2.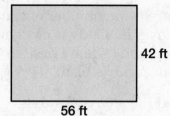
42 ft
56 ft

   A = _____

3.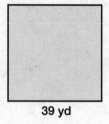
39 yd

   A = _____

4.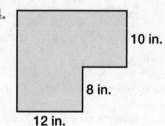
10 in.
8 in.
12 in.

   A = _____

Problem Solving

Solve each problem.

5. Carpet tiles cost $4.08 each. How much will it cost to cover a rectangular floor that uses 246 tiles?

6. A square floor is 4 yards on each side. A can of varnish covers 8 square yards. How many cans of varnish will be needed to cover the floor once?

7. The width of a rectangular ceiling is 18 feet. The length is 3 feet less than the width. What is the area of the ceiling?

8. The area of a rectangular wall is 192 square feet. The height of the wall is 12 feet. What is the width?

Use the ad to complete Problems 9 and 10.

9. Lori used 4 gallons of paint to cover 4,992 square feet of walls. What was the cost of her paint if she paid $2.03 in tax?

10. Lori bought a ladder, 3 brushes, and a roller. The tax was $1.68. She gave the clerk $30. How much change did she receive?

Al's Paint Store	
Paint	$ 7.80 per gallon
Brushes	$ 3.59 each
Rollers	$ 1.89 each
Ladders	$11.85 each

Name _____

Area of Parallelograms and Triangles

It's Algebra!

José changed a rectangle into a parallelogram. He cut along the dotted line and moved the shaded piece to the left side of the rectangle. Notice that the width of the rectangle becomes the height of the parallelogram.

Rectangle

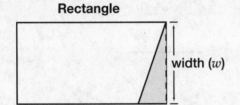

width (*w*)

length (*l*)

Parallelogram

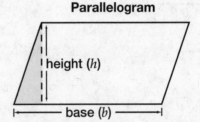

height (*h*)

base (*b*)

The area of the parallelogram is equal to the _____ of the rectangle.

José wrote the formula for the area of a rectangle. $A = l \times w$

Then, he rewrote the formula. He wrote *b* for *l* and *h* for *w*. $A = $ _____ $\times$ _____

The formula for the area of a parallelogram is: $A = b \times h$

Next, José showed how he found a formula for the area of a triangle. He began with the parallelogram and divided it in half. He wrote this formula.

$A = \frac{1}{2} b \times $ _____

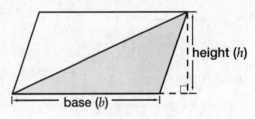

height (*h*)

base (*b*)

Getting Started

Find the area of each figure.

1.

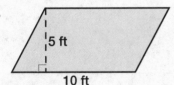

5 ft

10 ft

$A = $ _____

2.

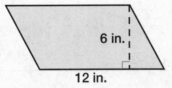

6 in.

12 in.

$A = $ _____

3.

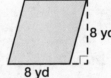

8 yd

8 yd

$A = $ _____

4.

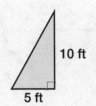

10 ft

5 ft

$A = $ _____

5.

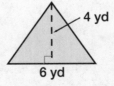

4 yd

6 yd

$A = $ _____

6.

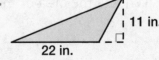

11 in.

22 in.

$A = $ _____

Practice

Find the area of each figure.

1.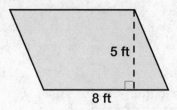

5 ft

8 ft

$A =$ _____

2.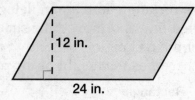

12 in.

24 in.

$A =$ _____

3.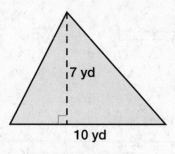

7 yd

10 yd

$A =$ _____

4.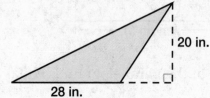

20 in.

28 in.

$A =$ _____

5.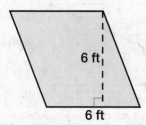

6 ft

6 ft

$A =$ _____

6.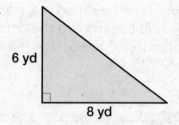

6 yd

8 yd

$A =$ _____

Problem Solving

Solve each problem.

7. The base of a parallelogram is 16 feet. The height is 6 feet less than the base. What is the area of the parallelogram?

8. The area of a parallelogram is 96 square feet. The height is 8 feet. What is the base?

Lesson 6-8 • Area of Parallelograms and Triangles

Name _____

Volume

It's Algebra!

The volume of a container is the number of cubic units it takes to fill the container. Jose's new hobby is raising tropical fish. What is the volume of Jose's aquarium?

We want to find the aquarium's volume in cubic units.

The aquarium is _____ units high, _____ units long, and _____ units wide.

We can find the volume by using a formula.

There are _____ times _____, or _____ cubes, on the bottom layer.

There are _____ layers.

To find the total number of cubes, we multiply the number of rows by the number of cubes in each, and again by the number of layers.

_____ × _____ × _____ = _____ cubes

REMEMBER If we multiply the length of a rectangular prism by its width, and again by its height, we will get its volume in cubic units.

The formula is: $V = l \times w \times h$.

There are _____ cubic units in Jose's aquarium.

Getting Started

Find the volume of each figure.

1.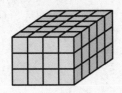

$V =$ _____

2.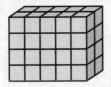

$V =$ _____

3.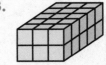

$V =$ _____

Complete the table.

4.

Length	3 yd	2 ft	27 in.	6 yd	4 ft
Width	6 yd	6 ft	9 in.	2 yd	12 ft
Height	8 yd	1 ft	15 in.	5 yd	25 ft
Volume					

Practice

Find the volume of each figure.

1.
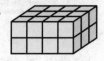

$V =$ _____

2.

$V =$ _____

3.
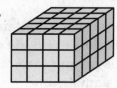

$V =$ _____

Complete the table.

4.

Length	6 yd	9 ft	24 in.	12 ft	14 in.	105 in.
Width	4 yd	12 ft	14 in.	12 ft	18 in.	45 in.
Height	3 yd	3 ft	8 in.	12 ft	24 in.	26 in.
Volume						

Now Try This!

Draw one of the diagonals of this rectangle to form two right triangles. Do you think these triangles are identical to each other? (Could you rotate or flip one triangle to fit exactly on the other?) _____

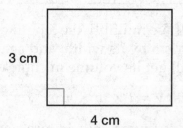

3 cm

4 cm

The area of one of these triangles can be obtained by multiplying the area of the rectangle by one-half.

_____ × _____ × $\frac{1}{2}$ = _____ sq cm

Complete each equation for finding the area of each right triangle.

1.
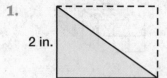

2 in.

3 in.

$A = \frac{1}{2} \times ($ _____ $\times 3) =$

_____ sq in.

2.
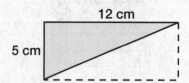

12 cm

5 cm

$A =$ _____ $\times (5 \times 12) =$

_____ sq cm

3.
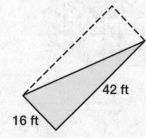

42 ft

16 ft

$A = \frac{1}{2} \times ($ _____ $\times$

_____ $) =$ _____ sq ft

Customary Units of Weight and Capacity

Martin Elliot drinks 12 pints of milk each week. Martin's mother buys milk in gallon containers. How many gallons does Mrs. Elliot buy for Martin each week?

We want to find the number of gallons of milk Mrs. Elliot must buy each week.

There are _____ pints in a quart and

_____ quarts in a gallon.

We find the number of pints in a gallon by

multiplying _____ by _____.

We find the number of gallons Mrs. Elliot needs by dividing the number of pints Martin drinks, by the number of pints in a gallon.

We divide _____ by _____.

$$\begin{array}{r} 1\ R4 \\ 8\overline{)12} \end{array} \qquad 12\ pt = 1\ gal\ 4\ pt$$

Since 12 pints is more than 1 gallon, Mrs. Elliot

must buy _____ gallons for Martin each week.

Capacity
1 cup (c) = 8 fluid ounces (fl oz)
1 pint (pt) = 2 c
1 pt = 16 fl oz
1 quart (qt) = 2 pt
1 qt = 32 fl oz
1 gallon (gal) = 4 qt

Weight
1 pound (lb) = 16 ounces (oz)
1 ton (T) = 2,000 lb

Getting Started

Rename each measurement.

1. 6 qt = _____ pt

2. 1 qt = _____ oz

3. 55 oz = _____ lb _____ oz

4. 5 gal = _____ qt

5. 3 qt 4 pt = _____ c

6. 2 gal 2 qt = _____ pt

Complete each sentence.

7. To change quarts to ounces,

   _____ by 32.

8. To change pounds and ounces to ounces, multiply the pounds by _____ and _____ the ounces.

Add or subtract. Simplify your answer.

9. $\quad$ 3 pt 2 c
    $+ $ 2 pt 3 c

10. $\quad$ 4 gal 3 qt
    $- $ 2 gal 5 qt

11. $\quad$ 3 qt
    $- $ 2 qt 5 oz

12. $\quad$ 15 lb 11 oz
    $+ $ 9 lb 15 oz

Practice

Rename each measurement.

1. 12 pt = _____ qt

2. 1 T = _____ oz

3. 59 oz = _____ lb _____ oz

4. 5 qt 3 pt = _____ c

5. 64 oz = _____ qt

6. 1 qt = _____ oz

7. 2 gal 1 qt = _____ qt

8. 80 oz = _____ lb

9. 73 lb 12 oz = _____ oz

10. 4 qt 5 pt 1 c = _____ oz

11. 23 pt = _____ gal _____ qt _____ pt

12. 3 T 250 lb = _____ lb

Complete each sentence.

13. To change gallons to pints, multiply by _____.

14. To change tons to pounds, multiply by _____.

15. To change quarts and pints to pints, multiply the quarts by _____ and _____ the pints.

16. To change ounces to gallons, _____ by 128.

Add or subtract. Simplify your answer.

17.   2 qt 1 pt
  + 3 qt 2 pt

18.   5 gal 3 qt
  − 2 gal 1 qt

19.   1 pt 9 oz
  + 5 pt 7 oz

20.   6 qt 3 pt
  − 2 qt 5 pt

21.   9 lb 8 oz
  − 3 lb 14 oz

22.   8 qt 24 oz
  + 5 qt 19 oz

23.   5 T 700 lb
  + 2 T 500 lb

24.   3 gal
  − 1 gal 3 qt

Problem Solving

Solve each problem.

25. Amy weighed nine pounds seven ounces at birth. Ricky's birth weight was eight pounds eleven ounces. How much more did Amy weigh?

26. Happy Juice is on sale in the 3-quart 8-ounce size for $7.28. The sale price for Super Juice in the 2-quart 9-ounce size is $5.84. Which brand is more expensive per ounce?

Measuring Length in Centimeters

The **centimeter** (cm) is used to measure lengths in the metric system. A smaller unit, the **millimeter** (mm) is used for more accurate measurements. How long is the paper clip to the nearest centimeter?

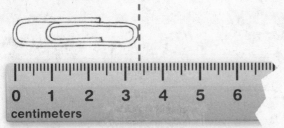

We are looking for the length of the paper clip to the nearest _____.

The millimeter lines help us determine whether the paper clip is

closer to _____ or _____ centimeters.

If the paper clip is less than 5 millimeters from the 3-centimeter line,

round _____. Round _____ to the next higher centimeter

if the paper clip is 5 millimeters or more from the 3-centimeter line.

Since the paper clip is _____ millimeters longer than the 3-centimeter

line, we say that it is _____ centimeters long, to the nearest centimeter.

Getting Started

Measure each item to the nearest centimeter.

1.

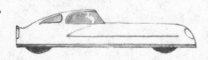

_____

2.

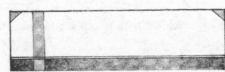

_____

3.

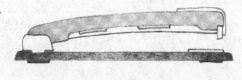

_____

4.

_____

Circle the best estimate.

5. The width of this page

    22 mm   22 cm   220 cm

6. The width of a dime

    18 mm   180 mm   180 cm

Practice

Measure each item to the nearest centimeter.

1.

   _____

2.

   _____

3.

   _____

4.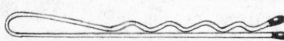

   _____

5.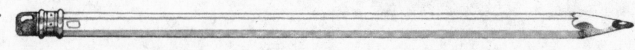

   _____

6.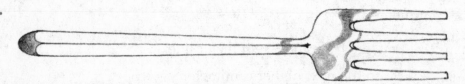

   _____

7.

   _____

8.

   _____

Circle the best estimate.

9. The width of a fingernail

   10 mm   100 mm   10 cm

10. The height of a chair

    45 mm   45 cm   450 cm

Problem Solving

Solve each problem.

11. Find the perimeter of a picture frame that is 150 millimeters long and 125 millimeters wide.

12. The area of a rectangle is 108 square centimeters. If the length of the rectangle is 12 centimeters, what is the width?

Metric Units of Length

Kathryn is training for the spring
marathon. For practice, she ran a
5-kilometer race. How many meters
did she run?

Length
1 meter (m) = 100 cm
1 kilometer (km) = 1,000 m

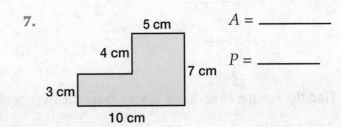

We are looking for the number of meters
Kathryn ran.

One kilometer equals _____ meters.

Kathryn ran _____ kilometers.

To find the total meters Kathryn ran, we
multiply the number of meters in a kilometer
by the number of kilometers she ran.

We multiply _____ by _____.

$1,000 \times 5 =$ _____

Kathryn ran _____ meters.

Getting Started

Circle the best estimate.

1. A person can walk ___?___ in 10 minutes.   1 cm   1 m   1 km

2. The United States is about ___?___ wide.   4,000 cm   4,000 m   4,000 km

3. A pair of scissors is about ___?___ long.   20 cm   20 m   20 km

Rename each measurement.

4. 6 kilometers = _____ meters

5. 10,000 meters = _____ kilometers

Find the perimeter and the area of each figure.

6. $A =$ _____

2 m
7 m $P =$ _____

7. $A =$ _____

5 cm
4 cm
7 cm
3 cm
10 cm $P =$ _____

Find the volume of each box having these measurements.

8. length = 15 cm $V =$ _____
   width = 20 cm
   height = 10 cm

9. length = 6 m $V =$ _____
   width = 9 m
   height = 5 m

Practice _____

Circle the best estimate.

1. This page is about ___?___ long.

   28 cm   28 m   28 km

2. The distance from Chicago to Los Angeles is about ___?___.

   2,800 cm   2,800 m   2,800 km

3. The distance around a running track is about ___?___.

   400 cm   400 m   400 km

4. The English Channel is about ___?___ long.

   560 cm   560 m   560 km

5. A necktie is about ___?___ long.

   60 cm   60 m   60 km

6. A staple is about ___?___ long.

   1 cm   1 m   1 km

Rename each measurement.

7. 2,000 meters = _____ kilometers

8. 200 meters = _____ centimeters

9. 3,000 centimeters = _____ meters

10. 1 kilometer = _____ centimeters

Find the perimeter and the area of each figure.

11.
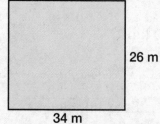
26 m
34 m

   A = _____

   P = _____

12.
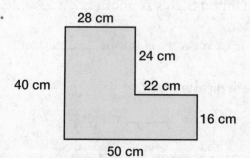
28 cm
24 cm
40 cm
22 cm
16 cm
50 cm

   A = _____

   P = _____

Find the volume of each box having these measurements.

13. length = 5 m   V = _____
    width = 9 m
    height = 4 m

14. length = 18 cm   V = _____
    width = 18 cm
    height = 18 cm

Metric Units of Mass and Capacity

In the metric system, there is a simple relationship between volume, capacity, and mass. One **cubic centimeter** holds 1 **milliliter** of water and has a mass of 1 **gram**.

Capacity
1 liter (l) = 1,000 milliliters (mL)

Mass
1 kilogram (kg) = 1,000 grams (g) 1 metric ton = 1,000 kg

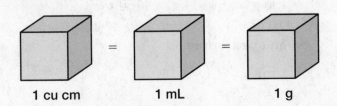

1 cu cm = 1 mL = 1 g

What does a container of water hold if it measures 20 centimeters on each edge?

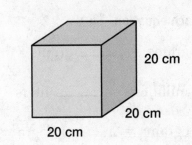

20 cm
20 cm
20 cm

Since 1 cubic centimeter holds 1 milliliter of water, 8,000 cubic centimeters will hold _____ milliliters

or _____ liters of water.

Since 1 milliliter of water has a mass of 1 gram, 8,000 milliliters of water has a mass of _____ grams.

The mass of the container is _____ grams

or _____ kilograms.

Getting Started

Circle the answer that seems most reasonable.

1. A small puppy

   450 g   450 kg   450 t

2. A compact auto

   1,500 g   1,500 kg   1,500 t

3. A bathtub

   320 mL   320 L

4. A bottle of milk

   2 mL   2 L

Complete each equation.

5. 6,000 grams = _____ kilograms

6. 3 liters = _____ milliliters

Solve this problem.

7. How many milliliters of water will a container hold that is 4 centimeters long, 9 centimeters wide, and 7 centimeters in height?

Practice

Circle the answer that seems most reasonable.

1. a container that holds milk

   4 mL   4 L

2. this book

   1 g   1 kg   1 t

3. a can of soup

   150 g   150 kg   150 t

4. a basketball

   150 g   150 kg   150 t

5. a comb

   60 g   60 kg   60 t

6. an eyedropper

   1 mL   1 L

Complete each equation.

7. 3 kilograms = _____ grams

8. 10 milliliters = _____ grams

9. 8,000 milliliters = _____ liters

10. 15 liters = _____ milliliters

11. 11,000 grams = _____ kilograms

12. 1 metric ton = _____ grams

13. 6,000 kilograms = _____ metric tons

14. 2 metric tons = _____ kilograms

15. 500 cubic centimeters = _____ milliliters

16. 60 grams = _____ cubic centimeters

Problem Solving

Solve each problem.

17. If a dairy produces 24,000 milliliters of chocolate milk each minute, how many 2-liter bottles can be filled each minute?

18. A container is 15 centimeters long, 12 centimeters wide, and 6 centimeters in height. How many milliliters of water will the container hold? What is the mass of the water?

19. Which container would hold more: a tin that measures 10 by 8 by 8 centimeters or a bottle that contains 1 liter?

20. How many milliliters of water do you need to fill a container that measures 7 by 8 by 9 centimeters?

Name _____

Problem Solving: Draw a Diagram

The desks in our classroom are in straight rows with the same number of desks in each row. Unless someone is absent, each desk is filled. Fred sits in the second row from the front and the fourth row from the back. He is the third student from the left end of the room and the fourth student from the right end. How many students are in the class?

★ **SEE**

We want to know how many students are in the class.

There is a student at each desk.

The number of desks equals the number of _____.

There are the same number of desks in each row.

Fred's desk is in the _____ row from the front.

His desk is in the _____ row from the back.

His desk is the _____ from the left side of the room.

His desk is the _____ from the right side of the room.

★ **PLAN**

We can understand all of this information by drawing a picture.

★ **DO**

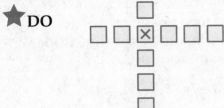

There are _____ students in the class.

★ **CHECK**

Compare your drawing with the clues in the problem. Is Fred's desk in the right place in relation to the four sides of the classroom? _____

Draw in the missing desks so that there are straight rows and the number of students in each row is the same.

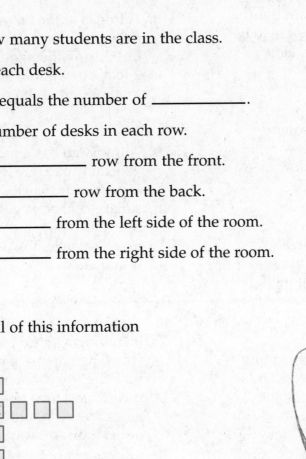

Apply

Draw a picture or diagram to help solve each problem.

1. There are 6 flags equally spaced around the track. It takes Susan 20 seconds to run from the first to the second flag. If she continues at the same rate, how long will it take Susan to run the complete track?

2. The school driveway is 90 meters long. The fifth grade decided to plant trees along each side of it. The trees are to be evenly spaced 5 meters apart. How many trees will be needed?

3. Mrs. Nolanski fenced in her square vegetable garden. There were 15 fence posts on each side. How many fence posts did she use?

4. Farmer Anderson has 9 pigs in a pigpen. Draw a plan for him to use 4 straight lines to put each pig in its own individual pen.

5. How much will it cost to cut a log into 8 pieces, if cutting it into 4 pieces costs $0.75? (Hint: You are charged by the number of cuts.)

6. Timothy is on a ladder leaning against a wall that he is painting. He starts on the middle rung, goes up 5 rungs, down 7 rungs, up 4 rungs, and up 9 more rungs to reach the top bar. How many rungs are on the ladder?

7. Samuel's father wants to build a fence around his patio. The fence will be in the shape of a rectangle 60 feet long and 48 feet wide. The posts will be 6 feet apart. How many posts will be needed?

8. A frog is at the bottom of a 20-foot deep well. Each day he jumps 5 feet but during the night he slides down 2 feet. How many days will it take him to jump out of the well?

9. Aunt Sarah has a rectangular-shaped vegetable patch that is 48 feet long and 16 feet wide. Uncle Norman has a square-shaped vegetable patch. If his patch has the same perimeter as Aunt Sarah's patch, how long is one side of his patch?

10. Cousin Caroline has 64 feet of fence, including a gate. She wants to enclose a rectangular space in her yard for a flower garden. She wants to enclose the greatest area possible with her fence. What should be the dimensions of her garden?

11. Percy has a picture of his pet poodle. He decides to have it enlarged by doubling both the length and the width. How does this affect the area?

12. Betty is making a box for her bows. She decides to make it larger by doubling all three of its dimensions. How does this affect the volume?

Rename each measurement.

1. 5 hours 15 minutes = _____ minutes

2. 3 hours = _____ seconds

3. 5 feet 9 inches = _____ inches

4. 79 feet = _____ yards _____ feet

5. 39 ounces = _____ pounds _____ ounces

6. 3 gallons = _____ quarts

7. 3 kilometers = _____ meters

8. 5,000 milliliters = _____ liters

Solve each problem.

9. Find the elapsed time between 6:30 A.M. and 11:15 A.M.

10. Find the elapsed time between 9:45 A.M. and 3:30 P.M.

11. Find the area of a square that is 16 feet on each side.

12. Find the volume of a box that is 24 inches long, 16 inches wide, and 9 inches high.

13. Find the area of a triangle that has a height of 12 inches and a base of 7 inches.

14. Find the area of a parallelogram that has a height of 5 inches and a base of 6 inches.

Find the perimeter.

15.

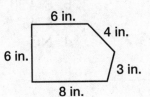

$P =$ _____

Write the temperature.

16.

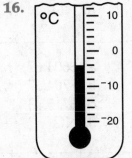

_____

Add or subtract.

17.   6 ft 9 in.
    + 3 ft 8 in.

18.   8 yd 2 ft
    − 5 yd 3 ft

Circle the letter of the correct answer.

1 What is the place value of the 7 in 326,475?
- **a.** ones
- **b.** tens
- **c.** hundreds
- **d.** NG

2 13,605 ◯ 13,506
- **a.** >
- **b.** <
- **c.** =

3
596
+ 437
- **a.** 933
- **b.** 1,023
- **c.** 1,033
- **d.** NG

4
$637.15
+ 209.18
- **a.** $836.33
- **b.** $846.33
- **c.** $946.33
- **d.** NG

5
7,462
− 6,847
- **a.** 625
- **b.** 1,425
- **c.** 1,625
- **d.** NG

6
$923.06
− 218.39
- **a.** $604.67
- **b.** $704.67
- **c.** $715.33
- **d.** NG

7 408 × 9
- **a.** 3,672
- **b.** 3,762
- **c.** 36,072
- **d.** NG

8
39
× 28
- **a.** 390
- **b.** 1,092
- **c.** 1,292
- **d.** NG

9 What is the GCF of 21 and 36?
- **a.** 7
- **b.** 9
- **c.** 3
- **d.** NG

10 Find the average of 36, 39, and 42.
- **a.** 36
- **b.** 39
- **c.** 42
- **d.** NG

11 46)2,900
- **a.** 63
- **b.** 63 R2
- **c.** 63 R46
- **d.** NG

12 47)$349.21
- **a.** $7.43
- **b.** $74.30
- **c.** $743
- **d.** NG

13 Find the area.

16 ft

21 ft
- **a.** 74 ft
- **b.** 336 ft
- **c.** 336 sq ft
- **d.** NG

score

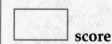
STOP

Name _____

Fractions

Writing Fractions

Fractions are used to show a part of a region or a part of a set.

What part of the flag is green?

The flag is divided into _____ equal parts.

_____ parts are colored green.

A fraction shows what part is green.

number of green parts → $\frac{3}{4}$ ← numerator
total number of parts →   ← denominator

Three-fourths of the flag is green.

What part of the set is green pennants?

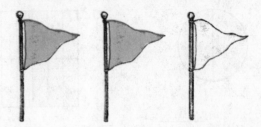

There are _____ objects in the set.

_____ of the objects are green pennants.

A fraction shows what part is green pennants.

number of green pennants → $\frac{2}{3}$ ← numerator
total number of objects →   ← denominator

Two-thirds of the set is green pennants.

REMEMBER When writing a fraction to name parts of a region or parts of a set, the numerator always represents the portion of the region or set we are naming in the fraction. The denominator always represents the total number of parts or objects in the set.

Getting Started

Write the word-name for each fraction.

1. $\frac{1}{3}$ _____

2. $\frac{2}{5}$ _____

3. $\frac{2}{9}$ _____

Write the fraction.

4. three-fourths

5. five-eighths

6. five-sixths

7. one-fourth

Write the fraction for each green part.

8.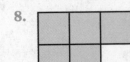

9.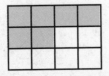

Write a fraction to answer the question.

10. What part of the set of apples is green?

Practice

Write the word-name for each fraction.

1. $\frac{1}{4}$ _____

2. $\frac{7}{8}$ _____

3. $\frac{1}{10}$ _____

4. $\frac{5}{6}$ _____

Write the fractions

5. seven-eighths

6. four-fifths

7. one-half

8. three-tenths

Write the fraction for each green part.

9.

_____

10.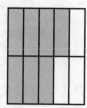

_____

11.

_____

12.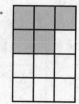

_____

Write a fraction to answer each question.

13. What part of all figures is boxes?

_____

14. What part of all the numbers is greater than 10?

1 3 11 2 6 15   _____

Shade the objects each fraction represents.

15. $\frac{2}{3}$

16. $\frac{7}{8}$

Now Try This!

To make bookshelves, Mari cut boards she bought at a lumber store. A whole board and a cut board are shown on the right. What part of the whole board was cut for a bookshelf?

Think about fractional parts of a whole.

About $\frac{3}{4}$ of the board was cut.

	1		
$\frac{1}{4}$	$\frac{1}{4}$	$\frac{1}{4}$	$\frac{1}{4}$

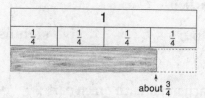

about $\frac{3}{4}$

Estimate the shaded part of each.

1.

2.

3.

Lesson 7-1 • Writing Fractions

Equivalent Fractions

Craig has a recipe that calls for $\frac{2}{4}$ of a cup of milk. He only has a $\frac{1}{2}$ measuring cup. How many times should Craig fill his measuring cup to measure the right amount?

We want to find a way Craig can measure the correct amount with his cup.

His cup measures _____ of a cup and he needs to measure _____ of a cup of milk.

We need to compare _____ and _____

 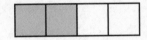

_____ and _____ measure the same amount.

They are **equivalent fractions** because both fractions represent the same amount.

We write: $\frac{1}{2} = \frac{2}{4}$.

Craig can fill his measuring cup _____ time because _____ of a cup is equal to _____ of a cup.

Getting Started

Write the equivalent fractions for the green parts.

1.

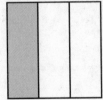 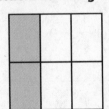

$\frac{}{3} = \frac{}{6}$

2.

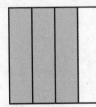 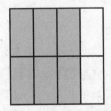

$\frac{}{4} = \frac{}{8}$

3.

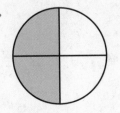 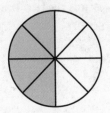

$\frac{}{4} = \frac{}{8}$

4.

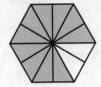 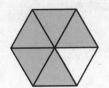

$\frac{}{12} = \frac{}{6}$

Practice

Write the equivalent fractions for the green parts.

1.

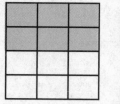

$$\frac{}{12} = \frac{}{4}$$

2.

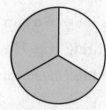 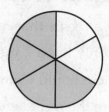

$$\frac{}{3} = \frac{}{6}$$

3.

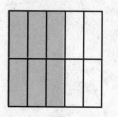 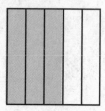

$$\frac{}{10} = \frac{}{5}$$

4.

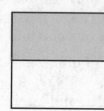 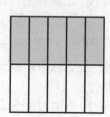

$$\frac{}{2} = \frac{}{10}$$

5.

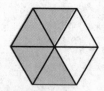 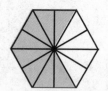

$$\frac{}{6} = \frac{}{12}$$

6.

$$\frac{}{10} = \frac{}{5}$$

7.

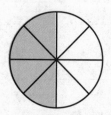

$$\frac{}{8} = \frac{}{4}$$

8.

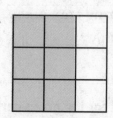 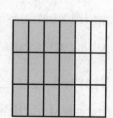

$$\frac{}{9} = \frac{}{18}$$

Now Try This!

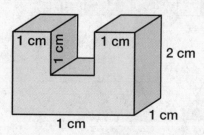

Find the surface area of this 3-dimensional figure by finding the area of each of its faces. You will have to imagine the faces that are not visible to you, such as the back face, the bottom face, and so on.

Name _____

Multiplying to Find Equivalent Fractions

Chang said $\frac{3}{4}$ of the cars were green, but Raul thought $\frac{9}{12}$ of them were green. The teacher said both boys were correct. Why are they both right?

They are both right because $\frac{3}{4}$ and $\frac{9}{12}$ are equivalent fractions.

To understand this, we need to consider the **identity element of multiplication**. Whenever the same non-zero number appears in both the numerator and denominator, the fraction is equal to 1.

Thus, $\frac{2}{2} = 1$, $\frac{3}{3} = 1$, $\frac{4}{4} = 1$ and $\frac{7}{7} =$ _____.

REMEMBER The number 1 is the identity element of multiplication. This means that whenever we multiply a number by 1, we get the same number.

To prove that $\frac{3}{4}$ and $\frac{9}{12}$ are equivalent fractions, we need to show how $\frac{3}{4}$ has been multiplied by 1 to get $\frac{9}{12}$.

$$\frac{3}{4} \times \frac{\square}{\square} = \frac{3 \times \square}{4 \times \square} = \frac{9}{12}$$

REMEMBER Equivalent fractions can be found by multiplying both the numerator and denominator by the same non-zero number.

Getting Started

Write the missing factors.

1. $\frac{5}{6} \times \frac{\square}{\square} = \frac{20}{24}$ 2. $\frac{1}{5} \times \frac{\square}{\square} = \frac{3}{15}$ 3. $\frac{3}{4} \times \frac{\square}{\square} = \frac{6}{8}$ 4. $\frac{2}{7} \times \frac{\square}{\square} = \frac{6}{21}$

Write the equivalent fraction.

5. $\frac{2}{3} = \frac{}{9}$ 6. $\frac{3}{7} = \frac{}{14}$ 7. $\frac{2}{5} = \frac{}{15}$ 8. $\frac{3}{8} = \frac{}{40}$

Are these fractions equivalent?

9. $\frac{1}{2}$ $\frac{4}{8}$ _____   10. $\frac{2}{9}$ $\frac{5}{27}$ _____   11. $\frac{2}{3}$ $\frac{4}{12}$ _____   12. $\frac{2}{4}$ $\frac{8}{16}$ _____

Practice

Write the missing factors.

1. $\frac{3}{4} \times \frac{\square}{\square} = \frac{6}{8}$

2. $\frac{1}{2} \times \frac{\square}{\square} = \frac{6}{12}$

3. $\frac{2}{5} \times \frac{\square}{\square} = \frac{8}{20}$

4. $\frac{5}{7} \times \frac{\square}{\square} = \frac{25}{35}$

5. $\frac{1}{4} \times \frac{\square}{\square} = \frac{4}{16}$

6. $\frac{5}{6} \times \frac{\square}{\square} = \frac{30}{36}$

7. $\frac{6}{15} \times \frac{\square}{\square} = \frac{24}{60}$

8. $\frac{3}{8} \times \frac{\square}{\square} = \frac{24}{64}$

9. $\frac{2}{3} \times \frac{\square}{\square} = \frac{10}{15}$

10. $\frac{1}{6} \times \frac{\square}{\square} = \frac{7}{42}$

11. $\frac{3}{10} \times \frac{\square}{\square} = \frac{15}{50}$

12. $\frac{4}{9} \times \frac{\square}{\square} = \frac{28}{63}$

13. $\frac{2}{9} \times \frac{\square}{\square} = \frac{6}{27}$

14. $\frac{3}{11} \times \frac{\square}{\square} = \frac{12}{44}$

15. $\frac{7}{8} \times \frac{\square}{\square} = \frac{49}{56}$

16. $\frac{3}{14} \times \frac{\square}{\square} = \frac{9}{42}$

Write the equivalent fraction.

17. $\frac{7}{8} = \frac{}{16}$

18. $\frac{3}{5} = \frac{}{25}$

19. $\frac{2}{3} = \frac{}{12}$

20. $\frac{7}{8} = \frac{}{24}$

21. $\frac{3}{4} = \frac{}{20}$

22. $\frac{7}{9} = \frac{}{45}$

23. $\frac{3}{8} = \frac{}{64}$

24. $\frac{3}{10} = \frac{}{100}$

25. $\frac{5}{6} = \frac{}{36}$

26. $\frac{5}{12} = \frac{}{60}$

27. $\frac{7}{15} = \frac{}{30}$

28. $\frac{9}{16} = \frac{}{64}$

29. $\frac{1}{3} = \frac{}{12}$

30. $\frac{2}{5} = \frac{}{15}$

31. $\frac{5}{12} = \frac{}{36}$

32. $\frac{4}{9} = \frac{}{18}$

33. $\frac{1}{2} = \frac{}{60}$

34. $\frac{4}{5} = \frac{}{45}$

35. $\frac{1}{4} = \frac{}{64}$

36. $\frac{3}{7} = \frac{}{56}$

Are these fractions equivalent?

37. $\frac{2}{3}$ $\frac{6}{9}$ _____

38. $\frac{1}{3}$ $\frac{8}{12}$ _____

39. $\frac{7}{8}$ $\frac{14}{16}$ _____

40. $\frac{1}{2}$ $\frac{9}{20}$ _____

41. $\frac{1}{4}$ $\frac{6}{24}$ _____

42. $\frac{3}{5}$ $\frac{15}{25}$ _____

43. $\frac{5}{6}$ $\frac{30}{42}$ _____

44. $\frac{5}{6}$ $\frac{30}{36}$ _____

45. $\frac{1}{2}$ $\frac{14}{24}$ _____

46. $\frac{2}{3}$ $\frac{12}{18}$ _____

47. $\frac{7}{10}$ $\frac{49}{70}$ _____

48. $\frac{5}{9}$ $\frac{35}{64}$ _____

49. $\frac{2}{7}$ $\frac{21}{49}$ _____

50. $\frac{3}{8}$ $\frac{27}{72}$ _____

51. $\frac{2}{9}$ $\frac{18}{81}$ _____

52. $\frac{1}{11}$ $\frac{11}{121}$ _____

Lesson 7-3 • Multiplying to Find Equivalent Fractions

Simplifying Fractions

Mrs. Phillips has a full busload of children this morning. If 32 boys are riding the bus today, what fraction of the children on the bus are boys?

CAPACITY 48

We want to find what fraction of the busload is boys.

The bus holds _____ children.

There are _____ boys on the bus.

REMEMBER The numerator of a fraction represents a portion of the total set. The denominator represents the total number of objects in the set.

$$\frac{\quad}{\quad} = \frac{\text{the number of boys on the bus}}{\text{the total number of children on the bus}}$$

The numerator and denominator of a fraction are called the **terms** of the fraction. The terms in this fraction can be **simplified**. To simplify a fraction, divide each term by a single number that will divide evenly into both the numerator and the denominator. We call this divisor a **common factor**.

A fraction is in simplest terms if the greatest common factor of the terms is 1.

$$\frac{32}{48} \div \frac{8}{8} = \frac{4}{6} \qquad \frac{4}{6} \div \frac{2}{2} = \overset{\text{simplest terms}}{\underset{\downarrow}{\frac{2}{3}}}$$

> 1 is the greatest common factor or only number that will divide into both 2 and 3 evenly.

The fraction of children on the bus that is boys is _____.

Getting Started

Write each fraction in simplest terms.

1. $\dfrac{4}{8} \div \dfrac{4}{4} = \dfrac{\square}{\square}$

2. $\dfrac{6}{9} \div \dfrac{3}{3} = \dfrac{\square}{\square}$

3. $\dfrac{8}{12} \div \dfrac{4}{4} = \dfrac{\square}{\square}$

4. $\dfrac{5}{15} \div \dfrac{5}{5} = \dfrac{\square}{\square}$

Write each fraction in simplest terms.

5. $\dfrac{4}{20} = $ _____

6. $\dfrac{6}{12} = $ _____

7. $\dfrac{10}{25} = $ _____

8. $\dfrac{9}{27} = $ _____

Practice

Write each fraction in simplest terms.

1. $\frac{2}{6} \div \frac{2}{2} = \frac{\square}{\square}$

2. $\frac{21}{24} \div \frac{3}{3} = \frac{\square}{\square}$

3. $\frac{6}{18} \div \frac{6}{6} = \frac{\square}{\square}$

4. $\frac{16}{20} \div \frac{4}{4} = \frac{\square}{\square}$

5. $\frac{12}{16} \div \frac{4}{4} = \frac{\square}{\square}$

6. $\frac{20}{32} \div \frac{4}{4} = \frac{\square}{\square}$

7. $\frac{4}{10} \div \frac{2}{2} = \frac{\square}{\square}$

8. $\frac{25}{35} \div \frac{5}{5} = \frac{\square}{\square}$

9. $\frac{6}{9} \div \frac{3}{3} = \frac{\square}{\square}$

10. $\frac{16}{40} \div \frac{8}{8} = \frac{\square}{\square}$

11. $\frac{8}{12} \div \frac{4}{4} = \frac{\square}{\square}$

12. $\frac{27}{63} \div \frac{9}{9} = \frac{\square}{\square}$

Write each fraction in simplest terms.

13. $\frac{4}{20} = $ _____

14. $\frac{4}{16} = $ _____

15. $\frac{15}{25} = $ _____

16. $\frac{3}{12} = $ _____

17. $\frac{10}{15} = $ _____

18. $\frac{4}{8} = $ _____

19. $\frac{6}{12} = $ _____

20. $\frac{21}{28} = $ _____

21. $\frac{6}{9} = $ _____

22. $\frac{32}{40} = $ _____

23. $\frac{9}{12} = $ _____

24. $\frac{6}{18} = $ _____

25. $\frac{24}{48} = $ _____

26. $\frac{14}{16} = $ _____

27. $\frac{15}{60} = $ _____

28. $\frac{27}{36} = $ _____

29. $\frac{96}{100} = $ _____

30. $\frac{72}{81} = $ _____

31. $\frac{96}{144} = $ _____

32. $\frac{20}{100} = $ _____

Problem Solving

Solve each problem.

33. Mrs. Phillips drove 16 boys and 20 girls to a ball game. What fraction of the children were girls?

34. The baseball team has 18 players. There are 15 right-handed players. What fraction of the team is not right-handed?

Name _____

Comparing and Ordering Fractions

It's Algebra!

Martina and Joan are members of the track team. During practice, Martina ran $\frac{2}{3}$ of a mile and Joan ran $\frac{3}{4}$ of a mile. Who ran farther?

We want to find which of the two distances is greater.

Martina ran _____ of a mile and Joan ran

_____ of a mile.

A number line can be used to compare these fractions.

Since $\frac{3}{4}$ is closer to 1 mile than $\frac{2}{3}$, we write $\frac{3}{4}$ ◯ $\frac{2}{3}$.

_____ ran farther.

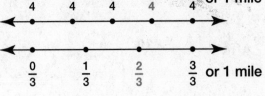

Fractions can also be compared by changing them to equivalent fractions with a common denominator and comparing the numerators. The greater fraction is the one with the greater numerator.

$\frac{3}{4} = \frac{9}{12}$ and $\frac{2}{3} = \frac{8}{12}$

$\frac{9}{12}$ ◯ $\frac{8}{12}$ because $9 > 8$.

$\frac{3}{4}$ ◯ $\frac{2}{3}$

Since $\frac{9}{12}$ is greater than $\frac{8}{12}$, _____ is greater than $\frac{2}{3}$.

Getting Started

Use a number line to compare the fractions.

Write > or < in each circle.

1. $\frac{1}{4}$ ◯ $\frac{1}{5}$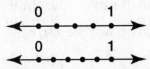

2. $\frac{3}{5}$ ◯ $\frac{2}{3}$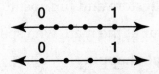

Write > or < in each circle.

3. $\frac{3}{4}$ ◯ $\frac{5}{8}$

4. $\frac{1}{2}$ ◯ $\frac{1}{3}$

5. $\frac{4}{5}$ ◯ $\frac{3}{4}$

6. $\frac{2}{3}$ ◯ $\frac{5}{8}$

Write the fractions in order from least to greatest.

7. $\frac{1}{2}, \frac{2}{8}, \frac{4}{12}$ _____, _____, _____

8. $\frac{3}{4}, \frac{5}{8}, \frac{4}{7}$ _____, _____, _____

Practice

Use a number line to compare the fractions.
Write > or < in each circle.

1. $\frac{3}{4}$ ◯ $\frac{5}{6}$

2. $\frac{3}{6}$ ◯ $\frac{3}{4}$

3. $\frac{1}{2}$ ◯ $\frac{4}{10}$

4. $\frac{2}{3}$ ◯ $\frac{5}{8}$

Write > or < in the circle.

5. $\frac{5}{8}$ ◯ $\frac{3}{4}$

6. $\frac{2}{3}$ ◯ $\frac{4}{5}$

7. $\frac{1}{3}$ ◯ $\frac{3}{8}$

8. $\frac{3}{4}$ ◯ $\frac{8}{10}$

9. $\frac{2}{5}$ ◯ $\frac{4}{15}$

10. $\frac{5}{6}$ ◯ $\frac{1}{2}$

11. $\frac{11}{12}$ ◯ $\frac{7}{8}$

12. $\frac{1}{3}$ ◯ $\frac{3}{8}$

13. $\frac{2}{3}$ ◯ $\frac{9}{15}$

14. $\frac{5}{6}$ ◯ $\frac{3}{4}$

15. $\frac{5}{9}$ ◯ $\frac{6}{12}$

16. $\frac{2}{5}$ ◯ $\frac{4}{6}$

17. $\frac{3}{12}$ ◯ $\frac{4}{15}$

18. $\frac{9}{10}$ ◯ $\frac{89}{100}$

19. $\frac{5}{12}$ ◯ $\frac{6}{10}$

20. $\frac{7}{20}$ ◯ $\frac{15}{50}$

Write the fractions in order from least to greatest.

21. $\frac{3}{4}, \frac{2}{3}, \frac{3}{5}$

22. $\frac{5}{6}, \frac{3}{4}, \frac{3}{8}$

23. $\frac{2}{3}, \frac{5}{9}, \frac{7}{12}$

Problem Solving

Solve each problem.

24. If Susan spent $\frac{2}{3}$ of an hour at the drugstore and Jim spent $\frac{7}{12}$ of an hour at the mall, who spent more time shopping?

25. While Ellen ran $\frac{3}{4}$ miles in 9 minutes, Josh ran $\frac{5}{9}$ miles in the same time. Who ran the farthest?

26. Of the fractions $\frac{3}{4}, \frac{2}{3}, \frac{7}{8}, \frac{5}{6}, \frac{4}{5}$, and $\frac{6}{7}$, which is the largest? Which is the smallest?

27. Arrange the fractions in Question 26 from the least to the greatest. Name a fraction larger than any in this series.

Lesson 7-5 • Comparing and Ordering Fractions

Name _____

Mixed Numbers

Irwin is building a model airplane to scale. How many quarter inches long is the propeller of Irwin's airplane?

We want to find how long Irwin's propeller is to the nearest $\frac{1}{4}$ of an inch. The propeller is exactly three-fourths of an inch longer than

_____ inches.

We write this measurement as a **mixed number**.

whole number $\rightarrow$ $3\frac{}{4}$ $\leftarrow$ fraction

We use a number line to help us understand this mixed number and rename it as a fraction.

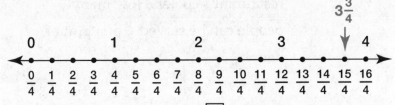

$3\frac{3}{4} = \frac{}{4}$ The propeller is $\frac{\Box}{\Box}$ inches long.

We can use a shortcut to rename a mixed number as a fraction.

Multiply the denominator by the whole number.	Add the numerator.	Write the sum over the denominator.

$3\frac{3}{4}$ $3 \times 4 =$ _____ $3\frac{3}{4}$ $12 + 3 =$ _____ $\frac{15}{4}$

Any fraction whose numerator is larger than the denominator is an **improper fraction**.

Getting Started

Write each mixed number as an improper fraction.

1. $4\frac{1}{2} =$ _____   2. $1\frac{7}{8} =$ _____   3. $5\frac{2}{3} =$ _____   4. $6\frac{7}{8} =$ _____   5. $7\frac{3}{10} =$ _____

6. $9\frac{1}{3} =$ _____   7. $3\frac{1}{12} =$ _____   8. $6\frac{4}{7} =$ _____   9. $8\frac{4}{5} =$ _____   10. $3\frac{5}{16} =$ _____

Practice

Write each mixed number as an improper fraction.

1. $1\frac{3}{4} =$ _____
2. $3\frac{1}{2} =$ _____
3. $5\frac{1}{8} =$ _____
4. $4\frac{3}{5} =$ _____
5. $6\frac{3}{8} =$ _____

6. $5\frac{2}{3} =$ _____
7. $2\frac{3}{8} =$ _____
8. $8\frac{3}{5} =$ _____
9. $6\frac{7}{10} =$ _____
10. $4\frac{5}{6} =$ _____

11. $4\frac{5}{12} =$ _____
12. $3\frac{7}{9} =$ _____
13. $6\frac{1}{4} =$ _____
14. $9\frac{4}{5} =$ _____
15. $7\frac{9}{10} =$ _____

16. $8\frac{8}{5} =$ _____
17. $4\frac{3}{7} =$ _____
18. $6\frac{1}{9} =$ _____
19. $5\frac{7}{12} =$ _____
20. $8\frac{9}{16} =$ _____

Problem Solving

Solve each problem.

21. It took Patti $3\frac{1}{4}$ hours to ride the train to her cousin's home. How many quarter-hours did it take?

22. There are $5\frac{1}{3}$ pints of juice in the restaurant's cooler. How many people can be served $\frac{1}{3}$ of a pint of juice?

(Now Try This!)

Simplify these fractions by first writing both the numerator and denominator as products of primes. Then cross out common factors in the numerator and denominator. Multiply the remaining factors in the numerator and denominator to get the simplified fraction. The first one has been done for you.

1. $\frac{84}{90} = \frac{2 \times 2 \times 3 \times 7}{2 \times 3 \times 3 \times 5} = \frac{2 \times 7}{3 \times 5} = \frac{14}{15}$

2. $\frac{16}{80} =$ _____ $=$ ___

3. $\frac{72}{90} =$ _____ $=$ _____ $=$ ___

4. $\frac{9}{51} =$ _____ $=$ ___

5. $\frac{36}{42} =$ _____ $=$ _____ $=$ ___

6. $\frac{57}{70} =$ _____ $=$ ___

7. $\frac{33}{121} =$ _____ $=$ ___

8. $\frac{24}{45} =$ _____ $=$ _____ $=$ ___

9. $\frac{12}{30} =$ _____ $=$ ___

10. $\frac{30}{48} =$ _____ $=$ _____ $=$ ___

Writing Quotients as Mixed Numbers

Crystal runs the packaging line at Bubbly Soap Works. Each hour, 327 bottles of liquid detergent are packed into cases. How many cases does Crystal pack each hour?

We need to find the number of cases Crystal packs each hour.

Each case holds _____ bottles, and Crystal can pack _____ bottles in an hour.

To find the number of cases she packs in an hour, we divide the bottles packed per hour by the number in each case. We divide _____ by _____.

$$\begin{array}{r} 27\ \text{R}3 \\ 12\overline{)327} \\ -24 \\ \hline 87 \\ -84 \\ \hline 3 \end{array}$$

The remainder can be written as a fraction.

$\dfrac{}{12}$ ← remainder
← divisor

We rewrite the quotient as the mixed number, _____.

We can simplify the fraction by dividing both the numerator and denominator by the greatest common factor, _____.

Crystal packs _____ cases of Bubbly Soap each hour.

Getting Started

Divide. Write each quotient as a mixed number. Simplify the fraction if necessary.

1. $4\overline{)218}$

2. $9\overline{)321}$

3. $14\overline{)395}$

4. $25\overline{)960}$

5. $46\overline{)2,921}$

6. $21\overline{)16,933}$

Copy and divide.

7. $593 \div 12$

8. $87,813 \div 51$

9. $3,021 \div 67$

Practice _____

Divide. Write each quotient as a mixed number. Simplify the fraction if necessary.

1. $3\overline{)58}$

2. $6\overline{)93}$

3. $4\overline{)130}$

4. $9\overline{)4,169}$

5. $18\overline{)654}$

6. $35\overline{)1,230}$

7. $28\overline{)2,360}$

8. $48\overline{)2,696}$

9. $85\overline{)36,225}$

Copy and divide.

10. $1,400 \div 26$

11. $3,111 \div 34$

12. $3,069 \div 45$

13. $10,575 \div 29$

14. $13,878 \div 15$

15. $14,670 \div 27$

16. $30,640 \div 48$

17. $32,388 \div 64$

18. $62,050 \div 75$

Problem Solving _____

Solve each problem.

19. A sidewalk along French Street is 500 inches wide. How many feet wide is the sidewalk?

20. A car gets 371 miles on 14 gallons of gas. How many miles does the car get for each gallon of gas?

21. Yoko weighs 1,380 ounces. How many pounds does Yoko weigh?

22. Wayne is making juice bars. Each bar weighs 8 ounces. If juices cost $1.65 a pint, how much will it cost to make 12 juice bars?

23. A farmer is preparing to ship 950 pounds of potatoes. He ships them in 50 pound sacks. How many sacks does he need for today's shipment?

24. A cement block weighs 65 pounds. If a crane can lift 1,040 pounds at a time, how many blocks can the crane lift?

Lesson 7-7 • Writing Quotients as Mixed Numbers

Renaming Improper Fractions

Cleve uses his computer to play math games. Each game takes $\frac{1}{4}$ of an hour. How long has Cleve been playing the computer games today?

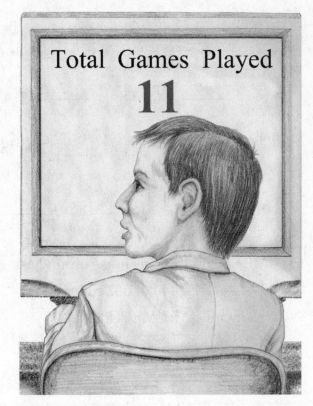

Total Games Played
11

We are looking for how long Cleve has been playing games on the computer today.

Each game takes _____ of an hour.

Cleve has played _____ games.

To find his total game time, we multiply the time it takes for one game by the number of games.

He has played for _____ quarters of an hour.

We write the fraction $\frac{}{4}$ hours to show how long Cleve has played.

$\frac{11}{4}$ is called an **improper fraction** because

the numerator, _____ is larger than the

denominator, _____.

$\frac{11}{4}$ can also represent division. We can read the

fraction as **eleven divided by four**.

REMEMBER To simplify an improper fraction, rename it as a whole or mixed number by dividing the denominator into the numerator. Write any remainder as a simplified fraction.

$$\frac{11}{4} \rightarrow 4\overline{)11} \begin{array}{r} 2\ \text{R}3 \\ \hline 11 \\ -8 \\ \hline 3 \end{array} \rightarrow 2\frac{3}{4}$$

Cleve has played computer games for $\frac{11}{4}$ or _____ hours.

Getting Started

Rename each improper fraction as a whole or mixed number.

1. $\frac{7}{6} =$ _____

2. $\frac{5}{5} =$ _____

3. $\frac{9}{5} =$ _____

4. $\frac{8}{6} =$ _____

5. $\frac{16}{12} =$ _____

6. $\frac{15}{10} =$ _____

7. $\frac{3}{2} =$ _____

8. $\frac{11}{3} =$ _____

9. $\frac{12}{4} =$ _____

10. $\frac{12}{8} =$ _____

Practice

Rename each improper fraction as a whole or mixed number.

1. $\frac{6}{5} =$ _____

2. $\frac{12}{3} =$ _____

3. $\frac{7}{4} =$ _____

4. $\frac{10}{8} =$ _____

5. $\frac{12}{5} =$ _____

6. $\frac{18}{6} =$ _____

7. $\frac{20}{12} =$ _____

8. $\frac{16}{10} =$ _____

9. $\frac{24}{16} =$ _____

10. $\frac{21}{7} =$ _____

11. $\frac{44}{8} =$ _____

12. $\frac{25}{15} =$ _____

13. $\frac{20}{6} =$ _____

14. $\frac{18}{4} =$ _____

15. $\frac{21}{9} =$ _____

16. $\frac{40}{16} =$ _____

17. $\frac{63}{18} =$ _____

18. $\frac{70}{20} =$ _____

19. $\frac{105}{35} =$ _____

20. $\frac{145}{10} =$ _____

Problem Solving

Solve each problem.

21. Mr. Seldon rode his horse around a $\frac{1}{2}$-mile track a total of 7 times. How many miles did Mr. Seldon ride?

22. Monica practices the piano for $\frac{25}{3}$ hours each month. Julia practices the violin $\frac{33}{4}$ hours each month. Who practices her instrument longer each month?

[Now Try This!]

When simplifying a fraction, test to see if 3 divides evenly into both the numerator and denominator. A number has 3 as a factor if the sum of its digits has 3 as its factor. For example, 1,551 is divisible by 3 because $1 + 5 + 5 + 1 = 12$ and 12 is divisible by 3.

Write the sums of the digits for each number. Write *yes* if the number is divisible by 3. Write *no* if it does not have 3 as a factor.

1. 151 _____ _____

2. 243,171 _____ _____

3. 7,015,206 _____ _____

4. 1,731 _____ _____

5. 111,222,444 _____ _____

6. 9,201,555 _____ _____

7. 222 _____ _____

8. 987,654,321 _____ _____

9. 687,490,100 _____ _____

10. If 3 is a factor of Tom's number and 3 is a factor of Jim's number, will 3 be a factor of the product of their numbers? _____

11. Will 3 be a factor of the sum of their numbers? _____

Lesson 7-8 • Renaming Improper Fractions

Name _____

Problem Solving: Identify a Subgoal

The Terrific T-Shirt Shop is having a sale. In the morning, T-shirts are on sale for $4.00 each. The shop sells $240 worth of shirts in the morning. After lunch, the price is dropped to $3.00 and the shop sells twice as many shirts. How much money does the shop take in on T-shirts that day?

⭐ SEE

We want to know how much money the shop took in on the day of the sale.

In the morning, the shirts cost _____ each.

The store took in _____ in the morning.

In the afternoon, the price of a shirt is _____ .

In the afternoon, the shop sold _____ times as many shirts as in the morning.

⭐ PLAN

- We need to answer several questions before we can reach a solution to the problem. This is known as **identifying a subgoal**.

- We find the number of shirts sold in the morning by dividing the money from the morning by the cost of a T-shirt.

- We double this number to get the number of shirts sold in the afternoon.

- We find the amount of money made from the afternoon sales by multiplying the number of shirts sold by the cost of one.

- We add the morning and the afternoon money to find the total.

⭐ DO

1. $240 ÷ $4 = _____

2. _____ × 2 = _____

3. _____ × $3 = _____

4. _____ + _____ = _____

The Terrific T-Shirt Shop took in _____ the day of the sale.

⭐ CHECK

We can work backward. If the shop took in $600 on the day of the sale, how many T-shirts did they sell in the afternoon?

$240 + _____ = $600   _____ ÷ $3 = _____   Is _____ twice 60? _____

Apply

Identify a subgoal to help solve each problem then solve.

1. A ballot box that is 1 foot long, 7 inches wide and 5 inches high, is taped along the length of each edge. If tape costs 10 cents per foot, what is the cost of the tape used?

2. A used car cost $800, but it needed four new tires and painting. Each new tire's original cost was $60, but they were on sale for one-third off. A new paint job costs $129. Mr. Sands had $500 to pay down on the car and will have to borrow the rest. How much will he have to borrow to pay for the car, the tires, and the paint job?

6. Carrie Consumer buys butter in pound boxes. Each box has 4 bars that weigh $\frac{1}{4}$ pound each. Carrie and her family use an average of $\frac{1}{8}$ pound of butter each week. Explain how to compute only with whole numbers to tell how much butter they use in 48 weeks.

3. Frosted doughnuts sell for $2.85 per dozen and doughnut holes for $0.60 per dozen. If you buy 2 dozen frosted doughnuts and 6 dozen doughnut holes, what would be the fewest number of coins in change you could receive from a ten-dollar bill?

7. How do the numerator and denominator of a fraction compare when the fraction is
   a. close to 1?
   b. close to $\frac{1}{2}$?
   c. close to 0?

4. What is the ones digit of the product when seven is used as a factor one hundred times?

8. There are 15 boxes on a shelf. One box has 7 toys in it. Half of the remaining boxes have 4 toys in each of them. The rest have 5 toys in each of them. Explain how to use the Distributive Property to find the number of toys in the boxes altogether.

5. Woody Weed has a rectangular lawn 48 by 75 feet. The Green Pear Company will weed and feed the lawn for one season for 1¢ per square foot. The Jolly Onion Company will do the same thing for 10¢ per square yard. Assuming both do good work, which company offers the better buy?

Calculator: Unit Prices

Mrs. Nordquist is shopping for the best buy in dog food. She uses her calculator to find the cost of one pound of dog food for each brand. Which brand is the best buy?

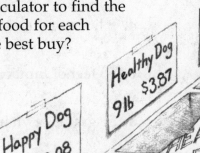

When we find the price of one pound of dog food we are finding the unit price.

REMEMBER To find the unit price, we divide the price by the number of units of measurement in the bag. The lower the unit price, the better the buy for the shopper.

Complete this code.

Happy Dog   3.08 [÷] 7 [=] [   ]

0.44 means $0.44 or _____ ¢

The unit price of Happy Dog is _____.

Complete these codes.

Healthy Dog   _____ [÷] _____ [=] [   ]

The unit price of Healthy Dog is _____.

Best Dog   _____ [÷] _____ [=] [   ]

The unit price of Best Dog is _____.

The best buy is the brand _____.

Getting Started

Use a calculator to find the total cost of each purchase.
The symbol @ is frequently used before the unit price.

1. 5 lb @ $0.36 a pound _____

2. 10 gal @ $0.96 a gallon _____

3. 7 oz @ $4.52 an ounce _____

4. 75 lb @ $1.45 a pound _____

Practice

Find the unit price.

1. 6 pounds of hamburger, $11.34 _____

2. 16 pounds of apples, $7.84 _____

3. 5 kilograms of potatoes, $4.95 _____

4. 8 liters of oil, $16.48 _____

5. 25 ounces of soap, $4.25 _____

6. 96 feet of lumber, $218.88 _____

7. 32 liters of gasoline, $15.68 _____

8. 56 grams of vitamins, $36.40 _____

9. 9 tons of coal, $211.95 _____

10. 28 meters of trim, $97.72 _____

Use a calculator to find the total cost of each purchase.

11. 15 oz @ $0.47 an ounce _____

12. 46 T @ $14.50 a ton _____

13. 25 yd @ $1.99 a yard _____

14. 12 qt @ $1.01 a quart _____

15. 256 mi @ $0.18 a mile _____

16. 360 pt @ $0.26 a pint _____

Problem Solving

Use a calculator to solve each problem. Use estimation to be sure the answer seems correct.

17. Midway Electric had two brands of videotapes on sale. One brand was selling at 6 tapes for $28.50 and the other was 8 tapes for $37.52. Which brand was the best buy?

18. Grass seed can be purchased in three sizes: 15 pounds for $18.75, 18 pounds for $23.76, or 25 pounds for $32.25. Which size is the best buy?

19. The West Side Market is selling 24 bottles of cola for $13.68. The East End Market is selling 36 bottles of the same cola brand for $20.52. Which has the better buy?

20. Ben's Butcher Shop ran this advertisement. Which is the best meat buy?

T-Bone	3 pounds for $11.37
Porterhouse	5 pounds for $17.45
New York	2 pounds for $7.18

21. China plates that usually sell at 8 plates for $98.80 are sold at a fire sale for $6.79 each. How much is saved on each plate?

22. Soap that usually sells for $2.15 a pound is on sale at 3 pounds for $5.85. How much is saved when 6 pounds of soap is bought on sale?

Write the equivalent fraction.

1. $\frac{2}{3} = \frac{}{12}$ 2. $\frac{3}{8} = \frac{}{16}$ 3. $\frac{4}{5} = \frac{}{20}$ 4. $\frac{5}{6} = \frac{}{60}$

Write each fraction in simplest terms.

5. $\frac{5}{10} = $ _____   6. $\frac{8}{12} = $ _____   7. $\frac{4}{20} = $ _____   8. $\frac{9}{27} = $ _____

9. $\frac{24}{30} = $ _____   10. $\frac{16}{18} = $ _____   11. $\frac{35}{49} = $ _____   12. $\frac{32}{40} = $ _____

Write < or > in each circle.

13. $\frac{5}{8}$ ◯ $\frac{2}{3}$ 14. $\frac{5}{12}$ ◯ $\frac{9}{16}$ 15. $\frac{1}{2}$ ◯ $\frac{4}{7}$ 16. $\frac{3}{8}$ ◯ $\frac{1}{3}$

Write each mixed number as an improper fraction.

17. $6\frac{2}{3} = $ _____   18. $5\frac{3}{8} = $ _____   19. $5\frac{4}{7} = $ _____   20. $8\frac{5}{12} = $ _____

21. $3\frac{4}{9} = $ _____   22. $4\frac{5}{11} = $ _____   23. $7\frac{2}{5} = $ _____   24. $9\frac{5}{8} = $ _____

Write each quotient as a mixed number. Simplify if necessary.

25. $5\overline{)27}$ 26. $8\overline{)188}$ 27. $35\overline{)308}$ 28. $16\overline{)740}$

29. $15\overline{)607}$ 30. $12\overline{)461}$ 31. $41\overline{)856}$ 32. $14\overline{)295}$

Rename each improper fraction as a whole or mixed number.

33. $\frac{9}{6} = $ _____   34. $\frac{15}{7} = $ _____   35. $\frac{36}{4} = $ _____   36. $\frac{63}{12} = $ _____

37. $\frac{56}{7} = $ _____   38. $\frac{95}{7} = $ _____   39. $\frac{49}{8} = $ _____   40. $\frac{54}{7} = $ _____

Circle the letter of the correct answer.

1 7,326 ◯ 7,236

    a. <
    b. >
    c. =

2
$$\begin{array}{r} 259 \\ + \ 186 \\ \hline \end{array}$$

    a. 335
    b. 444
    c. 445
    d. NG

3
$$\begin{array}{r} 13,296 \\ + \ 8,474 \\ \hline \end{array}$$

    a. 2,177
    b. 21,760
    c. 21,770
    d. NG

4
$$\begin{array}{r} 5,036 \\ - \ 2,984 \\ \hline \end{array}$$

    a. 2,052
    b. 2,952
    c. 3,952
    d. NG

5
$$\begin{array}{r} \$436.18 \\ - \ \ \ \ 82.86 \\ \hline \end{array}$$

    a. $343.32
    b. $352.32
    c. $454.72
    d. NG

6
$$\begin{array}{r} \$6.15 \\ \times \ \ \ \ \ \ 8 \\ \hline \end{array}$$

    a. $48.02
    b. $48.20
    c. $49.20
    d. NG

7 27 × 56

    a. 297
    b. 1,512
    c. 11,592
    d. NG

8 Find the average.
28, 16, 20, 24

    a. 20
    b. 22
    c. 24
    d. NG

9 6)60,326

    a. 154 R2
    b. 1,052 R2
    c. 10,054 R2
    d. NG

10 4,518 ÷ 36

    a. 12 R18
    b. 125 R18
    c. 126 R18
    d. NG

11 Find the perimeter.

5 cm   4 cm
6 cm

    a. 15 cm
    b. 120 cm
    c. 120 sq cm
    d. NG

12
$$\begin{array}{r} 6 \text{ ft} \ \ 3 \text{ in.} \\ + \ 2 \text{ ft} \ 10 \text{ in.} \\ \hline \end{array}$$

    a. 8 ft 3 in.
    b. 9 ft 1 in.
    c. 9 ft 3 in.
    d. NG

13 Find the missing
number.
$\frac{3}{5} = \frac{?}{15}$

    a. 3
    b. 5
    c. 9
    d. NG

 score

Add and Subtract Fractions

Adding Fractions

Elmwood School's theme for this year's All-American Week is patriotism. Jaime is decorating some of the windows in his fifth grade classroom. He will put stars on 3 more windows. What fractional part of the classroom windows will be covered with stars?

We are looking for a fraction that shows the part of all the windows that will be covered with stars.

We know there are _____ windows in the classroom. Jaime has covered 1 window with stars and will put stars on _____ more windows.

The fractional part of windows already decorated is _____.

The fraction representing the additional windows

Jaime plans to cover with stars is _____.

To find the fraction for the total number of decorated windows, we add the fraction for the window completed to the fractional part Jaime plans to do.

We add the fractions _____ and _____.

REMEMBER To add fractions with common denominators, add the numerators and write the sum over the denominator. Simplify if necessary.

$\frac{1}{8} + \frac{3}{8} = \frac{4}{8} = \frac{1}{2}.$

$$\begin{array}{r} \frac{1}{8} \\ + \frac{3}{8} \\ \hline \frac{4}{8} = \frac{1}{2} \end{array}$$

Jaime will cover _____ of the windows with stars.

Getting Started

Add. Simplify if necessary.

1. $\frac{5}{8}$
$+ \frac{1}{8}$

2. $\frac{1}{2}$
$+ \frac{1}{2}$

3. $\frac{5}{9}$
$+ \frac{1}{9}$

4. $\frac{5}{6}$
$+ \frac{3}{6}$

Copy and add.

5. $\frac{3}{12} + \frac{4}{12}$

6. $\frac{2}{3} + \frac{2}{3}$

7. $\frac{3}{5} + \frac{2}{5}$

Practice

Add. Simplify if necessary.

1. $\dfrac{7}{12}$ $+ \dfrac{1}{12}$

2. $\dfrac{3}{4}$ $+ \dfrac{2}{4}$

3. $\dfrac{7}{8}$ $+ \dfrac{3}{8}$

4. $\dfrac{7}{16}$ $+ \dfrac{7}{16}$

5. $\dfrac{9}{12}$ $+ \dfrac{7}{12}$

6. $\dfrac{4}{7}$ $+ \dfrac{3}{7}$

7. $\dfrac{5}{10}$ $+ \dfrac{7}{10}$

8. $\dfrac{5}{9}$ $+ \dfrac{6}{9}$

9. $\dfrac{5}{8}$ $+ \dfrac{7}{8}$

10. $\dfrac{13}{16}$ $+ \dfrac{7}{16}$

11. $\dfrac{3}{10}$ $+ \dfrac{5}{10}$

12. $\dfrac{1}{6}$ $+ \dfrac{3}{6}$

13. $\dfrac{5}{7}$ $+ \dfrac{6}{7}$

14. $\dfrac{1}{6}$ $+ \dfrac{5}{6}$

15. $\dfrac{8}{15}$ $+ \dfrac{12}{15}$

16. $\dfrac{3}{8}$ $+ \dfrac{7}{8}$

17. $\dfrac{2}{5}$ $+ \dfrac{3}{5}$

18. $\dfrac{3}{12}$ $+ \dfrac{3}{12}$

19. $\dfrac{8}{9}$ $+ \dfrac{4}{9}$

20. $\dfrac{9}{10}$ $+ \dfrac{7}{10}$

Copy and add.

21. $\dfrac{5}{8} + \dfrac{3}{8}$

22. $\dfrac{3}{7} + \dfrac{2}{7}$

23. $\dfrac{5}{9} + \dfrac{3}{9}$

24. $\dfrac{7}{12} + \dfrac{3}{12}$

25. $\dfrac{3}{5} + \dfrac{4}{5}$

26. $\dfrac{1}{4} + \dfrac{2}{4}$

27. $\dfrac{5}{6} + \dfrac{2}{6}$

28. $\dfrac{3}{16} + \dfrac{5}{16}$

Problem Solving

Solve each problem. Simplify if necessary.

29. Katie and Dale worked together on a poster for All-American Week. Katie painted $\dfrac{5}{12}$ of the poster red and Dale painted $\dfrac{3}{12}$ of it blue. They left the rest of the white poster board unpainted. What fractional part of the poster did Katie and Dale paint?

30. Sun Lin made a quilt for her sister's cradle using leftover fabric. She used $\dfrac{7}{8}$ of a yard of blue calico, $\dfrac{5}{8}$ of a yard of rose calico, and $\dfrac{3}{8}$ of a yard of white cloth. How many yards of material did Sun Lin use for her quilt?

Lesson 8-1 • Adding Fractions

Subtracting Fractions

Neil and Todd explored two different trails near their campsite on Bear Mountain. Neil hiked to Bear View and Todd hiked to Vista Point. How much farther did Neil have to hike to his destination?

We want to find how much farther Neil had to walk.

Neil hiked _____ of a mile and Todd

hiked _____ of a mile.

To find the difference in distance, we need to subtract Todd's distance from the distance hiked by Neil.

We subtract _____ from _____.

We can use a number line to help us subtract.

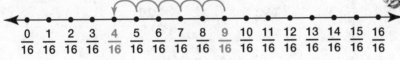

$$\frac{9}{16} - \frac{5}{16} = \frac{4}{16} = \frac{1}{4}$$

Neil hiked _____ of a mile farther than Todd.

REMEMBER To subtract fractions with common denominators, subtract the numerators. Write the difference over the denominator. Simplify if necessary.

If the difference is an improper fraction, simplify by renaming it as a whole or mixed number.

$$\begin{array}{r} \frac{9}{16} \\ - \frac{5}{16} \\ \hline \frac{4}{16} = \frac{1}{4} \end{array}$$

Getting Started

Subtract. Simplify if necessary.

1. $\frac{15}{9}$
    $- \frac{4}{9}$

2. $\frac{21}{12}$
    $- \frac{9}{12}$

3. $\frac{9}{8}$
    $- \frac{9}{8}$

4. $\frac{12}{5}$
    $- \frac{4}{5}$

Copy and subtract.

5. $\frac{7}{8} - \frac{1}{8}$

6. $\frac{9}{4} - \frac{3}{4}$

7. $\frac{4}{15} - \frac{3}{15}$

Practice

Subtract. Simplify if necessary.

1. $\dfrac{5}{7}$
$-\dfrac{3}{7}$

2. $\dfrac{8}{9}$
$-\dfrac{2}{9}$

3. $\dfrac{11}{4}$
$-\dfrac{3}{4}$

4. $\dfrac{7}{2}$
$-\dfrac{1}{2}$

5. $\dfrac{15}{8}$
$-\dfrac{3}{8}$

6. $\dfrac{9}{16}$
$-\dfrac{5}{16}$

7. $\dfrac{9}{10}$
$-\dfrac{4}{10}$

8. $\dfrac{9}{15}$
$-\dfrac{3}{15}$

9. $\dfrac{12}{5}$
$-\dfrac{3}{5}$

10. $\dfrac{10}{6}$
$-\dfrac{1}{6}$

11. $\dfrac{7}{12}$
$-\dfrac{3}{12}$

12. $\dfrac{17}{4}$
$-\dfrac{2}{4}$

13. $\dfrac{13}{9}$
$-\dfrac{2}{9}$

14. $\dfrac{23}{10}$
$-\dfrac{16}{10}$

15. $\dfrac{15}{16}$
$-\dfrac{7}{16}$

16. $\dfrac{17}{6}$
$-\dfrac{11}{6}$

17. $\dfrac{25}{4}$
$-\dfrac{15}{4}$

18. $\dfrac{27}{10}$
$-\dfrac{15}{10}$

19. $\dfrac{17}{3}$
$-\dfrac{11}{3}$

20. $\dfrac{37}{15}$
$-\dfrac{25}{15}$

Copy and subtract.

21. $\dfrac{7}{8} - \dfrac{4}{8}$

22. $\dfrac{13}{16} - \dfrac{9}{16}$

23. $\dfrac{7}{5} - \dfrac{1}{5}$

24. $\dfrac{2}{3} - \dfrac{1}{3}$

25. $\dfrac{5}{4} - \dfrac{1}{4}$

26. $\dfrac{5}{6} - \dfrac{1}{6}$

27. $\dfrac{4}{3} - \dfrac{2}{3}$

28. $\dfrac{9}{12} - \dfrac{1}{12}$

Problem Solving

Use the graph to solve each problem. Simplify if necessary.

29. How much farther did Mike run than Bess?

30. How much farther did Annie run than Bess?

31. Altogether, how many miles did Bess and Annie run?

32. How many total miles did all three children run?

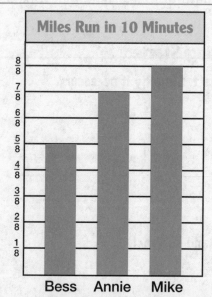

Finding Common Multiples

Ken and Dex are hiking the same trail.
Ken stops every 4 miles for a rest, while
Dex stops every 3 miles. At which point
will they both be stopping for a rest at
the same place?

We want to know where both hikers will rest.

Ken stops every _____ miles.

Dex stops every _____ miles.

To find their common resting points, we list the
multiples of each number and look for common
multiples in the two sets.

Multiples of 3: 3, 6, 9, **12**, 15, 18, 21, **24**, 27, ...

Multiples of 4: 4, 8, **12**, 16, 20, **24**, 28, 32, 36, ...

Ken and Dex will both be resting at the points on the

trail marked _____ miles and _____ miles.

The smallest possible multiple that can be evenly
divided by the numbers is called the **least common
multiple**. It is sometimes called the **LCM**.

Getting Started _____

Find the first three common multiples of each set.

1. 2 and 3   **2.** 5 and 10   **3.** 8 and 10   **4.** 7 and 5

Find the least common multiple of each set.

5. 3 and 7   **6.** 3 and 9   **7.** 10 and 12   **8.** 10 and 16

Practice

Find the first three common multiples of each set.

1. 5 and 3
2. 7 and 14
3. 4 and 10
4. 6 and 9

5. 8 and 12
6. 2 and 5
7. 4 and 8
8. 3 and 12

9. 6 and 15
10. 8 and 9
11. 4 and 6
12. 5 and 20

Find the least common multiple of each set.

13. 4 and 9
14. 3 and 12
15. 6 and 18
16. 7 and 8

17. 10 and 15
18. 12 and 15
19. 8 and 12
20. 6 and 7

21. 9 and 15
22. 6 and 4
23. 9 and 21
24. 10 and 25

Problem Solving

Solve each problem.

25. Mr. Phelps is buying bolts and washers. He needs to have the same number of each. Bolts are sold in packages of 8. Washers are sold in packages of 20. How many packages of each should he buy?

26. Tom, Alice, and Nancy are hiking the same trail. Tom rests every 5 kilometers, Alice rests every 4 kilometers, and Nancy rests every 3 kilometers. At what point is the first rest stop where all three hikers stop together?

[Now Try This!]

The least common multiple of two numbers can also be found by multiplying the numbers and dividing the product by the largest common factor of the two numbers.

The least common multiple of 4 and 16 is $4 \times 16 \div 4$. LCM = 16

The least common multiple of 8 and 12 is $8 \times 12 \div$ _____. LCM = 24

The least common multiple of 4 and 5 is $4 \times 5 \div$ _____. LCM = 20

Find the least common multiple of each set.

1. 15 and 25
2. 12 and 40
3. 24 and 30
4. 15 and 16

LCM = _____   LCM = _____   LCM = _____   LCM = _____

Adding Fractions With Unlike Denominators

Veronica made fruit bread for the bake sale. She used dates and raisins in her batter. How many cups of fruit did her bread contain?

We want to find the total number of cups of fruit in Veronica's bread.

Veronica added _____ of a cup of dates and _____ of a cup of raisins.

To find the total amount of fruit, we add the amounts of dates and raisins.

We add _____ and _____.

REMEMBER To add fractions with unlike denominators, first write them as equivalent fractions having a common denominator.

The common denominator is the **least common multiple** of the denominators.

Find the least common denominator.	Write equivalent fractions.	Add.

$\dfrac{3}{5} = \dfrac{}{20}$
$+\dfrac{3}{4} = \dfrac{}{20}$

The least common multiple of 5 and 4.

$\dfrac{3}{5} \dfrac{\times 4}{\times 4} = \dfrac{12}{20}$
$+\dfrac{3}{4} \dfrac{\times 5}{\times 5} = \dfrac{15}{20}$

A fractional name for 1

$\dfrac{3}{5} = \dfrac{12}{20}$
$+\dfrac{3}{4} = \dfrac{15}{20}$
$\rule{2cm}{0.4pt}$
$\dfrac{27}{20} = 1\dfrac{7}{20}$

REMEMBER Simplify improper fractions by dividing the denominator into the numerator. Write any remainders as simplified fractions.

Veronica put _____ cups of fruit in her bread.

Getting Started

Add. Simplify if necessary.

1. $\dfrac{3}{5}$
   $+\dfrac{1}{3}$

2. $\dfrac{1}{2}$
   $+\dfrac{3}{4}$

3. $\dfrac{5}{6}$
   $+\dfrac{3}{8}$

Copy and add.

4. $\dfrac{3}{7} + \dfrac{4}{5}$

5. $\dfrac{7}{10} + \dfrac{40}{100}$

Practice

Add. Simplify if necessary.

1. $\dfrac{1}{5}$
$+\dfrac{1}{3}$

2. $\dfrac{3}{4}$
$+\dfrac{5}{8}$

3. $\dfrac{3}{8}$
$+\dfrac{1}{2}$

4. $\dfrac{5}{6}$
$+\dfrac{5}{9}$

5. $\dfrac{7}{10}$
$+\dfrac{1}{5}$

6. $\dfrac{2}{3}$
$+\dfrac{7}{8}$

7. $\dfrac{9}{10}$
$+\dfrac{1}{2}$

8. $\dfrac{11}{4}$
$+\dfrac{4}{6}$

9. $\dfrac{9}{16}$
$+\dfrac{5}{8}$

10. $\dfrac{15}{12}$
$+\dfrac{3}{8}$

11. $\dfrac{15}{16}$
$+\dfrac{1}{6}$

12. $\dfrac{9}{15}$
$+\dfrac{7}{10}$

13. $\dfrac{25}{30}$
$+\dfrac{6}{10}$

14. $\dfrac{3}{6}$
$+\dfrac{7}{12}$

15. $\dfrac{8}{9}$
$+\dfrac{3}{7}$

16. $\dfrac{5}{8}$
$+\dfrac{8}{9}$

Copy and add.

17. $\dfrac{4}{5} + \dfrac{7}{10}$

18. $\dfrac{7}{8} + \dfrac{1}{4}$

19. $\dfrac{2}{3} + \dfrac{5}{9}$

20. $\dfrac{5}{6} + \dfrac{7}{9}$

21. $\dfrac{7}{8} + \dfrac{1}{6}$

22. $\dfrac{3}{6} + \dfrac{3}{4}$

23. $\dfrac{5}{16} + \dfrac{3}{4}$

24. $\dfrac{9}{6} + \dfrac{2}{4}$

25. $\dfrac{7}{10} + \dfrac{13}{15}$

26. $\dfrac{7}{3} + \dfrac{9}{4}$

27. $\dfrac{3}{9} + \dfrac{7}{12}$

28. $\dfrac{6}{7} + \dfrac{1}{3}$

29. $\dfrac{18}{100} + \dfrac{5}{10}$

30. $\dfrac{15}{8} + \dfrac{7}{12}$

31. $\dfrac{17}{21} + \dfrac{5}{6}$

32. $\dfrac{14}{6} + \dfrac{21}{9}$

Problem Solving

Solve each problem. Simplify if necessary.

33. Ruth practices her piano $\dfrac{3}{4}$ of an hour each day and Bert practices his violin $\dfrac{2}{3}$ of an hour each day. How long do Ruth and Bert together practice each day?

34. Leon used $\dfrac{2}{3}$ of a quart of blue paint, $\dfrac{1}{4}$ of a quart of red paint, and $\dfrac{1}{2}$ of a quart of yellow paint on his soap box derby car. How much paint did Leon use?

Subtracting Fractions With Unlike Denominators

The average height for a 10-year-old American child is $4\frac{1}{2}$ feet. Cindy kept track of her height for 4 months during one year. How much more did Cindy grow in October than in November?

We need to find how much more Cindy grew in October than in November.

In October, Cindy grew _____ of an inch.

She grew _____ of an inch in November.

To find her difference in growth, we subtract her growth in November from her growth in October. To subtract fractions with unlike denominators, first write them as equivalent fractions having **common denominators**.

Find the least common denominator.	Write equivalent fractions.	Subtract.
$\frac{1}{2} = \frac{}{8}$ $-\frac{3}{8} = \frac{}{8}$	$\frac{1}{2} \times \frac{4}{\times 4} = \frac{4}{8}$ $-\frac{3}{8} \times \frac{1}{\times 1} = \frac{3}{8}$	$\frac{1}{2} \times \frac{4}{\times 4} = \frac{4}{8}$ $-\frac{3}{8} \times \frac{1}{\times 1} = \frac{3}{8}$ $\frac{1}{8}$

Cindy grew _____ of an inch more in October than she did in November.

Getting Started

Subtract. Simplify if necessary.

1. $\frac{5}{9}$
$-\frac{1}{3}$

2. $\frac{5}{6}$
$-\frac{1}{4}$

3. $\frac{4}{5}$
$-\frac{3}{10}$

4. $\frac{13}{4}$
$-\frac{2}{3}$

Copy and subtract.

5. $\frac{11}{6} - \frac{4}{9}$

6. $\frac{60}{100} - \frac{2}{10}$

7. $\frac{12}{9} - \frac{13}{45}$

8. $\frac{2}{4} - \frac{1}{3}$

Practice

Subtract. Simplify if necessary.

1. $\frac{3}{4}$
   $-\frac{1}{2}$

2. $\frac{7}{9}$
   $-\frac{1}{3}$

3. $\frac{8}{3}$
   $-\frac{5}{6}$

4. $\frac{5}{8}$
   $-\frac{1}{4}$

5. $\frac{1}{3}$
   $-\frac{1}{5}$

6. $\frac{5}{6}$
   $-\frac{3}{8}$

7. $\frac{2}{3}$
   $-\frac{3}{5}$

8. $\frac{7}{8}$
   $-\frac{1}{3}$

9. $\frac{5}{8}$
   $-\frac{2}{5}$

10. $\frac{18}{5}$
    $-\frac{6}{4}$

11. $\frac{85}{100}$
    $-\frac{5}{10}$

12. $\frac{3}{2}$
    $-\frac{2}{3}$

Copy and subtract.

13. $\frac{7}{12} - \frac{1}{4}$

14. $\frac{21}{15} - \frac{6}{5}$

15. $\frac{87}{100} - \frac{3}{4}$

16. $\frac{9}{16} - \frac{3}{8}$

17. $\frac{2}{3} - \frac{1}{4}$

18. $\frac{9}{10} - \frac{2}{3}$

19. $\frac{5}{8} - \frac{2}{6}$

20. $\frac{4}{5} - \frac{3}{4}$

21. $\frac{3}{4} - \frac{1}{5}$

22. $\frac{2}{3} - \frac{3}{8}$

23. $\frac{3}{4} - \frac{2}{3}$

24. $\frac{9}{8} - \frac{5}{6}$

25. $\frac{9}{10} - \frac{5}{6}$

26. $\frac{11}{6} - \frac{8}{9}$

27. $\frac{13}{9} - \frac{25}{36}$

28. $\frac{12}{10} - \frac{9}{15}$

Problem Solving

Solve each problem. Simplify if necessary.

29. Ronnie had $\frac{3}{4}$ of a gallon of house paint. He used $\frac{1}{3}$ of a gallon on the doors. How much paint did Ronnie have left?

30. The Sterns started their trip with $\frac{7}{8}$ of a tank of gas. They returned home with $\frac{1}{6}$ of a tank. What part of a tank of gas did the Sterns use on their trip?

Lesson 8-5 • Subtracting Fractions With Unlike Denominators

Adding Mixed Numbers

Runners can improve their stamina by gradually increasing their running distance. Ryan keeps a log of his jogging distances. How far did Ryan jog on Friday and Sunday?

We are looking for how far Ryan ran on Friday and Sunday.

Ryan jogged _____ miles on Friday and $4\frac{1}{10}$ miles on Sunday.

To find the total number of miles jogged, we add the mileage for both days.

We add _____ and _____.

REMEMBER To add fractions with unlike denominators, first write them as equivalent fractions having common denominators.

Write equivalent fractions.	Add the fractions.	Add the whole numbers. Simplify.

$$3\frac{2}{5} = 3\frac{4}{10}$$
$$+\ 4\frac{1}{10} = 4\frac{1}{10}$$

$$3\frac{2}{5} = 3\frac{4}{10}$$
$$+\ 4\frac{1}{10} = 4\frac{1}{10}$$
$$\overline{\phantom{3\frac{2}{5}}\ \frac{5}{10}}$$

$$3\frac{2}{5} = 3\frac{4}{10}$$
$$+\ 4\frac{1}{10} = 4\frac{1}{10}$$
$$\overline{7\frac{5}{10} = 7\frac{1}{2}}$$

Ryan jogged _____ miles on Friday and Sunday.

Getting Started

Add. Simplify if necessary.

1. $5\frac{3}{8}$
    $+\ 2\frac{1}{8}$

2. $7\frac{10}{15}$
    $+\ 6\frac{4}{15}$

3. $9\frac{1}{2}$
    $+\ 8\frac{1}{4}$

4. $6\frac{1}{4}$
    $+\ 9\frac{1}{3}$

Copy and add.

5. $5\frac{3}{7} + 4\frac{3}{7}$

6. $6\frac{2}{8} + 5\frac{2}{12}$

7. $9\frac{1}{2} + 7\frac{1}{3}$

8. $4\frac{1}{4} + 1\frac{1}{5}$

Practice

Add. Simplify if necessary.

1. $3\frac{5}{9}$
    $+\ 8\frac{2}{9}$

2. $6\frac{2}{5}$
    $+\ 9\frac{1}{5}$

3. $7\frac{1}{4}$
    $+\ 8\frac{1}{8}$

4. $9\frac{5}{9}$
    $+\ 7\frac{1}{3}$

5. $7\frac{5}{8}$
    $+\ 6\frac{1}{6}$

6. $7\frac{1}{3}$
    $+\ 9\frac{2}{5}$

7. $6\frac{7}{10}$
    $+\ 4\frac{1}{5}$

8. $7\frac{1}{4}$
    $+\ 8\frac{1}{6}$

9. $6\frac{1}{8}$
    $+\ 5\frac{2}{3}$

10. $2\frac{2}{5}$
    $+\ 5\frac{1}{4}$

11. $4\frac{1}{3}$
    $+\ 9\frac{1}{6}$

12. $7\frac{2}{7}$
    $+\ 8\frac{3}{5}$

Copy and add.

13. $6\frac{1}{3} + 6\frac{1}{2}$

14. $4\frac{3}{8} + 9\frac{1}{6}$

15. $9\frac{2}{3} + 6\frac{1}{4}$

16. $1\frac{2}{3} + 6\frac{1}{5}$

17. $7\frac{1}{9} + 6\frac{2}{3}$

18. $8\frac{7}{10} + 8\frac{1}{5}$

19. $4\frac{3}{4} + 2\frac{1}{6}$

20. $6\frac{1}{2} + 9\frac{3}{10}$

Now Try This!

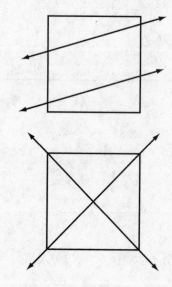

The two figures shown here are each partitioned into smaller regions by two straight lines. Where the lines are parallel, three regions are formed. Where the lines intersect, four regions are formed.

On another sheet of paper, draw all the possible ways that three lines can separate an area into regions. Consider only the number of regions formed and not their sizes or shapes.

What is the highest possible number of regions that can be formed in an area using three straight lines? _____

Renaming Mixed Numbers in Sums

Many students work after school but have to save time for homework. Juanita works part time three days a week, but never works more than 11 hours in any week. How many hours did Juanita work this week?

We want to find the number of hours Juanita worked this week.

She worked _____ hours on Monday, _____ hours on Tuesday, and _____ hours on Friday.

To find the total hours, we add her hours for all 3 days.

We add _____, _____, and _____.

The fractions in a set of mixed numbers must have a **common denominator** before they can be added.

Juanita
WORK SCHEDULE
Monday $2\frac{1}{2}$
Tuesday $3\frac{3}{4}$
Friday $3\frac{2}{3}$

Find the least common denominator.		Write equivalent fractions.	Add. Simplify the mixed number.

$2\frac{1}{2} = 2\frac{}{12}$

$3\frac{3}{4} = 3\frac{}{12}$

$+ 3\frac{2}{3} = 3\frac{}{12}$

12 is the last common multiple of 2, 4, and 3.

$2\frac{1}{2} = 2\frac{6}{12}$

$3\frac{3}{4} = 3\frac{9}{12}$

$+ 3\frac{2}{3} = 3\frac{8}{12}$

$2\frac{1}{2} = 2\frac{6}{12}$

$3\frac{3}{4} = 3\frac{9}{12}$

$+ 3\frac{2}{3} = 3\frac{8}{12}$

$8\frac{23}{12} = 9\frac{11}{12}$

REMEMBER When an improper fraction appears in the mixed number, simplify the mixed number by dividing the fraction's denominator into the numerator. Add this renamed fraction to the original whole number.

$8\frac{23}{12} = 8 + 1\frac{11}{12} = 9\frac{11}{12}$

Juanita worked _____ hours.

Getting Started

Simplify these mixed numbers.

1. $5\frac{7}{4} =$ _____   **2.** $6\frac{9}{3} =$ _____

Add. Simplify if necessary.

3. $4\frac{2}{3}$
        $5\frac{1}{3}$
     $+ 4\frac{2}{3}$
     _____

4. $7\frac{1}{8}$
        $4\frac{1}{2}$
     $+ 6\frac{1}{4}$
     _____

Copy and add.

5. $2\frac{1}{7} + 4 + 2\frac{13}{14}$

Practice

Simplify these mixed numbers.

1. $2\frac{7}{2} =$ _____

2. $5\frac{14}{10} =$ _____

3. $6\frac{9}{6} =$ _____

4. $5\frac{12}{8} =$ _____

5. $1\frac{16}{10} =$ _____

6. $2\frac{18}{4} =$ _____

7. $10\frac{25}{15} =$ _____

8. $2\frac{40}{16} =$ _____

Add. Simplify if necessary.

9. $\begin{array}{r} 7\frac{5}{6} \\ 4\frac{2}{3} \\ +\ 6\frac{1}{3} \\ \hline \end{array}$

10. $\begin{array}{r} 8\frac{1}{5} \\ 6\frac{4}{5} \\ +\ 7\frac{5}{10} \\ \hline \end{array}$

11. $\begin{array}{r} 2\frac{3}{4} \\ 7\frac{5}{8} \\ +\ 6\frac{1}{2} \\ \hline \end{array}$

12. $\begin{array}{r} 9\frac{7}{8} \\ 2\frac{3}{4} \\ +\ 5\frac{2}{3} \\ \hline \end{array}$

13. $\begin{array}{r} 4\frac{1}{2} \\ 5\frac{2}{3} \\ +\ 6\frac{1}{6} \\ \hline \end{array}$

14. $\begin{array}{r} 7\frac{1}{5} \\ 6 \\ +\ 8\frac{3}{4} \\ \hline \end{array}$

15. $\begin{array}{r} 9\frac{2}{3} \\ 7\frac{7}{15} \\ +\ 6\frac{4}{5} \\ \hline \end{array}$

16. $\begin{array}{r} 6\frac{1}{2} \\ 7\frac{2}{3} \\ +\ 8\frac{5}{8} \\ \hline \end{array}$

Copy and add.

17. $9\frac{5}{8} + 8\frac{3}{4} + 6\frac{1}{3}$

18. $2\frac{5}{7} + 1\frac{2}{3} + 9\frac{7}{21}$

19. $1\frac{7}{10} + 9\frac{3}{5} + 4\frac{1}{4}$

20. $8 + 2\frac{2}{3} + 5\frac{5}{8}$

21. $8\frac{4}{5} + 5\frac{7}{8} + 2\frac{3}{10}$

22. $5\frac{1}{2} + 6\frac{2}{3} + 5\frac{5}{6}$

Problem Solving

Solve each problem. Simplify if necessary.

23. Find the perimeter of the triangle.

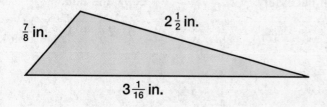

$\frac{7}{8}$ in. $2\frac{1}{2}$ in. $3\frac{1}{16}$ in.

24. Marissa rode her unicycle $3\frac{1}{2}$ miles on Monday. On Tuesday she rode $2\frac{2}{3}$ miles farther than she did on Monday. How far did Marissa ride on Monday and Tuesday?

Subtracting Mixed Numbers

Bruce bought $5\frac{5}{6}$ yards of denim to make some clothes.

He needs $2\frac{1}{3}$ yards to make one jacket. How many

yards of denim will Bruce have left?

We want to find how many yards of denim Bruce will have left.

He bought _____ yards and the pattern calls for _____ yards.

To find the yards left, we subtract the number of yards he will use from the number of yards he bought.

We subtract _____ from _____.

REMEMBER The fractions in a set of mixed numbers must have common denominators before they can be subtracted.

Write equivalent fractions.	Subtract the fractions.	Subtract the whole numbers. Simplify.
$5\frac{5}{6} = 5\frac{5}{6}$ $-2\frac{1}{3} = 2\frac{2}{6}$	$5\frac{5}{6} = 5\frac{5}{6}$ $-2\frac{1}{3} = 2\frac{2}{6}$ $\frac{3}{6}$	$5\frac{5}{6} = 5\frac{5}{6}$ $-2\frac{1}{3} = 2\frac{2}{6}$ $3\frac{3}{6} = 3\frac{1}{2}$

Bruce will have _____ yards of denim left.

Getting Started

Subtract. Simplify if necessary.

1. $4\frac{5}{9}$
   $-1\frac{3}{9}$

2. $16\frac{7}{8}$
   $-9\frac{3}{8}$

3. $8\frac{5}{6}$
   $-3\frac{1}{4}$

4. $16\frac{3}{4}$
   $-9\frac{2}{3}$

Copy and subtract.

5. $10\frac{3}{7} - 3\frac{2}{14}$

6. $15\frac{2}{5} - 8\frac{1}{15}$

7. $5\frac{2}{3} - 3\frac{4}{8}$

8. $9\frac{4}{5} - 4\frac{2}{6}$

Practice

Subtract. Simplify if necessary.

1. $7\frac{9}{16}$
   $-3\frac{5}{16}$

2. $8\frac{3}{4}$
   $-2\frac{1}{4}$

3. $11\frac{7}{9}$
   $-3\frac{4}{9}$

4. $5\frac{7}{8}$
   $-2\frac{1}{4}$

5. $9\frac{4}{5}$
   $-7\frac{3}{10}$

6. $11\frac{2}{3}$
   $-6\frac{1}{6}$

7. $10\frac{4}{5}$
   $-7\frac{1}{3}$

8. $13\frac{2}{3}$
   $-6\frac{1}{4}$

9. $6\frac{5}{8}$
   $-3\frac{1}{5}$

10. $12\frac{4}{5}$
    $-6\frac{1}{2}$

11. $18\frac{2}{3}$
    $-9\frac{1}{2}$

12. $12\frac{7}{8}$
    $-7\frac{1}{6}$

Copy and subtract.

13. $3\frac{5}{7} - 2\frac{1}{7}$

14. $9\frac{2}{3} - 2\frac{1}{9}$

15. $8\frac{1}{2} - 6\frac{1}{8}$

16. $18\frac{3}{4} - 9\frac{1}{5}$

17. $13\frac{5}{6} - 4\frac{3}{8}$

18. $13\frac{46}{100} - 5\frac{3}{20}$

19. $13\frac{9}{10} - 8\frac{5}{6}$

20. $16\frac{3}{4} - 7\frac{2}{3}$

21. $12\frac{7}{8} - 8\frac{5}{6}$

22. $11\frac{9}{16} - 6\frac{3}{8}$

23. $5\frac{5}{6} - 3\frac{5}{9}$

24. $12\frac{9}{10} - 8\frac{7}{15}$

Problem Solving

Solve each problem. Simplify if necessary.

25. Mr. Roberts felt tired on the second day of his trip. Although he drove $6\frac{3}{4}$ hours on Monday, he drove only $4\frac{1}{3}$ hours on Tuesday. How much longer did Mr. Roberts drive on Monday?

26. Gerri worked $3\frac{2}{3}$ hours on Monday and $4\frac{1}{2}$ hours on Tuesday. She knows she must work a total of $10\frac{1}{2}$ hours to earn enough money to pay for a set of school pictures. How many more hours does Gerri need to work?

Subtracting From a Whole Number

The winners of the athletic club's annual swim-a-thon were posted. Diane was the top swimmer this year. How much farther did Diane swim than Cheryl?

SWIM-A-THON
Diane - 3 miles
Cheryl - $1\frac{7}{8}$ miles

We want to find how many more miles Diane swam than Cheryl.

Diane swam _____ miles and Cheryl swam _____ miles.

To find out how many more miles Diane swam, we subtract Cheryl's distance from Diane's.

We subtract _____ from _____.

REMEMBER The whole number 1 can be renamed as a fraction whose numerator and denominator are the same, such as

$$1 = \frac{8}{8}$$

Rename the whole number.	Subtract the mixed numbers.

$3 = 2 + 1$
or $2 + \frac{8}{8}$

$$\begin{array}{r} 3 = 2\frac{8}{8} \\ -1\frac{7}{8} = 1\frac{7}{8} \\ \hline \end{array}$$

$$\begin{array}{r} 3 = 2\frac{8}{8} \\ -1\frac{7}{8} = 1\frac{7}{8} \\ \hline 1\frac{1}{8} \end{array}$$

Diane swam _____ miles farther than Cheryl.

Getting Started

Rename each whole number as a mixed number.

1. $8 = 7\frac{}{5}$

2. $4 = 3\frac{}{6}$

3. $7 = 6\frac{}{3}$

4. $12 = 11\frac{}{10}$

Subtract. Simplify if necessary.

5. $\begin{array}{r} 5 \\ -2\frac{1}{2} \\ \hline \end{array}$

6. $\begin{array}{r} 7 \\ -3\frac{3}{4} \\ \hline \end{array}$

7. $\begin{array}{r} 5 \\ -2\frac{2}{3} \\ \hline \end{array}$

8. $\begin{array}{r} 10 \\ -1\frac{3}{8} \\ \hline \end{array}$

Copy and subtract.

9. $9 - 2\frac{3}{4}$

10. $7 - 3\frac{1}{5}$

11. $17 - 9\frac{4}{12}$

12. $12 - 8\frac{8}{16}$

Practice

Rename each whole number as a mixed number.

1. $6 = 5\frac{}{8}$

2. $4 = 3\frac{}{9}$

3. $8 = 7\frac{}{7}$

4. $5 = 4\frac{}{12}$

Subtract. Simplify if necessary.

5. $\begin{array}{r} 9 \\ -\ 3\frac{1}{3} \\ \hline \end{array}$

6. $\begin{array}{r} 10 \\ -\ 3\frac{1}{5} \\ \hline \end{array}$

7. $\begin{array}{r} 12 \\ -\ 7\frac{3}{8} \\ \hline \end{array}$

8. $\begin{array}{r} 16 \\ -\ 9\frac{3}{5} \\ \hline \end{array}$

9. $\begin{array}{r} 11 \\ -\ 5\frac{5}{7} \\ \hline \end{array}$

10. $\begin{array}{r} 16 \\ -\ 7\frac{5}{10} \\ \hline \end{array}$

11. $\begin{array}{r} 16 \\ -\ 8\frac{5}{12} \\ \hline \end{array}$

12. $\begin{array}{r} 15 \\ -\ 9\frac{1}{2} \\ \hline \end{array}$

Copy and Subtract.

13. $8 - 2\frac{3}{5}$

14. $8 - 7\frac{5}{9}$

15. $15 - 7\frac{7}{8}$

16. $9 - 8\frac{3}{4}$

17. $7 - 5\frac{7}{12}$

18. $16 - 8\frac{15}{16}$

19. $13 - 5\frac{3}{10}$

20. $10 - 4\frac{9}{15}$

Problem Solving

Solve each problem. Simplify if necessary.

21. Rosalie estimated that it would take 12 days to thoroughly clean every room, window, drawer, and closet in her house. She finished in $9\frac{3}{4}$ days. How early did Rosalie finish her work?

22. Devin gave $\frac{2}{3}$ of his stamp collection to Belva and $\frac{1}{5}$ of his collection to Rosita. What fraction of his collection does Devin have left?

(Now Try This!)

Imagine this scene at the zoo.

In one area there are peacocks and camels. All together there are 30 eyes and 46 feet.

How many of each animal are there? _____ camels _____ peacocks

Suppose there were 528 eyes and 752 feet, then how many of each animal would there be? _____ camels _____ peacocks

Name _____

Subtracting Mixed Numbers With Renaming

A prize is awarded at the carnival to the person who comes closest to correctly guessing the weight of this jar. The jar of beans weighs $6\frac{1}{4}$ pounds. How close is Marty's estimate?

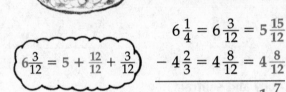
$4\frac{2}{3}$ pounds?

We need to find the difference between Marty's estimate and the actual weight of the jar.

The jar of beans weighs _____ pounds.

Marty estimated _____ pounds.

To find how close Marty's estimate was, we subtract it from the actual weight.

GUESS THE WEIGHT

Write equivalent fractions.	Regroup if needed.	Subtract.

$$6\frac{1}{4} = 6\frac{3}{12}$$
$$- 4\frac{2}{3} = 4\frac{8}{12}$$

$$6\frac{1}{4} = 6\frac{3}{12} = 5\frac{15}{12}$$
$$- 4\frac{2}{3} = 4\frac{8}{12} = 4\frac{8}{12}$$
$$\left(6\frac{3}{12} = 5 + \frac{12}{12} + \frac{3}{12}\right)$$

$$6\frac{1}{4} = 6\frac{3}{12} = 5\frac{15}{12}$$
$$- 4\frac{2}{3} = 4\frac{8}{12} = 4\frac{8}{12}$$
$$\overline{1\frac{7}{12}}$$

Marty's estimate is _____ pounds less than the actual weight of the jar.

Getting Started

Rename as mixed numbers with improper fractions.

1. $5\frac{2}{3} = 4\frac{}{3}$

2. $7\frac{3}{10} = 6\frac{}{10}$

3. $9\frac{1}{5} = 8\frac{}{5}$

4. $4\frac{4}{8} = 3\frac{}{8}$

Subtract. Simplify if necessary.

5. $8\frac{1}{3}$
   $- 4\frac{5}{6}$

6. $11\frac{1}{8}$
   $- 6\frac{3}{8}$

7. $14\frac{2}{5}$
   $- 8\frac{3}{4}$

8. $16\frac{1}{4}$
   $- 7\frac{2}{3}$

Copy and subtract.

9. $16\frac{1}{5} - 9\frac{2}{4}$

10. $11\frac{3}{7} - 4\frac{13}{14}$

11. $12\frac{5}{12} - 7\frac{5}{8}$

12. $15\frac{2}{9} - 8\frac{5}{6}$

Practice

Rename as mixed numbers with improper fractions.

1. $6\frac{1}{4} = 5\frac{}{4}$

2. $7\frac{2}{3} = 6\frac{}{3}$

3. $11\frac{3}{5} = 10\frac{}{5}$

4. $3\frac{7}{9} = 2\frac{}{9}$

5. $17\frac{5}{8} = 16\frac{}{8}$

6. $5\frac{1}{2} = 4\frac{}{2}$

7. $6\frac{7}{10} = 5\frac{}{10}$

8. $7\frac{7}{12} = 6\frac{}{12}$

Subtract. Simplify if necessary.

9. $\begin{array}{r} 5\frac{1}{6} \\ -\ 4\frac{5}{6} \\ \hline \end{array}$

10. $\begin{array}{r} 8\frac{3}{8} \\ -7\frac{5}{8} \\ \hline \end{array}$

11. $\begin{array}{r} 9\frac{2}{3} \\ -7\frac{5}{6} \\ \hline \end{array}$

12. $\begin{array}{r} 14\frac{1}{5} \\ -\ 9\frac{9}{10} \\ \hline \end{array}$

13. $\begin{array}{r} 14\frac{1}{4} \\ -\ 6\frac{1}{3} \\ \hline \end{array}$

14. $\begin{array}{r} 10\frac{1}{5} \\ -\ 6\frac{3}{4} \\ \hline \end{array}$

15. $\begin{array}{r} 15\frac{3}{8} \\ -\ 6\frac{5}{6} \\ \hline \end{array}$

16. $\begin{array}{r} 7\frac{2}{15} \\ -5\frac{7}{10} \\ \hline \end{array}$

17. $\begin{array}{r} 16\frac{1}{2} \\ -\ 9\frac{3}{5} \\ \hline \end{array}$

18. $\begin{array}{r} 17\frac{1}{8} \\ -\ 8\frac{7}{12} \\ \hline \end{array}$

19. $\begin{array}{r} 13\frac{5}{12} \\ -\ 6\frac{7}{9} \\ \hline \end{array}$

20. $\begin{array}{r} 16\frac{3}{8} \\ -\ 9\frac{1}{2} \\ \hline \end{array}$

Copy and subtract.

21. $12\frac{1}{3} - 7\frac{3}{5}$

22. $9\frac{3}{8} - 7\frac{3}{4}$

23. $18\frac{1}{5} - 9\frac{1}{6}$

24. $13\frac{3}{4} - 7\frac{5}{6}$

25. $10\frac{1}{2} - 5\frac{2}{3}$

26. $15\frac{1}{3} - 6\frac{3}{4}$

27. $9\frac{1}{2} - 1\frac{3}{5}$

28. $16\frac{4}{9} - 8\frac{1}{2}$

Problem Solving

Solve each problem. Simplify if necessary.

29. A recent Olympic record for pole vaulting is $19\frac{17}{24}$ feet. The earliest recorded vault was $10\frac{5}{6}$ feet in the year 1896, by William Hoyt of the USA. How far from the current record was Hoyt's vault?

30. Last Sunday, Jamie spent $5\frac{1}{3}$ hours on homework. She spent $1\frac{1}{2}$ hours on math, $2\frac{1}{2}$ hours reading, and the rest of the time on spelling. How many hours did Jamie spend on spelling homework?

31. The bean jar at the carnival weighs $6\frac{1}{4}$ pounds. Pete guessed that it weighed $5\frac{3}{8}$ pounds. How far off was his estimate?

32. Rita worked on the party decorations for $2\frac{1}{2}$ hours, but Walt worked $1\frac{3}{4}$ hours longer. How long did Walt work on the decorations?

Estimating Sums and Differences of Mixed Numbers

Eiji wants to make a vegetable salad.

About how many cups of beans will he need?

We are looking for an **estimate**. The word *about* tells you to estimate.

We know he will need _____ cups of yellow beans and _____ cups of green beans. To find about how many beans there are in all, we estimate the sum.

First, we need to round each mixed number to a whole number. We can use a number line to help.

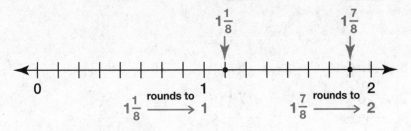

$$1\frac{1}{8} + 1\frac{7}{8} \text{ rounds to } \underline{\hspace{1cm}} + \underline{\hspace{1cm}} = \underline{\hspace{1cm}}.$$

Eiji will need about _____ cups of beans for the salad.

REMEMBER To estimate the sum or difference of mixed numbers, round the mixed numbers to whole numbers. Then, add or subtract.

Getting Started

Round each mixed number to the nearest whole number.

1. $5\frac{3}{4}$ _____

2. $7\frac{1}{3}$ _____

3. $9\frac{4}{5}$ _____

4. $12\frac{2}{7}$ _____

Estimate each sum or difference.

5. $\quad 4\frac{3}{4}$
$\quad + 2\frac{3}{4}$

6. $\quad 8\frac{1}{6}$
$\quad - 2\frac{5}{6}$

7. $\quad 7\frac{5}{8}$
$\quad + 3\frac{1}{5}$

8. $\quad 12\frac{4}{5}$
$\quad - 7\frac{3}{10}$

Practice

Estimate each sum or difference.

1. $5\frac{1}{3}$
    $+ 3\frac{2}{3}$

2. $7\frac{4}{5}$
    $+ 3\frac{1}{5}$

3. $6\frac{8}{9}$
    $+ 5\frac{5}{6}$

4. $9\frac{1}{4}$
    $+ 4\frac{2}{7}$

5. $8\frac{7}{8}$
    $+ 6\frac{5}{6}$

6. $9\frac{1}{6}$
    $- 3\frac{5}{6}$

7. $10\frac{3}{4}$
    $- 6\frac{7}{8}$

8. $15\frac{3}{10}$
    $- 8\frac{4}{5}$

9. $12\frac{6}{7}$
    $- 4\frac{3}{4}$

10. $14\frac{2}{9}$
    $- 6\frac{3}{15}$

11. $10\frac{4}{5}$
    $+ 5\frac{1}{3}$

12. $17\frac{1}{5}$
    $- 9\frac{2}{7}$

13. $13\frac{5}{6}$
    $- 6\frac{1}{3}$

14. $9\frac{7}{8}$
    $+ 7\frac{4}{5}$

15. $11\frac{2}{5}$
    $- 8\frac{7}{9}$

16. $14\frac{5}{7}$
    $- 5\frac{9}{10}$

17. $9\frac{4}{5}$
    $+ 7\frac{2}{9}$

18. $15\frac{3}{8}$
    $- 6\frac{5}{6}$

19. $8\frac{2}{3}$
    $+ 7\frac{1}{9}$

20. $16\frac{5}{6}$
    $- 9\frac{2}{5}$

Copy. Then, estimate each sum or difference.

21. $7\frac{9}{10} + 5\frac{3}{8}$

22. $10\frac{2}{7} - 3\frac{7}{9}$

23. $6\frac{1}{4} + 7\frac{4}{5}$

24. $13\frac{5}{6} - 5\frac{1}{4}$

25. $15\frac{1}{3} - 6\frac{5}{7}$

26. $8\frac{5}{6} + 5\frac{7}{8}$

27. $11\frac{7}{9} - 6\frac{3}{4}$

28. $9\frac{2}{9} + 6\frac{4}{5}$

Problem Solving

Use the recipe to solve each problem.

29. About how many more cups of strawberries are needed than oranges?

30. Altogether, about how much fruit is needed?

Fruit Salad

$2\frac{3}{4}$ cups	strawberries
$1\frac{1}{3}$ cups	sliced oranges
$2\frac{1}{4}$ cups	grapes
$1\frac{2}{3}$ cups	sliced peaches

Adding and Subtracting Mixed Numbers

Tracy needs to mail a letter at the post office before she goes to the library. How much farther is Tracy's trip to the library past the post office, than her trip directly from home?

We want to find how many more miles Tracy will travel on her way to the library if she stops at the post office.

It is _____ miles to the post office from home, and

_____ miles from the post office to the library. We add the two distances.

We add _____ and _____.

$$3\frac{1}{3} = 3\frac{}{6}$$
$$+ 2\frac{5}{6} = 2\frac{}{6}$$
$$\rule{2cm}{0.4pt}$$
$$\rule{1.5cm}{0.4pt} = \rule{1cm}{0.4pt}$$

It is _____ miles to the library via the post office.

It is _____ miles from the library to home directly. To find how many more miles Tracy traveled, we find the difference between the lengths of the two trips.

We subtract _____ from _____.

$$6\frac{1}{6} = 6\frac{}{12} =$$
$$- 5\frac{1}{4} = 5\frac{}{12} = 5\frac{}{12}$$
$$\rule{2cm}{0.4pt}$$

Tracy's trip was _____ of a mile farther going to the library past the post office.

$2\frac{5}{6}$ miles

$5\frac{1}{4}$ miles

$3\frac{1}{3}$ miles

Getting Started

Add or subtract. Simplify if necessary.

1. $20\frac{1}{5}$
    $- 7\frac{7}{15}$

2. $8\frac{3}{4}$
    $+ 7\frac{2}{9}$

Copy, and add or subtract.

3. $\left(3\frac{1}{2} + 2\frac{5}{8}\right) - 2\frac{1}{2}$

4. $\left(8\frac{1}{10} - 3\frac{2}{5}\right) + 6\frac{1}{2}$

Practice

Add or subtract. Simplify if necessary.

1. $3\frac{2}{3}$
   $-2\frac{1}{2}$

2. $7\frac{3}{8}$
   $+4\frac{5}{6}$

3. $9\frac{1}{4}$
   $+7\frac{1}{6}$

4. $14\frac{1}{2}$
   $-6\frac{3}{8}$

5. $13\frac{7}{8}$
   $+5\frac{1}{3}$

6. $19\frac{1}{10}$
   $-12\frac{5}{15}$

7. $13\frac{2}{3}$
   $-7\frac{7}{8}$

8. $8\frac{1}{8}$
   $+4\frac{3}{10}$

Copy, and add or subtract.

9. $\left(2\frac{1}{2} + 3\frac{1}{4}\right) - 1\frac{2}{3}$

10. $\left(7\frac{3}{8} - 1\frac{1}{4}\right) + 5\frac{1}{3}$

11. $21\frac{1}{4} - \left(4\frac{2}{3} + 5\frac{1}{2}\right)$

12. $\left(17\frac{1}{8} - 11\frac{5}{6}\right) + 10\frac{7}{12}$

13. $13\frac{2}{3} + \left(10\frac{1}{4} - 4\frac{5}{6}\right)$

14. $19\frac{2}{3} - \left(6\frac{1}{4} - 3\frac{5}{8}\right)$

Problem Solving

Solve each problem. Simplify if necessary.

15. The record snowfall in Portland, Maine, for a 24-hour period is $15\frac{5}{16}$ inches. If $3\frac{1}{4}$ inches of snow falls between 7 A.M. and noon on Monday, then $5\frac{1}{2}$ more inches accumulate by midnight, and $7\frac{1}{3}$ additional inches are on the ground as of 6:59 A.M. on Tuesday, by how much will this snowfall exceed the record?

16. Margo bought stock in the Tops Are Top Clothing Company for $19\frac{1}{4}$ on Friday. The stock moved up $1\frac{1}{8}$ on Monday, $2\frac{1}{2}$ on Tuesday, and dropped $1\frac{3}{4}$ on Wednesday. What was Margo's stock worth after Wednesday?

[Now Try This!]

Division can be represented as a fraction: $\left(\frac{\text{dividend}}{\text{divisor}} = \text{quotient} \longrightarrow \frac{30}{6} = 5\right)$

Write the quotients. Then write each division equation as a fraction.

1. $42 \div 7 =$ _____ $\longrightarrow$ _____ $=$ _____

2. $32 \div 4 =$ _____ $\longrightarrow$ _____ $=$ _____

3. $54 \div 6 =$ _____ $\longrightarrow$ _____ $=$ _____

4. $63 \div 9 =$ _____ $\longrightarrow$ _____ $=$ _____

Name _____

Problem Solving: Choose a Strategy

Andy has an eight-cup container of sugar. He also
has an empty five-cup container and an empty
three-cup container. None of the containers has any
markings. How can Andy measure exactly four cups
of sugar using only these three containers?

 SEE

We want to know how Andy can measure exactly
four cups of sugar. He has a 5-cup and a 3-cup
container that are empty. He has an 8-cup container
that is filled with sugar.

 PLAN

Since the solution to this problem requires showing
how Andy can get exactly four cups of sugar, we will
need to record how he transfers sugar from container
to container. We can do this by using three numbers
to show the amount of sugar in each container. The
first number will represent the amount of sugar in
the 8-cup container. The second number will
represent the amount of sugar in the 5-cup container.
The third number will represent the amount of sugar

in the _____ -cup container.

 DO

8, 0, 0   There are 8 cups of sugar in the _____ -cup container.

3, 5, 0   Andy transfers _____ cups of sugar into the 5-cup container.

3, 2, ?   He transfers 3 cups of sugar from the _____ -cup to the _____ -cup container.

6, 2, ?   He transfers _____ cups of sugar from the _____ -cup to the 8-cup container.

6, 0, ?   He transfers _____ cups of sugar from the _____ -cup to the 3-cup container.

1, ?, 2   He transfers 5 cups of sugar from the 8-cup to the _____ -cup container.

1, 4, 3   He transfers 1 cup of sugar from the _____ -cup to the 3-cup container.

Andy now has _____ cups of sugar in the _____ -cup container.

 CHECK

We can check our work by reviewing each step.

Apply

Solve each problem.

1. You have two pails: one that will hold 4 quarts of water and one that will hold 9 quarts. There are no markings on either pail to indicate smaller quantities. How can you measure out 6 quarts of water using only these two pails?

2. How can you cook an egg for exactly 15 minutes, if all you have is a 7-minute hourglass and an 11-minute hourglass?

3. Joe and Sam like to trade. They agree that six peanuts are worth two suckers, and ten suckers are worth five apples. How many peanuts should Joe give Sam in trade for three apples?

4. You have a 7-gallon pail and a 5-gallon pail. How can you measure exactly four gallons of water using only these two pails?

5. All students in the class like milkshakes. Sixteen like vanilla, 16 like chocolate, and 20 like strawberry, 5 like both chocolate and strawberry, 4 like both strawberry and vanilla, and 2 like both vanilla and chocolate. Three students like all three. How many are in the class?

6. Palmer, Smith, and West are a teacher, a doctor, and a lawyer, but not necessarily in that order. Their first names are Anne, Frank, and Ed. Smith is neither a teacher nor a doctor. West is not the doctor and Anne is not the teacher. Ed is older than Smith and West. Give the full name and occupation of each person.

7. The Basset Hound Musicians practiced $1\frac{3}{4}$ hours on Friday and $2\frac{2}{3}$ hours on Saturday. Do not use pencil and paper to compute. Was the total time that they practiced more or less than 4 hours? Explain how you know.

8. Adelle added two fractions with unlike denominators. She used a denominator of one of the fractions as a common denominator for both of the fractions. What had to be true about the two denominators so that she could do this?

9. If the sum of two like fractions is equal to 1, what is true about the sum of the numerators?

10. If the sum of any two fractions is less than 1, what is true about the fractions?

Add or subtract. Simplify if necessary.

1. $\dfrac{2}{5}$
$+ \dfrac{1}{5}$
_____

2. $\dfrac{3}{8}$
$- \dfrac{1}{8}$
_____

3. $\dfrac{7}{8}$
$- \dfrac{1}{8}$
_____

4. $\dfrac{9}{4}$
$- \dfrac{3}{4}$
_____

5. $\dfrac{8}{4}$
$+ \dfrac{1}{3}$
_____

6. $\dfrac{1}{2}$
$+ \dfrac{3}{5}$
_____

7. $\dfrac{7}{10}$
$- \dfrac{1}{2}$
_____

8. $\dfrac{7}{8}$
$- \dfrac{1}{6}$
_____

9. $4\dfrac{3}{5}$
$+ 6\dfrac{7}{10}$
_____

10. $8\dfrac{1}{2}$
$+ 9\dfrac{2}{3}$
_____

11. $6\dfrac{3}{8}$
$+ 5\dfrac{5}{6}$
_____

12. $6\dfrac{9}{10}$
$+ 8\dfrac{7}{15}$
_____

13. $9\dfrac{2}{3}$
$- 6\dfrac{1}{2}$
_____

14. $12\dfrac{7}{8}$
$- 5\dfrac{1}{4}$
_____

15. $13\dfrac{9}{10}$
$- 4\dfrac{3}{5}$
_____

16. $14\dfrac{7}{16}$
$- 8\dfrac{5}{16}$
_____

17. 8
$- 6\dfrac{3}{4}$
_____

18. $10\dfrac{1}{6}$
$- 8\dfrac{2}{3}$
_____

19. $17\dfrac{2}{5}$
$- 8\dfrac{3}{4}$
_____

20. $16\dfrac{3}{10}$
$- 7\dfrac{5}{6}$
_____

Rename as mixed numbers.

21. $2 = $ _____ $\dfrac{12}{12}$

22. $10\dfrac{3}{4} = 9\dfrac{}{4}$

23. $3 = $ _____ $\dfrac{5}{5}$

24. $5\dfrac{3}{5} = 4\dfrac{}{5}$

Simplify each mixed number.

25. $11\dfrac{12}{10} = $ _____

26. $1\dfrac{4}{16} = $ _____

27. $10\dfrac{43}{30} = $ _____

28. $10\dfrac{63}{81} = $ _____

Circle the letter of the correct answer.

1
$$563$$
$$+ 739$$
- a. 1,202
- b. 1,292
- c. 1,302
- d. NG

2
$$15,763$$
$$+ 9,839$$
- a. 24,602
- b. 25,602
- c. 27,602
- d. NG

3
$$6,248$$
$$- 951$$
- a. 5,297
- b. 5,397
- c. 6,717
- d. NG

4
$$\$708.15$$
$$- 429.38$$
- a. $221.23
- b. $278.77
- c. $288.77
- d. NG

5
$$\$9.06$$
$$\times 7$$
- a. $63.42
- b. $64.14
- c. $630.42
- d. NG

6
$$75$$
$$\times 36$$
- a. 675
- b. 2,570
- c. 2,900
- d. NG

7 $4\overline{)48,084}$
- a. 1,212
- b. 1,221
- c. 12,021
- d. NG

8 $49\overline{)11,768}$
- a. 24 R8
- b. 240 R8
- c. 240
- d. NG

9 Find the area.

9 in.

6 in.
- a. 30 in.
- b. 30 sq in.
- c. 54 sq in.
- d. NG

10
$$7 \text{ gal } 3 \text{ qt}$$
$$+ 4 \text{ gal } 2 \text{ qt}$$
- a. 11 gal
- b. 11 gal 1 qt
- c. 12 gal 1 qt
- d. NG

11 Simplify.

$\frac{5}{25}$
- a. $\frac{1}{5}$
- b. $\frac{1}{3}$
- c. $\frac{5}{25}$
- d. NG

12 Simplify.

$\frac{20}{6}$
- a. $\frac{1}{3}$
- b. $3\frac{1}{6}$
- c. $3\frac{1}{3}$
- d. NG

score

Multiply and Divide of Fractions

Finding Fractional Parts of a Number

Ysidra tries to save as much money as she can for her college expenses. She earns $48 each week tutoring history students at the campus learning center. How much does she save each week?

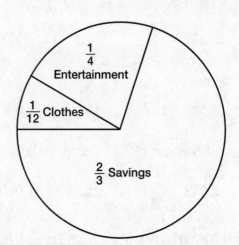

We want to find the amount Ysidra saves each week.

We know Ysidra earns _____ each week.

She saves _____ of her earnings. We need

to find _____ of _____.

First, we divide the number by the denominator, 3.	Then we multiply the quotient by the numerator, 2.

$\frac{1}{3}$ of 48 $3\overline{)48}$ $\frac{2}{3}$ of 48 $2 \times 16 =$ _____

We can draw a picture to help us understand this.

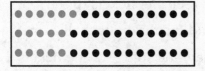 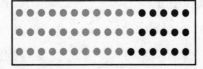 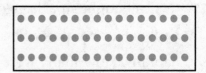

$\frac{1}{3}$ of 48 = 16 $\frac{2}{3}$ of 48 = 32 $\frac{3}{3}$ of 48 = 48

REMEMBER To find a fraction of a number, divide the number by the denominator and multiply that result by the numerator.

Ysidra saves _____ each week.

Getting Started

Write the number for each fractional part.

1. $\frac{1}{8}$ of 16 =

2. $\frac{1}{10}$ of $100 =

3. $\frac{1}{12}$ of 96 =

Copy and solve.

4. $\frac{3}{4}$ of 24

5. $\frac{5}{6}$ of 96

6. $\frac{9}{16}$ of $288

Practice

Write the number for each fractional part.

1. $\frac{1}{3}$ of 21 =
2. $\frac{1}{2}$ of 24 =
3. $\frac{4}{7}$ of $84 =

4. $\frac{5}{6}$ of 36 =
5. $\frac{3}{4}$ of 36 =
6. $\frac{3}{8}$ of 64 =

7. $\frac{4}{5}$ of $35 =
8. $\frac{2}{3}$ of 21 =
9. $\frac{1}{12}$ of 24 =

10. $\frac{1}{7}$ of $49 =
11. $\frac{3}{10}$ of 40 =
12. $\frac{7}{8}$ of 56 =

Copy and do.

13. $\frac{2}{3}$ of 42
14. $\frac{1}{8}$ of 80
15. $\frac{3}{7}$ of 84
16. $\frac{4}{5}$ of 75

17. $\frac{1}{12}$ of $48
18. $\frac{1}{16}$ of 608
19. $\frac{1}{2}$ of 806
20. $\frac{3}{8}$ of $496

21. $\frac{3}{4}$ of 948
22. $\frac{3}{5}$ of $1,080
23. $\frac{3}{16}$ of 1,792
24. $\frac{7}{15}$ of 1,905

Problem Solving

Solve each problem.

25. Winston bought $\frac{1}{2}$ dozen macaroni and cheese dinners. If he eats one dinner each day, how many days will his supply of dinners last?

26. It took Dean $\frac{3}{5}$ of an hour to walk home from basketball practice. How many minutes did it take?

27. Jessica bought a package of 36 paper napkins for her party. She used $\frac{2}{3}$ of the napkins. How many were left in the package?

28. Tina has to sell 144 tickets to the student and faculty volleyball game. On Monday, she sold $\frac{3}{8}$ of the tickets. On Tuesday, she sold $\frac{1}{6}$ of the original number of tickets. How many did Tina have left to sell on Wednesday?

Use the ad to solve Problems 29 and 30.

29. What is the sale price of a coat that usually sells for $87?

30. A pair of shoes costs $72 and a jacket costs $116. How much is saved if Paul buys the shoes and jacket on sale?

Sale	
Coats	$\frac{2}{3}$ off
Shoes	$\frac{1}{2}$ off
Jackets	$\frac{2}{4}$ off

Lesson 9-1 • Finding Fractional Parts of a Number

Multiplying Fractions

Ricardo has all the ingredients ready to bake three batches of corn muffins. Ricardo needs to use $\frac{2}{3}$ of his milk to make the first two batches. He had $\frac{1}{2}$ cup of milk. What part of a full cup of milk will Ricardo use in the first two batches?

We want to find what fraction of a cup of milk Ricardo will use in the first two batches.

The measuring cup is $\frac{1}{2}$ full. Ricardo needs to use $\frac{2}{3}$ of the milk.

We need to find $\frac{2}{3}$ of _____.

We can draw a picture to help us understand the problem.

Total Milk Available

$\frac{1}{2}$

$\frac{1}{2}$

Milk for Two Batches

$\frac{1}{6}$ $\frac{1}{6}$ $\frac{1}{6}$

We can also multiply to find $\frac{2}{3}$ of $\frac{1}{2}$.

Multiply the numerators to find the part used.	Multiply the denominators to find how many parts in all. Simplify.
$\frac{2}{3} \times \frac{1}{2} = \frac{2}{}$	$\frac{2}{3} \times \frac{1}{2} = \frac{2}{6} = \frac{1}{3}$

Ricardo will use _____ of a cup of milk for two batches.

Getting Started

Multiply. Simplify if necessary.

1. $\frac{3}{4} \times \frac{5}{8} =$ _____

2. $\frac{1}{5} \times \frac{3}{4} =$ _____

3. $\frac{7}{3} \times \frac{2}{5} =$ _____

4. $\frac{6}{10} \times \frac{2}{3} =$ _____

5. $\frac{7}{8} \times \frac{4}{5} =$ _____

6. $\frac{2}{3} \times \frac{9}{10} =$ _____

7. $\frac{2}{5} \times \frac{5}{2} =$ _____

8. $\frac{7}{2} \times \frac{6}{7} =$ _____

Copy and multiply.

9. $\frac{1}{3} \times \frac{2}{5}$ _____

10. $\frac{5}{9} \times \frac{7}{9}$ _____

11. $\frac{9}{15} \times \frac{5}{3}$ _____

12. $\frac{9}{4} \times \frac{2}{6}$ _____

Practice

Multiply. Simplify if necessary.

1. $\frac{3}{4} \times \frac{2}{5} =$ _____

2. $\frac{1}{8} \times \frac{3}{8} =$ _____

3. $\frac{6}{5} \times \frac{2}{3} =$ _____

4. $\frac{4}{5} \times \frac{5}{8} =$ _____

5. $\frac{8}{9} \times \frac{3}{4} =$ _____

6. $\frac{7}{8} \times \frac{8}{7} =$ _____

7. $\frac{3}{12} \times \frac{6}{10} =$ _____

8. $\frac{3}{7} \times \frac{7}{15} =$ _____

9. $\frac{9}{10} \times \frac{5}{3} =$ _____

10. $\frac{6}{10} \times \frac{5}{12} =$ _____

11. $\frac{5}{16} \times \frac{8}{10} =$ _____

12. $\frac{2}{3} \times \frac{9}{16} =$ _____

Copy and multiply.

13. $\frac{8}{5} \times \frac{5}{4}$ _____

14. $\frac{7}{3} \times \frac{9}{14}$ _____

15. $\frac{4}{9} \times \frac{12}{16}$ _____

16. $\frac{7}{12} \times \frac{8}{21}$ _____

17. $\frac{10}{4} \times \frac{8}{15}$ _____

18. $\frac{9}{16} \times \frac{1}{3}$ _____

19. $\frac{3}{3} \times \frac{9}{10}$ _____

20. $\frac{5}{6} \times \frac{12}{5}$ _____

Problem Solving

Solve each problem. Simplify if necessary.

21. Dorothy is redecorating by painting $\frac{1}{4}$ of her room pink. She plans to cover $\frac{2}{3}$ of the pink wall with mirrors. What part of her room is covered with mirrors?

22. Ernie likes gardening and planted $\frac{3}{4}$ of his garden with melons. He planted $\frac{3}{5}$ of the melons on Friday. What part of the garden did Ernie plant on Friday?

23. The planning commission has determined that Parkville is $\frac{3}{16}$ park land. About $\frac{4}{9}$ of the park land is used for recreation. What part of Parkville is used for recreation?

24. Shasta lives $\frac{7}{8}$ of a mile from school. She walks $\frac{2}{3}$ of the way with Joan. How far does Shasta walk alone?

Now Try This!

Here is a **factoring method** for multiplying fractions.

First, write the prime factors for each numerator and denominator.

$$\frac{9}{14} \times \frac{21}{6} = \frac{3 \times 3}{2 \times 7} \times \frac{3 \times 7}{2 \times 3}$$

Next, cross out primes that are common in the numerators and denominators.

$$\frac{3 \times 3}{2 \times 7} \times \frac{\cancel{3} \times \cancel{7}}{2 \times \cancel{3}}$$

Multiply the remaining primes to get the product.

$$\frac{3 \times 3}{2 \times 2} = \frac{9}{4} = 2\frac{1}{4}$$

Multiply. Use the factoring method.

1. $\frac{12}{13} \times \frac{5}{18} =$

2. $\frac{7}{12} \times \frac{18}{21} =$

3. $\frac{6}{7} \times \frac{5}{3} =$

4. $\frac{72}{49} \times \frac{21}{16} =$

5. $\frac{121}{45} \times \frac{15}{33} =$

6. $\frac{3}{7} \times \frac{5}{14} \times \frac{49}{30} =$

Multiplying Fractions and Mixed Numbers

Yong is applying for a part-time job at Sam's Sandwich Shop. The waiter's position pays $4 per hour. How much can Yong make each week as a waiter?

SAM'S SANDWICH SHOP

We want to know the weekly amount Yong can earn as a waiter.

The waiter's position pays _____ per hour

and is available for _____ hours a week.

To find the weekly earnings for this position, we multiply the hourly rate by the total working hours per week. We multiply _____

by _____.

Wanted Part-Time	Hours per Week
Cook	12
Waiter	$8\frac{1}{4}$
Hostess	$6\frac{2}{3}$

Rename the factors as fractions.	Multiply numerators and denominators.	Simplify the product as a whole or mixed number.
$4 \times 8\frac{1}{4}$ $\frac{4}{1} \times \frac{33}{4}$	$\frac{4}{1} \times \frac{33}{4} = \frac{132}{4}$	$\frac{4}{1} \times \frac{33}{4} = \frac{132}{4} = 33$

REMEMBER To rename a whole number as a fraction, we write the whole number in the numerator and 1 in the denominator, such as $4 = \frac{4}{1}$.

Yong can make _____ each week as a waiter.

Getting Started

Multiply. Simplify if necessary.

1. $\frac{2}{3} \times 3\frac{1}{3} =$ _____

2. $7 \times 1\frac{1}{2} =$ _____

3. $2\frac{3}{4} \times \frac{1}{2} =$ _____

4. $5\frac{1}{3} \times \frac{3}{4} =$ _____

Copy and multiply.

5. $4\frac{1}{2} \times \frac{5}{9}$

6. $\frac{3}{5} \times 6\frac{1}{3}$

7. $\frac{2}{9} \times 7$

8. $8 \times \frac{3}{16}$

9. $3\frac{5}{7} \times 3$

10. $\frac{1}{5} \times 9\frac{1}{2}$

Practice

Multiply. Simplify if necessary.

1. $\frac{3}{4} \times 2\frac{1}{2} =$ _____

2. $1\frac{2}{3} \times \$6 =$ _____

3. $\frac{3}{8} \times 1\frac{1}{3} =$ _____

4. $5\frac{1}{3} \times 15 =$ _____

5. $4\frac{2}{3} \times \frac{1}{4} =$ _____

6. $\frac{5}{12} \times 1\frac{1}{5} =$ _____

7. $6\frac{1}{3} \times 9 =$ _____

8. $1\frac{1}{2} \times \frac{4}{5} =$ _____

9. $3\frac{1}{3} \times \frac{2}{5} =$ _____

10. $\$10 \times 4\frac{1}{5} =$ _____

11. $2\frac{1}{6} \times 3 =$ _____

12. $9\frac{1}{2} \times \frac{2}{3} =$ _____

13. $5\frac{1}{8} \times 4 =$ _____

14. $\frac{5}{7} \times 1\frac{3}{4} =$ _____

15. $\$12 \times 5\frac{1}{3} =$ _____

16. $\frac{5}{8} \times \$16 =$ _____

Copy and multiply.

17. $1\frac{1}{5} \times \frac{5}{6}$

18. $15 \times 2\frac{1}{3}$

19. $8\frac{1}{2} \times \$20$

20. $\frac{4}{5} \times 12$

21. $3\frac{1}{8} \times \frac{2}{5}$

22. $\frac{5}{7} \times \frac{1}{10}$

23. $1\frac{2}{3} \times 8$

24. $3\frac{3}{5} \times \$25$

25. $2\frac{1}{12} \times \frac{3}{10}$

26. $48 \times \frac{5}{8}$

27. $18 \times 2\frac{1}{9}$

28. $6\frac{1}{4} \times \frac{1}{10}$

Problem Solving

Use the recipe for griddle cakes to solve each problem.

29. How much baking powder and baking soda is needed for 4 servings?

30. How much milk is needed for 8 servings?

31. How much more sugar than baking soda is used for 4 servings?

32. How much flour is needed for 10 servings?

GRIDDLE CAKES 4 servings
$\frac{1}{2}$ cup flour
$2\frac{2}{3}$ teaspoons sugar
$\frac{1}{3}$ teaspoon baking powder
$\frac{3}{4}$ teaspoon baking soda
1 egg
$2\frac{1}{2}$ cups milk

Lesson 9-3 • Multiplying Fractions and Mixed Numbers

Multiplying Mixed Numbers

Mrs. Reynolds is buying wall-to-wall carpeting for her dining room. Carpeting is sold by the square yard. How many square yards of carpeting will Mrs. Reynolds need?

We want to know the number of square yards of carpeting needed.

To know this we need to find the area of Mrs. Reynolds' dining room.

The length is _____ yards and the width is

_____ yards.

To find the area, we multiply the length of the room by the width.

We multiply _____ by _____.

Rename the factors as fractions.	Multiply numerators and denominators.	Simplify the product.
$2\frac{1}{4} \times 3\frac{1}{3}$ $\frac{9}{4} \times \frac{10}{3}$	$\frac{9}{4} \times \frac{10}{3} = \frac{90}{12}$	$\frac{9}{4} \times \frac{10}{3} = \frac{90}{12} = \frac{15}{2} = 7\frac{1}{2}$

Mrs. Reynolds will need _____ square yards of carpeting.

REMEMBER To rename a mixed number as an improper fraction, we write the numerator as the product of the denominator and whole number plus the numerator.

$2\frac{1}{4} = \frac{4 \times 2 + 1}{4} = \frac{9}{4}$

Getting Started

Multiply. Simplify if necessary.

1. $2\frac{1}{5} \times 3\frac{1}{2} =$ _____

2. $1\frac{1}{8} \times 3\frac{1}{9} =$ _____

3. $1\frac{1}{3} \times 2\frac{1}{2} =$ _____

4. $2\frac{3}{8} \times 1\frac{1}{3} =$ _____

Copy and multiply.

5. $1\frac{1}{6} \times 1\frac{1}{8}$

6. $2\frac{1}{2} \times 3\frac{3}{4}$

7. $5\frac{3}{7} \times 2\frac{1}{5}$

8. $2\frac{1}{3} \times 1\frac{3}{5}$

9. $3\frac{1}{3} \times 1\frac{7}{10}$

10. $3\frac{2}{3} \times 4\frac{2}{12}$

Practice

Multiply. Simplify if necessary.

1. $2\frac{1}{3} \times 1\frac{1}{2} =$ _____

2. $1\frac{1}{5} \times 1\frac{1}{6} =$ _____

3. $4\frac{1}{2} \times 1\frac{5}{9} =$ _____

4. $3\frac{1}{7} \times 1\frac{3}{11} =$ _____

5. $7\frac{1}{2} \times 1\frac{3}{5} =$ _____

6. $1\frac{1}{5} \times 1\frac{3}{4} =$ _____

7. $4\frac{1}{3} \times 1\frac{1}{3} =$ _____

8. $1\frac{4}{5} \times 3\frac{1}{3} =$ _____

9. $1\frac{1}{3} \times 2\frac{1}{5} =$ _____

10. $2\frac{1}{2} \times 2\frac{1}{2} =$ _____

Copy and multiply.

11. $2\frac{1}{4} \times 2\frac{2}{5}$

12. $1\frac{3}{4} \times 1\frac{1}{7}$

13. $2\frac{2}{5} \times 5\frac{5}{6}$

14. $3\frac{2}{3} \times 2\frac{1}{4}$

15. $2\frac{3}{4} \times 1\frac{5}{11}$

16. $2\frac{1}{2} \times 2\frac{3}{4}$

17. $1\frac{1}{4} \times 3\frac{3}{5}$

18. $2\frac{4}{5} \times 1\frac{3}{7}$

19. $4\frac{2}{3} \times 7\frac{1}{2}$

20. $5\frac{5}{12} \times 4\frac{2}{5}$

21. $9\frac{1}{7} \times 2\frac{5}{8}$

22. $15\frac{1}{3} \times 17\frac{1}{4}$

Problem Solving

Solve each problem.

23. A bottle of Fruity Grape Juice will fill $3\frac{1}{3}$ four-ounce glasses. How many four-ounce glasses will $1\frac{1}{2}$ bottles fill?

24. Elmer devotes more time to his studies than to his hobbies. He spent $3\frac{3}{4}$ hours on homework and $1\frac{3}{5}$ hours labeling his shell collection. How much longer did Elmer spend on homework?

Use the rectangle to solve Problems 25 through 28.

25. Find the perimeter of the rectangle.

26. Find the area of the rectangle.

27. Rename the dimensions of the rectangle in feet.

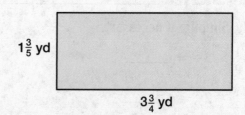

$1\frac{3}{5}$ yd

$3\frac{3}{4}$ yd

28. It costs $1.25 per foot to buy molding for the walls. How much will it cost to buy molding for a room with the same dimensions as the rectangle?

Writing Reciprocals

When the product of two fractions is 1, the
fractions are called **reciprocals**.

$$\frac{1}{2} \times \frac{2}{1} = 1 \qquad\qquad \frac{2}{3} \times \frac{3}{2} = 1 \qquad\qquad \frac{3}{4} \times \frac{4}{3} = 1$$

reciprocals   reciprocals   reciprocals

REMEMBER To find the reciprocal of a fraction,
invert it, or exchange the positions of the
numerator and denominator.

Fraction	Reciprocal	Check. Multiply the fraction and its reciprocal.
$\frac{4}{5}$	$\frac{5}{4}$ or $1\frac{1}{4}$	$\frac{4}{5} \times \frac{5}{4} = \frac{4 \times 5}{5 \times 4} = \frac{20}{20} = 1$

REMEMBER To find the reciprocal of a whole
or mixed number, first rename it as a fraction,
then invert the fraction.

Number	Reciprocal	Check.
$7 = \frac{7}{1}$	___	$\frac{7}{1} \times$ ___ $=$ ___ $=$ ___
$4\frac{1}{3} = \frac{13}{3}$	___	$\frac{13}{3} \times$ ___ $=$ ___ $=$ ___

Getting Started

Write the reciprocal.

1. $\frac{3}{8}$

2. $\frac{7}{3}$

3. $1\frac{5}{6}$

4. 8

5. $2\frac{4}{5}$

Circle each pair of reciprocals.

6. $\frac{4}{5}$, $1\frac{1}{4}$

7. $\frac{1}{12}$, 12

8. $2\frac{1}{3}$, $\frac{7}{3}$

9. $3\frac{1}{2}$, $\frac{2}{7}$

10. $4\frac{3}{8}$, $\frac{8}{35}$

Practice

Write the reciprocal.

1. $\frac{3}{5}$ 2. $\frac{1}{9}$ 3. 4   4. $1\frac{1}{2}$ 5. $3\frac{4}{5}$

6. $\frac{8}{7}$ 7. $5\frac{1}{3}$ 8. $\frac{2}{7}$ 9. 10   10. $3\frac{5}{12}$

Circle each pair of reciprocals.

11. $\frac{3}{8}, \frac{8}{2}$ 12. $\frac{3}{4}, \frac{4}{3}$ 13. $3\frac{1}{5}, \frac{5}{16}$ 14. $6\frac{1}{2}, \frac{13}{2}$ 15. $4\frac{1}{3}, \frac{3}{13}$

16. $2\frac{1}{4}, \frac{4}{9}$ 17. $4\frac{3}{8}, \frac{35}{8}$ 18. $6\frac{2}{3}, \frac{6}{20}$ 19. $9, \frac{1}{9}$ 20. $7\frac{1}{2}, \frac{15}{2}$

21. $\frac{7}{5}, \frac{12}{7}$ 22. $\frac{7}{12}, 1\frac{5}{12}$ 23. $\frac{9}{10}, \frac{90}{100}$ 24. $\frac{5}{8}, 1\frac{3}{8}$ 25. $\frac{4}{15}, 3\frac{3}{4}$

Now Try This!

The **Fundamental Theorem of Counting** can help us determine the total number of ways a problem can be solved. The theorem states we must first determine what steps are necessary to solve the problem. Then multiply the number of choices in each step.

For example: How many 3-digit area codes are possible if no code starts with zero?

Step 1: How many different digits can be used in the first place? _____

Step 2: How many can be used in the second place? _____

Step 3: How many can be used in the third place? _____

Then we multiply: _____ × _____ × _____ = _____

We can form _____ different 3-digit area codes.

Apply the Fundamental Theorem to solve these problems.

1. How many license plates are possible if each one has three numbers and three letters of the alphabet?

2. How many ways can you choose a president, vice-president, and secretary from a class of 25 fifth graders? (No person can hold more than one office at a time.)

3. An auto dealer offers 15 exterior colors, 10 interior fabrics, and 12 accessory packages on its latest model luxury car. How many different combinations are possible for the customer to choose from?

Name _____

Dividing Fractions

Eve is serving fruit punch at the school graduation party. Each glass holds $\frac{2}{3}$ of a pint of liquid. Eve is anxious to empty her punch bowl so that she can join the fun. How many full glasses must she pour?

We want to know how many full glasses Eve must serve to empty her punch bowl.

There are _____ pints of fruit punch in the bowl and each glass will hold _____ of a pint.

To find how many glasses of fruit punch Eve must serve, we divide the total pints of fruit punch by the capacity of one glass.

We divide _____ by _____.

To divide when either the dividend or divisor is a fraction, multiply by the reciprocal of the divisor.

$8 \div \frac{2}{3}$ is the same as $8 \times \frac{3}{2} = \frac{24}{2} = 12$

We can use a picture to help us understand this.

We have divided 8 by $\frac{2}{3}$. What is the number of $\frac{2}{3}$s in 8? _____

Eve should pour _____ glasses of punch.

REMEMBER Whole numbers can be renamed as fractions.

$\frac{5}{6} \div 30 = \frac{5}{6} \div \frac{30}{1} = \frac{5}{6} \times \frac{1}{30} = \frac{5}{180} = \frac{1}{36}$

Getting Started

Complete each division problem. Simplify if necessary.

1. $\frac{3}{4} \div \frac{1}{2} = \frac{3}{4} \times \frac{2}{1} = $ _____

2. $\frac{5}{8} \div \frac{3}{8} = \frac{5}{8} \times \frac{8}{3} = $ _____

Divide. Simplify if necessary.

3. $\frac{3}{7} \div \frac{5}{8}$

4. $\frac{5}{8} \div 10$

Copy and divide.

5. $10 \div \frac{1}{2}$

6. $\frac{2}{3} \div \frac{1}{4}$

Practice

Complete each division problem. Simplify if necessary.

1. $\frac{2}{7} \div \frac{5}{6} = \frac{2}{7} \times \frac{6}{5} = $ _____

2. $\frac{5}{8} \div \frac{5}{6} = \frac{5}{8} \times \frac{6}{5} = $ _____

3. $\frac{2}{3} \div 12 = \frac{2}{3} \times \frac{1}{12} = $ _____

4. $\frac{5}{6} \div \frac{5}{6} = \frac{5}{6} \times \frac{6}{5} = $ _____

5. $\frac{2}{3} \div \frac{5}{6} = \frac{2}{3} \times \frac{6}{5} = $ _____

6. $15 \div \frac{3}{5} = 15 \times \frac{5}{3} = $ _____

Divide. Simplify if necessary.

7. $9 \div \frac{9}{10}$

8. $\frac{2}{3} \div \frac{2}{5}$

9. $\frac{1}{2} \div \frac{2}{3}$

10. $\frac{3}{4} \div 8$

11. $\frac{5}{8} \div \frac{1}{4}$

12. $\frac{3}{1} \div \frac{6}{7}$

13. $\frac{5}{9} \div \frac{2}{3}$

14. $15 \div \frac{3}{4}$

Copy and divide.

15. $\frac{4}{5} \div \frac{3}{10}$

16. $\frac{5}{8} \div 15$

17. $12 \div \frac{2}{3}$

18. $\frac{1}{8} \div \frac{1}{4}$

19. $\frac{1}{4} \div \frac{1}{8}$

20. $\frac{5}{6} \div \frac{5}{9}$

21. $\frac{4}{7} \div \frac{5}{14}$

22. $\frac{7}{12} \div \frac{1}{6}$

23. $16 \div \frac{4}{5}$

24. $\frac{5}{10} \div \frac{2}{3}$

25. $18 \div \frac{5}{6}$

26. $\frac{7}{9} \div \frac{14}{15}$

Problem Solving

Solve each problem. Draw a picture to help you if necessary.

27. A bag of dinner rolls contains 6 rolls and weighs $\frac{2}{3}$ of a pound. What is the weight of 1 roll in pounds?

28. Alan walks for exercise, at the rate of $\frac{2}{3}$ of a mile each 15 minutes. How far can Alan walk in 1 hour?

29. Mei Ling has just received unexpected guests and has only $\frac{3}{4}$ of a pound of nuts for 4 people. What part of a pound will that be for each person?

30. The cafeteria is offering applesauce as an extra dessert today. There are 48 cups of applesauce. Each serving is $\frac{2}{3}$ of a cup. How many servings can be made?

31. Elena uses $\frac{2}{3}$ cup of milk to make custard for 6 people. How much milk will she need if she doubles the recipe?

32. David uses $1\frac{3}{4}$ cups of milk to make pudding. How much milk will he need if he doubles the recipe?

Dividing Mixed Numbers

Roberta is preparing miniature cornhusk dolls for the school craft show. She is using small wooden dowels to make the arms. Each one measures $1\frac{1}{8}$ inches in length. How many dowels can she cut from a piece of wood $5\frac{1}{4}$ inches long?

We are looking for the number of dowels Roberta can cut from a piece of wood.

We know the wood is _____ inches long.

She needs to cut dowels that are _____ inches long. To find the possible number of dowels that can be cut, we divide the length of the wood by the length of one dowel.

We divide _____ by _____.

Rename the mixed numbers as fractions.	Multiply the dividend by the reciprocal of the divisor. Simplify.	Check. Multiply the divisor by the quotient.
$5\frac{1}{4} \div 1\frac{1}{8}$ $\frac{21}{4} \div \frac{9}{8}$	$\frac{21}{4} \times \frac{8}{9} = \frac{168}{36} = 4\frac{24}{36} = 4\frac{2}{3}$	$1\frac{1}{8} \times 4\frac{2}{3}$ $\frac{9}{8} \times \frac{14}{3} = \frac{126}{24} = 5\frac{1}{4}$

dividend

Roberta will cut _____ dowels $1\frac{1}{8}$ inches long.

She will have _____ of a dowel left over.

REMEMBER Whole numbers can be renamed as fractions.

$7 \div 2\frac{1}{4} = \frac{7}{1} \times \frac{4}{9} = \frac{28}{9} = 3\frac{1}{9}$ or $3\frac{4}{10} \div 2 = \frac{34}{10} \times \frac{1}{2} = \frac{34}{20} = 1\frac{7}{10}$

Getting Started

Divide and check.

1. $\frac{5}{9} \div 1\frac{1}{2}$

2. $2\frac{1}{3} \div \frac{3}{5}$

Copy and divide.

3. $2\frac{1}{5} \div 1\frac{1}{3}$

4. $3 \div 4\frac{1}{5}$

5. $6\frac{5}{8} \div 4$

6. $10\frac{6}{9} \div 3\frac{1}{3}$

Practice

Divide and check.

1. $7 \div 2\frac{1}{3}$

2. $1\frac{5}{8} \div 13$

3. $9 \div 1\frac{4}{5}$

4. $6 \div 1\frac{2}{3}$

5. $2\frac{3}{4} \div 1\frac{1}{8}$

6. $4\frac{1}{5} \div 2\frac{3}{5}$

7. $2\frac{5}{8} \div 5\frac{1}{4}$

8. $1\frac{1}{7} \div 1\frac{1}{3}$

9. $5\frac{1}{3} \div \frac{8}{9}$

10. $7 \div 1\frac{3}{4}$

11. $4\frac{1}{2} \div 2\frac{7}{10}$

12. $3\frac{1}{5} \div 3\frac{1}{10}$

13. $6\frac{2}{3} \div 5$

14. $9 \div 3\frac{2}{3}$

15. $5\frac{1}{4} \div 2\frac{1}{3}$

16. $4\frac{1}{8} \div 2\frac{1}{4}$

17. $8\frac{1}{3} \div 6\frac{1}{2}$

18. $7\frac{1}{5} \div 3\frac{3}{4}$

Copy and divide.

19. $12 \div 2\frac{2}{3}$

20. $1\frac{3}{4} \div 2\frac{1}{2}$

21. $5\frac{1}{2} \div 9$

22. $4\frac{1}{8} \div 1\frac{4}{7}$

23. $1\frac{3}{5} \div 1\frac{1}{15}$

24. $3\frac{2}{3} \div 2\frac{1}{6}$

25. $1\frac{3}{16} \div 1\frac{1}{2}$

26. $1\frac{3}{4} \div 2\frac{5}{6}$

27. $21 \div 3\frac{1}{2}$

28. $\frac{9}{10} \div 2\frac{2}{5}$

29. $1\frac{5}{9} \div 1\frac{3}{4}$

30. $2\frac{2}{5} \div 1\frac{1}{3}$

Problem Solving

Solve each problem.

31. Naomi's favorite blouse pattern requires $1\frac{2}{3}$ yards of material. How many blouses can she make from 10 yards?

32. It took Mr. and Mrs. Williams $4\frac{1}{2}$ hours to drive their son to camp. They took turns driving. If Mr. Williams drove $1\frac{1}{2}$ hours, what part of the way did Mr. Williams drive?

33. After avoiding sweets and exercising regularly, Jerry lost $7\frac{1}{5}$ pounds in 6 weeks. What was Jerry's average weekly loss?

34. Mr. and Mrs. Brightwater are planning to build a patio sidewalk using a single row of $\frac{2}{3}$ of a foot square blocks. How many blocks will be needed to build a walk $10\frac{2}{3}$ feet long?

Name _____

Estimating Products and Quotients

Adena wants to make 72 biscuits for a family reunion. She can make 2 dozen biscuits using the recipe on the right. About how much flour will Adena need to make 3 times the recipe?

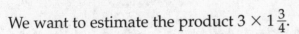

Best Biscuits

$1\frac{3}{4}$	cups	sifted flour
2	teaspoon	salt
2	tablespoons	baking powder
6	tablespoons	cold butter
$\frac{2}{3}$	cup	milk

We want to estimate the product $3 \times 1\frac{3}{4}$.

One way to estimate the product is to round the mixed number.

$1\frac{3}{4}$ rounds to _____   We multiply 3 by _____. $3 \times$ _____ = _____

Using rounding, we estimate Adena needs about _____ cups of flour.

Another way to estimate the product is to change the whole number to a compatible number.

A **compatible number** is a number that is close to the original number, but is easier to use.

Use a number that is close to 3 and makes multiplying by $1\frac{3}{4}$ easy.

_____ is compatible to $1\frac{3}{4}$. We multiply _____ by $1\frac{3}{4}$. _____ $\times 1\frac{3}{4} =$ _____

Using a compatible number, we estimate Adena needs about _____ cups of flour.

We can also use a compatible number to estimate quotients of mixed numbers. To estimate $11 \div 3\frac{1}{3}$, we replace the whole number 11.

First find the reciprocal of $3\frac{1}{3}$. _____

Look for a number that is close to 11 and makes multiplying by $\frac{3}{10}$ easy. $10 \times \frac{3}{10}$ is easy to multiply. Replace 11 with _____ and divide.

$10 \div 3\frac{1}{3} = 10 \times \frac{3}{10} =$ _____

$11 \div 3\frac{1}{3}$ is about _____

Getting Started

Estimate each product or quotient. Use rounding.

1. $1\frac{7}{8} \times 16$ **2.** $5\frac{1}{4} \times 6$ **3.** $12 \div 3\frac{5}{7}$ **4.** $5 \div 9\frac{3}{4}$

Estimate each product or quotient. Use a compatible number.

5. $9 \times \frac{4}{5}$ **6.** $13 \times 1\frac{5}{7}$ **7.** $14 \div \frac{5}{6}$ **8.** $17 \div 2\frac{1}{4}$

Practice

Estimate each product or quotient. Use rounding.

1. $2\frac{5}{6} \times 8$

2. $3\frac{1}{9} \times 7$

3. $9 \times 5\frac{2}{7}$

4. $12 \times 10\frac{3}{4}$

5. $18 \div 1\frac{9}{10}$

6. $32 \div 4\frac{1}{6}$

7. $42 \div 6\frac{1}{8}$

8. $27 \div 2\frac{4}{5}$

9. $4 \div 12\frac{1}{5}$

10. $4\frac{7}{8} \times 6\frac{1}{7}$

11. $15\frac{1}{8} \div 4\frac{7}{9}$

12. $5\frac{6}{7} \times \frac{9}{10}$

Estimate each product or quotient. Use a compatible number.

13. $21 \times 2\frac{2}{5}$

14. $7 \times 1\frac{3}{4}$

15. $8 \times 3\frac{1}{3}$

16. $13 \times \frac{5}{6}$

17. $11 \div 1\frac{1}{5}$

18. $23 \div \frac{8}{9}$

19. $31 \div 2\frac{1}{7}$

20. $17 \div 1\frac{1}{8}$

21. $26 \times 2\frac{1}{4}$

22. $19 \times 1\frac{4}{5}$

23. $39 \div 2\frac{2}{3}$

24. $48 \div 1\frac{3}{4}$

Problem Solving

Use the recipe to solve each problem.

25. Aaron wants to make 4 times the recipe. About how much milk will he need?

26. Mari wants to make 48 popovers. About how much milk will she need?

27. Rewrite the recipe to show the ingredients needed for 8 popovers.

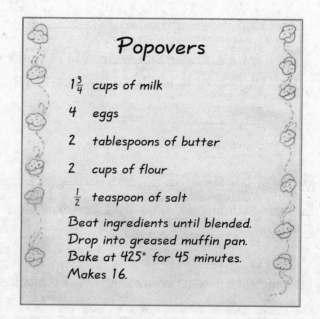

Popovers

$1\frac{3}{4}$ cups of milk

4 eggs

2 tablespoons of butter

2 cups of flour

$\frac{1}{2}$ teaspoon of salt

Beat ingredients until blended.
Drop into greased muffin pan.
Bake at 425° for 45 minutes.
Makes 16.

Name _____

Problem Solving: Use a Formula

A plane flight from Miami to New York City takes 4 hours.
If the total distance in the air is 2,140 miles, what is the
average speed of the plane?

⭐**SEE**

We want to know the rate of speed of the plane.

The flight from Miami to New York City takes _____ hours.

The distance the plane travels is _____ miles.

We can use the formula for finding distance to help us solve
this problem.

The formula is: **Rate × Time = Distance**

The TIME of the trip is _____ hours.

The DISTANCE the plane travels is _____ miles.

⭐**PLAN**

We can use this information and a formula to write an open
sentence. We need to fill in the numbers we know.

   Rate × Time = Distance
     ? × 4 = 2,140

Since we are missing a factor in this problem, we need to
divide to find the rate. **Distance ÷ Time = Rate**

⭐**DO**

$4\overline{)2,140}$

The rate the plane travels is _____ miles per hour.

⭐**CHECK**

We can check our work by using the original formula.

   Rate × Time = Distance
   535 × 4 = _____

**New York
City**

Miami

Apply

Use a formula or open sentence to help solve each problem.

1. The first successful gas-powered car was a three-wheeler, built in 1886 by Carl Benz. If the car could travel 54 miles in 6 hours, how fast was the car traveling?

2. Miss Prentiss won a bicycle race by traveling 168 miles in 8 hours. What was Miss Prentiss' average speed?

3. The Queen Ann ocean liner travels at an average rate of 32 miles per hour. How far would the Queen Ann travel in a 24-hour day?

4. A train travels at an average rate of 80 miles per hour. How long would it take the train to travel between two cities that are 560 miles apart? Hint: Distance ÷ Rate = Time.

5. Miss Muffet's pet spider can travel at an average rate of 55 yards per hour. How many hours would it take the spider to travel 495 yards?

6. The first flight across the Atlantic Ocean took 33 hours and covered a distance of 3,610 miles. What was the plane's approximate rate of speed?

7. Superwoman can circle the Earth five times in a one-hour period. If one trip around the Earth is 25,000 miles, how fast can Superwoman travel?

8. At 7:00 in the morning, Mr. Rash took his dog for a walk around the block. Mr. Rash and his dog returned at 7:30, one half-hour later. The two walked at an average rate of 4 miles per hour. How far did they walk?

9. Anita wants to make a circular tablecloth for a table. The radius of the circular top of the table is 4 feet. She wants the tablecloth to hang down 3 feet all around. Use $A = \frac{22}{7} \times r \times r$ to find the area of the fabric that Anita needs.

10. Ernie multiplied two fractions and wrote the following:

    $$\frac{3}{5} \times \frac{7}{8} = \frac{21}{40}$$

    Did it matter in what order Ernie multiplied the numerators and the denominators? Explain why or why not.

11. If each of two fractions is less than 1, how does their product compare to 1?

12. If each of two fractions is less than 1, how does their product compare to each fraction?

Calculator: Sale Price

Robin always takes her calculator with
her shopping and uses it to help find
the sale prices. What will Robin pay for
the radio if she buys it on sale?

We want to find the sale price of the radio.

The original price was _____.

The price has been reduced by _____.

To find the new price we multiply the original price by
the fraction it is reduced, and subtract that number
from the original price.

We multiply _____ by _____ and divide by _____.

Then we subtract that result from _____.

Complete the codes.

Amount Off

$\frac{2}{3}$ of $49.50   49 $\boxed{\cdot}$ 5 $\boxed{\times}$ 2 $\boxed{\div}$ 3 $\boxed{=}$ $\boxed{}$

Sale Price

$49.50 − _____   49 $\boxed{\cdot}$ 5 $\boxed{−}$ _____ $\boxed{=}$ $\boxed{}$

Robin will play _____ for the radio.

Robin's sister, Ann, uses another method to find the sale price.
She knows that if the sale price is $\frac{2}{3}$ off the original price, the sale
price must be $\frac{1}{3}$ of the original price.

Complete the code to show how Ann thinks.

$\frac{1}{3}$ of $49.50   49.5 $\boxed{\div}$ 3 $\boxed{=}$ $\boxed{}$

Use Ann's method to find the sale price of a stereo costing
$275.25 and being reduced by $\frac{2}{3}$ of the original price.

_____ $\boxed{\div}$ _____ $\boxed{=}$ $\boxed{}$

The sale price of the stereo is _____.

Practice

Use Robin's method to find the sale price.

1. $429, $\frac{1}{3}$ off

2. $625, $\frac{2}{5}$ off

3. $720, $\frac{3}{4}$ off

4. $9.30, $\frac{1}{6}$ off

5. $952.40, $\frac{5}{8}$ off

6. $2,025, $\frac{2}{3}$ off

Use Ann's method to find the sale price.

7. $640, $\frac{3}{4}$ off

8. $984, $\frac{7}{8}$ off

9. $2,082, $\frac{5}{6}$ off

10. $1,674, $\frac{2}{3}$ off

11. $5,224, $\frac{3}{8}$ off

12. $182.95, $\frac{3}{5}$ off

Problem Solving

Solve each problem.

13. Ron saw an ad that gave $\frac{2}{3}$ off all games and books. If games originally sold for $12 and books sold for $9 what were the sale prices?

14. Elaine went to a clothing sale that advertised $\frac{1}{5}$ off. She bought a skirt that originally sold for $56 and a sweater that originally sold for $32.50. How much did Elaine spend on the two items?

Use the ad to solve Problems 15 and 16.

15. Kerry bought a pair of shoes that originally sold for $75. If Kerry paid cash, how much did the shoes cost?

16. Nancy bought a coat that originally sold for $145. If Nancy paid cash, how much did the coat cost?

Write the number for each fractional part.

1. $\frac{2}{3}$ of 9 = _____
2. $\frac{1}{8}$ of $96 = _____
3. $\frac{3}{5}$ of 35 = _____
4. $\frac{1}{10}$ of 640 = _____

5. $\frac{1}{4}$ of $128 = _____
6. $\frac{3}{4}$ of 72 = _____
7. $\frac{2}{5}$ of $125 = _____
8. $\frac{7}{8}$ of 160 = _____

9. $\frac{2}{7}$ of 217 = _____
10. $\frac{4}{5}$ of $195 = _____
11. $\frac{5}{6}$ of $252 = _____
12. $\frac{4}{7}$ of 483 = _____

13. $\frac{3}{10}$ of 820 = _____
14. $\frac{4}{9}$ of $603 = _____
15. $\frac{9}{9}$ of 504 = _____
16. $\frac{3}{7}$ of $406 = _____

Multiply. Simplify if necessary.

17. $\frac{3}{4} \times \frac{5}{6} = _____
18. $\frac{2}{3} \times \frac{1}{4} = _____
19. $\frac{5}{8} \times \frac{7}{10} = _____
20. $\frac{3}{5} \times \frac{10}{21} = _____

21. $7\frac{1}{2} \times 8 = _____
22. $4\frac{1}{2} \times 2\frac{2}{3} = _____
23. $6\frac{1}{2} \times \frac{8}{9} = _____
24. $2\frac{1}{7} \times 4\frac{1}{5} = _____

25. $4\frac{1}{3} \times \frac{3}{8} = _____
26. $5\frac{3}{4} \times \frac{1}{2} = _____
27. $\frac{3}{7} \times 3\frac{3}{4} = _____
28. $\frac{7}{9} \times 2\frac{1}{4} = _____

29. $8\frac{1}{10} \times 2\frac{1}{3} = _____
30. $3\frac{1}{2} \times 4\frac{4}{5} = _____
31. $7\frac{1}{6} \times 8\frac{1}{4} = _____
32. $10\frac{1}{3} \times 6\frac{2}{3} = _____

Write the reciprocal.

33. $\frac{1}{7}$
34. 9
35. $\frac{4}{6}$
36. $5\frac{1}{6}$

37. $\frac{2}{16}$
38. $2\frac{4}{7}$
39. 10
40. $9\frac{2}{5}$

41. $\frac{5}{3}$
42. $5\frac{1}{3}$
43. $\frac{1}{8}$
44. $10\frac{1}{4}$

Divide. Simplify if necessary.

45. $\frac{1}{2} \div \frac{1}{3}$
46. $\frac{2}{3} \div \frac{5}{6}$
47. $\frac{3}{5} \div \frac{9}{10}$
48. $\frac{4}{5} \div \frac{2}{9}$

49. $8 \div 1\frac{1}{5}$
50. $4\frac{2}{3} \div 7$
51. $3\frac{1}{3} \div 2\frac{1}{2}$
52. $6\frac{1}{4} \div 2\frac{1}{2}$

Circle the letter of the correct answer.

1
$421.36
+   89.57

a. $500.93
b. $510.93
c. $511.93
d. NG

2
7,901
− 837

a. 6,974
b. 7,064
c. 7,136
d. NG

3
43,215
− 11,941

a. 31,274
b. 31,374
c. 32,734
d. NG

4
$4.25
×   9

a. $36.25
b. $37.25
c. $38.25
d. NG

5 28 × 74

a. 308
b. 2,052
c. 2,072
d. NG

6 6)7,206

a. 131
b. 1,301
c. 10,301
d. NG

7 63)6,630

a. 15 R15
b. 105 R15
c. 150 R15
d. NG

8 Find the perimeter.

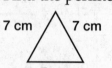

7 cm   7 cm
7 cm

a. 21 cm
b. 21 sq cm
c. 29 sq cm
d. NG

9
5 ft 9 in.
+ 3 ft 8 in.

a. 9 ft 7 in.
b. 9 ft 5 in.
c. 9 ft 3 in.
d. NG

10
$6 \frac{1}{4}$
$+ 7 \frac{5}{8}$

a. $13 \frac{1}{4}$
b. $13 \frac{7}{8}$
c. $14 \frac{1}{8}$
d. NG

11
$9 \frac{1}{3}$
$- 4 \frac{2}{3}$

a. $4 \frac{1}{3}$
b. $4 \frac{2}{3}$
c. $5 \frac{1}{3}$
d. NG

12
$7 \frac{1}{5}$
$- 6 \frac{2}{3}$

a. $\frac{8}{15}$
b. $1 \frac{7}{15}$
c. $1 \frac{8}{15}$
d. NG

score

STOP

Add and Subtract Decimals

Tenths

Ramon agreed to help his father by painting the back and one side of their garage white. What decimal represents the amount Ramon has painted so far?

We want to know how many walls are painted. Each side of the garage has _____ equal boards. Ramon painted _____ boards on the back and _____ boards on the side of the garage.

To write the number of walls painted so far as a decimal, we rename the mixed number $1\frac{3}{10}$. We write $1\frac{3}{10}$ as the decimal **1.3**. We say: **one and three tenths**.

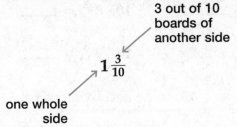

3 out of 10 boards of another side

$1\frac{3}{10}$

one whole side

decimal point

1.3

whole number   decimal number

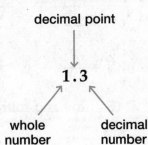

ones	tenths
1	3

Ramon has painted _____ garage walls so far.

Decimal numbers can name parts less than 1. Ramon still has **0.7** of a side of the garage to paint. We say: **seven tenths**.

0 ones → **0.7** ← 7 tenths

Whole numbers can be written as decimal numbers. When Ramon completes both sides, he will have painted **2.0** sides of the garage. We say: **two**.

2 ones → **2.0** ← 0 tenths

Getting Started

Write the decimal for the green part.

1.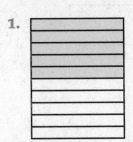

_____

Write a decimal for each number.

2. $6\frac{6}{10} =$ _____

3. $\frac{4}{10} =$ _____

4. five and six tenths _____

Write the decimal in words.

5. 8.1 _____

Practice

Write the decimal for each green part.

1.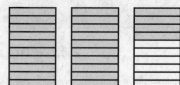

_____

2.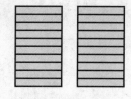

_____

3.

_____

4.

_____

5.

_____

6.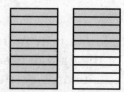

_____

Write a decimal for each number.

7. $2\frac{3}{10} =$ _____

8. $9\frac{9}{10} =$ _____

9. $6\frac{5}{10} =$ _____

10. $8\frac{2}{10} =$ _____

11. $7\frac{1}{10} =$ _____

12. $2\frac{7}{10} =$ _____

13. $6\frac{4}{10} =$ _____

14. $9\frac{8}{10} =$ _____

15. three and one tenth

_____

16. nine and four tenths

_____

17. nine and five tenths

_____

18. six tenths

_____

19. eight

_____

20. four and seven tenths

_____

Write each decimal in words.

21. 7.3 _____

22. 8.6 _____

23. 0.3 _____

24. 5.7 _____

25. 8.9 _____

26. 2.5 _____

27. 9.0 _____

28. 10.1 _____

29. 5.2 _____

30. 9.8 _____

Name _____

Hundredths

Donna is using graph paper to design a floor plan for her living room. What decimal represents the portion of her living room that will be filled with furniture?

We want to know what part of Donna's floor plan is filled with furniture.

The graph paper is divided into _____ equal squares.

Donna filled _____ of these squares with furniture.

To find the decimal number that represents the part that will be filled with furniture, we rename the fraction $\frac{26}{100}$.

We write $\frac{26}{100}$ as the decimal **0.26**. We say: **twenty-six hundredths**.

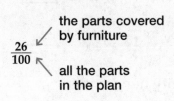

the parts covered by furniture

$\frac{26}{100}$

all the parts in the plan

decimal point

0.26

whole number   decimal number

ones	tenths	hundredths
0	2	6

Donna will fill _____ of the room with furniture.

Getting Started

Write the decimal for each green part.

1.

2. _____

3. _____

Write a decimal for each number.

4. $5\frac{3}{100} =$ _____   5. $\frac{37}{100} =$ _____   6. $\frac{6}{100} =$ _____   7. $9\frac{5}{100} =$ _____

8. two and twenty-five hundredths

_____

9. eighty-five hundredths

_____

Write each decimal in words.

10. 5.03 _____   11. 0.74 _____

12. 2.25 _____   13. 0.86 _____

Practice

Write the decimal for each green part.

1.

2. 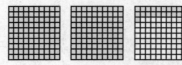 _____

3. _____

4.  _____

5. 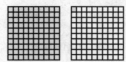 _____

6. _____

Write a decimal for each number.

7. $\frac{67}{100} =$ _____

8. $\frac{4}{100} =$ _____

9. $3\frac{25}{100} =$ _____

10. $2\frac{1}{100} =$ _____

11. $6\frac{96}{100} =$ _____

12. $3\frac{10}{100} =$ _____

13. $4\frac{2}{100} =$ _____

14. $5\frac{19}{100} =$ _____

15. six and nine hundredths

_____

16. fifteen and seventy hundredths

_____

17. four hundredths

_____

18. nine and ninety-nine hundredths

_____

Write each decimal in words.

19. 9.06 _____

20. 0.65 _____

21. 3.75 _____

22. 7.90 _____

Problem Solving

Solve each problem.

23. There are 100 centimeters in 1 meter. Write 48 centimeters as a decimal part of a meter.

24. Bob shot 100 free throws. He missed 14. What decimal represents the number of free throws Bob made?

Thousandths

Fred is hiking to High Ridge to go on a rock hunt. What decimal can be used to represent the distance to High Ridge in kilometers?

We are looking for the hiking distance in kilometers.

It is _____ meters to High Ridge.

There are _____ meters in 1 kilometer.

To write the distance we must rename meters as kilometers by dividing the number of meters by 1,000.

Fractions can represent division. Thus, **1,000$\overline{)465}$** can be written as $\frac{465}{1000}$.

We rename $\frac{465}{1000}$ as the decimal **0.465**.

We say: **four hundred sixty-five thousandths**.

$\frac{465}{1000}$ ← meters hiked
← meters in a kilometer

ones	tenths	hundredths	thousandths
0 .	4	6	5

Fred is hiking _____ of a kilometer to High Ridge.

Getting Started

Write a decimal for each number.

1. $\frac{405}{1000}$ = _____

2. $\frac{136}{1000}$ = _____

3. $\frac{75}{1000}$ = _____

4. $\frac{6}{1000}$ = _____

5. $6\frac{15}{1000}$ = _____

6. $7\frac{120}{1000}$ = _____

7. $12\frac{500}{1000}$ = _____

8. $16\frac{10}{1000}$ = _____

9. seven and three thousandths

_____

10. eight and one hundred seven thousandths

_____

Write each decimal in words.

11. 0.064 _____

12. 9.245 _____

Practice

Write a decimal for each number.

1. $\frac{325}{1000} = $ _____

2. $\frac{16}{1000} = $ _____

3. $\frac{150}{1000} = $ _____

4. $\frac{6}{1000} = $ _____

5. $4\frac{3}{1000} = $ _____

6. $5\frac{214}{1000} = $ _____

7. $8\frac{29}{1000} = $ _____

8. $3\frac{1}{1000} = $ _____

9. $87\frac{4}{1000} = $ _____

10. $12\frac{100}{1000} = $ _____

11. $495\frac{495}{1000} = $ _____

12. $21\frac{86}{1000} = $ _____

13. two hundred fifteen thousandths

_____

14. six and twelve thousandths

_____

15. nine thousandths

_____

16. seven and fifty-six thousandths

_____

17. nine and forty-eight thousandths

_____

18. seven and two hundred nine thousandths

_____

19. seventeen and four thousandths

_____

20. three hundred eleven thousandths

_____

Write each decimal in words.

21. 0.531 _____

22. 4.004 _____

23. 5.230 _____

24. 2.015 _____

25. 7.216 _____

26. 66.033 _____

Problem Solving

Solve each problem.

27. In a poll of 1,000 teenagers, 428 preferred the color blue. What decimal represents the number of teens that did not prefer blue?

28. Mr. Ellis returned $1,000 he had borrowed from his credit union. He paid $88 in interest. What decimal represents the amount of interest paid by Mr. Ellis?

Name _____

Place Value to Thousandths

Janice is the timekeeper for the Blue Team in the Road Runner Relay. She must use a very accurate timer. How long has it taken for the Blue Team to finish the first 5 laps?

We want to read the decimal number that tells the Blue Team's time for the first 5 laps.

The timer shows _____ seconds have passed.

We use the place value chart to help us understand this number.

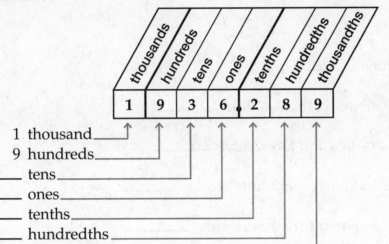

1 thousand
9 hundreds
_____ tens
_____ ones
_____ tenths
_____ hundredths
_____ thousandths

The Blue Team took _____

_____

seconds to run the 5 laps.

Getting Started

Write the place value of each green digit.

1. 7.25 6   **2.** 23.92   **3.** 157.834   **4.** 16.840

_____   _____   _____   _____

5. 2,365.381   **6.** 526.3   **7.** 19.003   **8.** 374.218

_____   _____   _____   _____

Write the decimal for each number.

9. three hundred ninety-five and one hundred eight thousandths _____

10. six thousand seven and nineteen thousandths _____

Practice

Write the place value of each green digit.

1. 5.231

_____

2. 16.205

_____

3. 0.96

_____

4. 751.6

_____

5. 852.14

_____

6. 396.21

_____

7. 47.304

_____

8. 2,158.05

_____

9. 3,341.9

_____

10. 7,298.51

_____

11. 26.395

_____

12. 765.27

_____

Write the decimal for each number.

13. five hundred sixteen and six tenths _____

14. eighty-nine and eight hundred twenty-six thousandths _____

15. one thousand, three hundred thirty-five and five tenths _____

16. six thousand, two hundred nine and thirty-eight hundredths _____

17. one hundred seventeen and two hundred fifty thousandths _____

Now Try This!

If our place-value system were based on five instead of ten, we would regroup after every five units and the place-value positions would be 1, 5, 25 (five 5s), 125 (five 25s), and so on instead of 1, 10, 100, 1000, ... We can rewrite our base-ten numbers as base-five numbers by thinking of them as groups of 125s, 25s, 5s and 1s.

Base 10 Numbers

$7 = (1 \times 5) + (2 \times 1)$

$69 = (2 \times 25) + (3 \times 5) + (4 \times 1)$

$234 = (1 \times 125) + (4 \times 25) + (1 \times 5) + (4 \times 1)$

Base Five Values			
125	25	5	1
		1	2
	2	3	4
1	4	1	4

Write the base-five numbers for the base-ten counting numbers 1 to 26.

_____

_____

Lesson 10-4 • Place Value to Thousandths

Name _____

Comparing and Ordering Decimals

It's Algebra!

The top three competitors in the county track meet ran faster than 12 seconds in the 100-meter dash. List them in order by their finishing times.

We need to list the three competitors in the order of fastest to slowest.

Williams finished in _____ seconds, Harrison in _____ seconds and Jones in _____ seconds.

To compare their finishing times, we find and label _____, _____, and _____ on a number line.

```
        11.7                  Jones                              11.9
                              11.8
    ←——┼──┼──┼──┼──┼──┼──┼──┼──┼──┼──┼──┼──┼──┼──┼──┼──→
      11.70        11.75      ↑    11.80        11.85↑    11.90
                            11.78                 11.86
                           Harrison              Williams
```

REMEMBER Zeros to the far right of a decimal number do not change its value.

Thus, **11.8 = 11.80**.

We can also compare these times using place values.

Same number of tens and ones	11.78 has less tenths.	11.80 has less hundredths.	Arranged from greatest to smallest
	11.7 ◯ 11.8	11.80 ◯ 11.86	
11.**86**	11.**86**	11.**86**	11.**86**
11.**78**	11.**78**	11.**80**	11.**80**
11.**80**	11.**80**		11.**78**

Since the runner with the shortest time places first, the order of finish is first place: _____, second place: _____ and last: _____.

Getting Started

Compare. Write >, =, or < in each circle.

1. 7.215 ◯ 7.251   **2.** 9.8 ◯ 9.800   **3.** 15.531 ◯ 15.315

Write in order from least to greatest.

4. 6.21, 6.12, 6.1, 6.15

5. 48.334, 48.33, 48.343, 48.3

_____   _____

Practice

Compare. Write >, =, or < in each circle.

1. 9.315 ◯ 9.215

2. 5.036 ◯ 5.306

3. 14.21 ◯ 14.26

4. 0.024 ◯ 0.026

5. 9.20 ◯ 9.200

6. 125 ◯ 125.6

7. 3.761 ◯ 3.706

8. 7.003 ◯ 7.03

9. 5.1 ◯ 5.100

10. 19.5 ◯ 19.36

11. 112.06 ◯ 110.06

12. 48.7 ◯ 48.763

13. 126.41 ◯ 126.1

14. 29 ◯ 29.02

15. 14.374 ◯ 14.375

Write in order from least to greatest.

16. 9.11, 9.10, 9.01

17. 17.095, 17.19, 17.509

18. 38.271, 38.27, 38.197

_____

_____

_____

Problem Solving

Solve each problem.
Use the table of winning records to answer Problems 19 through 21.

19. Which team has the best record?

_____

20. Which team has the worst record?

_____

21. Write the decimals in order from least to greatest.

_____ _____ _____ _____ _____

Long Jump Winning Records	
Team	**Distance**
Lincoln	0.689
Washington	0.750
King	0.721
Anthony	0.685
Jefferson	0.769

Use the table of metric equivalents for Exercise 22 and 23.

22. Carol lives 2.65 kilometers from school. Heather lives 2,650 meters from school. Who lives farther from school?

_____

23. Which is larger, 5.96 centimeters or 596 millimeters?

_____

Metric Equivalents
1 kilometer = 1,000 meters
1 meter = 100 centimeters
1 meter = 1,000 millimeters
1 centimeter = 10 millimeters

Lesson 10-5 • Comparing and Ordering Decimals

Name _____

Adding Decimals

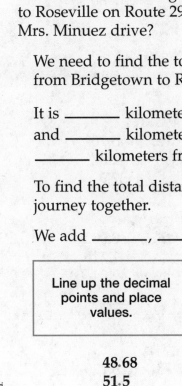

Bridgetown

Mrs. Minuez is driving from Bridgetown to Roseville on Route 29. How far will Mrs. Minuez drive?

48.68 km

Centerville

We need to find the total driving distance from Bridgetown to Roseville.

It is _____ kilometers from Bridgetown to Centerville, and _____ kilometers from Centerville to Gilman, and _____ kilometers from Gilman to Roseville.

51.5 km

To find the total distance, we add the three stages of the journey together.

We add _____, _____ and _____.

Gilman

37.25 km

Roseville

Line up the decimal points and place values.	Zeros may be placed to the far right without changing the decimal's value.	Add from right to left. Place the decimal point between the ones and the tenths.

$$
\begin{array}{r}
48.68 \\
51.5 \\
+\ 37.25 \\
\hline
\end{array}
\qquad
\begin{array}{r}
48.68 \\
51.50 \\
+\ 37.25 \\
\hline
\end{array}
\qquad
\begin{array}{r}
48.68 \\
51.50 \\
+\ 37.25 \\
\hline
\end{array}
$$

Mrs. Minuez drove _____ kilometers from Bridgetown to Roseville.

REMEMBER When adding a whole number to a decimal number, place a decimal point and zeros after the whole number.

54.72 + 31 should be set up:
$$
\begin{array}{r}
54.72 \\
+\ 31.00 \\
\hline
\end{array}
$$

Getting Started

Add.

1.
$$
\begin{array}{r}
4.36 \\
+\ 2.59 \\
\hline
\end{array}
$$

2.
$$
\begin{array}{r}
12.9 \\
+\ 7.38 \\
\hline
\end{array}
$$

3.
$$
\begin{array}{r}
4.739 \\
+\ 1.821 \\
\hline
\end{array}
$$

4.
$$
\begin{array}{r}
11.24 \\
6.1 \\
+\ 9.306 \\
\hline
\end{array}
$$

Copy and add.

5. 15 + 1.51

6. 4.018 + 91.79

7. 13 + 0.57 + 2.14

Practice

Add.

1. 6.81
      + 4.75

2. 29.7
      + 48.6

3. 39.21
      + 14.7

4. 4.372
      + 1.985

5. 12.762
      + 9.36

6. 18.4
      + 75.329

7. 27.8
      + 39.2

8. 78
      + 6.06

9. 4.372
      2.189
      + 8.754

10. 9.62
      11.8
      + 18.375

11. 18.28
      29
      + 56.3

12. 45.702
      42.37
      + 37.9

13. 751.06
      90.24
      + 872.16

14. 234.31
      178.31
      + 800.07

15. 12
      0.07
      + 123.45

16. 0.002
      1.713
      + 42.04

Copy and add.

17. 18.6 + 17.3

18. 29.65 + 38.29

19. 12.731 + 18.296

20. 15.27 + 28.9

21. 7.593 + 18.2

22. 49.75 + 85.392

23. 13.721 + 12.58 + 26.85

24. 6.475 + 8.21 + 9.323 + 8.4

25. 12.14 + 61.96 + 5.115

26. 1.183 + 19.31 + 720 + 8.04

27. 14.92 + 1.812 + 106.6

28. 329.8 + 33.01 + 4.92

29. 86.86 + 423 + 0.001 + 1.7

30. 289.76 + 22.22 + 4.007

Problem Solving

Solve each problem.

31. Find the perimeter of a rectangle that is 36.25 centimeters wide and 14.72 centimeters long.

32. One bucket holds 13.735 liters of water. Another bucket holds 4.815 liters more water than the first. How many liters of water will both buckets hold altogether?

Subtracting Decimals

Hilo has the highest rainfall average in Hawaii and Honolulu has the lowest average. How much more rain does Hilo average each year than Honolulu?

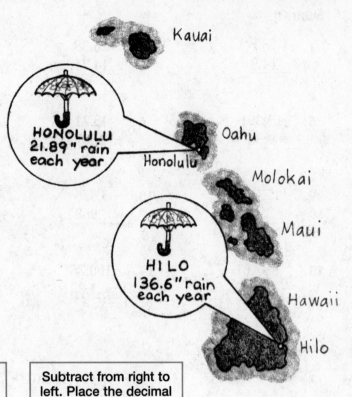

We want to find the difference in rainfall between the two cities.

Hilo averages _____ inches of rain each year.

Honolulu averages _____ inches of rain each year.

To find the difference, we subtract Honolulu's average rainfall from that of Hilo.

We subtract _____ from _____.

Line up the decimal points and place values.	Zeros may be placed to the far right without changing the decimal's value.	Subtract from right to left. Place the decimal point between the ones and the tenths.

$$\begin{array}{r} 136.6 \\ -\ 21.89 \\ \hline \end{array}$$

$$\begin{array}{r} 136.60 \\ -\ 21.89 \\ \hline \end{array}$$

$$\begin{array}{r} 136.60 \\ -\ 21.89 \\ \hline 114.71 \end{array}$$

On the average, it rains _____ inches more each year in Hilo than in Honolulu.

Getting Started

Subtract.

1. $\begin{array}{r} 9.8 \\ -\ 6.4 \\ \hline \end{array}$

2. $\begin{array}{r} 127.34 \\ -\ 68.5 \\ \hline \end{array}$

3. $\begin{array}{r} 3.926 \\ -\ 1.581 \\ \hline \end{array}$

4. $\begin{array}{r} 5.8 \\ -\ 2.785 \\ \hline \end{array}$

Copy and subtract.

5. $29.372 - 14.785$

6. $18 - 7.328$

7. $493.8 - 237.46$

8. $127.5 - 4.98$

9. $254.09 - 31.799$

10. $572.34 - 28.3$

Practice

Subtract.

1. 18.7
   − 14.9

2. 26.38
   − 14.71

3. 38.421
   − 16.549

4. 73.5
   − 16.68

5. 15.391
   − 9.36

6. 48.21
   − 12.875

7. 74.32
   − 18.7

8. 89.8
   − 14.962

9. 125
   − 8.75

10. 3.876
    − 1.968

11. 4.003
    − 2.96

12. 15.21
    − 7.857

13. 987.01
    − 42.99

14. 100.78
    − 1.87

15. 17.341
    − 16.279

16. 87.47
    − 83.81

Copy and subtract.

17. 49.75 − 39.87

18. 146.01 − 57.376

19. 59.327 − 16.9

20. 25 − 3.721

21. 67.39 − 58.5

22. 86.215 − 19.392

23. 50.06 − 39.781

24. 375.9 − 148.48

25. 939.6 − 758.972

26. 17.76 − 12.02

27. 4.86 − 2.99

28. 86.67 − 86.66

29. 751.06 − 30.31

30. 184.14 − 125.09

31. 111.07 − 99.9

Problem Solving

Solve each problem.

32. A jar that held 3.348 liters of water now is holding 1.5 liters. How much water has been poured out?

33. In two hours, the barometer dropped 0.15. The current reading is 29.89. What was the reading before it began to drop two hours ago?

34. Lin bought a pair of pants for $39.95 and a shirt for $8.45. How much change did he receive from a fifty-dollar bill?

35. Roxanne purchased 4.5 kilograms of ground beef yesterday. She froze some of it in 2 packs, one weighing 2.6 kilograms and the other 1.5 kilograms. She made hamburgers out of the remaining beef. How much beef was made into hamburgers?

Rounding Decimals

Measurements are never exact. They are only approximate numbers. Rounding decimal numbers, such as these weight measurements, makes them easier to add or subtract. Round each of the pictured measurements to the nearest tenth.

We want to round the decimal numbers, _____ and _____, to the nearest tenth.

To round a decimal, look at the digit to the right of the place you want to round to.

If the digit to the right is **less than 5**, the digit you are rounding to stays the same and you drop all digits to the right.	If the digit to the right is **5 or more**, add 1 to the digit you are rounding to and drop all digits to the right.
42.71$\longrightarrow$ 42.7	32.481$\longrightarrow$ 32.5

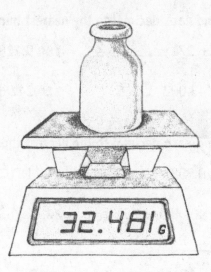

42.71
32.481
Round $\uparrow\uparrow$ Look
here.   here.

42.71 rounded to the nearest tenth is _____.

32.481 rounded to the nearest tenth is _____.

Getting Started

Round each decimal to the nearest whole number.

1. 17.8 _____ **2.** 9.63 _____ **3.** 11.05 _____ **4.** 6.591 _____

Round each decimal to the nearest tenth.

5. 26.73 _____ **6.** 7.05 _____ **7.** 27.391 _____ **8.** 14.51 _____

Round each decimal to the nearest hundredth.

9. 6.078 _____ **10.** 19.999 _____ **11.** 16.834 _____ **12.** 4.009 _____

Round each decimal to the nearest thousandth.

13. 16.5834 _____ **14.** 20.0045 _____ **15.** 7.1395 _____ **16.** 9.1996 _____

Practice

Round each decimal to the nearest whole number.

1. 14.2 _____
2. 6.85 _____
3. 17.061 _____
4. 4.37 _____

5. 89.76 _____
6. 32.4 _____
7. 96.54 _____
8. 128.276 _____

Round each decimal to the nearest tenth.

9. 6.25 _____
10. 9.387 _____
11. 11.006 _____
12. 58.715 _____

13. 215.87 _____
14. 903.99 _____
15. 76.508 _____
16. 15.75 _____

Round each decimal to the nearest hundredth.

17. 6.271 _____
18. 9.128 _____
19. 14.375 _____
20. 49.666 _____

21. 43.002 _____
22. 24.964 _____
23. 72.411 _____
24. 105.315 _____

Round each decimal to the nearest thousandth.

25. 0.3587 _____
26. 1.7625 _____
27. 8.0946 _____
28. 5.1515 _____

29. 4.5994 _____
30. 2.7333 _____
31. 6.0007 _____
32. 0.9999 _____

Now Try This!

When a number is multiplied by itself several times, a special notation called an **exponent** is used as a shorthand form. In the equation, $3 \times 3 \times 3 \times 3 = 3^4$, 3 is called the **base** and 4 is the **exponent**. The exponent indicates how many times to use the base as a factor. Write the standard product for each of the following exponential expressions. The first one is done for you.

1. $5^4 = 5 \times 5 \times 5 \times 5 = 625$

2. $3^4 \times 3^2 =$ _____ = _____

3. $1^8 \times 5^2 \times 2^2 =$ _____ = _____

4. $2^3 \times 3^2 =$ _____ = _____

5. $10^4 =$ _____ = _____

6. $5^2 \times 5^2 =$ _____ = _____

Lesson 10-8 • Rounding Decimals

Estimating Sums and Differences

Elena bought lunch in the cafeteria each day. About how much money did she spend on food the first three days of the week?

Lunch	
Mon	$ 2.85
Tues	$ 3.55
Wed	$ 3.19

We can use rounding or front-end estimation to estimate sums.

Use rounding. Round to the nearest whole number.	Use front-end estimation. Add the dollars.

$$\begin{array}{ccc} \$2.85 & \rightarrow & \$3 \\ 3.55 & \rightarrow & 4 \\ + 3.19 & \rightarrow & + 3 \\ \hline \end{array}$$

$$\begin{array}{c} \$2.85 \\ 3.55 \\ + 3.19 \\ \hline \end{array}$$

Elena spent about _____.

Elena spent more than $8. How do you know?

_____

Elena paid for her lunch on Tuesday with a ten-dollar bill. About how much change did she receive?

We can use rounding or front-end estimation to estimate differences.

Use rounding. Round to the nearest whole number.	Use front-end estimation. Add the dollars.

$$\begin{array}{ccc} \$10.00 & \rightarrow & \$10 \\ - 3.57 & \rightarrow & - 4 \\ \hline \end{array}$$

$$\begin{array}{c} \$10.00 \\ - 3.57 \\ \hline \end{array}$$

Elena received about _____ in change.

Elena received less than $7 in change. How do you know?

_____

Getting Started

Estimate each sum or difference. Tell how you estimated.

1.	2.	3.	4.
$25.67 + 12.05	8.37 + 0.9	17.32 − 8.53	3.65 − 0.8

about _____

about _____

about _____

about _____

_____

_____

_____

_____

Practice

Estimate each sum or difference. Tell how you estimated.

1. $4.25
    + 1.98

    about _____

    _____

2. 5.12
    + 2.8

    about _____

    _____

3. 2.4
    + 3.3

    about _____

    _____

4. 1.18
    + 0.67

    about _____

    _____

5. 10.86
    + 5.4

    about _____

    _____

6. 28.2
    + 12.95

    about _____

    _____

7. 5.07
    + 2.59

    about _____

    _____

8. $1.89
    + 0.35

    about _____

    _____

9. 2.75
    − 1.05

    about _____

    _____

10. 4.37
    − 2.8

    about _____

    _____

11. 18.01
    − 15.68

    about _____

    _____

12. $4.37
    − 1.78

    about _____

    _____

13. 3.8
    − 1.2

    about _____

    _____

14. $9.05
    − 0.75

    about _____

    _____

15. 5.15
    − 3.2

    about _____

    _____

16. 10.01
    − 7.28

    about _____

    _____

Copy, and use rounding to estimate each sum or difference.

17. 1.4 + 6.83

18. $9 + $2.59

19. 3.1 + 4.68 + 2.05

20. $5.30 − $2.75

21. 4.08 − 0.98

22. 6.14 − 3.56

Problem Solving

Use the price list to solve each problem.

23. Pilar bought a postcard, a lighthouse, and a magnet. About how much did she spend?

24. About how much more does it cost to buy a lighthouse than a magnet?

25. Tyrell bought a crab pin and a magnet. He paid with a ten-dollar bill. About how much change should he get back?

Gift Shop

Postcards $0.55

Lighthouses $4.75

Magnets $1.89

Crab Pin $2.40

Lesson 10-9 • Estimating Sums and Differences

Practice: Adding and Subtracting Decimals

On her business trips to Los Angeles and San Francisco, Mrs. Banks travels around the cities by cab. How much more per mile does it cost her to ride a cab in Los Angeles than San Francisco?

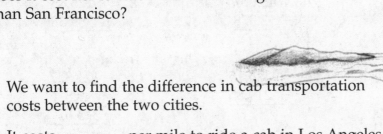

We want to find the difference in cab transportation costs between the two cities.

It costs _____ per mile to ride a cab in Los Angeles and _____ per mile to ride in San Francisco.

To find the difference, we subtract the cost per mile of a cab ride in San Francisco from the cost per mile in Los Angeles.

We subtract _____ from _____.

Line up the decimal points and place values.	Subtract from right to left. Place the decimal point between the ones and the tenths.
60.69¢ − 58.16¢	60.69¢ − 58.16¢ 2.53¢

REMEMBER Use a cent symbol, ¢, when the digits to the left of the decimal point refer to cents.

We read **2.53¢** as **two and fifty-three hundredths cents** and understand that the amount is between 2¢ and 3¢.

It costs _____ per mile more to ride a cab in Los Angeles.

Getting Started

Add or subtract.

1. $37.48
   − 16.95

2. 7.862
   + 1.38

3. $217.15
   + 622.48

4. 19.73
   − 8.285

Copy, and add or subtract.

5. 79 − 0.79

6. $447.23 + $138.15

7. 560.19 − 8.7

8. 103.01 + 0.59

Practice

Add or subtract.

1. 29.7
   + 16.85

2. $30.15
   −   9.86

3. 4.8
   − 2.796

4. 39.751
   + 18.56

5. $138.50
   −   79.97

6. 182.47
   + 96.5

7. 45.007
   − 12.378

8. $126.85
   + 589.38

9. 67.85
   38.4
   + 15.76

10. 59
   − 7.85

11. $475.15
   − 219.85

12. 121.327
   9.8
   + 375.67

Copy, and add or subtract.

13. 159.46 − 83.75

14. 379.2 + 186.38

15. $457.56 − $196.88

16. 486.5 − 97.964

17. $49.68 + $800.41

18. 752.4 + 379.621

19. 758.85 − 147.975

20. 365 − 29.76

21. 189.5 + 79.95 + 265.4

Problem Solving

Solve each problem.

22. A molding machine accepts steel cut into lengths of 17.36 centimeters. A piece cut into 17.365 centimeters is rejected. What is the difference in the length of the two pieces?

23. The average cost of T-bone steak was $4.05 a pound in 1985. By 1991, the average price was $5.21 a pound. If the price continues to climb at the same rate, how much will the meat cost per pound in 1997?

Use the graph of snowfall to answer Problems 24 and 25.

24. How much less did it snow in the two months of November and December than in the three months of January, February, and March?

25. The record snowfall in Skiville in one year is 25 feet. How close to the record is this year's snowfall?

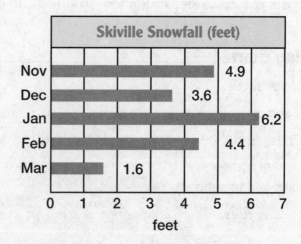

Skiville Snowfall (feet)

Nov 4.9
Dec 3.6
Jan 6.2
Feb 4.4
Mar 1.6

0 1 2 3 4 5 6 7
feet

Problem Solving: Work Backward

Ann spent half of her money on a birthday present for her mother. She then spent half of what was left on two CDs for herself. On the way home, Ann met Pat who returned the five dollars Ann had lent her. Ann now had $20. How much money did she have at the start?

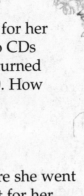

⭐ SEE

We want to know how much money Ann had before she went shopping. She spent half of her money on a present for her mother. She spent half of what was left for two CDs.

She got _____ from a friend. Ann ended up with _____ left.

⭐ PLAN

Since we know that Ann had $20 in the end, and we know how Ann spent her money, we can work backward to find out how much she had to start.

⭐ DO

$20 − $5 = $15   This is the amount of money Ann had before Pat returned $5.00.

$15 × 2 = $30   Since Ann spent half of what was left on CDs, we can double what she had left to find out what she had before buying the CDs.

$30 × 2 = _____   Since Ann spent half of her money on a present for her mother, we can double what she had after buying the gift to find the amount she started with.

Ann had _____ at the start.

⭐ CHECK

We can check our solution by working forward.

$\frac{1}{2}$ of $60 = _____ (The amount Ann spent on the gift)

$60 − $30 = _____ (The amount of money Ann had left after buying the gift)

$\frac{1}{2}$ of $30 = _____ (The amount Ann spent on CDs)

$30 − $15 = _____ (The amount of money Ann had left after buying the CDs)

$15 + $5 = _____ (The amount of money Ann had left after the $5.00 was returned)

Apply

Solve each problem.

1. If I multiply my age by three and add 40, I get 85. How old am I?

2. Jenny bought a compass for $0.59. Then she bought a notebook that cost four times as much as the compass. She received $2.05 in change. How much money did she give the clerk?

3. Mark spent 30 minutes eating dinner, 15 minutes helping with the dishes, and 1 hour practicing piano. He then spent one and one-half hours on homework, and 30 minutes reading. He went to bed at 9:00. What time did Mark start eating dinner?

4. The perimeter of a rectangle is 58 inches. One half of the width is 6 inches. What is the length of the rectangle?

5. In a Silly-Day contest, George made 100 paper hats in 5 hours. Each hour he made 6 less than he did the previous hour. How many hats did he make during each hour?

6. At the Farmer's Market, a farmer sold half of all the watermelons he had plus half of another watermelon. He had 8 watermelons left. How many watermelons did he have to start with?

> **Problem-Solving Strategy:**
> **Using the Four-Step Plan**
> ★ **SEE** What do you need to find?
> ★ **PLAN** What do you need to do?
> ★ **DO** Follow the plan.
> ★ **CHECK** Does your answer make sense?

7. Puff Dragon's tail is 1.84 meters long. Poof Dragon's tail is 1.57 meters long. Without calculating tell whether the difference in the lengths of the tails is greater or less than 1 meter.

8. Puff Dragon worked a subtraction problem with decimals and found the correct answer to be 37.6. If he increased each of the two numbers in the subtraction problem by 3.4, what answer would he get?

9. Poof Dragon eats 8.5 apples a day to keep the dragon doctor away. Tell whether this is more or less than 260 apples per month and explain how you got your answer.

Lesson 10-11 • Problem Solving: Work Backward

Write a decimal for each number.

1. $7\frac{9}{10}$ = _____

2. $6\frac{5}{100}$ = _____

3. $\frac{8}{1000}$ = _____

4. seventy-four hundredths = _____

5. five and six thousandths _____

6. fourteen thousandths = _____

7. five and seven hundredths _____

Write the place value of each green digit.

8. 29.461

9. 3,485.1

10. 6.009

11. 138.756

_____   _____   _____   _____

Write <, =, or > in each circle.

12. 19.2 ◯ 19.20

13. 6.75 ◯ 6.7

14. 3.006 ◯ 3.018

15. 0.621 ◯ 0.612

Add.

16. 742.6
   + 139.24

17. 16.308
   + 9.75

18. 421.326
   + 385.775

19.   7.09
      4.276
   + 8.932

Subtract.

20. 39.754
   − 15.296

21. 2.039
   − 0.75

22. 29
   − 6.75

23. 126.35
   − 97.482

Round each decimal to the nearest tenth.

24. 17.39 _____

25. 32.985 _____

26. 8.31 _____

Round each decimal to the nearest hundredth.

27. 126.372 _____

28. 829.085 _____

29. 283.192 _____

Round each decimal to the nearest thousandth.

30. 5.3645 _____

31. 12.1993 _____

32. 25.0996 _____

CUMULATIVE ASSESSMENT

Circle the letter of the correct answer.

1 12,375
    + 8,196
   a. 10,461
   b. 20,461
   c. 20,571
   d. NG

2 7,046
    − 2,685
   a. 4,361
   b. 5,381
   c. 5,641
   d. NG

3 $6.25
    ×   9
   a. $55.85
   b. $56.25
   c. $58.25
   d. NG

4 39×57
   a. 468
   b. 2,123
   c. 2,423
   d. NG

5 $3\overline{)30,603}$
   a. 121
   b. 10,201
   c. 1,201
   d. NG

6 $27\overline{)1,300}$
   a. 48
   b. 48 R4
   c. 48 R6
   d. NG

7 Find the volume.
Length = 9 cm
Width = 6 cm
Height = 2 cm
   a. 17 cu cm
   b. 56 cu cm
   c. 108 cu cm
   d. NG

8 6 ft 9 in.
    + 2 ft 6 in.
   a. 8 ft 3 in.
   b. 9 ft 3 in.
   c. 9 ft 5 in.
   d. NG

9 Simplify.
$\frac{28}{6}$
   a. $\frac{14}{3}$
   b. $4\frac{2}{3}$
   c. $4\frac{3}{4}$
   d. NG

10 $5\frac{1}{3}$
    $+ 2\frac{5}{8}$
   a. $7\frac{3}{4}$
   b. $8\frac{1}{24}$
   c. $8\frac{3}{4}$
   d. NG

11 $9\frac{7}{8}$
    $- 3\frac{1}{8}$
   a. $5\frac{3}{4}$
   b. $7\frac{3}{4}$
   c. $7\frac{7}{8}$
   d. NG

12 $11\frac{1}{3}$
    $- 9\frac{2}{5}$
   a. $\frac{14}{15}$
   b. $1\frac{1}{15}$
   c. $1\frac{14}{15}$
   d. NG

score

STOP

Name _____

Multiply and Divide Decimals

Estimating Decimal Products

Paul and his father catch and sell lobsters to earn money. How much will they earn for a lobster that weighs 1.75 pounds?

We can use rounding or compatible numbers to estimate products.

REMEMBER Compatible numbers are numbers that are close to the original numbers, but that are easier to use.

Lobster Today
$ 3.49 lb

Use rounding

┌─────────────────────────┐
│ Round each factor to   │
│ the nearest whole   │
│ number.   │
└─────────────────────────┘

$$\begin{array}{r} \$3.49 \rightarrow \quad 3 \\ \times\ 1.75 \rightarrow \times\ 2 \\ \hline \underline{} \end{array}$$

They will earn about _____.

Use compatible numbers

┌─────────────────────────┐
│ Substitute numbers that │
│ are easier to multiply. │
└─────────────────────────┘

$$\begin{array}{r} \$3.49 \rightarrow \quad 3.5 \\ \times\ 1.75 \rightarrow \times\ 2 \\ \hline \underline{} \end{array}$$

They will earn about _____.

Getting Started

Estimate by rounding.

1. $\begin{array}{r} 18 \\ \times\ 2.1 \\ \hline \end{array}$

    about _____

2. $\begin{array}{r} 4.8 \\ \times\ 3 \\ \hline \end{array}$

    about _____

3. $\begin{array}{r} \$2.85 \\ \times\ 1.38 \\ \hline \end{array}$

    about _____

4. $\begin{array}{r} 9.6 \\ \times\ 2.09 \\ \hline \end{array}$

    about _____

Use compatible numbers to estimate. Write the numbers you used.

5. $\begin{array}{r} 9.03 \\ \times\ 1.5 \\ \hline \end{array}$

    about _____

6. $\begin{array}{r} 18.25 \\ \times\ 2.39 \\ \hline \end{array}$

    about _____

7. $\begin{array}{r} 2.5 \\ \times\ 8 \\ \hline \end{array}$

    about _____

8. $\begin{array}{r} \$123.42 \\ \times\ 4.18 \\ \hline \end{array}$

    about _____

Practice

Estimate by rounding.

1. 8.6
    × 2.8

    about _____

2. 2.37
    × 1.9

    about _____

3. $72.55
    ×   5

    about _____

4. 17
    × 0.89

    about _____

5. 7.32
    × 3.9

    about _____

6. $9.87
    ×   6

    about _____

7. $8.20
    × 0.93

    about _____

8. 40.1
    × 4.68

    about _____

Use compatible numbers to estimate. Write the numbers you used.

9. $13.95
    ×   1.5

    about _____

10. 3.18
    × 26.2

    about _____

11. 23
    × 5.6

    about _____

12. 9.29
    × 2.8

    about _____

13. 5.8
    × 9.6

    about _____

14. 9.9
    × 4.3

    about _____

15. $105.98
    ×   3.8

    about _____

16. 18
    × 4.5

    about _____

Copy and estimate each product by rounding.

17. 3.9 × 4.21

18. 1.98 × 7

19. 9.2 × 6.4

20. 12.05 × 2.89

21. 5.3 × $7.99

22. 27.05 × 4.54

23. 8.3 × 6.72

24. 1.72 × 15

25. 2.35 × 1.85

Problem Solving

Use the price list to solve each problem.

26. About how much will 4 pounds of cheese cost?

27. About how much will 1.35 pounds of turkey cost?

28. Rose has $5.00. Does she have enough money to
    buy 3 pounds of potato salad? Explain.

29. Mike buys 2.25 pounds of ham and 1.67 pounds
    of cheese. About how much will it cost altogether?

Deli Sale
Ham $4.49 lb
Turkey $4.79 lb
Swiss Cheese
        $5.25 lb
Potato Salad
    $1.99 lb

Multiplying a Whole Number and a Decimal

Rita has 4 gallons of water to carry to her garden. Each gallon weighs 8.33 pounds. What is the total weight of the water?

We want to know the total weight of all the water.

Each gallon of water weighs _____ pounds.

Rita will carry _____ gallons of water.

To find the total weight, we multiply the weight of one gallon by the number of gallons carried.

We multiply _____ by _____.

$$
\begin{array}{rl}
8.33 & \text{2 decimal places} \\
\times\ \ 4 & \text{0 decimal places} \\
\hline
33.32 & \text{2 decimal places}
\end{array}
$$

Four gallons of water will weigh _____ pounds.

REMEMBER To multiply a decimal and a whole number, multiply as if they were both whole numbers. The product will have the same number of decimal places as the decimal factor.

Getting Started

Place the decimal point in each product.

1. 3.45
    × 7
    ────
    2 4 1 5

2. 2.365
    × 3
    ────
    7 0 9 5

3. 1.5
    × 93
    ────
    1 3 9 5

4. 8.05
    × 124
    ────
    9 9 8 2 0

Multiply.

5. 2.7
    × 8

6. $4.26
    × 24

7. 148
    × 3.6

8. 7.215
    × 7

Copy and multiply.

9. 6 × 5.18

10. 9.5 × 1,340

11. 20 × 1.271

12. 8,561 × 1.2

Practice

Place the decimal point in each product.

1.
$$\begin{array}{r} 23 \\ \times\ 0.6 \\ \hline 138 \end{array}$$

2.
$$\begin{array}{r} 5.8 \\ \times\ 7 \\ \hline 406 \end{array}$$

3.
$$\begin{array}{r} \$1.59 \\ \times\ 8 \\ \hline \$1272 \end{array}$$

4.
$$\begin{array}{r} 654 \\ \times\ 0.5 \\ \hline 3270 \end{array}$$

5.
$$\begin{array}{r} 8.39 \\ \times\ 26 \\ \hline 21814 \end{array}$$

6.
$$\begin{array}{r} 361 \\ \times\ 4.6 \\ \hline 1,6606 \end{array}$$

7.
$$\begin{array}{r} 6.248 \\ \times\ 34 \\ \hline 212432 \end{array}$$

8.
$$\begin{array}{r} 462 \\ \times\ 1.84 \\ \hline 85008 \end{array}$$

Multiply.

9.
$$\begin{array}{r} 7.3 \\ \times\ 8 \\ \hline \end{array}$$

10.
$$\begin{array}{r} \$6.91 \\ \times\ 7 \\ \hline \end{array}$$

11.
$$\begin{array}{r} 18.6 \\ \times\ 5 \\ \hline \end{array}$$

12.
$$\begin{array}{r} 39 \\ \times\ 1.4 \\ \hline \end{array}$$

13.
$$\begin{array}{r} 862 \\ \times\ 4.8 \\ \hline \end{array}$$

14.
$$\begin{array}{r} 2.76 \\ \times\ 47 \\ \hline \end{array}$$

15.
$$\begin{array}{r} 1.804 \\ \times\ 27 \\ \hline \end{array}$$

16.
$$\begin{array}{r} 64.9 \\ \times\ 347 \\ \hline \end{array}$$

Copy and multiply.

17. 8×6.15

18. 13×9.5

19. 4×2.658

20. 3.56×27

21. 47×6.4

22. 7.5×137

23. 9×7.8

24. 6.105×9

25. 8.25×49

26. 57×3.721

27. $3,270 \times 5.9$

28. 7.125×46

Problem Solving

Solve each problem.

29. In one year, Americans consumed an average of 22.4 pounds of cheese per person. What is the weight of the cheese eaten by a family of 4 that year?

30. Union Pacific's fastest scheduled freight train runs from North Platte to Cheyenne at a speed of 66 miles per hour. The Santa Fe Railroad's fastest freight run is 62.9 miles per hour between Gallup and Winslow. How many miles per hour faster is the Union Pacific run?

31. Stay-n-Shop is selling sirloin steak this week for $3.95 a pound. How much will a 2-pound sirloin cost?

32. Mr. Aerts pressed 46 sheets of metal on his shift at the steel mill. How thick is his stack of metal if each sheet is 0.125 centimeters thick?

Multiplying Decimals

Debra says she weighs 0.85 as much as Randall. How much does Debra weigh?

We want to know Debra's weight.

Randall weighs _____ kilograms.

Debra weighs _____ as much.

To find how much Debra weighs, we multiply Randall's weight by the decimal part of it representing Debra's weight.

We multiply _____ by _____.

RANDALL 68.5 kg.
DEBRA _____ kg.

Multiply like whole numbers.	The product has the same number of decimal places as the sum of the decimal factors.

$$\begin{array}{r} 68.5 \\ \times\ 0.85 \\ \hline 3425 \\ 5480 \\ \hline 58225 \end{array}$$

$$\begin{array}{r} 68.5 \leftarrow 1 \text{ decimal place} \\ \times\ 0.85 \leftarrow 2 \text{ decimal places} \\ \hline 3425 \\ 5480 \\ \hline 58.225 \leftarrow 3 \text{ decimal places} \end{array}$$

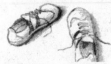

Debra weighs _____ kilograms.

Getting Started

Place the decimal point in each product.

1. $\begin{array}{r} 5.6 \\ \times\ 3.2 \\ \hline 1792 \end{array}$

2. $\begin{array}{r} 1.58 \\ \times\ 7.3 \\ \hline 11534 \end{array}$

3. $\begin{array}{r} 92.3 \\ \times\ 8.51 \\ \hline 785473 \end{array}$

4. $\begin{array}{r} 14.25 \\ \times\ 9.4 \\ \hline 133950 \end{array}$

Multiply.

5. $\begin{array}{r} 59.1 \\ \times\ 0.7 \end{array}$

6. $\begin{array}{r} 19.31 \\ \times\ 2.6 \end{array}$

7. $\begin{array}{r} 8.07 \\ \times\ 4.9 \end{array}$

8. $\begin{array}{r} 75.2 \\ \times\ 36.5 \end{array}$

Copy and multiply.

9. 4.3×7.1

10. 4.32×1.5

11. 3.3×2.72

12. 92.5×2.4

Practice

Place the decimal point in each product.

1. 7.21
    × 8.5
    6 1 2 8 5

2. 3.98
    × 1.6
    6 3 6 8

3. 146.2
    × 3.07
    4 4 8 8 3 4

4. 19.1
    × 24.6
    4 6 9 8 6

5. 13.24
    × 4.3
    5 6 9 3 2

6. 285.6
    × 6.24
    1 7 8 2 1 4 4

7. 13.85
    × 0.8
    1 1 0 8 0

8. 112.5
    × 0.43
    4 8 3 7 5

Multiply.

9. 5.2
    × 0.9

10. 7.28
    × 2.1

11. 57.7
    × 4.6

12. 126.8
    × 7.5

13. 28.2
    × 11.1

14. 52.81
    × 4.6

15. 423.2
    × 25.91

16. 3.25
    × 0.8

Copy and multiply.

17. 5.3×2.6

18. 1.18×0.9

19. 12.3×7.8

20. 21.36×0.5

21. 2.73×4.6

22. 5.1×8.09

23. 51.3×17.6

24. 9.53×1.8

25. 631.5×0.81

26. 0.46×59.7

27. 27.3×85.4

28. 426.21×0.8

Problem Solving

Solve each problem.

29. Between 1951 and 1980 in Dawson, Yukon, the average wind speed was 3.7 kilometers per hour. The highest recorded speed was approximately 1.5 times faster. About how fast was Dawson's highest wind during that period?

30. Mr. Harris's car averages 32.43 miles to a gallon of gas. His tank holds 10.5 gallons. How many miles can Mr. Harris travel on a full tank?

31. A rectangle is 9.5 inches wide and 15.8 inches long. What is its perimeter?

32. It takes 8.25 pounds of sand to make a bucket of concrete. How much sand is needed to make 6.5 buckets of concrete?

Zeros in the Product

A human hair is about 0.04 as thick as the
wire in a paper clip. What is the thickness
of a human hair?

We want to know the thickness of a human hair.

The wire in a paper clip is about _____ of a
centimeter thick.

A human hair is about _____ as thick as this wire.

To find how thick a human hair is, we multiply the
thickness of the wire by the decimal part of that
wire representing the human hair.

We multiply _____ by _____.

Multiply like whole numbers.

The product has the same number of decimal places as the sum of the decimal places in the factors.

$$\begin{array}{r} 0.1 \\ \times\ 0.04 \\ \hline 4 \end{array}$$

$$\begin{array}{r} 0.1 \leftarrow \text{1 decimal place} \\ \times\ 0.04 \leftarrow \text{2 decimal places} \\ \hline 0.004 \leftarrow \text{3 decimal places} \end{array}$$

REMEMBER If there are not enough places in the
product, annex zeros to the left of the number
before placing the decimal point.

A human hair is _____ of a centimeter thick.

Getting Started

Multiply.

1. $\begin{array}{r} 0.6 \\ \times\ 0.2 \\ \hline \end{array}$	2. $\begin{array}{r} 0.004 \\ \times\ \quad 9 \\ \hline \end{array}$	3. $\begin{array}{r} 45 \\ \times\ 0.002 \\ \hline \end{array}$	4. $\begin{array}{r} 0.03 \\ \times\ 1.4 \\ \hline \end{array}$
5. $\begin{array}{r} 8.5 \\ \times\ 0.4 \\ \hline \end{array}$	6. $\begin{array}{r} 0.1 \\ \times\ 0.23 \\ \hline \end{array}$	7. $\begin{array}{r} 0.005 \\ \times\ \quad 7 \\ \hline \end{array}$	8. $\begin{array}{r} 3.4 \\ \times\ \quad 9 \\ \hline \end{array}$

Copy and multiply.

9. 0.003×6 10. 74×0.008 11. 0.6×0.06 12. 0.015×3.9

Practice

Multiply.

1.	0.3 × 0.01	**2.**	0.03 × 0.04	**3.**	0.18 × 0.5	**4.**	0.24 × 1.3

5.	0.008 × 9	**6.**	6.43 × 100	**7.**	0.05 × 0.3	**8.**	4.75 × 0.5

Copy and multiply.

9. 0.2 × 0.3   **10.** 7.8 × 0.02   **11.** 0.06 × 0.4   **12.** 3.8 × 0.21

13. 0.03 × 0.45   **14.** 0.001 × 28   **15.** 0.123 × 0.01   **16.** 4.8 × 0.03

17. 10 × 0.007   **18.** 5.8 × 43.8   **19.** 0.003 × 21   **20.** 0.9 × 0.09

Problem Solving

Use the rectangle to complete each problem.

21. The perimeter is _____ meters.

22. The area is _____ square meters.

0.3 meters

0.8 meters

(Now Try This!)

Here is a map of a town having a river with two islands and seven bridges. Is it possible for a person to go for a stroll, cross each bridge once and only once, and end up where he or she started? _____

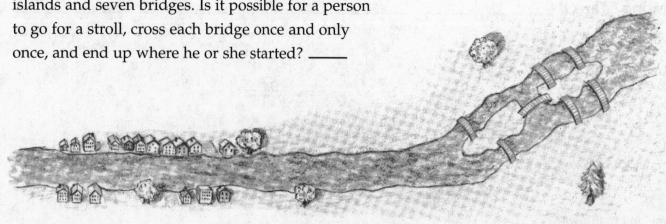

Multiplying by 10, 100, and 1,000

Adam won the long jump with his final attempt. Find how many centimeters long Adam's jump was.

We want to know the length of Adam's jump expressed in centimeters.

The jump was _____ meters long.

There are _____ centimeters in 1 meter.

To find the number of centimeters in the jump, we multiply the length of the jump in meters by the number of centimeters in one meter.

We multiply _____ by _____.

Complete the following patterns to find a shortcut for multiplying by 10, 100, or 1,000.

	Number of zeros in second factor	Move the decimal point to the right
$3.42 \times 10 = 34.2$	1	1 place
$3.42 \times 100 = 342$	2	2 places
$3.420 \times 1,000 = 3,420$	3	3 places

Notice, that when there are not enough digits to move the decimal point, zeros are annexed to the right.

Multiplying by 10 moves the decimal _____ place to the right.

Multiplying by 100 moves the decimal _____ places to the right.

Multiplying by 1,000 moves the decimal _____ places to the right.

$3.42 \times 100 =$ _____

Adam jumped _____ centimeters in his winning long jump.

Getting Started

Multiply.

1. $5.8 \times 100 =$ _____

2. $5.75 \times 1,000 =$ _____

Write the missing factor.

3. _____ $\times 325.4 = 3,254$

4. _____ $\times 1.06 = 1,060$

Write the missing number.

5. 3,742 meters = _____ centimeters

6. To change liters to milliliters, multiply by _____.

Practice

Multiply.

1. $6.32 \times 100 =$ _____

2. $10 \times 7.731 =$ _____

3. $19.21 \times 1{,}000 =$ _____

4. $100 \times 0.241 =$ _____

5. $13.1 \times 1{,}000 =$ _____

6. $100 \times 26 =$ _____

7. $10 \times 0.159 =$ _____

8. $1{,}000 \times 0.001 =$ _____

9. $10 \times 8.37 =$ _____

10. $14.29 \times 1{,}000 =$ _____

11. $100 \times 2.315 =$ _____

12. $0.39 \times 10 =$ _____

13. $400 \times 100 =$ _____

14. $10 \times 5.675 =$ _____

15. $0.48 \times 1{,}000 =$ _____

16. $100 \times 13.721 =$ _____

Write the missing factor.

17. $9.6 \times$ ___ $= 96$

18. $1.25 \times$ ___ $= 1{,}250$

19. ___ $\times 8.245 = 82.45$

20. ___ $\times 3.75 = 375$

21. $0.321 \times$ ___ $= 32.1$

22. $14.158 \times$ ___ $= 1{,}415.8$

Write the missing number.

23. 4.265 kilometers = _____ meters

24. 7.3 liters = _____ milliliters

25. 0.214 kilograms = _____ grams

26. 14.294 meters = _____ centimeters

27. To change meters to centimeters, multiply by _____.

28. To change kilometers to meters, multiply by _____.

(Now Try This!)

In a right triangle, if a and b are the sides that form the right angle and c is the side opposite the right angle, then $(a \times a) + (b \times b) = (c \times c)$. This is called the **Pythagorean Theorem**. It is usually expressed as $a^2 + b^2 = c^2$. Below, sides a and b of a right triangle are given. Use the Pythagorean Theorem to find the length of the third side.

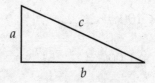

$a = 5$ mm $\qquad b = 12$ mm $\qquad c =$ ___ mm

Dividing a Decimal by a Whole Number

It took Cheryl 4 hours to drive from Clinton to San Remo. How many kilometers did she average per hour?

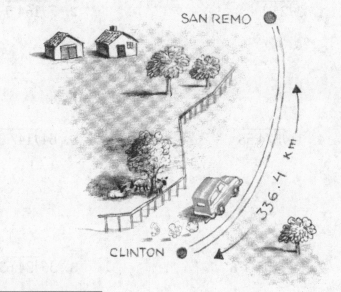

We want to know the kilometers per hour Cheryl drove between the two towns.

She drove _____ kilometers.

The trip took her a total of _____ hours.

To find the kilometers per hour, we divide the number of kilometers in the whole trip by the number of hours it took.

We divide _____ by _____.

Place the decimal point.	Divide like whole numbers.	Check by multiplication.

$$4\overline{)336.4}$$ with decimal point above

$$
\begin{array}{r}
84.1 \\
4\overline{)336.4} \\
\underline{32} \\
16 \\
\underline{16} \\
4 \\
\underline{4}
\end{array}
$$

$$
\begin{array}{r}
84.1 \\
\times 4 \\
\hline
336.4
\end{array}
$$

Cheryl averaged _____ kilometers per hour.

Getting Started

Divide and check.

1. $5\overline{)29.35}$

2. $6\overline{)\$6.72}$

3. $9\overline{)48.123}$

4. $54\overline{)34.668}$

5. $19\overline{)44.46}$

6. $65\overline{)36.40}$

Copy and divide.

7. $\$125.20 \div 5$

8. $20.360 \div 40$

9. $1{,}914.9 \div 13$

Practice

Divide and check.

1. $3\overline{)2.91}$

2. $7\overline{)164.5}$

3. $6\overline{)6.234}$

4. $11\overline{)\$74.58}$

5. $64\overline{)147.84}$

6. $25\overline{)382.5}$

7. $72\overline{)155.376}$

8. $36\overline{)34.632}$

9. $83\overline{)\$834.98}$

Copy and divide.

10. $143.4 \div 6$

11. $\$3.84 \div 4$

12. $107.95 \div 17$

13. $\$75.15 \div 45$

14. $550.8 \div 36$

15. $228 \div 38$

16. $2{,}321.16 \div 92$

17. $30.352 \div 56$

18. $143.898 \div 87$

Problem Solving

Solve each problem.

19. If a carton of 24 cans of soup weighs 7.32 kilograms, what is the weight of each can?

20. How many miles can a car travel in 6 hours if it averages 45.6 miles per hour?

21. Veann's share of her family's garage sale proceeds was $18.56 on Thursday, $16.21 on Friday, and $27.36 on Saturday. What was her average daily earnings?

22. Mrs. Aguire bought a chair for $426.38. She paid $115.50 as a down payment. She paid the balance in 4 monthly payments. How much was each payment?

Zeros in the Quotient

A scientist is using an electron microscope to measure several skin cells. One of the things she needs to know is the average width of the cells.

Specimen 1	0.04 mm
Specimen 2	0.05 mm
Specimen 3	0.04 mm
Specimen 4	0.05 mm
Specimen 5	0.05 mm

We want to know the average width of the skin cells.

The scientist made _____ recordings.

The widths were _____, _____, _____, _____, and _____ millimeters.

To find the average width, we add all the widths and divide by the number of recordings.

We add _____, _____, _____, _____, and _____ and divide that sum by _____.

Add the recordings.	Place the decimal point. Write zeros in place values when the dividend is too small. Divide.	Annex a zero in the dividend and divide again.
0.04 0.05 0.04 0.05 + 0.05 ――― 0.23	$\underset{\overline{}}{0.04}$ 5)0.23 $\underline{20}$	0.046 5)0.230 $\underline{20}$ 30 $\underline{30}$

The average width of a skin cell is _____ millimeters.

Getting Started

Divide. Annex a zero if necessary.

1. 7)0.21

2. 4)0.048

3. 5)0.37

Copy and divide.

4. 0.003 ÷ 6

5. 0.042 ÷ 14

6. 2.08 ÷ 52

Practice

Divide. Annex a zero if necessary.

1. $8\overline{)0.128}$

2. $12\overline{)0.384}$

3. $7\overline{)0.602}$

4. $15\overline{)0.135}$

5. $24\overline{)8.76}$

6. $56\overline{)19.88}$

7. $4\overline{)0.02}$

8. $16\overline{)0.112}$

9. $32\overline{)0.16}$

Copy and divide.

10. $0.015 \div 3$

11. $0.56 \div 10$

12. $1.08 \div 9$

13. $0.84 \div 28$

14. $1.92 \div 64$

15. $4.05 \div 75$

16. $2.22 \div 37$

17. $2.08 \div 80$

18. $3.15 \div 35$

19. $2.496 \div 26$

20. $3.4 \div 50$

21. $0.45 \div 75$

(Now Try This!)

Complete the table to find a shortcut for dividing decimals by 10, 100, and 1,000.

Dividends	7.15	265.3	8	5,750.1
Divided by 10	0.715		0.8	
Divided by 100	0.0715	2.653		
Divided by 1,000	0.00715			

To divide a decimal number by 10, 100, or 1,000, count the number of _____ in the

divisor to determine how many places the decimal point will be moved to the _____.

Dividing by a Decimal

Mr. Sanduski bought a new sedan. How many miles
per gallon can he expect if he drives the average
range with a full tank of gas?

Type of Car	Tank Capacity (gallons)	Average Range (miles)	Miles per Gallon
Compact	10.5	327.6	?
Sedan	18.3	452.01	?
Sports	15.6	436.8	?

We want to know the number of miles Mr.
Sanduski's car will travel on one gallon of gas.

A sedan holds _____ gallons of gas.

The range of a sedan on a tank of gas is _____
miles.

To find the miles per gallon, we divide the range
by the tank's capacity.

We divide _____ by _____.

REMEMBER The divisor must be a whole number.
If it is a decimal number, it should be multiplied by
a 10, 100, or 1,000 to make it a whole number.
Multiply the dividend by the same number.

Multiply the divisor and the dividend by 10.	Divide.

$$18.3\overline{)452.01}$$

$$\begin{array}{r} 24.7 \\ 18.3\overline{)452.01} \\ \underline{366} \\ 86\ 0 \\ \underline{73\ 2} \\ 12\ 81 \\ \underline{12\ 81} \end{array}$$

The sedan should average _____ miles to the gallon.

Getting Started

Divide.

1. $4.8\overline{)43.2}$　　　　2. $0.6\overline{)3.36}$　　　　3. $1.2\overline{)3.912}$

Copy and divide.

4. $532.8 \div 3.6$　　　　5. $31.08 \div 51.8$　　　　6. $133.95 \div 9.4$

Practice

Divide.

1. $0.3\overline{)6.96}$

2. $1.2\overline{)0.048}$

3. $6.4\overline{)230.4}$

4. $3\overline{)5.418}$

5. $3.6\overline{)21.744}$

6. $2.5\overline{)15.875}$

7. $9.5\overline{)30.115}$

8. $6.7\overline{)20.636}$

9. $7.7\overline{)482.02}$

Copy and divide.

10. $5.4 \div 1.5$

11. $2.6 \div 1.3$

12. $201.6 \div 6.3$

13. $7.596 \div 3.6$

14. $12.838 \div 4.9$

15. $69.12 \div 7.2$

16. $35.316 \div 5.4$

17. $1.143 \div 1.8$

18. $43.51 \div 3.8$

Problem Solving

Solve each problem.

19. Hal worked a total of 18.75 hours last month as an auxiliary policeman. If he worked in shifts of about 2.5 hours each, how many days did Hal work last month?

20. Paula's average stride is 0.5 of a meter. How many steps will it take for Paula to walk 241.2 meters?

[Now Try This!]

Write a number between each pair whose value is higher than the number on the left, but lower in value than the number on the right.

1. 2.1352, _____, 2.137

2. 0.01, _____, 0.021

3. $5\frac{1}{2}$, _____, 5.545

4. 567.23, _____, 568.95

5. 2.25, _____, 2.33

6. $2\frac{1}{4}$, _____, $2\frac{1}{3}$

Rounding Quotients

A jet aircraft flew from San Francisco to Kansas City in
3 hours. What was the average speed of the plane to the
nearest tenth of a mile?

1,506.5 miles   KANSAS CITY

We want to know the approximate speed of the
airplane to the nearest tenth of a mile.

It is _____ miles from San Francisco to Kansas City.

It took the jet _____ hours to fly that distance.

To find the average speed, we divide the distance
between the cities by the length of time it took to
make the trip.

Divide until you run out of digits.	Annex a zero in hundredths place and divide again.	Round the quotient to tenths.

$$\begin{array}{r} 502.1 \\ 3\overline{)1{,}506.5} \\ \underline{15} \\ 006 \\ \underline{6} \\ 0\,5 \\ \underline{3} \end{array}$$

$$\begin{array}{r} 502.16 \\ 3\overline{)1{,}506.50} \\ \underline{15} \\ 006 \\ \underline{6} \\ 0\,5 \\ \underline{3} \\ 20 \\ \underline{18} \end{array}$$

$502.16 \rightarrow$ _____

REMEMBER You must divide to one place value beyond
the place in which you want to express the quotient.

The average speed of the jet was _____ miles per hour.

Getting Started

**Divide. Round the quotient to the
nearest whole number.**

1. $5\overline{)9.2}$

2. $3.6\overline{)25.92}$

**Divide. Round the quotient to the
nearest tenth.**

3. $4\overline{)3.33}$

4. $7.6\overline{)44.08}$

Practice

Divide. Round the quotient to the nearest whole number.

1. $7\overline{)47.6}$

2. $3.5\overline{)23.45}$

3. $7.2\overline{)25.2}$

4. $6.4\overline{)19.968}$

5. $8\overline{)55.2}$

6. $45\overline{)283.5}$

Divide. Round the quotient to the nearest tenth.

7. $9\overline{)6.66}$

8. $12\overline{)3.5}$

9. $5.4\overline{)14.094}$

10. $3.7\overline{)8.732}$

11. $1.6\overline{)2.57}$

12. $7.6\overline{)41.368}$

Problem Solving

Solve each problem.

13. A plumber needs to cut a piece of pipe 2.5 meters long into 3 equal pieces. About how long will each piece be?

14. A carpenter used a board 3.4 feet long to estimate the length of some laminated plastic he needed. He needed a piece of laminated plastic 2.7 times the length of the board. What is the length of the needed laminated plastic?

Now Try This!

Circle the correct value for each letter to make the equation true.

$I = 6$

$J = \frac{1}{2}$ or $\frac{2}{3}$

$K = 3$ or 1

$L = \frac{1}{4}$ or $\frac{3}{4}$

$$(I \times J) - (I \div K) = L \times (I - K + 2J)$$

Name _____

Problem Solving: Collect Data

Which of the following is the tallest structure: Sears Tower in Chicago, CN Tower in Toronto, Empire State Building in New York City, or the John Hancock Center in Chicago?

Sears Tower

⭐ **SEE**

We want to find out which is the tallest structure.

We do not have enough information to solve this problem.

CN Tower

⭐ **PLAN**

We need to find the height of each structure.

We can find this information by looking in

_____.

Once we have this information we can compare the heights to find the tallest structure.

John Hancock Center

⭐ **DO**

Use a reference book such as an almanac or look on the Internet to find the height of each structure.

Sears Tower _____

CN Tower _____

Empire State Building _____

John Hancock Center _____

The _____ is the tallest of the four structures.

⭐ **CHECK**

We can check by verifying this data in another reference book, and by listing the heights of the four structures in order from largest to smallest.

Empire State Building

Apply

Solve each problem.

1. Roll a single number cube 50 times and record the outcomes. Perform the experiment a second time and record the outcomes. What number appears most often? What number appears least often?

2. Roll a pair of number cubes 30 times and record the number of times each sum appears. Perform the experiment a second time. What sum appears most often? What sum appears least often?

3. Record the number of pages in your daily newspaper for a week. Explain why some days the papers are larger or smaller.

4. Toss a coin 50 times and record the number of heads and tails. Which side of the coin appears more often?

5. Near the front of your classroom textbooks is a copyright date. Find the latest copyright date of each of five books and arrange them in order of newest to oldest.

6. Record the dates of the coins available in your classroom. How many years difference exist between the newest and oldest coin?

> **Problem-Solving Strategy:
> Using the Four-Step Plan**
>
> ★ **SEE** What do you need to find?
>
> ★ **PLAN** What do you need to do?
>
> ★ **DO** Follow the plan.
>
> ★ **CHECK** Does your answer make sense?

7. Jeff and Karen have the same amount of money. Jeff's is all in one-dollar bills. Karen's is all in five-dollar bills. Both of them spend one-half of their money. Who has more money now?

8. Cindy Loo used a calculator to multiply 35.45×2.18. The display showed only 3 decimal places in the product. Does this mean that she made an error? Why or why not?

9. Without multiplying, tell which has the greater product. 2.79×1.28 or 27.9×0.128

10. In Exercise 4, if you tossed the coins 100 times, how would the results differ?

Calculator: Rates

Gene is selling his car by placing a three-line ad in the *Daily News*. He is going to advertise for 5 days. How much will the ad cost Gene?

Daily News Ad Rates Charge per Line, per Day (2-line minimum)	
9+ days	$1.98
8 days	$2.20
7 days	$2.51
4 to 6 days	$3.09
1 to 3 days	$4.12

We want to figure the cost of Gene's ad. He is placing his ad for _____ days at a cost of _____ for each line, each day. He is writing a _____-line ad.

Complete this code to find the cost of the ad.

3 $\boxed{\cdot}$ 09 $\boxed{\times}$ 5 $\boxed{\times}$ 3 $\boxed{=}$ $\boxed{}$

The ad will cost _____.

Use a calculator to find the cost of these ads.

1. 6 lines for 6 days _____

2. 13 lines for 2 days _____

3. 9 lines for 7 days _____

4. 4 lines for 8 days _____

We have been using a calculator to add, subtract, multiply, and divide with money. A calculator can be used to do these operations with any decimals.

Complete the following:

5. 6 $\boxed{\cdot}$ 48 $\boxed{\times}$ 12 $\boxed{\cdot}$ 9 $\boxed{=}$ $\boxed{}$

6. 5 $\boxed{\cdot}$ 32 $\boxed{\times}$ 16 $\boxed{\cdot}$ 4 $\boxed{=}$ $\boxed{}$

7. 93 $\boxed{\cdot}$ 6 $\boxed{\div}$ $\boxed{\cdot}$ 3 $\boxed{=}$ $\boxed{}$

8. 75 $\boxed{\cdot}$ 8 $\boxed{\div}$ $\boxed{\cdot}$ 2 $\boxed{=}$ $\boxed{}$

9. 17 $\boxed{\cdot}$ 9 $\boxed{+}$ 36 $\boxed{\cdot}$ 72 $\boxed{=}$ $\boxed{}$

10. 39 $\boxed{\cdot}$ 7 $\boxed{+}$ 18 $\boxed{\cdot}$ 6 $\boxed{=}$ $\boxed{}$

11. 44 $\boxed{\cdot}$ 5 $\boxed{\times}$ 13 $\boxed{\cdot}$ 7 $\boxed{-}$ 496 $\boxed{\cdot}$ 376 $\boxed{=}$ $\boxed{}$

12. 73 $\boxed{\cdot}$ 9 $\boxed{\times}$ 8 $\boxed{\cdot}$ 4 $\boxed{-}$ 63 $\boxed{\cdot}$ 49 $\boxed{\times}$ $\boxed{\cdot}$ 2 $\boxed{=}$ $\boxed{}$

Practice

Use a calculator to complete each equation.
Don't forget to use the decimal key when necessary.

1. $49.6 + 39.7 =$ _____

2. $85.14 - 57.38 =$ _____

3. $4.7 \times 3.9 =$ _____

4. $393.96 \div 14.7 =$ _____

5. $39.3 \times 16.7 =$ _____

6. $0.177 \div 5.9 =$ _____

7. $268.15 - 199.57 =$ _____

8. $615.2 + 189.475 =$ _____

9. $476.2 + 89.7 - 112.25 =$ _____

10. $126.5 - 96.13 - 7.06 =$ _____

11. $(9.62 + 4.21) \times 0.85 =$ _____

12. $(124.3 - 68.8) \div 0.5 =$ _____

Problem Solving

Solve each problem.

13. Pat bought a shirt for $10.75 and a belt for $8.35. How much change did Pat receive from a twenty dollar bill?

14. Ms. Garcia kept track of how much gas she used in one month. Her records show weekly amounts of 41.36 liters, 36.72 liters, 44.9 liters, and 26.81 liters. How much gas did Ms. Garcia use?

15. Mr. Petit rented a car with 15,748.9 miles on the odometer. He drove the car 212.6 miles on Monday, 307.8 miles on Tuesday, and 189.6 miles on Thursday. How many miles were on the odometer when Mr. Petit returned the car?

16. On February 1, Karen had $374.68 in her account. On February 9, she wrote a check for $8.75. On February 28, she wrote a check for $26.18. How much does Karen have left in her account?

Use the ad rates on page 253 to solve each problem.

17. Find the cost of a 2-line ad run for 7 days.

18. Find the cost of a 4-line ad run for 2 days.

Estimate by rounding.

1. $3.89
  × 12

2. $5.25
  × 6

3. $7.55
  × 11

4. $9.95
  × 20

Multiply.

5. 4.7
  × 1.8

6. 3.21
  × 0.6

7. 21.3
  × 1.9

8. 6.24
  × 0.35

9. 0.5
  × 0.1

10. 0.003
   × 8

11. 0.09
   × 1.2

12. 0.007
   × 10

Divide.

13. $6\overline{)2.94}$

14. $8\overline{)\$52.64}$

15. $8\overline{)0.048}$

16. $21\overline{)0.819}$

17. $0.3\overline{)6.66}$

18. $2.4\overline{)3.84}$

19. $1.5\overline{)0.405}$

20. $5.9\overline{)0.354}$

Divide. Round the quotient to the nearest tenth.

21. $6\overline{)3.21}$

22. $8\overline{)1.2}$

23. $1.8\overline{)3.5}$

24. $3.3\overline{)11.11}$

Circle the letter of the correct answer.

1
36,318
+ 14,273

a. 40,591
b. 50,591
c. 51,591
d. NG

2
13,653
− 6,948

a. 6,315
b. 6,605
c. 6,705
d. NG

3 48 × 39

a. 576
b. 1,672
c. 1,872
d. NG

4 38)8,172

a. 215
b. 215 R2
c. 215 R20
d. NG

5 Find the area.

9 in.

6 in.

a. 30 in.
b. 15 sq in.
c. 54 sq in.
d. NG

6
7 ft 3 in.
− 2 ft 8 in.

a. 4 ft 5 in.
b. 4 ft 7 in.
c. 5 ft 5 in.
d. NG

7 Simplify.
$\frac{42}{10}$

a. $\frac{21}{5}$
b. $4\frac{2}{5}$
c. $4\frac{1}{5}$
d. NG

8
$3\frac{1}{2}$
$+ 2\frac{3}{8}$

a. $5\frac{1}{8}$
b. $5\frac{2}{5}$
c. $5\frac{7}{8}$
d. NG

9 $15\frac{1}{3} - 8\frac{2}{5}$

a. $7\frac{2}{3}$
b. $8\frac{1}{5}$
c. $8\frac{2}{3}$
d. NG

10
14.36
+ 2.9

a. 17.26
b. 17.2
c. 27.26
d. NG

11
20.1
− 9.73

a. 10.37
b. 11.43
c. 11.63
d. NG

score

Name _____

Geometry

Points, Lines, and Planes

Points, lines, line segments, rays, and planes are geometric ideas. What geometric idea does the beacon light suggest?

A **point** is a position in space.

We say: point *A*.

•*A*

A **line segment** is a straight path between two points. It is named by its two endpoints.

We say: **segment *XY*.**   We write: $\overline{XY}$.

A **line** has no endpoints. It extends indefinitely in both directions.

We say: **line *MN*.**   We write: $\overleftrightarrow{MN}$.

A **ray** is part of a line. It has one endpoint and extends indefinitely in one direction.

We say: **ray *RS*.**   We write: $\overrightarrow{RS}$.

To name a ray, write the endpoint first.

A **plane** is a flat surface that extends indefinitely in all directions. It contains points, lines, line segments and rays. A plane is named by any three points in the plane.

We say: **plane *ABC*.**

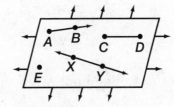

The beacon light suggests a _____ because it seems to start at a point and go indefinitely in one direction.

Getting Started

Write the name for each figure.

Draw and label each figure.

1.

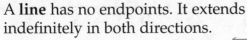

_____

2.

L   *M*

_____

3. Plane *PQR*

4. $\overleftrightarrow{AB}$

Practice

Write the name for each figure.

1.

   _____

2.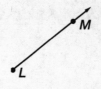

   _____

3.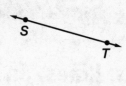

   _____

4.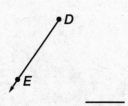

   _____

5.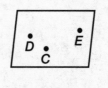

   _____

6.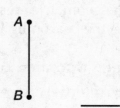

   _____

7.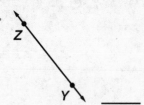

   _____

8.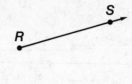

   _____

9.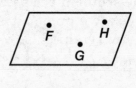

   _____

Draw and label each figure.

10. Line *CD*

11. Point *Q*

12. Plane *ABC*

13. Ray *AB*

14. Segment *MN*

15. $\overrightarrow{XY}$

16. $\overleftrightarrow{LM}$

17. Plane *XYZ*

18. $\overline{ST}$

Lesson 12-1 • Points, Lines, and Planes

Angles

The clock hands suggest an angle. Is the angle straight, right, obtuse, or acute?

An **angle** is formed by two rays with a common endpoint. The common endpoint is called the **vertex**. An angle is usually named by 3 points, the vertex and one on each ray.

We say: **angle** *ABC*.   We write: ∠*ABC*.

Notice, in naming an angle, the vertex is always named as the center letter.

Angles are measured in degrees.

We say: **180 degrees**.   We write: **180°**.

straight angle	right angle	obtuse angle	acute angle
180°	90°	greater than 90° less than 180°	less than 90°

The clock hands suggest a _____ angle.

Getting Started

**Write the name for each angle, its vertex, and its rays.
Then, identify the type of angle.**

1.

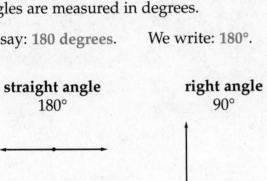

Angle _____

Vertex _____

Rays _____ _____

Type _____

2.

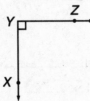

Angle _____

Vertex _____

Rays _____ _____

Type _____

3.

Angle _____

Vertex _____

Rays _____ _____

Type _____

Practice

Write the name for each angle, its vertex, and its rays.
Then, identify the type of angle.

1.

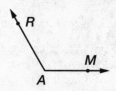

Angle _____

Vertex _____

Rays ____ ____

Type _____

2.

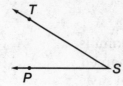

Angle _____

Vertex _____

Rays ____ ____

Type _____

3.

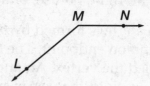

Angle _____

Vertex _____

Rays ____ ____

Type _____

4.

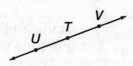

Angle _____

Vertex _____

Rays ____ ____

Type _____

5.

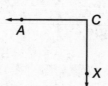

Angle _____

Vertex _____

Rays ____ ____

Type _____

6.

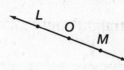

Angle _____

Vertex _____

Rays ____ ____

Type _____

7.

Angle _____

Vertex _____

Rays ____ ____

Type _____

8.

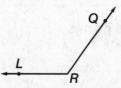

Angle _____

Vertex _____

Rays ____ ____

Type _____

9.

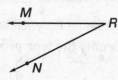

Angle _____

Vertex _____

Rays ____ ____

Type _____

10. Name all the angles.

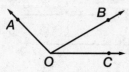

_____

_____

_____   _____

11. Draw an obtuse angle. Draw a ray that divides the angle into two equal parts. What type of angles are formed?

Measuring Angles

A **protractor** can be used to measure an angle. How many degrees are in the angle formed by the hands of the clock?

The protractor is divided into 180 degrees. Some protractors give the degrees in both directions.

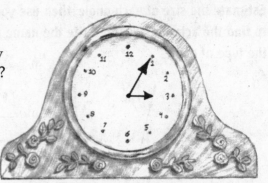

To measure an angle:

1. Extend the rays to make them long enough to go through the grid on the protractor.

2. Place the zero edge along one side of the angle.

3. Place the vertex at the center of the protractor.

4. Read the number of degrees on the same scale as the 0 degree mark.

The hands of the clock form a _____ angle.

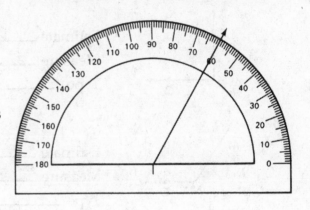

To draw an angle:

1. Place the zero edge along the bottom ray.

2. Place the vertex at the center of the protractor.

3. Mark a point at the degree on the same scale as the 0 degree mark.

4. Use a straight edge to draw the second ray from the vertex through that point.

Getting Started

Estimate the size of each angle. Then, use your protractor to find the actual measure. Write the name that identifies the type of angle.

1.
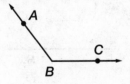

Estimate _____

Measure _____

Type _____

2.
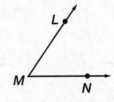

Estimate _____

Measure _____

Type _____

Use your protractor to draw each angle.

3. ∠*TIP* measures 80°.

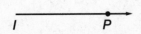

4. ∠*MAT* measures 145°.

Practice

Estimate the size of each angle, then use your protractor
to find the actual measure. Write the name that identifies
the type of angle.

1.

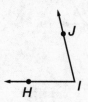

Estimate _____

Measure _____

Type _____

2.

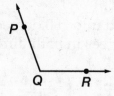

Estimate _____

Measure _____

Type _____

3.

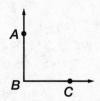

Estimate _____

Measure _____

Type _____

4.

Estimate _____

Measure _____

Type _____

5.

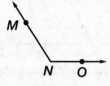

Estimate _____

Measure _____

Type _____

6.

Estimate _____

Measure _____

Type _____

Use your protractor to draw each angle.

7. $\angle GCQ$ measures 75°.

8. $\angle FGH$ measures 120°.

9. $\angle CDE$ measures 30°.

10. $\angle MIN$ measures 149°.

11. $\angle KLM$ measures 17°.

12. $\angle QRS$ measures 67°.

13. $\angle IJK$ measures 113°.

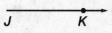

14. $\angle VWX$ measures 98°.

15. $\angle SQT$ measures 41°.

Lesson 12-3 • Measuring Angles

Name _____

Parallel, Intersecting, and Perpendicular Lines

Two lines in the same plane are either parallel or they intersect at a point. Do the rungs in the ladder suggest parallel or intersecting lines?

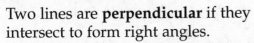

Two lines are **parallel** if they are in the same plane and never meet.

We say: line *AB* is **parallel** to line *CD*.

We write: $\overleftrightarrow{AB} \parallel \overleftrightarrow{CD}$

Two lines **intersect** if they eventually meet or cross each other.

We say: line *XY* **intersects** line *MN* at point *P*.

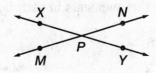

Two lines are **perpendicular** if they intersect to form right angles.

We say: line *RS* is **perpendicular** to line *TU*.

We write: $\overleftrightarrow{RS} \perp \overleftrightarrow{TU}$

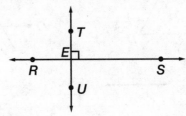

The rungs in the ladder suggest _____ lines.

Getting Started _____

Identify each pair of lines by writing the word *parallel*, *intersecting*, or *perpendicular*.

1.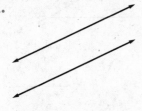

_____

2.

_____

3.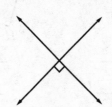

_____

4.

_____

5. Write the pairs of perpendicular segments.

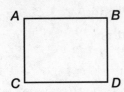

_____

_____

6. Write the pairs of parallel segments.

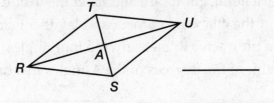

_____

_____

Practice

Identify each pair of lines by writing the word *parallel*, *intersecting*, or *perpendicular*.

1.

_____

2.

_____

3.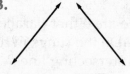

_____

4.

_____

5.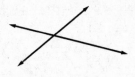

_____

6.

_____

7.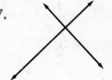

_____

8.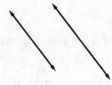

_____

Write the pairs of parallel segments in each figure.

9.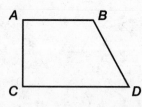

_____

10.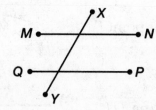

_____

11.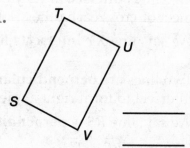

_____

Write the pairs of perpendicular segments in each figure.

12.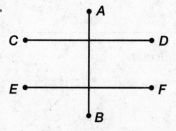

_____

_____

13.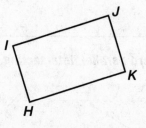

_____

_____

14.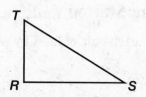

_____

Now Try This!

Find the sum of the degrees of the 4 angles in a quadrilateral. First, draw a quadrilateral, cut it out, and label the inside of the angles *A*, *B*, *C*, and *D*. Next, cut off the 4 labeled corners and lay them side to side with the vertices touching. Use a protractor to measure the four angles. Add the degrees together. What is the sum of the degrees of the 4 angles in a quadrilateral? _____

Lesson 12-4 • Parallel, Intersecting, and Perpendicular Lines

Name _____

Parts of a Circle

A compass can be used to draw a circle. How many degrees are in a circle?

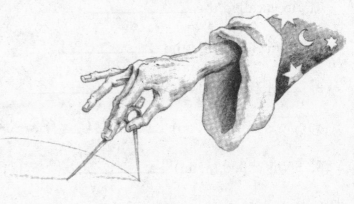

To draw a circle:

1. Place the tip of the compass on a point.

2. Move the pencil completely around the tip.

The point is called the **center** of the circle. The circle is named by the point in the center. The distance around a circle is called the **circumference**. The segment from the center to the circumference is called the **radius**. Any segment connecting two points on the circle is called a **chord**. A chord through the center is called the **diameter**. The angle formed by the center and two radii is called a **central angle**. The part of the circumference between two points is called an **arc**. An arc contains the same number of degrees as its central angle.

We say: **arc** *BC*. We write: $\overset{\frown}{BC}$.

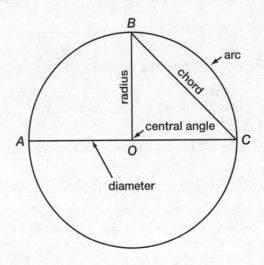

The circle is divided by the diameter into two arcs. One arc starts at *A*, goes through *B*, and stops at *C*. It contains 180°. The other arc starts at *A*, goes the other direction, and stops at *C*. It contains _____ degrees.

The complete circle has _____ degrees.

We say this is **circle** *O*
with **radius** $\overline{OB}$,
diameter $\overline{AC}$,
chord $\overline{BC}$,
central angle $\angle BOC$, and
arc $\overset{\frown}{BC}$.

Getting Started

Use circle O to do Exercises 1 through 5.

1. Name the diameter. _____

2. The length of the diameter is _____.

3. Name one central angle that is right. _____

4. The measure of $\overset{\frown}{AC}$ is _____.

5. Name the chord that is not a diameter. _____

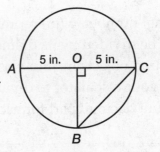

Practice

Use circle A to do Exercises 1 to 5.

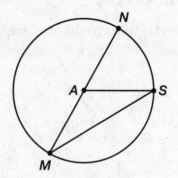

1. $\overline{AS}$ is called the _____.

2. Point A is called the _____.

3. $\angle NAS$ is called (a, an) _____.

4. $\overline{SM}$ is called (a, an) _____.

5. $\overset{\frown}{SN}$ is called (a, an) _____.

Use circle P to do Exercises 6 to 10.

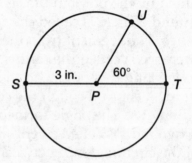

6. Name one radius. _____

7. Name one central angle. _____

8. Name the diameter. _____

9. How long is the diameter? _____

10. What is the measure of arc UT? _____

Use your compass to draw and label each of the following.

11. Circle A with chord $\overline{MN}$.

12. Circle O with radius $\overline{OA}$.

13. Circle P with diameter $\overline{AB}$.

14. Circle R with central angle $\angle LRM$.

Now Try This!

The irrational number π (pi) represents the number of times the circumference (c) of a circle can be divided by its diameter (d). Thus, $\pi = \frac{c}{d}$. Use a metric measuring tape on some round objects in your classroom to find the circumference and diameter. To find π, use your calculator to divide these circumferences by their diameters and record the full decimal part for each calculation.

Lesson 12-5 • Parts of a Circle

Bisecting Segments and Angles

To bisect a figure is to divide it into two equal parts. How can we bisect a line segment and an angle using only a compass and a straightedge?

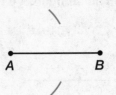

To bisect a line segment:

1. With your compass select a radius which is larger than half the length of $\overline{AB}$. With point A as center, construct an arc above and below $\overline{AB}$.

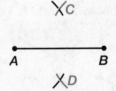

2. Use the same radius you used in Step 1. With point B as center, construct two arcs which intersect the arcs constructed in Step 1. Label the intersections C and D.

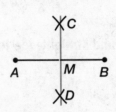

3. Draw $\overline{CD}$. $\overline{CD}$ bisects $\overline{AB}$. M is the midpoint of $\overline{AB}$.

To bisect an angle:

1. Construct an arc intersecting the rays at points M and N.

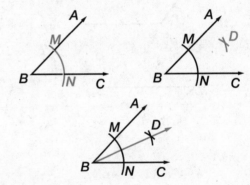

2. With M and N as center, construct two arcs intersecting in the interior of $\angle ABC$. Label the intersection D.

3. Draw $\overline{BD}$. $\overline{BD}$ bisects $\angle ABC$.

Getting Started

Use your compass and straightedge to bisect each figure.

1.

$A \bullet\!\!-\!\!-\!\!-\!\!-\!\!\bullet B$

2.

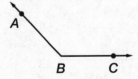

Draw each angle using your protractor. Use your compass and straightedge to bisect it. Use your protractor to check the results.

3. $\angle FGH = 20°$

4. $\angle QRS = 98°$

Practice _____

Use your compass and straightedge to bisect each segment.

1.

2.

3.

4.

Use your compass and straightedge to bisect each angle.

5.

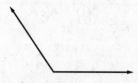

6.

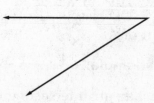

7.

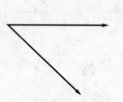

8.

Draw each angle using your protractor. Use your compass and straightedge to bisect it. Use your protractor to check the results.

9. $\angle ABC = 170°$

10. $\angle DEF = 16°$

B   C

E ——————→ F

11. $\angle HIJ = 100°$

12. $\angle MNO = 61°$

I   J

N ——————→ O

Name _____

Problem Solving: Make a List or Table

The greenhouse is having a problem with insects. On each spider plant there are 7 insects. On each rubber tree there are 13 insects. If there are a total of 115 insects in the greenhouse, how many spider plants are there? How many rubber trees are there?

 SEE

We want to know the number of spider plants and the number of rubber trees.

There are _____ insects on each spider plant.

There are _____ insects on each rubber tree.

There are _____ insects altogether.

 PLAN

We make a table that shows the possible combinations of spider plants and rubber trees. We show the total number of insects on each type of plant. By adding the number of insects we show the total number of insects for each combination.

 DO

Number of Rubber Trees	1	2	3	4	5	6	7
Number of Insects	13	____	____	____	____	____	____
Remaining Number of Insects	102	____	____	____	____	____	____
Number of Groups of 7 Insects	14.6	____	____	____	____	____	____

There are _____ spider plants and _____ rubber trees in the greenhouse.

 CHECK

There are _____ spider plants. $9 \times 7 =$ _____ insects

There are _____ rubber trees. $4 \times 13 =$ _____ insects

$63 + 52 =$ _____ insects

Apply

Solve each problem.

1. In a stable there are men and horses. In all, there are 22 heads and 72 feet. How many men and how many horses are in the stable?

2. A pen and an eraser cost a dollar and a dime. The pen costs a dollar more than the eraser. How much does each cost?

3. Your heart pumps about 60 cubic centimeters of blood each time it beats. How many times would your heart have to beat to pump 6 liters of blood? (Hint: 100 cubic centimeters = 1 liter)

4. Brad has seven coins in his pocket: 4 pennies, a nickel, a dime, and a quarter. What amounts of money less than 44¢ is he unable to make using one or any combinations of the coins?

5. You are a contestant waiting to appear on a new game show. You know the stage will be filled with prizes priced from $1 to $500. You will be allowed to keep each prize with a price tag whose digits add up to 10. You will only have 1 minute to select your prizes. Make a list of all winning price tags. What is the most expensive prize? What is the least expensive prize?

6. People began arriving at the circus in groups. The closer that it came to showtime, the larger each group became. The first group consisted only of Joey. Each group after that had two more persons than the group that arrived before it. How many people attended the circus if altogether 10 groups came?

7. Read Problem 1 again. What if the number of heads and feet were doubled? How would this change the answer?

8. Read Problem 1 again. Change the situation so that the correct answer to the problem would be 4 men and 7 horses.

9. Henny said that two lines must either intersect or be parallel. Penny said that she can show two lines that do not intersect and are not parallel. How can she do this?

10. Jim drew a triangle and showed it to Lila. He said the triangle had two right angles. Lila said that this was not possible. Explain why Lila is correct.

Draw and label each figure.

1. Ray *PQ*

2. Line segment *AB*

3. Plane *STU*

4. $\overleftrightarrow{CD}$

5. Line *CD* ⊥ line *MN*

6. $\overleftrightarrow{TU} \parallel \overleftrightarrow{RS}$

7. Circle *O* with chord *ST*

8. Circle *B* with radius *BA*

Use a protractor to measure each angle, then write the word that identifies the type of angle.

9.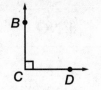

Measure _____
Type _____

10.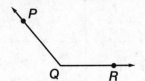

Measure _____
Type _____

11.

Measure _____
Type _____

Write the names for the vertex and rays of angle *GHI*.

12. Vertex _____

13. Rays _____
_____

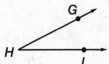

Bisect segment *AB* and angle *PQR*.

14.

15.

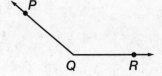

Circle the letter of the correct answer.

1
$$17,041 - 9,272$$
a. 7,879
b. 17,769
c. 7,769
d. NG

2 73×58
a. 4,234
b. 4,134
c. 131
d. NG

3 $42\overline{)2,175}$
a. 51 R3
b. 51
c. 51 R33
d. NG

4
$$3 \text{ hr } 5 \text{ min} - 1 \text{ hr } 8 \text{ min}$$
a. 2 h 3 min
b. 1 h 57 min
c. 1 h 7 min
d. NG

5 $5\frac{1}{2} + \frac{6}{7}$
a. $6\frac{5}{14}$
b. $6\frac{8}{14}$
c. $5\frac{9}{14}$
d. NG

6
$$10 - 2\frac{7}{12}$$
a. $7\frac{5}{12}$
b. $12\frac{7}{12}$
c. $8\frac{5}{12}$
d. NG

7
$$64.03 + 8.7$$
a. 72.10
b. 64.703
c. 72.73
d. NG

8
$$51.2 - 4.86$$
a. 56.06
b. 46.34
c. 4.634
d. NG

9 Round 16.71 to the nearest whole number.
a. 16
b. 17
c. 20
d. NG

10 1.36×100
a. 136
b. 100.36
c. 1.3600
d. NG

11 $0.0168 \div 12$
a. 0.014
b. 0.14
c. 0.0014
d. NG

12 $3.2\overline{)3.36}$
a. 1.25
b. 0.105
c. 1.05
d. NG

score

STOP

Polygons

Classifying Triangles

It's Algebra!

A **triangle** is a 3-sided figure that also has 3 interior angles. The sum of the measures of these 3 angles is always 180 degrees. How many degrees are there in angle *ACB*?

Triangle *ABC*
or
△ *ABC*

We want to find the measurement of angle *ACB*.

Angle *CAB* measures _____ degrees, and angle *ABC* measures _____ degrees.

To find the measurement of angle *ACB*, we add the measurements of the two known angles and subtract the total from the sum of the interior angles.

We add _____ and _____ and subtract that sum from _____.

$$\begin{array}{r} 90° \\ + 45° \\ \hline 135° \end{array} \qquad \begin{array}{r} 180° \\ - 135° \\ \hline 45° \end{array}$$

Angle *ACB* measures _____.

There is a relationship between the angles and the sides in a triangle.

Equilateral

All 3 angles are equal in measure. All 3 sides are equal in length.

Isosceles

Two angles are equal in measure. The 2 sides opposite these angles are equal in length.

Scalene

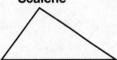

No angles are equal in measure. No sides are equal in length.

Getting Started

Calculate the missing angle measure. Identify the triangle as *equilateral*, *isosceles*, or *scalene*.

1. ∠*TRS* = _____

_____

2. ∠*XZY* = _____

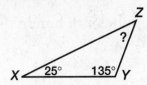

_____

3. ∠*ABC* = _____

_____

Practice

Calculate the missing angle measure. Identify the triangle as *equilateral*, *isosceles*, or *scalene*.

1. ∠*ACB* = _____

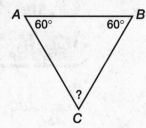

_____

2. ∠*RST* = _____

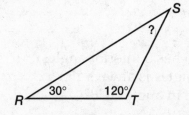

_____

3. ∠*MPO* = _____

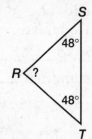

_____

4. ∠*YZX* = _____

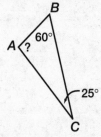

_____

5. ∠*SRT* = _____

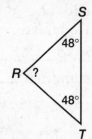

_____

6. ∠*BAC* = _____

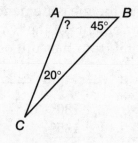

_____

7. ∠*BAC* = _____

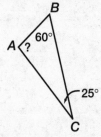

_____

8. ∠*SRT* = _____

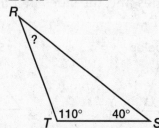

_____

9. ∠*XYZ* = _____

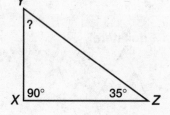

_____

Now Try This!

Find the hidden number.

1. The number of hundreds plus the number of thousands is 1.

2. The number of tens is 6 times the number of thousands.

3. The number of ones is the same as the number of hundreds.

4. The number is greater than 101.

Answer _____ _____ _____ _____

Classifying Quadrilaterals

It's Algebra!

A **quadrilateral** is a 4-sided figure. The sum of the 4 angles is always 360 degrees. Some quadrilaterals are given special names. What special name does figure *ABCD* have?

Parallelogram

A quadrilateral with opposite sides parallel and equal in length

Rectangle

A parallelogram with 4 right angles and opposite sides equal in length

Rhombus

A parallelogram with 4 sides equal in length

Square

A rectangle with 4 sides equal in length

Trapezoid

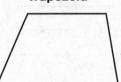

A quadrilateral with exactly one pair of parallel sides

Figure *ABCD* has _____ pair of parallel sides. It is called a _____.

Getting Started

Write the kind of quadrilateral. Identify each kind of angle.

Draw a trapezoid with one right angle. Label the corners *WXYZ*. Write the names of the sides.

1.

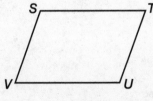

_____

∠S_____   ∠T_____

∠U_____   ∠V_____

2.

_____ _____

_____ _____

Complete the sentence.

3. The only figure that is not a parallelogram on this page is the _____.

Practice _____

Write the kind of quadrilateral. Identify each kind of angle.

1.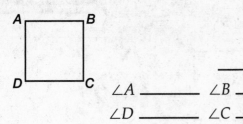

∠A _____ ∠B _____
∠D _____ ∠C _____

2.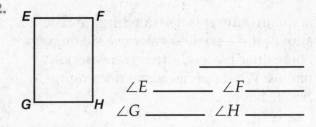

∠E _____ ∠F _____
∠G _____ ∠H _____

3.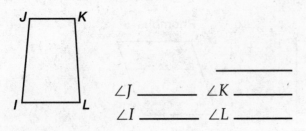

∠J _____ ∠K _____
∠I _____ ∠L _____

4.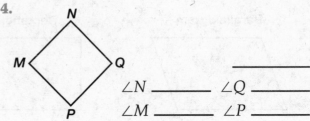

∠N _____ ∠Q _____
∠M _____ ∠P _____

5.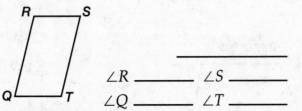

∠R _____ ∠S _____
∠Q _____ ∠T _____

6.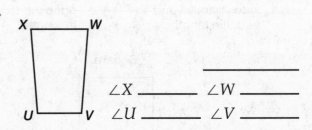

∠X _____ ∠W _____
∠U _____ ∠V _____

Calculate the missing angle measure.

7.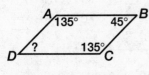

_____

8.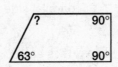

_____

9.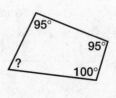

_____

Complete each sentence.

10. A quadrilateral having 2 unparallel sides is the _____.

11. Two parallelograms that have 4 sides of equal length are
the _____ and _____.

12. Two parallelograms having 4 right angles are the _____
and _____.

Lesson 13-2 • Classifying Quadrilaterals

Classifying Polygons

Triangles and quadrilaterals are polygons. A **polygon** is a plane figure with sides that are line segments that meet at a **vertex**. Which of these figures is not a polygon?

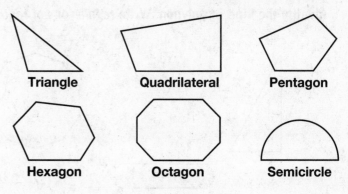

Triangle   **Quadrilateral**   **Pentagon**

Hexagon   **Octagon**   **Semicircle**

A polygon has straight sides. Since the _____ has a curved side, it is not a polygon.

A **diagonal** of a polygon joins two vertices of a polygon but is not a side of the polygon.

$\overline{AC}$ and $\overline{AD}$ are two diagonals of the polygon *ABCDE*.

A **regular polygon** has all sides of equal length and all angles of equal measure.

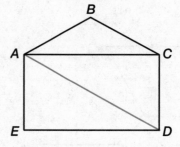

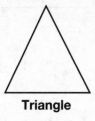 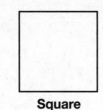 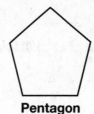 

Triangle   **Square**   **Pentagon**   **Hexagon**

Getting Started

Identify the kind of polygon. Write *regular* or *not regular*.

1. _____

2. _____

3. _____

Draw all possible diagonals. Write the name of each diagonal. Then, complete the chart.

4.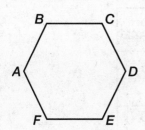

5. _____ _____ _____

   _____ _____ _____

   _____ _____ _____

6.

Name of figure	
Number of sides	
Number of angles	
Number of diagonals from one vertex	
Total number of diagonals	

Practice _____

Identify the kind of polygon. Write *regular* or *not regular*.

1.

   _____

   _____

2.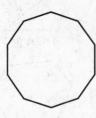

   _____

   _____

3.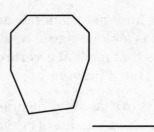

   _____

   _____

4.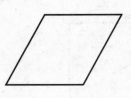

   _____

   _____

5.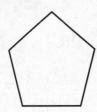

   _____

   _____

6.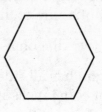

   _____

   _____

Draw all possible diagonals. Write the name of each diagonal.

7.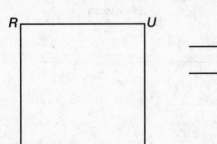

   _____

8.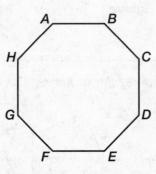

   _____ _____ _____

   _____ _____ _____

   _____ _____ _____

   _____ _____ _____

   _____ _____ _____

   _____ _____ _____

Complete the chart.

9.

Name	Number of Sides	Number of Angles	Number of Diagonals from 1 Vertex	Total Number of Diagonals
Triangle	3	3	0	0
Quadrilateral	4	4	1	2
Pentagon	5			
Hexagon	6			
Heptagon	7			

Congruent Polygons

Two plane figures are **congruent** if they have the same size and shape. One figure will fit on top of the other. The parts that fit together are called **corresponding parts**. Which angle corresponds to angle *ABC*?

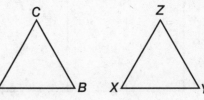

We can use tracing paper to show which parts will fit. Place the paper over triangle *ABC* and trace it. Slide this over triangle *XYZ*.

The angle that fits on angle *ABC* is angle _____.

Angles *ABC* and _____ are corresponding angles.

Corresponding Sides	*Corresponding Angles*
$\overline{AC}$ and $\overline{XZ}$	∠*ABC* and ∠*XYZ*
$\overline{CB}$ and _____	∠*CAB* and _____
$\overline{AB}$ and _____	∠*ACB* and _____

The corresponding parts of congruent figures are also congruent. The symbol for "is congruent to" is ≅. **Triangle *ABC* is congruent to triangle *XYZ*** is written: △***ABC*** ≅ △***XYZ***.

$\overline{AC} \cong \overline{XZ}$	∠*ABC* ≅ ∠*XYZ*
_____ ≅ $\overline{ZY}$	_____ ≅ ∠*ZXY*
_____ ≅ $\overline{XY}$	_____ ≅ ∠*XZY*

Getting Started

Tell if these segments are congruent. Write *Yes* or *No*.

1. _____

Complete these statements about each set of congruent figures.

2. $\overline{AB} \cong$ _____

3. $\overline{DA} \cong$ _____

4. ∠*SVU* ≅ _____

5. ∠*UTS* ≅ _____

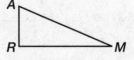

6. $\overline{AM} \cong$ _____

7. $\overline{YX} \cong$ _____

8. ∠*RAM* ≅ _____

9. ∠*YZX* ≅ _____

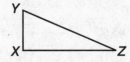

Practice

Tell if the figures are congruent. Write *Yes* or *No*.

1.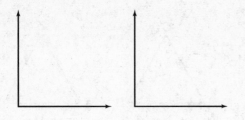

2.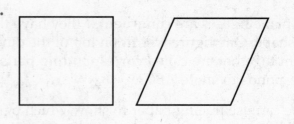

   _____

3.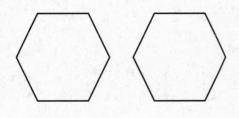

   _____

4.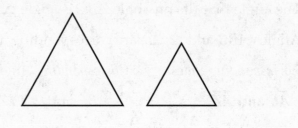

   _____

5.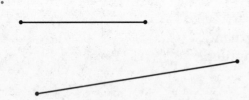

   _____

6.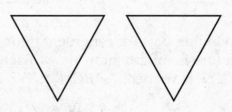

   _____

Complete these statements about each set of congruent figures.

7. $\overline{AB} \cong$ _____

8. $\angle ABC \cong$ _____

9. $\overline{MN} \cong$ _____

10. $\angle MLN \cong$ _____

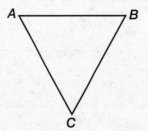 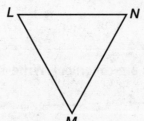

11. $\angle DGF \cong$ _____

12. $\angle TUV \cong$ _____

13. $\overline{ST} \cong$ _____

14. $\overline{GF} \cong$ _____

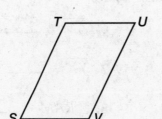 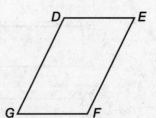

Lesson 13-4 • Congruent Polygons

Symmetry

If you can fold a figure so that the two parts match, the figure is called a **symmetric figure**. The line where the figure is folded is called a **line of symmetry**. Name the lines of symmetry for this rectangle.

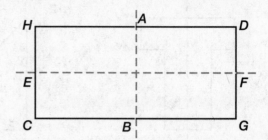

We can fold the rectangle along the dotted lines and each time make two congruent figures.

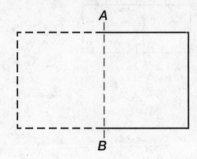 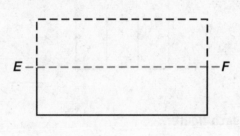

The lines of symmetry are _____ and _____.

Getting Started

Tell if the dotted line is a line of symmetry. Write *Yes* or *No*.

1.
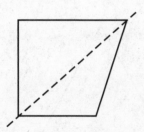

2.
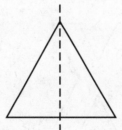

3.
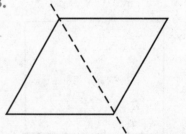

Draw all lines of symmetry for each figure.

4.
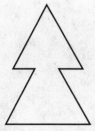

5.
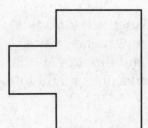

6.
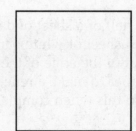

Practice

Tell if the dotted line is a line of symmetry. Write *Yes* or *No*.

1.
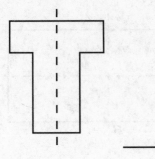
___

2.
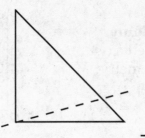
___

3.
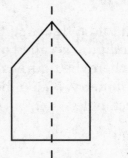
___

4.
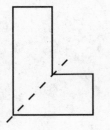
___

5.
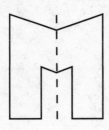
___

6.
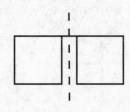
___

Draw all lines of symmetry for each figure.

7.
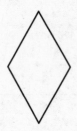

8.
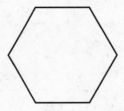

9.

10.

11.

12.

[Now Try This!]

Use one half of a sheet of dark colored paper, scissors, glue, and 1 full sheet of white paper to show congruence. Cut a shape out of the edge of the dark paper and flip it over onto white paper to make a reflection. Your reflections might look similar to this when completed.

Transformations

You can slide, flip, or turn a figure. Each move is called a **transformation**. The original figure and the transformed figure are congruent.

Slide

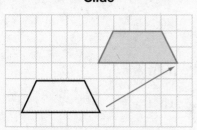

Another name for a slide is a **translation**.

Flip

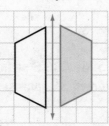

Another name for a flip is a **reflection**.

Turn

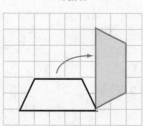

Another name for a turn is a **rotation**.

With each move, the trapezoid did not change its _____ or _____.

The original trapezoid and the resulting trapezoid are _____.

Getting Started

Write *translation*, *reflection*, **or** *rotation* **to describe each move.**

1.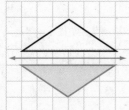

_____

2.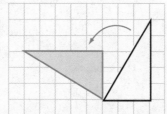

_____

3.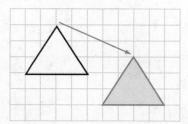

_____

4. **Slide ABCD 6 squares to the right.**

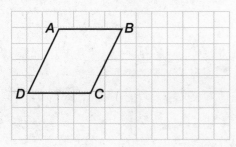

5. **Flip JKLM over line segment ML.**

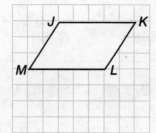

Practice

Write *translation*, *reflection*, or *rotation* to describe each move.

1.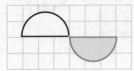

   _____

2.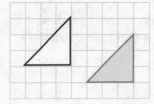

   _____

3.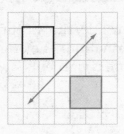

   _____

**Turn *ABC* to the right 90°.
The first line is drawn for you.**

4.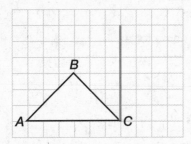

**Slide *ABC* 5 squares to the right and
down 3 squares.**

5.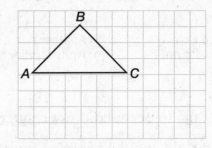

Flip *DEF* over line *a*.

6.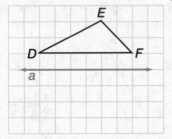

Flip *ABC* over line *b*.

7.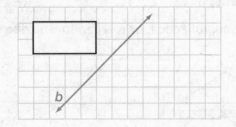

⟨ Now Try This! ⟩

You can combine two or more transformations. The single transformation
you produce is called a **composition**. These footsteps create a **glide reflection**.

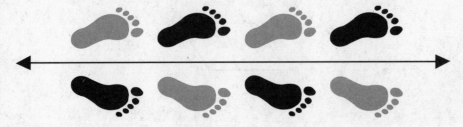

Create a glide reflection of your own.

Identifying Similar Polygons

Similar figures have the same shape but not necessarily the same size. Which two of these rectangles are similar?

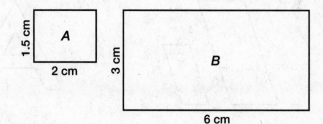

We want to identify the two figures that have the same shape.

Rectangle *A* is _____ cm by _____ cm.

Rectangle *B* is _____ cm by _____ cm.

Rectangle *C* is _____ cm by _____ cm.

Rectangle *D* is _____ cm by _____ cm.

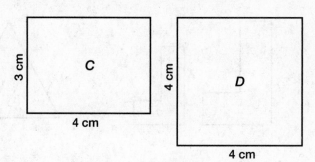

REMEMBER To be similar figures, each part of the first figure must get larger or smaller at the same rate as its corresponding part in the second figure.

Since each side of rectangle _____ is _____ times as large as the corresponding side of rectangle _____, rectangle _____ is similar to rectangle _____.

Getting Started

Which triangle is similar to triangle *A*?

1.

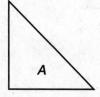 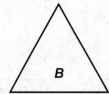   _____

Write *Yes* or *No* to tell if the pair is similar.

2.

   _____

3.

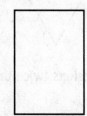   _____

Draw a similar square with dimensions twice the size.

4.

Practice

Write *Yes* or *No* to tell if the pair is similar.

1.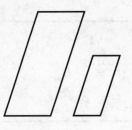
   ___

2.
   ___

3.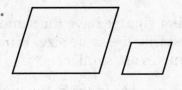
   ___

4.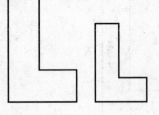
   ___

5.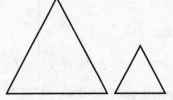
   ___

6.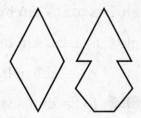
   ___

Which rectangle is similar to rectangle *A*?

7.
   ___

Which triangle is similar to triangle *A*?

8.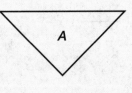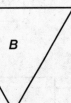
   ___

Draw a similar rectangle with dimensions twice the size.

9.

Lesson 13-7 • Identifying Similar Polygons

Classifying Solid Figures

Prisms and pyramids are examples of **solid figures**. They are named for the shape of the bases. The sides of the figures are called **faces** and include the **bases**. The faces meet at **edges**. The edges meet at **vertices**. How many faces, edges, and vertices does a rectangular prism have?

Triangular Prism

Rectangular Prism

If you were to flatten a rectangular prism, it would appear like this.

Square Prism or Cube

Rectangular Pyramid

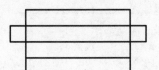

It has _____ faces.

It has _____ edges.

It has _____ vertices.

Triangular Pyramid

Square Pyramid

Some solid figures have curved surfaces.

Cone

Cylinder

Sphere

Getting Started

Use these figures to answer 1 through 5.

1. What solid figure does the pencil tip suggest? _____

2. Name the edges of base *EFGH*.

   ____ ____ ____ ____

3. Name the face congruent to *RTS*. _____

4. Name the vertices of face *PTR*.

   ____ ____ ____

Complete the chart.

5.

	Number of Faces	Number of Edges	Number of Vertices
Rectangular pyramid			
Rectangular prism			

Practice

Write the name of the solid figure each object suggests.

1.

   _____

2.

   _____

3.

   _____

4.

   _____

5.

   _____

6.

   _____

Use the figures on the right to complete Exercises 7 through 9.

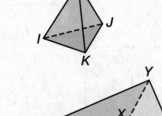

7. Name the edges of the triangular pyramid.

   ____ ____ ____ ____ ____ ____

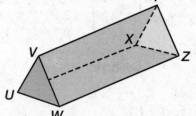

8. Name the faces congruent to *VYZW*.

   _____ _____

9. Name the vertices of *UVYX*.

   ____ ____ ____ ____

Use the figures on page 287 to complete the chart.

10.

	Number of Faces	Number of Edges	Number of Vertices
Square pyramid			
Cube			
Triangular pyramid			
Triangular prism			

⟦ Now Try This! ⟧

Enlarge this pattern on a sheet of paper. Cut along the solid lines. Fold on the dotted lines and tape together to form a cube. Design your own patterns and make other solid figures out of paper.

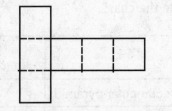

Lesson 13-8 • Classifying Solid Figures

Name _____

Problem Solving: Make a Tally and a Graph

Four students took a survey to find out which types of books were most popular with elementary school students in Grades 3 through 6. Their results are tallied here. Make a bar graph showing the results of the survey.

	Grade 3	Grade 4	Grade 5	Grade 6
Fairy tales	IIII III	IIII	IIII II	II
Science fiction	IIII	IIII III	IIII II	IIII IIII
Mysteries	IIII IIII II	IIII II	IIII IIII I	IIII IIII IIII
Animal stories	IIII IIII II	IIII IIII	IIII IIII	IIII II
Biographies	IIII IIII	IIII III	IIII IIII II	IIII IIII

SEE

We want to show on a bar graph the number of students who selected each kind of book. We know the results of each of the four surveys.

PLAN

Since the largest number of selections is 45, we choose to make the graph go from 0 to 50 with 10 selections per interval.

DO

Complete the graph below.

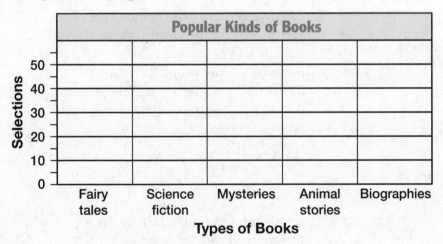

Popular Kinds of Books

Selections: 50, 40, 30, 20, 10, 0

Types of Books: Fairy tales, Science fiction, Mysteries, Animal stories, Biographies

CHECK

We can check our work by adding again the results of all four surveys for each type of book.

Fairy tales $8 + 4 + 7 + 2 =$ _____

Science fiction $5 + 8 + 7 + 9 =$ _____

Mysteries $12 + 7 + 11 + 15 =$ _____

Animal stories $12 + 10 + 9 + 7 =$ _____

Biographies $9 + 8 + 12 + 10 =$ _____

Apply

Solve each problem.

1. Read the following sentence and tally the number of times the vowels *a, e, i, o,* and *u* are used: "Four score and seven years ago our fathers brought forth on this continent a new nation, conceived in liberty and dedicated to the proposition that all men are created equal."

2. From your tally in Problem 1, make a bar graph to show the number of times each vowel was used.

3. Toss a coin 20 times and tally the number of heads and the number of tails.

4. Create a bar graph to show the number of heads and number of tails that you recorded in Problem 3.

5. Tally the results of the entire class for Problem 3. Have each student toss a coin 20 times and record the total number of heads and tails.

6. Roll a pair of dice 36 times and tally the sums. Create a bar graph to illustrate the results. Compare your graph with those of other students.

7. A single die, or number cube, has 6 faces. Does a rectangular prism have more, fewer, or the same number of faces as the number cube?

8. Which of these solid figures has more faces, a triangular prism or a rectangular pyramid? Prove that your answer is correct.

9. The Math Club tallied the lines of symmetry on different figures they saw in an art catalog. Does a square have more, fewer, or the same number of lines of symmetry as a rectangle that is not a square? Prove that your answer is correct.

10. The Math Club also tallied the different kinds of angles—right, acute, or scalene—found in the art catalog. Under which of these kinds would they put a tally mark for the angle formed by the two equal sides in an isosceles right triangle?

Calculator: Expressions and Formulas

A swimming pool in the shape of a rectangular prism is filled with water. What is the volume of the swimming pool?

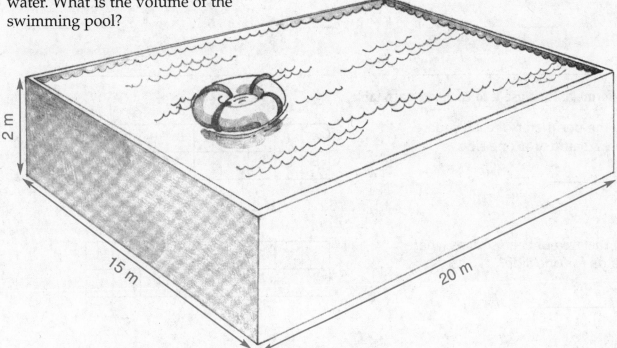

2 m

15 m

20 m

A **formula** is a special expression that helps you find particular measurements. The formula for finding volume is **length times width times height.** This is usually written as $V = l \times w \times h$, or simply $V = lwh$. To find the volume of the swimming pool we replace l by 20, w by 15, and h by 2. Complete this calculator code.

20 ⊠ 15 ⊠ 2 ⊟ ☐

The volume of the swimming pool is _____ cubic meters.

An **expression** is a mathematical sentence sometimes written with letters instead of numbers. If numbers are used to replace the letters we have **evaluated the expression**. We evaluate the expression $a \times b + c$ by replacing 12 for a, 9 for b, and 56 for c. Complete this code.

12 ⊠ 9 ⊞ 56 ⊟ ☐

Evaluate each of these expressions by replacing 17 for a, 28 for b, and 13 for c. Then compute the answers.

$a + b - c =$ _____ $5 \times a + c - b =$ _____

Practice

Evaluate each expression when *a* is 25, *b* is 12, and *c* is 9.

1. $a - b + c =$ _____

2. $5 \times a + b =$ _____

3. $9 \times b - a =$ _____

Evaluate each expression when *a* is 36, *b* is 6, and *c* is 12.

4. $a \div c \times b =$ _____

5. $a \times b \times b =$ _____

6. $5 \times c + a - b =$ _____

Apply

Write the formula. Then use it to complete each table.

7. Find the perimeter of each square where *s* stands for one side.

   _____

s	1	2	3	4	5	6	7	8
P	4							

8. Find the area of each square where *s* stands for one side.

   _____

s	1	2	3	4	5	6	7	8
A	1							

9. Find the surface area of each cube where *s* stands for one side of a face.

   _____

s	1	2	3	4	5	6	7	8
SA	6							

10. Find the volume of each cube where *e* stands for one edge.

    _____

e	1	2	3	4	5	6	7	8
V	1							

Now Try This!

1. What happens to the perimeter of a square if each side is doubled?

2. What happens to the area of a square if each side is doubled?

3. What happens to the volume of a cube if each edge is doubled?

Find the missing angle measure.

1.

_____

2.

_____

Identify the kind of quadrilateral.

3.

_____

4.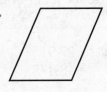

_____

Identify the kind of polygon. Draw all possible diagonals.

5.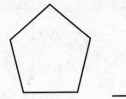

_____

6.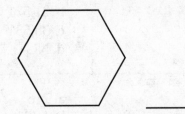

_____

Tell if the figures are congruent. Write *Yes* or *No*.

7.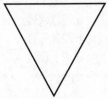

_____

The triangles are congruent. Write the name of the angle which is congruent to *BCA*.

8.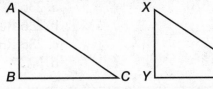

_____

Draw all possible lines of symmetry.

9.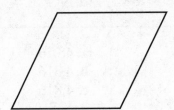

Are the figures similar? Write *Yes* or *No*.

10.

_____

Identify the kind of solid figure.

11.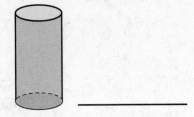

_____

Write the number of edges.

12.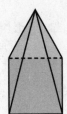

_____

Circle the letter of the correct answer.

1
27,915
+ 8,475

a. 35,380
b. 35,390
c. 36,390
d. NG

2
31,046
− 9,575

a. 21,471
b. 21,571
c. 38,531
d. NG

3 27 × 53

a. 216
b. 1,431
c. 13,581
d. NG

4 24)5,670

a. 236
b. 236 R4
c. 236 R6
d. NG

5 Find the volume.

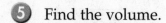

a. 7 cm
b. 12 sq cm
c. 12 cu cm
d. NG

6
$4\frac{4}{5}$
$+ 3\frac{2}{3}$

a. $7\frac{2}{15}$
b. $7\frac{7}{15}$
c. $7\frac{3}{4}$
d. NG

7
$21\frac{1}{4}$
$- 16\frac{2}{3}$

a. $4\frac{7}{12}$
b. $5\frac{7}{12}$
c. $5\frac{5}{12}$
d. NG

8 $2\frac{1}{2} \times 3\frac{1}{3}$

a. $5\frac{1}{6}$
b. $6\frac{1}{6}$
c. $8\frac{1}{3}$
d. NG

9
16.241
+ 4.79

a. 20.031
b. 20.931
c. 21.031
d. NG

10
16.36
− 4.788

a. 11.572
b. 11.588
c. 12.428
d. NG

11 1.06 × 3.6

a. 48.16
b. 4.816
c. 4,816
d. NG

score

Ratios and Percents

Writing Ratios

A **ratio** is a way of comparing two quantities. Washington has won 3 games and lost 2. The ratio of wins to losses is 3 to 2. What is the ratio of wins to total games played?

We want to express the relationship of games won to games played as a ratio.

Washington won _____ games.

They played _____ games.

The ratio of wins to games played is _____ to _____.

We can write the ratio of 3 to 5 in three ways.

3 to 5   **3:5** $\frac{3}{5}$

Three and five are called the **terms** of the ratio. The order in which the terms are expressed is very important. 3:5 is not the same as 5:3.

Getting Started

Write each ratio in three ways. Do not simplify fractions.

1. white marbles to green marbles

   _____ _____ _____

2. green marbles to all marbles

   _____ _____ _____

3. The U.S. flag has 7 red stripes and 6 white stripes. What is the ratio of red stripes to white stripes?

   _____ ____ ____

4. You can buy 6 candy bars for 89¢. What is the ratio of candy bars to money?

   _____ ____ ____

Write each ratio in fraction form. Do not simplify.

5. 7 to 5   6. 4:6   7. 5 to 10   8. 3:4

Practice

Write each ratio in three ways. Do not simplify fractions.

1. green cars to white cars

_____ _____ _____

2. handbags to hats

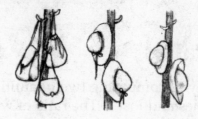

_____ _____ _____

3. cardinals to robins

robins   cardinals

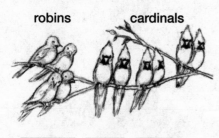

_____ _____ _____

4. bricks to blocks

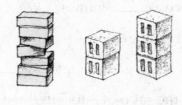

_____ _____ _____

Write each ratio in fraction form. Do not simplify.

5. 3 to 7 _____

6. 8 to 5 _____

7. 6:1 _____

8. 3 to 9 _____

9. 10:6 _____

10. 6 to 5 _____

11. 4 to 8 _____

12. 7:8 _____

Problem Solving

Solve each problem. Write each ratio in fraction form. Do not simplify

13. Rhoda got 4 hits in 7 times at bat. What is the ratio of hits to times at bat?

14. George lost 3 out of 8 golf matches. What is the ratio of wins to losses?

15. Lemons sell 3 for $1.00 at the grocery. What is the ratio of lemons to their cost?

16. It took Winston 2 hours to skate 15 miles. What is the ratio of distance to time?

17. Mrs. Yeager used 9 gallons of gas driving 216 miles on her weekend trip. What is the ratio of miles to gallons?

18. Marcie has $1.53 in coins in her pocket. If she has 6 quarters, what is the ratio of quarters to pennies?

19. What is the ratio of red stripes to stars on the U.S. flag?

20. What is the ratio of inches to feet in one yard?

Name _____

Using Ratio Tables

Manuel is running a 5-mile race. If he runs the same time for each mile, how long will it take Manuel to run the race?

We can make a ratio table to find how long it will take Manuel to run 5 miles.

Miles	1	2	3	4	5
Minutes	9	18	27		

We can complete the ratio table by finding equivalent fractions.

$$\frac{1 \times 2}{9 \times 2} = \frac{2}{18}$$

$$\frac{1 \times 3}{9 \times 3} = \frac{3}{27}$$

$$\frac{1 \times 4}{9 \times 4} = \frac{4}{\blacksquare}$$

$$\frac{1 \times 5}{9 \times 5} = \frac{5}{\blacksquare}$$

It will take _____ minutes for Manuel to run the race.

Getting Started

Complete each ratio table to answer the question.

1. One bolt costs 8¢. How much must be paid for 6 bolts?

Bolts	1	2	3	4	5	6
Cost	8¢	16¢				

2. Three mints cost 15¢. How much will it cost for 12 mints?

Mints	3	6	9	12
Cost	15¢	30¢		

3. Each girl in the parade is carrying a half-dozen roses. How many roses are 7 girls carrying?

Roses	6	12					
Girls	1	2	3	4	5	6	7

4. Walking uses about 200 calories for each 2 miles. How many calories are used in 12 miles?

Calories						
Miles	2	4	6	8	10	12

Practice

Complete each ratio table to answer the question.

1. Three cards cost $2. How much does it cost for 15 cards?

Cards	3	6	9	12	15
Cost	2	4	6		

2. Four boys and three girls make up each team. If there are 12 girls, how many boys are playing on the teams?

Boys	4	8		
Girls	3	6	9	12

3. A recipe calling for 2 eggs will make 7 pancakes. How many eggs will be needed for 28 pancakes?

Eggs	2			
Pancakes	7	14	21	28

4. There are 5 petals and 2 leaves on each silk flower. How many petals are in a bouquet having 10 leaves?

Petals	5				
Leaves	2	4	6	8	10

5. Each sweater has 5 buttons and 3 emblems. How many emblems are on a set of identical sweaters having 40 buttons?

Buttons	5	10	15	20	25	30	35	40
Emblems	3							

6. Sam walked 1 mile in 15 minutes. How long will it take him to walk 3 miles?

Miles	1	2	3	4
Minutes	15			

Now Try This!

A white cube, measuring three inches on each edge, is painted green on its outer surface. When the paint is dry, it is cut into one-inch cubes. How many little cubes will there be? _____

How many of the little cubes will have:

1. green on 3 sides? _____   2. green on 1 side? _____

3. green on 2 sides? _____   4. green on no sides? _____

Name _____

Equal Ratios

Adelina and her father are making concrete. Each batch of concrete requires 9 buckets of sand. The ratio of sand to gravel is 3 to 4 parts. How much gravel is needed for each batch of concrete?

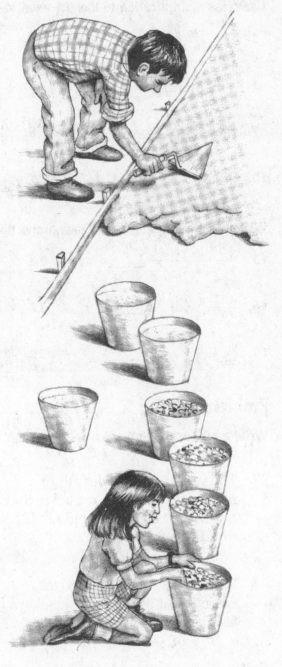

We need to find the amount of gravel needed for a batch of concrete.

There are _____ buckets of sand in a batch of concrete.

The ratio of sand to gravel is _____ to _____.

To find the amount of gravel in a batch, we write two equal ratios and solve for n by multiplying or dividing by the identity element.

$\dfrac{\text{sand}}{\text{gravel}}$ $\qquad$ $\dfrac{3}{4} = \dfrac{9}{n}$ $\qquad$ $\dfrac{3}{4} \times \dfrac{}{} = \dfrac{9}{}$

$\uparrow$
identity
element

Each batch requires _____ buckets of gravel. The equation that expresses two equal ratios is called a **proportion**.

REMEMBER We can cross multiply to see if two ratios are equal.

$\dfrac{2}{3} \bowtie \dfrac{4}{6}$

$2 \times 6 = 3 \times 4$

$12 = 12$

The ratios are equal. They are really a proportion.

Getting Started

Use cross multiplication to identify equal ratios. Write *Yes* or *No*.

1. $\dfrac{1}{2} = \dfrac{3}{4}$ _____

2. $\dfrac{2}{3} = \dfrac{10}{15}$ _____

3. $\dfrac{16}{24} = \dfrac{8}{12}$ _____

Write the missing number in each proportion.

4. $\dfrac{4}{5} = \dfrac{n}{20}$ $\quad n =$ _____

5. $\dfrac{2}{3} = \dfrac{12}{n}$ $\quad n =$ _____

6. $\dfrac{n}{8} = \dfrac{20}{40}$ $\quad n =$ _____

Practice

Use cross multiplication to identify equal ratios. Write *Yes* or *No*.

1. $\frac{3}{4} = \frac{12}{16}$ _____

2. $\frac{4}{5} = \frac{13}{15}$ _____

3. $\frac{6}{36} = \frac{1}{6}$ _____

4. $\frac{3}{2} = \frac{6}{4}$ _____

5. $\frac{9}{2} = \frac{72}{16}$ _____

6. $\frac{5}{8} = \frac{35}{54}$ _____

7. $\frac{12}{15} = \frac{8}{10}$ _____

8. $\frac{10}{15} = \frac{12}{18}$ _____

9. $\frac{25}{20} = \frac{10}{8}$ _____

10. $\frac{5}{7} = \frac{35}{42}$ _____

11. $\frac{8}{24} = \frac{6}{18}$ _____

12. $\frac{35}{100} = \frac{9}{25}$ _____

Write the missing number in each proportion.

13. $\frac{3}{4} = \frac{n}{12}$ $n =$ _____

14. $\frac{2}{3} = \frac{n}{9}$ $n =$ _____

15. $\frac{n}{5} = \frac{16}{20}$ $n =$ _____

16. $\frac{4}{n} = \frac{12}{15}$ $n =$ _____

17. $\frac{6}{8} = \frac{3}{n}$ $n =$ _____

18. $\frac{n}{10} = \frac{70}{100}$ $n =$ _____

19. $\frac{n}{56} = \frac{3}{7}$ $n =$ _____

20. $\frac{16}{n} = \frac{2}{5}$ $n =$ _____

21. $\frac{9}{3} = \frac{n}{6}$ $n =$ _____

Problem Solving

Write a proportion and solve each problem.

22. The width and the length of a rectangle are in the ratio 3 to 5. If the width of the rectangle is 12, find the length.

23. Each quilt square uses 5 red pieces and 3 white pieces of cloth. How many red pieces are sewn in a set of quilt squares containing 18 white pieces?

24. Raisins cost $3.20 for 2 boxes. Allen spent $4.80 on raisins. How many boxes of raisins did he buy?

25. Betsy averages 2 bites for every 5 times she casts her fishing rod. Betsy got 8 bites on her fishing trip. How many times did she cast her rod?

26. There are 36 paper plates in 3 packages. How many paper plates are there in 5 packages?

27. Eiji spent $2.00 for 12 ears of corn. How much would 15 ears of corn cost?

Scale Drawings

A map is an example of a scale drawing. The scale is a ratio. Actually how far is it from Artesia to Baldwin?

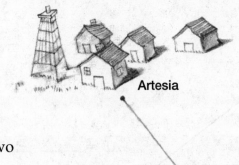

Artesia

We want to find the distance between the two towns.

On the map, it is _____ centimeters between Artesia and Baldwin.

The ratio of centimeters to kilometers is _____ to _____.

To find the actual distance between towns, we write and solve a proportion in which the scale is equal to the actual distances.

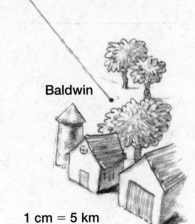

Baldwin

1 cm = 5 km

$$\frac{cm}{km} = \frac{1}{5} = \frac{5}{n} \qquad \frac{1}{5} \times \underline{\quad} = \frac{5}{n} \qquad n = \underline{\quad}$$

It is _____ kilometers from Artesia to Baldwin.

Getting Started

Use the scale 1 cm = 5 km to find the actual distance in kilometers of each of the following:

1. A distance of 6 cm _____

2. A distance of 10 cm _____

3. A distance of 7 cm _____

4. A distance of 1 cm _____

5. A distance of 2 cm _____

6. A distance of 9 cm _____

Use the scale below and a metric ruler to find the actual dimensions and area of the figure represented by this scale drawing.

7. 1 cm = 4 m $\overline{AB}$ = _____

   $\overline{BC}$ = _____

   The area is _____.

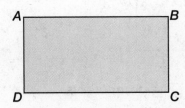

Practice

**Use each scale and a metric ruler to find the actual dimensions
of the figures represented by each scale drawing.**

1. 1 cm = 4 m

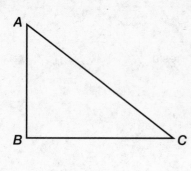

$\overline{AB}$ = _____

$\overline{BC}$ = _____

$\overline{AC}$ = _____

2. 2 cm = 3 km

$\overline{WX}$ = _____

$\overline{WZ}$ = _____

3. 1 cm = 5 m

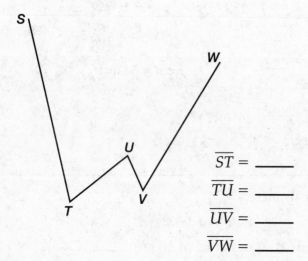

$\overline{ST}$ = _____

$\overline{TU}$ = _____

$\overline{UV}$ = _____

$\overline{VW}$ = _____

4. 1 cm = 9 km

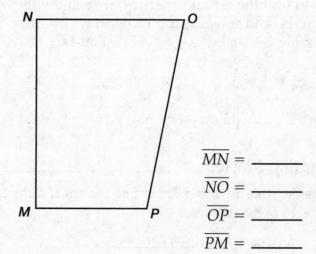

$\overline{MN}$ = _____

$\overline{NO}$ = _____

$\overline{OP}$ = _____

$\overline{PM}$ = _____

5. 1 cm = 2 m

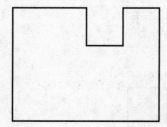

The perimeter is _____.

6. 3 cm = 5 m

The area is _____.

Name _____

Percents

A percent is a special ratio. The word **percent** means "per one hundred." The symbol for percent is %. What percent of pennies shown are heads?

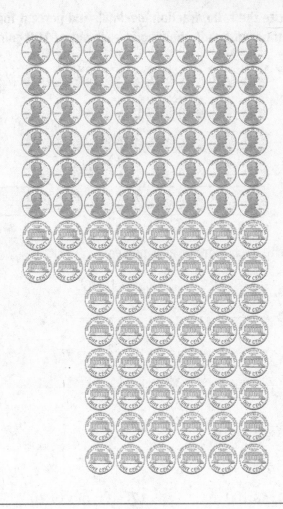

We want to express the ratio of pennies showing heads to all the pennies, as a percent.

There are _____ pennies altogether.

Heads are showing on _____ of the pennies.

To express this relationship as a percent, we first write it as a fraction and decimal. Then, to rename a decimal as a percent, we multiply it by 100.

Ratio	Fraction	Decimal	Percent
48 to 100	$\frac{48}{100}$	0.48	48%

Heads are showing on _____% of the pennies.

Getting Started

Write the ratio, fraction, decimal, and percent for the number of heads showing in each set of 100 coin tosses. (Tails are not shown.)

1.

2.

3.

_____ _____   _____ _____   _____ _____

_____ _____   _____ _____   _____ _____

Write each number as a percent.

4. 20 out of 100

5. 66 to 100

6. $\frac{89}{100}$

7. 0.36

Practice

Write the ratio, fraction, decimal, and percent for the number of heads showing in each set of 100 coin tosses. (Tails are not shown.)

1.

   _____ _____

   _____ _____

2.

   _____ _____

   _____ _____

3.

   _____ _____

   _____ _____

Write each number as a percent.

4. $\frac{17}{100}$

   _____

5. 11:100

   _____

6. 31 out of 100

   _____

7. 29 to 100

   _____

8. 0.12

   _____

9. $\frac{36}{100}$

   _____

10. $\frac{63}{100}$

    _____

11. 50:100

    _____

12. $\frac{37}{100}$

    _____

13. 0.15

    _____

14. $\frac{1}{100}$

    _____

15. 0.96

    _____

16. 43:100

    _____

17. 100 out of 100

    _____

18. 5:100

    _____

19. $\frac{67}{100}$

    _____

Problem Solving

Solve each problem.

20. In a recent poll, 65 out of every 100 people surveyed thought the president was doing a good job. What percent thought the president was doing a good job?

21. On a test containing 100 items, Brittany answered 87 questions correctly. What percent did Brittany get right? What percent did she get wrong?

[Now Try This!]

Write five ratios equivalent to 50%.

_____ _____ _____ _____ _____

Expressing Percents as Fractions

Headlines in newspapers often express number relationships in the form of percents. Express the rate that earnings have increased in the form of a fraction.

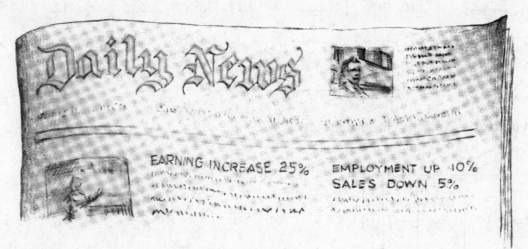

We want to write _____ as a fraction.

Any percent can be written as a fraction if you remember that percent means "per one hundred."

We drop the percent sign and express the number over 100. Remember, we must simplify the terms if we can.

Percent	Fraction	Simplified
25%	$\frac{25}{100}$	$\frac{1}{4}$

The earnings increased by _____.

Getting Started

Write each percent as a fraction in simplest terms.

1. 75% = _____   2. 32% = _____   3. 8% = _____   4. 12% = _____   5. 55% = _____

6. 19% = _____   7. 10% = _____   8. 87% = _____   9. 64% = _____   10. 91% = _____

Use the newspaper headlines to answer Exercises 11 and 12.

11. Write the employment figure as a fraction. _____

12. Write the sales drop as a fraction. _____

Practice

Write each percent as a fraction in simplest terms.

1. 16% = ＿＿＿ 2. 4% = ＿＿＿ 3. 13% = ＿＿＿ 4. 75% = ＿＿＿

5. 28% = ＿＿＿ 6. 57% = ＿＿＿ 7. 12% = ＿＿＿ 8. 48% = ＿＿＿

9. 89% = ＿＿＿ 10. 40% = ＿＿＿ 11. 36% = ＿＿＿ 12. 62% = ＿＿＿

13. 1% = ＿＿＿ 14. 70% = ＿＿＿ 15. 8% = ＿＿＿ 16. 37% = ＿＿＿

17. 5% = ＿＿＿ 18. 14% = ＿＿＿ 19. 32% = ＿＿＿ 20. 96% = ＿＿＿

Write each percent as a fraction in simplest terms.

21.

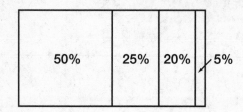

50% = ＿＿＿   25% = ＿＿＿

20% = ＿＿＿   5% = ＿＿＿

22.

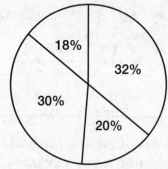

18% = ＿＿＿   20% = ＿＿＿

32% = ＿＿＿   30% = ＿＿＿

Problem Solving

Solve each problem.

23. In Rochester, New York, 40% of the population is 35 or older. What percent of the population is younger than 35?

24. Thirteen percent of the population of Rhode Island lives in rural areas. What percent of the people do not live in rural areas?

25. Ozzie's sold chocolate and cherry shakes to the Girl Scout troop. If 74% of the troop ordered chocolate shakes, what percent ordered cherry?

26. Eighteen percent of the pictures in Myles' photo album are black and white. The rest are in color. What percent of Myles' photos are in color?

Name _____

Expressing Fractions as Percents

The mathematics teacher took a poll of the favorite color of each of her students. Find the percent of the class that chose blue.

Favorite Color Survey	
Red	6
Yellow	4
Blue	8
Green	7

We want to express the part of the class that chose blue as a percent.

Blue was the favorite color of _____ students.

There are _____ students in the class altogether.

To express this relationship as a percent, we first write it as a fraction. We rename the fraction as a decimal by dividing the numerator by the denominator. Finally, we rename the decimal as a percent by multiplying it by 100 and affixing a percent sign.

Fraction	Decimal	Percent
$\frac{8}{25}$	$25\overline{)8.00}$ 0.32	$0.32 \times 100 = $ _____%

The survey showed that _____% of the class preferred blue.

Round all decimals to hundredths.

$\frac{1}{7}$ $7\overline{)1.000}$ $\frac{0.142}{} \approx 0.14$ 14%

Getting Started

Write each fraction as a percent.

1. $\frac{1}{2} = $ _____

2. $\frac{1}{3} = $ _____

3. $\frac{3}{8} = $ _____

4. $\frac{4}{5} = $ _____

5. $\frac{3}{7} = $ _____

6. $\frac{9}{10} = $ _____

7. $\frac{3}{25} = $ _____

8. $\frac{4}{50} = $ _____

Use the Favorite Color Survey to answer Exercises 9 and 10.

9. What percent chose red as their favorite color? _____

10. What percent chose green as their favorite color? _____

Practice

Write each fraction as a percent.

1. $\frac{1}{5} =$ _____

2. $\frac{2}{3} =$ _____

3. $\frac{3}{10} =$ _____

4. $\frac{1}{8} =$ _____

5. $\frac{5}{6} =$ _____

6. $\frac{3}{4} =$ _____

7. $\frac{7}{9} =$ _____

8. $\frac{1}{4} =$ _____

9. $\frac{3}{25} =$ _____

10. $\frac{4}{7} =$ _____

11. $\frac{17}{50} =$ _____

12. $\frac{11}{12} =$ _____

13. $\frac{7}{8} =$ _____

14. $\frac{14}{35} =$ _____

15. $\frac{19}{20} =$ _____

16. $\frac{3}{16} =$ _____

17. $\frac{7}{40} =$ _____

18. $\frac{3}{50} =$ _____

19. $\frac{7}{18} =$ _____

20. $\frac{5}{11} =$ _____

Problem Solving

Use the Favorite Team Survey to answer each question.

21. What percent voted for the Cowboys? _____

22. What percent voted for the Jets? _____

23. What percent voted for the Bears? _____

24. What percent voted for the Rams? _____

Favorite Team Survey	
Cowboys	16
Jets	8
Bears	10
Rams	6

(Now Try This!)

A **repeating decimal** is a decimal consisting of a finite series of digits that repeat infinitely. Examples of repeating decimals are $0.33\overline{3}$ and $3.2474\overline{47}$. The bar over the digits indicates that this series of digits repeats infinitely.

Write each fraction as a repeating decimal.

1. $\frac{1}{9} =$ _____

2. $\frac{2}{3} =$ _____

3. $\frac{3}{11} =$ _____

Estimating Percents

Mr. Martinez wants to buy a digital camera he saw advertised. If he buys it online he will save 23%. About how many dollars will he save if he buys it online?

Sale

$200.⁰⁰

We want to estimate _____% of $200 to find about how much Mr. Martinez will save.

Remember that we can write a percent as a fraction.

We can use the benchmark numbers below to help us estimate.

$20\% = \frac{1}{5}$ $25\% = \frac{1}{4}$ $33\frac{1}{3}\% = \frac{1}{3}$ $50\% = \frac{1}{2}$

To estimate 23% of 200, we choose a benchmark percent.

23% is about 25%. 25% written as a fraction is _____.

We solve the problem using the fraction equivalent.

$$25\% \text{ of } 200 = 25\% \times 200$$

$$= \frac{1}{4} \times 200 \longleftarrow \text{Think: divide 200 by 4}$$

$$= \underline{\qquad}$$

Mr. Martinez will save about _____.

Getting Started

Write the benchmark percent and equivalent fraction you could use to estimate using each percent below. Choose 20%, 25%, 33$\frac{1}{3}$%, or 50% for a benchmark.

1. 30% _____ = _____   **2.** 45% _____ = _____   **3.** 15% _____ = _____

Estimate.

4. 30% of 213 about _____   **5.** 45% of 300 about _____   **6.** 15% of 200 about _____

7. 23% of 812 about _____   **8.** 19% of 1,000 about _____   **9.** 52% of 2,400 about _____

Practice

Write the benchmark percent and equivalent fraction you could use to estimate using each percent below. Choose 20%, 25%, $33\frac{1}{3}$%, or 50% for a benchmark.

1. 55% ____ = ____

2. 18% ____ = ____

3. 24% ____ = ____

4. 38% ____ = ____

5. 21% ____ = ____

6. 35% ____ = ____

Estimate.

7. 55% of 148

   about ____

8. 18% of 75

   about ____

9. 24% of 92

   about ____

10. 38% of $144

    about ____

11. 21% of 300

    about ____

12. 17% of 250

    about ____

Copy and estimate.

13. 27% of 64

    about ____

14. 58% of 180

    about ____

15. 32% of 261

    about ____

16. 17% of 35

    about ____

17. 26% of $140

    about ____

18. 55% of 500

    about ____

Problem Solving

Solve each problem.

19. There are 80 cats at the animal shelter. Sixteen percent of the cats are grey. About how many cats are grey?

20. The shelter spends $650 a month for pet food. Cat food represents 54% of the cost. About how much is spent on cat food?

21. Pet vitamins cost $45 for the large container. The shelter saves 18% by buying vitamins and food from the same supplier. About how much do the vitamins cost after the 18% saving? (Hint: This problem has more than one step.)

Finding a Percent of a Number

Mr. Hirakawa bought a new color television.
He paid cash. In addition to the price of the
set, Mr. Hirakawa had to pay a sales tax of
7%. How much did Mr. Hirakawa pay for
the television set?

Color T.V.
$450

Small T.V.
$120

Stereo
$280

We are looking for the entire cost of the
television set.

The television set itself cost _____.

Mr. Hirakawa also paid _____ sales tax. To
find the total cost, we multiply the cost of
the set by the sales tax rate and add that to
the cost of the set.

We multiply _____ by _____ and add that to _____.

Change the percent to a decimal.	Multiply.	Add.
7% = 0.07	$450 × 0.07	$450.00 + _____

Mr. Hirakawa paid a total of _____ for the television set.

Getting Started

Find the part of each price represented by the percent.

1. 30% of $125 = _____ **2.** 25% of $86 = _____ **3.** 20% of $45 = _____

Copy and calculate.

4. 42% of $195   **5.** 16% of $59   **6.** 4% of $38

Use the ad to answer Exercises 7 and 8. Add 6% sales tax to each item purchased.

7. How much does a small TV cost?

8. Mr. Henry buys a stereo. He is going to make 4 payments. How much is each payment?

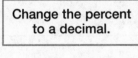

Practice

Find the part of each price represented by the percent.

1. 60% of $80 = _____
2. 25% of $120 = _____
3. 14% of $360 = _____

4. 48% of $96 = _____
5. 4% of $250 = _____
6. 10% of $73 = _____

7. 14% of $84 = _____
8. 61% of $13 = _____
9. 36% of $10 = _____

10. 2% of $368 = _____
11. 99% of $60 = _____
12. 86% of $65 = _____

13. 35% of $270 = _____
14. 43% of $43 = _____
15. 70% of $960 = _____

Copy and calculate.

16. 16% of $236
17. 23% of $94
18. 38% of $375

19. 6% of $88
20. 65% of $795
21. 45% of $226

22. 12% of $400
23. 3% of $115
24. 75% of $95

Problem Solving

Solve each problem.

25. Alex took a 90 item test. He got 90% correct. How many items did Alex get correct?

26. If sales tax is 5%, what is the cost of a suit that sells for $326?

(Now Try This!)

You can use a fraction to find a percent of a number. First you need to change the percent to a fraction. Here are some equivalents you should know.

Percent	10%	20%	40%	60%	80%	25%	75%	50%
Fraction	$\frac{1}{10}$	$\frac{1}{5}$	$\frac{2}{5}$	$\frac{3}{5}$	$\frac{4}{5}$	$\frac{1}{4}$	$\frac{3}{4}$	$\frac{1}{2}$

Find 50% of $400.

50% = $\frac{1}{2}$ $\frac{1}{2}$ of $400 = $200

So, 50% of $400 is $200.

Find 25% of $32.

25% = $\frac{1}{4}$ $\frac{1}{4}$ of $32 = $8

So, 25% of $32 is $8.

Find the part of each number represented by the percent.

1. 20% of $500
2. 10% of $780
3. 25% of $200

4. 60% of $250
5. 75% of $400
6. 80% of $350

Calculating Discount and Sale Prices

Store owners sometimes reduce the price of an item they wish to sell. This reduction is called a **discount**. The **rate of discount** is the percent of the original price that the customer does not pay. Tony bought a pair of skis at the big winter sale. The **list price** of the skis was originally $124. How much did Tony pay for the skis?

ALL SKI EQUIPMENT
25% OFF

We want to know what Tony actually paid for the skis.

The original price of the skis was _____.

The rate of discount was _____.

To find what Tony paid, we multiply the list price by the rate of discount to get the discount. Then we subtract the discount from the list price.

We multiply _____ by _____ and subtract that from _____.

$$\begin{array}{r} \$124 \\ \times\ 0.25 \\ \hline 620 \\ 248 \\ \hline \end{array}$$ ← list price
← rate of discount

← discount

$$\begin{array}{r} \$124 \\ -\quad 31 \\ \hline \end{array}$$ ← list price
← discount

← sale price

Tony actually paid _____ for the skis.

Getting Started

Write each sale price to complete the chart.

1.

List Price	$85	$156	$260	$148	$940
Rate of Discount	10%	15%	30%	20%	5%
Sale Price					

Practice

Write each sale price.

1. list price: $75

rate of discount: 20%

sale price = _____

2. list price: $216

rate of discount: 30%

sale price = _____

3. list price: $148

rate of discount: 12%

sale price = _____

4. list price: $212

rate of discount: 15%

sale price = _____

Write each sale price to complete the chart.

5.

List Price	$54	$125	$284	$635	$986	$1,865
Rate of Discount	5%	10%	25%	15%	40%	8%
Sale Price						

Problem Solving

Solve each problem.

6. At the Clothes Tree Apparel Store they offered a discount rate of 5%. Mary Lou bought a jacket that was listed at $29. How much did Mary Lou actually pay for the jacket?

7. The Favorite Foods Factory had a discount sale. Everything was on sale for 10% off. Dawn bought $48 worth of food. What did she actually pay for the food?

8. The Super Sounds Stereo Shop held a 15% off sale. Ivan bought a stereo that cost $186. He also bought $30 worth of tapes. What did Ivan actually pay for the stereo and tapes?

9. The Value Town Discount Store had a 20% reduction sale. Mario had saved $125 toward a new bike. The price of the bike Mario wanted was $186. How much more money does Mario still need to save to buy the bike on sale?

Name _____

Problem Solving: Solve a Simpler but Related Problem

How many angles are there in this figure?

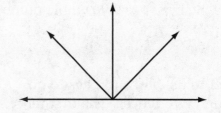

 SEE

We want to find the total number of angles.
There are _____ rays.

 PLAN

Since there are 5 rays in this figure, we should start with a simpler problem. We should make a table of our results to see if we can find a pattern that would help us to solve the problem.

⭐ **DO**

Number of Rays	Types of Angles	Number of Each Angle	Total Angles
2		1	1
3		2 ⎫ 1 ⎬	3
___		___ ⎫ ___ ⎬ ___ ⎭	6
___		___ ⎫ ___ ⎪ ___ ⎬ ___ ⎪ ___ ⎭	___

There are _____ different angles in this figure.

 CHECK

There is _____ ∠ angle.   There are _____ angles.

There are _____ angles.   There are _____ angles.

Apply

Solve each problem.

1. Use each of the digits from 0 to 9 to make the greatest possible whole number. Then use the ten digits to make the least possible whole number.

2. To get to its den, a fox has to go through two fences. The first fence has 2 holes in it and the second fence has 4 holes in it. How many different paths can the fox take?

3. How long would it take you to spend one million dollars if you spent $200 a day?

4. How long will it take to spend a million dollars if you can spend one dollar per second?

5. If one million dollar bills are placed end to end, how far will the line of bills stretch in miles? One dollar bill is about 6 inches long.

6. In how many ways can five different flavors of ice cream be arranged on an ice cream cone? (You can only have one scoop of each flavor.)

7. How many possible diagonals does an octagon have?

> ## Problem-Solving Strategy: Using the Four-Step Plan
> ★ **SEE** What do you need to find?
> ★ **PLAN** What do you need to do?
> ★ **DO** Follow the plan.
> ★ **CHECK** Does your answer make sense?

8. How many squares are in this figure? (The squares may be different sizes.)

9. Read Problem 2 again. What if the farmer builds another fence between the two fences already there? The new fence has 1 hole in it. Now how many different paths can the fox take?

10. Shelby and Justin picked some corn and now must shuck, or peel, the husks off the ears of corn. Shelby shucks 25% of 20 ears. Justin shucks 20% of 25 ears. Who shucked more corn?

11. There were 2 bags of peanuts in the barn. The fox ate 50% of the peanuts in the first bag and 75% of the peanuts in the second bag. The farmer said that the fox ate 125% of his peanuts. Tell if the farmer is correct or incorrect and explain why.

12. Chick Little has an egg farm 2 miles outside of town. Naturally he raises hens on this farm. Some of the hens he raises are white and the rest are red. The ratio of white hens to red hens is 3 to 2. What percent of Chick Little's hens are red?

Calculator: Interest

Most calculators have a percent key. Use the % key to solve the following problem. Mr. Ivers bought a used car for $6,500. To pay for the car, he had to borrow the money. When you borrow money, interest must be paid for the loan. How much did the new car actually cost Mr. Ivers?

INTEREST NOW **8%**
Buy a new car for less!
Take **4** years to pay.

We want to calculate the final cost of Mr. Ivers' car.

The list price of the car was _____.

The rate of interest was _____ per year.

The loan was for _____ years.

To find the actual cost, we find the amount of interest for 1 year,

6500 $\boxed{\times}$ 8 $\boxed{\%}$ $\boxed{}$

we find the amount of interest for 4 years,

520 $\boxed{\times}$ 4 $\boxed{=}$ $\boxed{}$

and we find the total cost by adding the interest and the list price.

2080 $\boxed{+}$ 6500 $\boxed{=}$ $\boxed{}$

The car cost Mr. Ivers _____.

We can also find the total cost with one code.

6500 $\boxed{\times}$ 8 $\boxed{\%}$ $\boxed{\times}$ 4 $\boxed{+}$ 6500 $\boxed{=}$ $\boxed{}$

Find the interest and total cost of a loan of $5,000 and 9.6% for 3 years.

_____ , _____

Practice

Use your calculator to find the given percent of each number.

1. 60% of 380

_____

2. 42% of $675

_____

3. 19% of 482

_____

4. 12% of 3,765

_____

5. 27% of 12,048

_____

6. 6% of $16,125

_____

7. 9% of 11,214

_____

8. 36% of $78,000

_____

9. 2% of 29,575

_____

10. 13% of $17,214

_____

11. 3% of $128,276

_____

12. 14% of $308, 210

_____

Problem Solving

Complete the table.

13.

Loan	$8,250	$7,275	$11,940	$15,000	$15,000	$125,000
Rate of interest	8%	9%	14%	16%	15%	11%
Years	3	5	2	4	4	20
Total cost of loan						

[Now Try This!]

1. If $5,000 is saved at 10% for 1 year, the **simple interest** can be found by using the code 5,000 $\boxed{\times}$ 10 $\boxed{\%}$. The total in the account can be found by using the code 5,000 $\boxed{\times}$ 110 $\boxed{\%}$. How much is in the account? _____

2. **Compound interest** is paid by most banks. The interest is paid on the original amount plus the interest earned. If 10% is compounded semi-annually, 5% is earned each 6 months. The total in the account starting with $5,000 can be found by using the code $5,000 $\boxed{\times}$ 105 $\boxed{\%}$ $\boxed{\times}$ 105 $\boxed{\%}$. How much is in the account after one year? _____

Write each ratio in fraction form. Do not simplify.

1. two to three _____

2. five to three _____

3. 6 to 4 _____

4. 3:8 _____

5. 9 out of 10 _____

6. 8:2 _____

Write the missing number in each proportion.

7. $\frac{4}{n} = \frac{6}{9}$

8. $\frac{n}{8} = \frac{8}{16}$

9. $\frac{9}{3} = \frac{n}{12}$

10. $\frac{4}{8} = \frac{2}{n}$

$n =$ _____

$n =$ _____

$n =$ _____

$n =$ _____

Use the scale and a metric ruler to find the actual dimensions of this figure.

11. $\overline{AB}$ _____

12. The perimeter of ABC is _____.

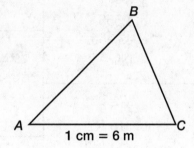

1 cm = 6 m

Write each number as a percent.

13. $0.15 =$ _____

14. $\frac{15}{100} =$ _____

15. $39:100 =$ _____

16. 25 out of 100 = _____

Write each percent as a fraction in simplest terms.

17. $30\% =$ _____

18. $25\% =$ _____

19. $84\% =$ _____

20. $6\% =$ _____

Write each fraction as a percent. Round to the nearest whole-number percent, if necessary.

21. $\frac{3}{5} =$ _____

22. $\frac{2}{3} =$ _____

23. $\frac{1}{8} =$ _____

24. $\frac{7}{25} =$ _____

Find the given percent of each number.

25. 16% of $80 =$ _____

26. 30% of $246 =$ _____

27. 5% of $\$235 =$ _____

Circle the letter of the correct answer.

1
$$\begin{array}{r} 7,248 \\ + 29,756 \end{array}$$
a. 36,004
b. 36,994
c. 37,004
d. NG

2
$$\begin{array}{r} 54,302 \\ - 19,658 \end{array}$$
a. 34,644
b. 34,654
c. 45,356
d. NG

3 86×53
a. 688
b. 4,558
c. 43,258
d. NG

4 $15\overline{)7,250}$
a. 215
b. 215 R2
c. 215 R20
d. NG

5
$$\begin{array}{r} 3\frac{3}{4} \\ + 5\frac{1}{2} \end{array}$$
a. $8\frac{1}{4}$
b. $8\frac{2}{3}$
c. $9\frac{1}{4}$
d. NG

6
$$\begin{array}{r} 14\frac{1}{3} \\ - 9\frac{3}{4} \end{array}$$
a. $4\frac{7}{12}$
b. $5\frac{3}{12}$
c. $5\frac{7}{12}$
d. NG

7 $2\frac{1}{3} \div \frac{5}{9}$
a. $\frac{7}{27}$
b. $1\frac{8}{27}$
c. $4\frac{1}{5}$
d. NG

8
$$\begin{array}{r} 2.079 \\ + 8.16 \end{array}$$
a. 10.23
b. 10.139
c. 10.239
d. NG

9
$$\begin{array}{r} 21.2 \\ - 8.346 \end{array}$$
a. 12.854
b. 12.946
c. 27.146
d. NG

10
$$\begin{array}{r} 3.2 \\ \times 0.06 \end{array}$$
a. 0.192
b. 1.92
c. 19.2
d. NG

11 $4.96 \div 3.1$
a. 0.16
b. 1.6
c. 16
d. NG

12 Find the measure of $\angle ABC$.
a. 33°
b. 45°
c. 57°
d. NG

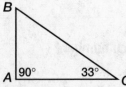

score

STOP

Graphs, Statistics, and Probability

Collecting Data

Data is numerical information collected for a purpose. One way to collect data is to ask a group of people questions to gather facts, such as age, or to gather opinions, such as favorite foods. This is called a survey.

Favorite Flavor	
Flavor	Response
Orange	8
Blueberry	0
Watermelon	5
Cherry	7

Best Fruit Ice Co. conducted a survey about ice pops. They asked people to decide which flavor of ice pop they prefer. The survey results are recorded on the right.

A **line plot** can be drawn to show this data. A line plot is a graph that shows each item of information on a number line. You can use an x to represent each response to the survey question.

How many xs should you make for Cherry? _____

How many xs should you make for Blueberry? _____

Complete the line plot to show the results of the Best Fruit Ice Co. survey.

Favorite Ice Pop Flavor

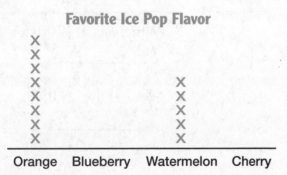

```
X
X
X
X          X
X          X
X          X
X          X
X          X
Orange  Blueberry  Watermelon  Cherry
```

Getting Started

Use the line plot to answer each question.

1. How many people were surveyed? Explain how you know. _____

2. Which flavor was the favorite? _____

3. Based on the results of the survey, should Best Fruit Ice Co. make more blueberry ice pops than any other flavor? Explain. _____

Practice

Write a survey question for each set of responses.

1.
Number of pets	Response
0	3
1	5
2	4
3	0
4 or more	1

Survey question: _____

_____

2.
Favorite color	Number
red	4
blue	7
green	6
yellow	1
orange	2

Survey question: _____

_____

Use the table to make a line plot. Then, answer Questions 4 through 7.

3.
Favorite After-School Sport	
Sport	**Number**
Basketball	5
Football	4
Soccer	5
Softball	7
Tennis	1
Track	3

Favorite After-School Sport

Basketball   Football   Soccer   Softball   Tennis   Track

4. Which sport is the most popular?

   _____

5. Which sport is the least popular?

   _____

6. Which sport is as popular as basketball?

   _____

7. How many students were surveyed?

   _____

Problem Solving

Use the data in the line plot to answer each question.

8. How tall are most of the fifth-grade basketball players at Glen School?

9. What is the difference in height between the shortest player and the tallest player?

10. How many players are 59 inches tall?

11. How many basketball players are less than 59 inches tall?

**Glen School
Height of Fifth-Grade
Basketball Players**

```
                      X
               X      X
        X      X  X   X
X       X  X   X  X
X       X  X   X  X         X
55  56  57 58  59 60 61 62  63
        Height (inches)
```

Using Tallies to Make Bar Graphs

The fifth-grade class voted for president.
Complete the table and the bar graph to
show the results of the election.
Who won the vote?

Votes for President		
Name	**Tally**	**Votes**
Beth	ⵌ l	
Aaron	ⵌ ⵌ	
Earl	ⵌ ll	
Jodi	ⵌ ⵌ ll	

Votes for President

Candidates														
Beth	▓	▓	▓	▓	▓	▓								
Aaron														
Earl														
Jodi														
	1	2	3	4	5	6	7	8	9	10	11	12	13	14

Votes

_____ won with _____ votes.

Getting Started

Use the bar graph above to answer each question.

1. How many votes did Aaron receive?

   _____

2. How many more votes did Jodi receive than Beth? _____

3. How many students voted?

   _____

4. How many less votes did Earl get than Aaron? _____

Use this tally to complete the graph.

5.

Favorite Color	
Blue	ⵌ llll
Red	ⵌ ⵌ ⵌ ll
Green	ⵌ ⵌ lll

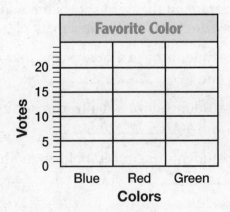

Favorite Color

Practice

Use this tally to complete the bar graph and answer each question.

1.

Favorite Kind of TV Show	
Drama	IIII
Comedy	IIII IIII
Sports	IIII IIII II
Movies	IIII III
Cartoons	IIII IIII II

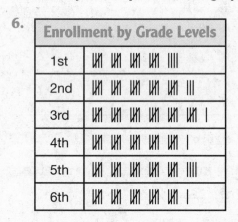

Favorite Kind of TV Show

Type of Show: Drama, Comedy, Sports, Movies, Cartoons
Votes: 2 4 6 8 10 12 14 16 18 20

2. How many votes did comedy receive?

_____

3. How many votes did movies receive?

_____

4. How many votes were taken?

_____

5. Which shows received the most votes?

_____

Use this tally to complete the bar graph.

6.

Enrollment by Grade Levels	
1st	IIII IIII IIII IIII IIII
2nd	IIII IIII IIII IIII IIII III
3rd	IIII IIII IIII IIII IIII IIII I
4th	IIII IIII IIII IIII IIII I
5th	IIII IIII IIII IIII IIII IIII
6th	IIII IIII IIII IIII IIII I

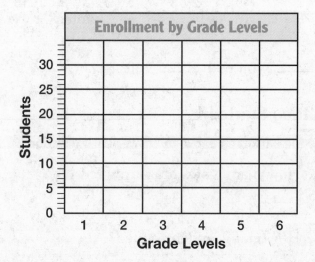

Enrollment by Grade Levels

Students: 0 5 10 15 20 25 30
Grade Levels: 1 2 3 4 5 6

Now Try This!

Sometimes you need to use a **histogram** to display data. The histogram on the right shows the math scores for the students in Mr. Philip's math class.

1. How many students have a math score that is between 71 and 80? _____

2. How many students have a math score that is between 81 and 90? _____

3. How many students are in Mr. Philip's math class? _____

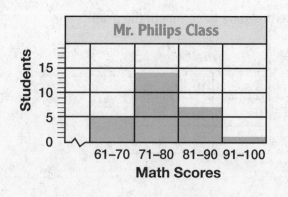

Mr. Philips Class

Students: 0 5 10 15
Math Scores: 61–70 71–80 81–90 91–100

Mean, Median, and Mode

Three statistics that help to understand the meaning of numbers are the mean, median, and mode. The **mean** is the average score, the **median** is the middle score, and the **mode** is the most frequent score. What are the mean and median scores for the Lincoln football team this year? What is the mode?

Lincoln Football Team	
Game	**Points Scored**
1	36
2	53
3	42
4	58
5	50
6	40
7	50

To find the mean, we find the sum of the scores.

36 + 53 + 42 + 58 + 50 + 40 + 50 = _____

We divide by the number of scores.

_____ ÷ _____ = _____

The mean score is _____.

To find the median, we list the scores from lowest to highest.

36, 40, 42, 50, 50, 53, 58

We select the middle score. If there are an even number of scores, the median is the mean of the two middle scores.

The median score is _____.

To find the mode, we look for the most frequent score.

_____ occurs more often than any other score.

The mode is _____.

A set of data can have no mode or more than one mode.

Getting Started

Find the mean, median, and mode of each set of numbers.

1. 118, 130, 114, 106, 118, 116

mean _____

median _____

mode _____

2. 86, 79, 105, 58, 97

mean _____

median _____

mode _____

3. 74, 68, 87, 62, 74, 66, 83, 62

mean _____

median _____

mode _____

4. $8.20, $7.12, $8.20, $12.63, $3.10

mean _____

median _____

mode _____

Practice

Find the mean, median, and mode of each set of numbers.

1. $6.40, $2.40, $3.18, $9.85, $4.57

   mean _____

   median _____

   mode _____

2. 84, 100, 75, 97, 84

   mean _____

   median _____

   mode _____

3. 24, 35, 22, 24, 68, 48, 43, 48

   mean _____

   median _____

   mode _____

4. $1.57, $2.48, $1.57, $4.51, $3.12

   mean _____

   median _____

   mode _____

Problem Solving

Use the table of students' heights to answer Questions 5 through 9.

5. Who is the tallest? _____

6. Who is the shortest? _____

7. How much taller is Diane than Tim? _____

8. What is the mean height? _____

9. What is the median height? _____

Selected Students' Heights	
Pupil	**Height in cm**
Vince	152
Diane	154
Marcia	143
Tim	146
Rich	155

Complete the bar graph of the students' heights.

10.

Selected Students' Heights								
Vince								
Diane								
Marcia								
Tim								
Rich								

Students

20 40 60 80 100 120 140 160
Height in Centimeters

Line Graphs

The high and low average temperatures in San Francisco
stay about the same throughout the year. In which months
is the difference between them 20 degrees or more?

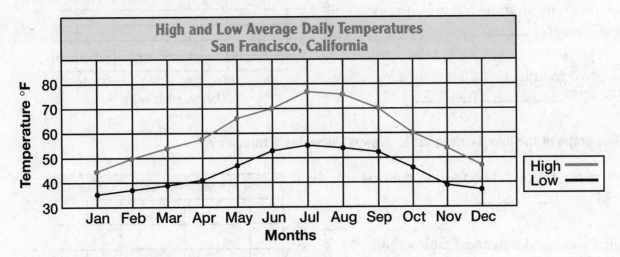

We want to examine the range of the high and low temperatures.
To find the range, we subtract the low temperature for the month
from the high temperature for the month.

January	45° − 35° = _____	July	_____ − _____ = _____
February	50° − 37° = _____	August	_____ − _____ = _____
March	54° − 39° = _____	September	_____ − _____ = _____
April	58° − 41° = _____	October	_____ − _____ = _____
May	66° − 47° = _____	November	_____ − _____ = _____
June	70° − 53° = _____	December	_____ − _____ = _____

The difference in the temperatures is 20 degrees or more during
the months of _____.

REMEMBER In a multi-line graph, it is important to use the code
provided with the graph to interpret the lines correctly.

Getting Started

Use the line graph of average daily temperatures to answer Questions 1 and 2.

1. Between which months is the high
   temperature increasing the most?

   _____

2. Between which months is the low
   temperature decreasing the most?

   _____

Practice

Use the line graph of this year's snowfall to answer Questions 1 through 3.

1. How much snow fell in January?
   _____

2. How much more snow fell in February than October? _____

3. What two months had the greatest snowfall? _____

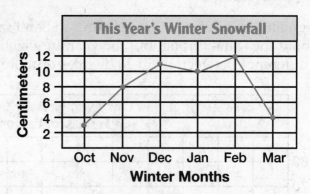

Use the line graph of the bike sale contest to answer Questions 4 through 7.

4. How many bikes did Ben sell in the first week? _____

5. Which week did Ben and Frank sell a total of 25 bikes? _____

6. Who reached sales of 50 bikes first? _____

7. Who won the contest? _____

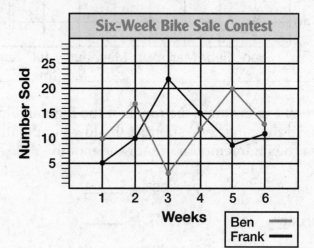

Problem Solving

Angie recorded the temperature every two hours during the school day. Complete this line graph showing the temperatures during school.

8.

Temperature During School	
Time	**Temperature**
8:00	57°F
10:00	63°F
12:00	73°F
2:00	75°F
4:00	62°F

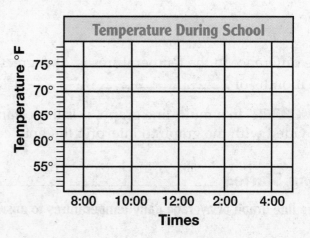

9. Find the mean and median of the temperatures that Angie recorded.

   mean _____   median _____

Lesson 15-4 • Line Graphs

Circle Graphs

Mr. Smith has $1,650 to budget for household
expenses each month. How much money does
Mr. Smith budget for family entertainment?

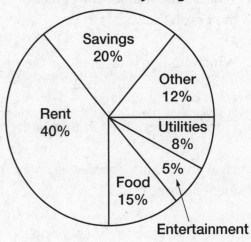

Mr. Smith's Monthly Budget

We want to find the amount the Smiths put
aside for entertainment each month.

The total monthly budget is _____.

The percent budgeted for entertainment is _____.

To find the amount to be used for entertainment, we
multiply the total budget by the percent used for that
purpose.

We multiply _____ by _____.

$$\begin{array}{r} \$1,650 \\ \times \quad 0.05 \\ \hline \end{array}$$

The amount budgeted for entertainment is _____.

Getting Started

**Use the circle graph of Mr. Smith's monthly budget
to answer Questions 1 through 8.**

1. What is the largest amount of money
   budgeted for? _____

2. What percent is budgeted for savings?
   _____

3. How much is budgeted for food?
   _____

4. How much money is budgeted for
   rent? _____

5. What percent is budgeted for food and
   utilities? _____

6. How much more money is spent on
   savings than on entertainment?
   _____

7. What is the sum of all the percents
   shown on the graph? _____

8. What is the sum of all the amounts
   budgeted? _____

Practice

Enrique earns $460 each month. Use the circle graph representing his budget to answer Questions 1 through 5.

1. What is the total of the percents shown on the graph? _____

2. Which item is budgeted for the most money? _____

3. How much is saved each month? _____

4. How much more money is spent on food than clothing? _____

5. How much money is spent on entertainment and food? _____

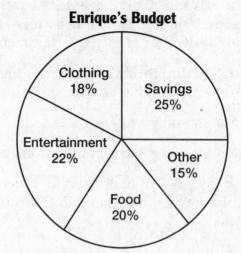

Enrique's Budget

A poll of 3,000 adults was taken to find their favorite recreation. Use the circle graph of the results to answer Questions 6 through 10.

6. What percent chose skiing? _____

7. How many people chose skiing? _____

8. What was the favorite recreation? _____

9. How many more people chose racquetball than tennis? _____

10. What fraction of the people polled chose jogging? _____

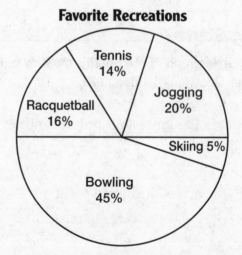

Favorite Recreations

[Now Try This!]

You want to tile a rectangular patio so that there is no space between tiles and no overlapping. Can this be done with a tile that is quadrilateral having no two sides the same length? _____. To prove your answer, draw and cut out a quadrilateral with no sides equal and use it to trace copies to show the pattern of your tiling. The tile may be flipped or rotated if necessary. Tiles on the border may be cut.

Stem-and-Leaf Plots

The health clinic serves people of all ages in the town. The data at the right shows the ages of the people who used the clinic on Sunday, October 19. The doctors want to organize the data to find which age group came to the clinic most often on that day.

Patients' Ages 10/19			
22,	8,	16,	25
24,	2,	30,	38
73,	22,	18,	55
63,	57,	22,	68

One way to organize data is to use a **stem-and-leaf plot**. In the stem and leaf plot below, the numbers are arranged in order from least to greatest.

Patients' Ages

The tens digit in ⟶ each number is the **stem**.

Stem	Leaf	⟵ The ones digit in each number is the **leaf**.
0	2 8	
1	6 8	
2	2 2 2 4 5	
3	0 8	
4		
5	5 7	
6	3 8	
7	3 ⟵ represents 73	

How many people in their teens came to the clinic on Sunday, October 19? _____

Which stem has the most leaves? _____

Which age group used the clinic most often that day? _____

Getting Started

Use the stem-and-leaf plot above to answer Questions 1 through 4.

1. For the number 30, which digit is written in the stem? _____

   The leaf? _____

2. How old was the oldest person to come to the clinic that day? _____

   The youngest? _____

3. In which age group are there 3 people the same age? _____

4. Did anyone in their 40s come to the clinic that day? Explain.

   _____

   _____

Practice

Write the stem and leaves for each set of numbers.

1. 15, 12, 18

2. 98, 90, 95, 93

3. 33, 36, 32, 33, 35

Use the data in the table to make a stem-and-leaf plot.
Then, answer Questions 4 through 7.

4.

Math Test Scores
75, 82, 85
90, 97, 84
78, 95, 80, 85
98, 85, 93, 89
72, 88, 82

Math Test Scores

Stem	Leaf

5. What is the lowest score on the math test? The highest?

6. How many students in the math class scored 90 or more on the test?

7. How many students received a score of 85 on the test?

8. How many students took the test?

Problem Solving

Use the data in the stem-and-leaf plot on the right to answer each question.

9. Anna recorded the low temperature each day in January. What is the difference between the lowest and highest temperatures?

Daily Low Temperature (°F) in January

Stem	Leaf
0	5 6 7
1	2 4 7 8 8 9
2	1 2 3 4 5 6 6 7 9
3	0 3 3 4 5 5 6 8 9
4	0 1 1 2

10. How many days had a low temperature of 18°F?

11. How many days did the temperature fall below freezing (32°F)?

12. How many days was the low temperature 40°F or warmer?

Probability

Su Linn is removing a marble from
the box. There are 12 possible outcomes
of different marbles she can take. If
Su Linn selects the color marble she
wants, that is called a **favorable
outcome**. Since there are 3 black
marbles, the chance of a favorable
outcome of taking a black marble is
3 out of 12. The **probability** of an
event taking place is the ratio of
favorable outcomes to the number of
possible outcomes. The probability of
taking a black marble is $\frac{3}{12}$ or $\frac{1}{4}$.

We write: $P(\text{black}) = \frac{1}{4}$.

What is the probability of taking a striped
marble?

There are _____ striped marbles.

There are _____ marbles altogether.

$$\frac{\text{favorable outcomes}}{\text{possible outcomes}} = \frac{\square}{\square}$$

$$P(\text{striped}) = \frac{\square}{\square}$$

What is the probability of not taking a black
marble?

There are _____ that are not black marbles.

There are _____ marbles altogether.

$$\frac{\text{favorable outcomes}}{\text{possible outcomes}} = \frac{\square}{\square}$$

$$P(\text{not black}) = \frac{\square}{\square}$$

Getting Started

Use the coins to write a ratio for each probability.

1. $P(\text{penny}) = $ _____

2. $P(\text{nickel}) = $ _____

3. $P(\text{dime}) = $ _____

4. $P(\text{penny or dime}) = $ _____

5. $P(\text{penny or nickel}) = $ _____

6. $P(\text{not dime}) = $ _____

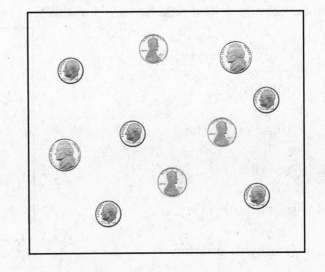

Practice

Use the geometric figures to write a ratio for each probability.

1. P(triangle) = _____

2. P(circle) = _____

3. P(triangle or circle) = _____

4. P(not circle) = _____

5. P(rectangle) = _____

6. P(not triangle) = _____

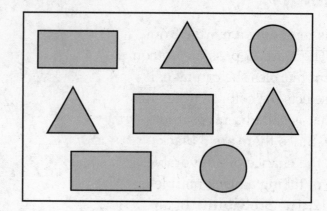

Use the letters to write a ratio for each probability.

7. P(A) = _____

8. P(B) = _____

9. P(C) = _____

10. P(D) = _____

11. P(A or B) = _____

12. P(C or D) = _____

13. P(not C) = _____

14. P(A or B or C) = _____

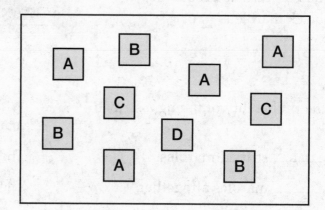

Use the coins to write a ratio for each probability.

15. P(penny) = _____

16. P(nickel) = _____

17. P(dime or quarter) = _____

18. P(not dime) = _____

19. P(not quarter) = _____

20. P(penny or quarter) = _____

Determining Possible Outcomes

John tossed a penny and a nickel 20 times. He made a chart to show the possible outcomes of the tosses and then recorded them. What ratios represent the following outcomes:

Possible Outcomes		Tally of Outcomes
(penny heads)	(nickel heads)	IIII
(penny heads)	(nickel tails)	ⅢI I
(penny tails)	(nickel heads)	ⅢI
(penny tails)	(nickel tails)	ⅢI

Both coins showing tails?

Outcome _____

Total tosses _____

Ratio _____

The penny showing heads and the nickel showing tails?

Outcome _____

Total tosses _____

Ratio _____

Toss a penny and a nickel 50 times and record your results. Write a simplified ratio to represent each situation.

1. Both coins show heads. _____

2. The penny shows heads and the nickel shows tails. _____

3. The penny shows tails and the nickel shows heads. _____

4. Both coins show tails. _____

Penny	Nickel	Tally
(heads)	(heads)	
(heads)	(tails)	
(tails)	(heads)	
(tails)	(tails)	

Practice

Toss 3 pennies 50 times. Record your results.
Write a simplified ratio to represent each situation.

Possible Outcomes	Tally

1. 3 heads _____

2. 2 heads, 1 tail _____

3. 1 head, 2 tails _____

4. 3 tails _____

Toss 1 penny, 1 nickel, and 1 dime 100 times. Record your results. Write a simplified ratio to represent each situation.

5. All coins show heads. _____

6. All coins show tails. _____

7. The penny shows heads.
   The nickel shows tails.
   The dime shows heads. _____

8. The dime shows heads. _____

9. The penny shows heads.
   The nickel shows tails. _____

10. The penny shows heads.
    The nickel shows tails.
    The dime shows tails. _____

11. The dime shows tails.
    The penny shows heads.
    The nickel shows heads. _____

12. The nickel shows heads.
    The other coins show tails. _____

13. The penny shows tails.
    The other coins show heads. _____

Penny	Nickel	Dime	Tally

Lesson 15-8 • Determining Possible Outcomes

Name _____

Determining Probability of Favorable Outcomes

Sammy listed the four possible outcomes when tossing a penny and a nickel. The probability of tossing a head on each coin is $\frac{1}{4}$. What is the probability of tossing one head and one tail?

Penny	Nickel		
Head	Head		
Head	Tail		
Tail	Head		
Tail	Tail		

We want to express the probability of tossing a head and a tail in a fraction.

The outcome is one head and one tail.

There are _____ ways to get this favorable outcome.

There are _____ possible outcomes.

$$P = \frac{\text{number of favorable outcomes}}{\text{possible outcomes}}$$

$$P = \underline{\quad} = \underline{\quad}$$

The probability of tossing one head and one tail is _____.

Getting Started

Write a fraction for the probability of each favorable outcome.

Activity	Possible Outcomes	Favorable Outcomes	Probability
Toss a penny.		1. Heads	$P = \underline{\quad}$
		2. Tails	$P = \underline{\quad}$
Spin the spinner.	1, 2, 3, 4	3. 1	$P = \underline{\quad}$
		4. 1 or 3	$P = \underline{\quad}$
		5. Number less than 3	$P = \underline{\quad}$
		6. Number greater than 4	$P = \underline{\quad}$

Practice _____

Write a fraction for the probability for each favorable outcome.

Activity	Possible Outcomes	Favorable Outcomes	Probability
Spin the spinner.	1, 2, 3, 4, 5, 6, 7, 8	**1.** 2	P = _____

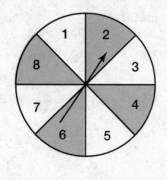

		2. 4	P = _____
		3. Number greater than 3	P = _____
		4. 5 or 7	P = _____
		5. Even number	P = _____
		6. Number between 3 and 8	P = _____

Toss a dime and spin the spinner.

Possible Outcomes	Favorable Outcomes	Probability
_____	**7.** Heads and a 3	P = _____
_____	**8.** Tails and a 2 or 3	P = _____
_____	**9.** Heads or tails and a 1 or a 3	P = _____
_____	**10.** Heads and an odd number	P = _____
_____	**11.** Heads and any number	P = _____
	12. Tails and a number greater than 1	P = _____

Spin two spinners.

Possible Outcomes	Favorable Outcomes	Probability
_____	**13.** Both numbers are even.	P = _____
_____	**14.** Sum of the spin is 4.	P = _____
_____	**15.** Both numbers are the same.	P = _____

Using Tree Diagrams

Shelby is getting ready for school. What possible combinations of blouses and skirts can Shelby wear?

> A **tree diagram** is a graphic picture of all possible outcomes in an activity.

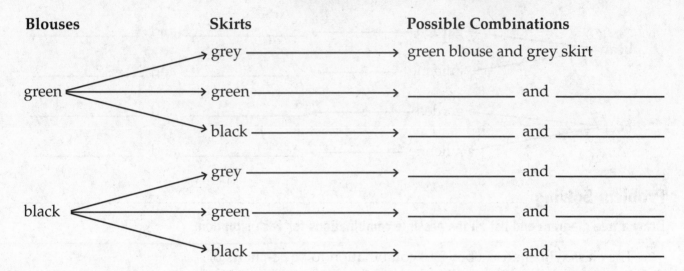

Blouses	Skirts	Possible Combinations
green	grey	green blouse and grey skirt
	green	_____ and _____
	black	_____ and _____
black	grey	_____ and _____
	green	_____ and _____
	black	_____ and _____

Getting Started

Complete the tree diagram and list all the possible combinations. Carlos is making a sandwich. He has ham, beef, and chicken with wheat or rye bread to choose from. List the possible sandwich combinations.

1. Meats   Breads   Possible Combinations

_____ → _____ → _____ → _____ and _____

→ _____ → _____ → _____ and _____

_____ → _____ → _____ → _____ and _____

→ _____ → _____ → _____ and _____

_____ → _____ → _____ → _____ and _____

→ _____ → _____ → _____ and _____

Practice

Complete the tree diagram and list the possible combinations. Elaine is ordering lunch from a menu. She can choose vegetable, mushroom, bean, or beef soup to eat with a garden or julienne salad.

1. **Soups**   **Salads**   **Possible Combinations**

vegetable

→ garden ——————→ vegetable soup and garden salad

→ julienne ——————→ _____ and _____

mushroom

→ garden ——————→ _____ and _____

→ julienne ——————→ _____ and _____

bean

→ garden ——————→ _____ and _____

→ julienne ——————→ _____ and _____

beef

→ garden ——————→ _____ and _____

→ julienne ——————→ _____ and _____

Problem Solving

Draw a tree diagram and list all the possible combinations for each situation.

2. The class will choose a boy-girl combination to be co-chairs of the carnival. The boy-candidates are Sal and Nate. The girls are Lois, Melissa, Theresa, Jackie, and Polly.

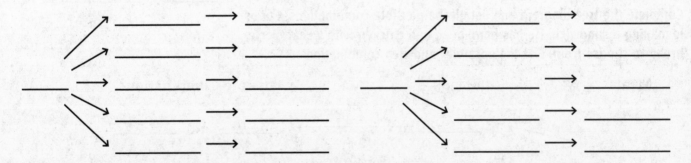

3. Use the single letters b, c, and f in combination with the double letters ad, ar, and at to form three-letter words.

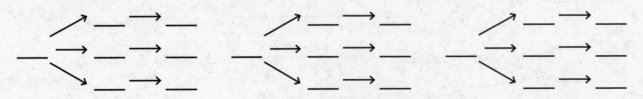

Problem Solving: Choose the Best Graph

Liz is growing a bean plant as part of a science project. She has collected data on the plant's growth. She needs to decide how best to display the data for her report. What type of graph should she use?

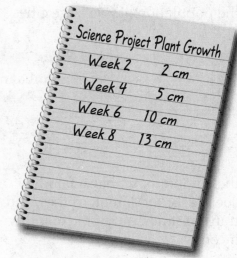

Science Project Plant Growth

Week 2	2 cm
Week 4	5 cm
Week 6	10 cm
Week 8	13 cm

SEE

We need to decide what kind of graph to use to display the data. What does the data show?

_____

PLAN

Think of the different kinds of graphs.

A bar graph uses bars to show data that can be compared. Does the data compare the heights of different plants?

_____

A line graph uses line segments to show data that changes over time. Does the data show change in the plant's height over time?

_____

A **circle graph** shows how an amount has been

divided into parts. Why didn't Liz make a circle

graph using her data? _____

_____

DO

Which type of graph should Liz use? _____

Explain your thinking. _____

Draw a line graph.

CHECK

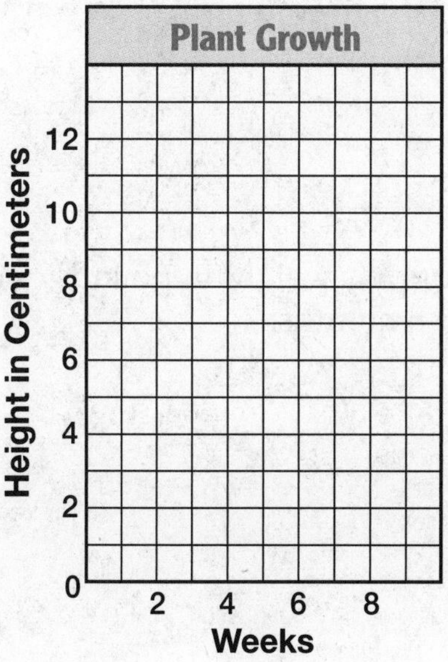

Did the plant continue to grow between week 2 and week 4?

_____

How tall was it in week 3? _____

Which graph shows the plant's growth best? _____

Plant Growth

(graph with vertical axis "Height in Centimeters" marked 0, 2, 4, 6, 8, 10, 12 and horizontal axis "Weeks" marked 2, 4, 6, 8)

Apply

Read the description of each set of data. Tell the kind of graph you would use to display the data. Write *bar graph*, *line graph*, or *circle graph*. Explain.

1. the population of five large cities

2. the amount of money a family spends for food, rent, clothes, and transportation out of the monthly income

3. the number of votes for each candidate in the school election

4. a puppy's weight in pounds over the past 8 months

5. Tell the kind of graph you would use to display the data in the table, Cookies Sold. Explain.

Cookies Sold	
Chocolate Chip	40 boxes
Almond	10 boxes
Oatmeal	30 boxes
Lemon	20 boxes

6. Draw a graph for the data in Problem 5.

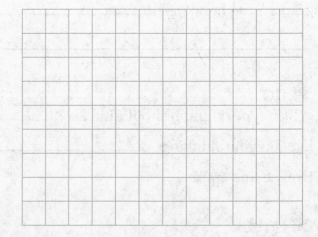

Lesson 15-11 • Problem Solving: Choose the Best Graph

Use the tally to complete Exercise 1.

1. Make a bar graph.

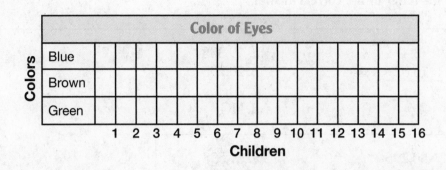

Color of Eyes	
Blue	卌 卌 IIII
Brown	卌 卌 卌
Green	卌 卌

Use the line graph to answer Questions 2 and 3.

2. Who received the higher reading score?

   _____

3. How many more science problems did Bill get correct than Tom?

   _____

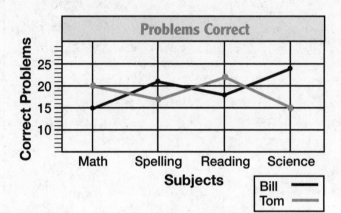

Use the circle graph of Ed's budget to answer Questions 4 and 5.

4. What percent is spent on clothes and fun? _____

5. If Ed earns $62 a week, how much does he save? _____

Use the stem-and-leaf plot to answer Questions 6 through 8.

Test Scores

Stem	Leaf
6	5 8 9
7	2 3 3 5 5 7 7 7 9
8	0 1 1 2 4 5 8
9	0 2 2 3 5 6

6. How many students received an 81 on the test? _____

7. What was the lowest score? _____

8. What is the mode for this data? _____

Solve each problem.

9. A penny and a quarter are tossed. List all the possible outcomes of heads and tails. _____

10. Write the probability that both coins show tails. _____

Circle the letter of the correct answer.

1 3,476
  + 16,829

    a. 19,305
    b. 20,295
    c. 20,305
    d. NG

2 80,296
  − 18,758

    a. 61,538
    b. 71,538
    c. 78,542
    d. NG

3 $2\frac{1}{2}$
  $+ 3\frac{3}{4}$

    a. $5\frac{2}{3}$
    b. $5\frac{1}{4}$
    c. $6\frac{1}{4}$
    d. NG

4 $7\frac{1}{3}$
  $- 4\frac{3}{4}$

    a. 3
    b. $3\frac{5}{12}$
    c. $3\frac{7}{12}$
    d. NG

5 $1\frac{1}{2} \times 5\frac{1}{3}$

    a. $5\frac{1}{6}$
    b. 8
    c. $8\frac{1}{6}$
    d. NG

6 $2\frac{1}{2} \div 3\frac{1}{2}$

    a. $\frac{2}{3}$
    b. $\frac{3}{7}$
    c. $8\frac{1}{6}$
    d. NG

7 4.2×36

    a. 1.512
    b. 15.12
    c. 151.2
    d. NG

8 $5.2\overline{)1.716}$

    a. 3.3
    b. 0.33
    c. 3
    d. NG

9 Find the area.

3 cm
6 cm

    a. 18 cm
    b. 18 sq cm
    c. 9 cm
    d. NG

10 Write 75% as a simplified fraction.

    a. $\frac{7}{10}$
    b. $\frac{75}{100}$
    c. $\frac{3}{4}$
    d. NG

 score

Equations, Integers, and Graphs

Variables

It's Algebra!

Madison had $50 in her savings account. She made a deposit into the account on May 30. How much did she have in her account after she made the deposit?

What information is missing? _____

THANK YOU FOR SAVING AT THE BANK

	DATE	DIVIDENDS	WITHDRAWLS	DEPOSITS	BALANCE
1	05/22				$50.00

We can use a **variable** to represent the unknown deposit. A variable is a symbol, usually a letter, that stands for an unknown number.

We will let d stand for the _____. Now we can write an **algebraic expression** to represent this situation. An algebraic expression contains at least one variable.

$50 + d$

Some other algebraic expressions are shown below.

$a + 15 \qquad 3 \times r \qquad x - 20 \qquad n \div 9$

We can omit the multiplication sign when one of the factors is a variable.

$3r \qquad 3 \bullet r \qquad (3)(r) \qquad \text{mean} \qquad 3 \times r$

A fraction bar can be used to show division.

$\dfrac{n}{9} \qquad \text{means} \qquad n \div 9$

Getting Started

Match the verbal expression with an algebraic expression.

1. seven times n a. $n - 7$

2. the sum of n and 7   b. $7n$

3. n divided by 7   c. $n + 7$

4. n decreased by 7   d. $\dfrac{n}{7}$

5. Write an algebraic expression for the verbal expression below. The words *less than* tell you to write what comes after those words first.

   7 less than n _____

Practice

Match the verbal expression with an algebraic expression.

1. the product of 15 and b **a.** $b - 15$

2. b increased by 15   **b.** $15 \div b$

3. the quotient of 15 and b **c.** $15b$

4. 15 less than b **d.** $b + 15$

Write an algebraic expression for each verbal expression.

5. the sum of x and 3   _____

6. k divided by 12   _____

7. the product of b and 9   _____

8. 5 multiplied by m _____

9. the total of y and 28   _____

10. 16 subtracted from c _____

Write a verbal expression for each algebraic expression. There is more than one correct answer for each exercise.

11. $21 \cdot a$ _____

12. $p - 5$ _____

Problem Solving

Write an algebraic expression for each situation.

13. Mr. Takeuchi had $150 in his account. He withdrew some money from his account on June 1. How much did he have in his account then?

14. Eiji is 9 years older than Aaron. How old is Eiji?

15. Mari has 3 times as many books as Riki. How many books does Mari have?

Evaluating Algebraic Expressions

It's Algebra!

Chance is 6 years older than Madison. How old is Chance?

An algebraic expression for this situation is _____.

We could find out how old Chance is if we knew Madison's age.

Suppose Madison is 3 years old. How old is Chance? To find Chance's age we can **substitute** 3 for m in the expression $m + 6$. Then find the value of the number expression.

$$m + 6 \quad = \quad \underline{\quad} + 6 \quad = \quad \underline{\quad}$$

Algebraic   Numerical   Value
Expression   Expression

If Madison is 3 years old, Chance is ____ years old.

Suppose Madison is 10 years old. How old is Chance?

$m + 6 =$ ____ $+ 6 =$ ____

If Madison is ____ years old, Chance is ____ years old.

REMEMBER To **evaluate** an algebraic expression, first substitute numbers for the variables. Then find the value of the numerical expression.

Getting Started

Evaluate each algebraic expression for $x = 5$.

1. $x + 5$ 2. $7x$ 3. $12 - x$ 4. $\dfrac{45}{x}$

Evaluate each algebraic expression for the given value of the variables.

5. $a - b$ when a is 32 and b is 9   6. $n + m - 17$ when n is 10 and m is 15

7. $6(p + r)$ when p is 8 and r is 4   8. $12y + 25$ when y is 6

Practice

Evaluate each algebraic expression for $c = 24$.

1. $c - 5$

2. $\frac{c}{8}$

3. $6 \cdot c$

4. $c + 39$

5. $3(c - 8)$

6. $(c + 16)10$

7. $5c - 20$

8. $\frac{3c}{4}$

9. $32 - c$

10. $7c + 2$

11. $\frac{1}{2}c$

12. $4c - 90$

Evaluate each algebraic expression for the given value of the variables.

13. $8x + 3y$ when x is 5 and y is 4.

14. $10a - 5b$ when a is 12 and b is 20.

15. $n(m + 15)$ when m is 5 and n is 8.

16. $p \div q + 9$ when p is 42 and q is 7

17. $\frac{1}{2}c + \frac{1}{4}d$ when c is 12 and d is 32

18. $x(z - 10)$ when x is 9 and z is 35

Problem Solving

Find the distance in each problem. Use the formula $d = rt$ where d is distance, r is rate, and t is time.

19. Mr. Kelly drove 50 miles an hour on the Parkway. How far did he travel if he drove for 3 hours?

20. It took Mrs. Miller $2\frac{1}{2}$ hours to drive from New City to Old Town. She drove at an average speed of 60 miles an hour on the highway. What is the distance between New City and Old Town?

21. Jon drove 45 miles an hour on a small road and 55 miles an hour on the Parkway. If he drove for 1 hour on the small road and 3 hours on the Parkway, how far did he travel?

Lesson 16-2 • Evaluating Algebraic Expressions

Properties of Equality

An **equation** is a mathematical sentence that contains the equals sign, = which is read, *is equal to*. The equals sign tells us that the values of the expressions on both sides of the symbol are equal.

$6 + 7$ is equal to _____.

Sometimes an equation contains a variable.

$n + 7 = 13$

To **solve** an equation, we find the value of the variable that makes the equation true. This value is a **solution** to the equation. We will use the following properties to help us to solve equations.

Properties of Equality and Numbers			
Property	**Example**	**Property**	**Example**
Addition We can add the same number to both sides of an equation.	$18 - 7 = 10 + 1$ $18 - 7 + 7 = 10 + 1 + 7$ $18 = 18$	**Multiplication** We can multiply both sides of an equation by the same number.	$36 \div 9 = 2 \times 2$ $36 \div 9 \times 9 = 2 \times 2 \times 9$ $36 = 36$
Subtraction We can subtract the same number from both sides of an equation.	$25 + 3 = 20 + 8$ $25 + 3 - 3 = 20 + 8 - 3$ $25 = 25$	**Division** We can divide both sides of an equation by the same number.	$8 \times 7 = 4 \times 14$ $8 \times 7 \div 7 = 4 \times 14 \div 7$ $8 = 8$

In the first example, adding _____ undoes subtracting _____.

In the second example, _____ undoes _____.

Getting Started

Tell how you can undo the operation in each expression.

1. 48×6 _____

2. $35 \div 5$ _____

3. $17 + 9$ _____

4. $26 - 12$ _____

5. Name the property shown by the equation
   $48 \div 8 \times 8 = 6 \times 8.$ _____

Practice

Tell how we can undo the operation in each expression.

1. $84 + 3$ _____

2. 15×10 _____

3. $54 - 7$ _____

4. $32 \div 4$ _____

5. $n - 6$ _____

6. $n + 3.8$ _____

7. $n \times \frac{1}{2}$ _____

8. $n \div 0.5$ _____

Name the property shown by each equation.

9. $38 + 5 - 5 = 30 + 8 - 5$ _____

10. $9 \times 7 \div 7 = 63 \div 7$ _____

11. $16 - 9 + 9 = 7 + 9$ _____

12. $24 \div 2 \times 2 = 12 \times 2$ _____

Use mental math to solve. Find the value of the variable that will make each equation true.

13. $10 + n = 19$

$n =$ _____

14. $15 - a = 7$

$a =$ _____

15. $2x = 20$

$x =$ _____

16. $36 \div m = 4$

$m =$ _____

17. $13 - b = 8$

$b =$ _____

18. $7y = 42$

$y =$ _____

Problem Solving

Solve each problem.

19. Jon has 42 rock CDs and 16 rap CDs. Maria has the same number of CDs as Jon. If Jon buys 3 new CDs, how many more CDs does Maria need to have the same total as Jon?

20. Write the missing number to make the number sentence true. Explain your thinking.

$(24 \div 6) \times 3 =$ _____ $\times 3$

Solving Addition and Subtraction Equations

Roberto took 9 photos so far with a new roll of film. How many more photos can he take before he reaches the end of the roll?

35 mm film

24 Exposures

We can write an equation to solve this problem.

$$9 + n = 24$$

The variable, *n*, represents the unknown number of exposures left on the roll.

We can use the properties of equality to find the value of the variable. This is called solving the equation.

$$9 + n = 24$$
$$9 - 9 + n = 24 - \underline{}$$
$$0 + n = \underline{}$$
$$n = \underline{}$$

To undo the addition, subtract _____.

To check your work, substitute the value you found for *n* in the original equation.

$$9 + \underline{} = 24$$
$$24 = 24$$

Roberto can take _____ more photos.

You can also solve a subtraction equation, such as $n - 12 = 30$. You need to _____ to undo the subtraction.

Getting Started

Solve and check each equation.

1. $n + 6 = 31$

   $n = $ _____

2. $n - 3 = 17$

   $n = $ _____

3. $15 + n = 48$

   $n = $ _____

4. $n - 28 = 54$

   $n = $ _____

Practice

Solve and check each equation.

1. $b + 7 = 22$

   $b =$ _____

2. $15 + n = 21$

   $n =$ _____

3. $49 = x + 27$

   $x =$ _____

4. $d + 33 = 76$

   $d =$ _____

5. $152 = m + 84$

   $m =$ _____

6. $12 + n = 6 + 8$

   $n =$ _____

7. $x - 8 = 26$

   $x =$ _____

8. $17 = y - 9$

   $y =$ _____

9. $b - 38 = 40$

   $b =$ _____

10. $c - 21 = 21$

    $c =$ _____

11. $175 = a - 29$

    $a =$ _____

12. $n - 6 = 7 + 5$

    $n =$ _____

Copy, solve, and check.

13. $x + 14 = 27$

    $x =$ _____

14. $76 = n + 38$

    $n =$ _____

15. $135 + y = 164$

    $y =$ _____

16. $n - 16 = 9$

    $n =$ _____

17. $83 = c - 15$

    $c =$ _____

18. $p - 46 = 105$

    $p =$ _____

19. $8 + n = 23 - 7$

    $n =$ _____

20. $b - 4 = 15 - 6$

    $b =$ _____

21. $9 + 8 = x - 7$

    $x =$ _____

Problem Solving

Write an equation for each problem, then solve.

22. There are 47 students on the school bus. There are 29 girls on the bus. How many boys are on the bus?

23. Mr. Orlando bought a camera for $138 and a camera case. He spent a total of $153. How much did the camera case cost?

Lesson 16-4 • *Solving Addition and Subtraction Equations*

Solving Multiplication and Division Equations

Vans shuttle campers and supplies from the train station to base camp. How many vans are needed for 56 campers?

We can write an equation to represent the problem.

$7n = 56$

The variable, n, represents the number of vans needed.

$7n$ is a way to show 7 times n. Other ways to show this multiplication are $7 \cdot n$ and $7 \times n$.

We can use the properties of equality to solve the equation.

$$7n = 56$$
$$\frac{7n}{7} = \frac{56}{7}$$
$$n = \frac{56}{7}$$
$$n = \underline{\quad}$$

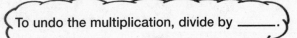

To undo the multiplication, divide by _____.

To check your work, substitute the value you found for **n** in the original equation.

$$7 \times \underline{\quad} = 56$$
$$56 = 56$$

_____ vans are needed.

You also can solve a division equation, such as $a \div 6 = 9$. You need to _____ to undo the division.

Getting Started

Solve and check each equation.

1. $5n = 45$

    $n = \underline{\quad}$

2. $9x = 72$

    $x = \underline{\quad}$

3. $b \div 7 = 6$

    $b = \underline{\quad}$

4. $m \div 8 = 7$

    $m = \underline{\quad}$

Practice

Solve and check each equation.

1. $6a = 24$

   $a =$ _____

2. $72 = 8 \times n$

   $n =$ _____

3. $y \times 11 = 132$

   $y =$ _____

4. $70 = 14n$

   $n =$ _____

5. $b \times 12 = 60$

   $b =$ _____

6. $15c = 105$

   $c =$ _____

7. $n \div 7 = 8$

   $n =$ _____

8. $x \div 8 = 6$

   $x =$ _____

9. $5 = n \div 8$

   $n =$ _____

10. $p \div 12 = 4$

    $p =$ _____

11. $15 = m \div 8$

    $m =$ _____

12. $n \div 13 = 12$

    $n =$ _____

Copy, solve, and check.

13. $y \times 18 = 180$

    $y =$ _____

14. $12b = 300$

    $b =$ _____

15. $128 = 8n$

    $n =$ _____

16. $n \div 4 = 9$

    $n =$ _____

17. $18 = c \div 9$

    $c =$ _____

18. $y \div 16 = 7$

    $y =$ _____

19. $x \div 7 = 9$

    $x =$ _____

20. $5 \times m = 45$

    $m =$ _____

21. $a \div 8 = 6$

    $a =$ _____

Problem Solving

Write an equation for each problem, then solve.

22. At base camp, the campers live in 4-person tents. How many tents are needed for 56 campers?

23. Sara made some sandwiches to take on a hike. She packed 4 sandwiches in a bag. She had 7 bags of sandwiches. How many sandwiches did she make?

Integers

A thermometer uses positive and negative numbers
to show the temperature. Look at the thermometer.

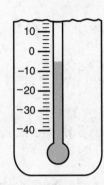

The temperature is _____.

The temperature is 5° **below** zero.

Numbers such as ⁻5, 0, and ⁺5 are **integers**. Integers
are used to describe many real-life situations.

A deposit of $10 is ⁺10. A gain of 3 yards in football is _____.

A withdrawal of $5 is ⁻5. A loss of 9 yards in football is _____.

We can show integers on a number line.

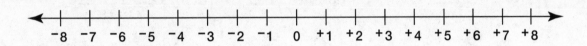

Each integer has an **opposite**.

⁻2 is the opposite of ⁺2.

What is the opposite of ⁺5? _____

Zero is its own opposite.

Getting Started

Write an integer to represent each situation.

1. 3°F below zero _____

2. a deposit of $5 _____

3. 4 feet above sea level _____

4. a loss of $6 _____

5. a gain of 7 yards during a football game _____

Write the opposite of each number. Use the number line to help.

6. ⁺3 _____   7. ⁻2 _____   8. ⁻5 _____   9. ⁺4 _____   10. 0 _____

Practice

Write an integer to represent each situation.

1. an increase of $25 _____

2. a debt of $10 _____

3. a loss of 15 yards _____

4. winning 8 points _____

5. 60 feet above see level _____

6. 70°C below zero _____

7. down 3 floors _____

8. up 5 floors _____

Write the opposite of each integer. Use the number line to help you.

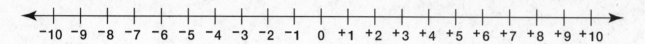

⁻10 ⁻9 ⁻8 ⁻7 ⁻6 ⁻5 ⁻4 ⁻3 ⁻2 ⁻1 0 ⁺1 ⁺2 ⁺3 ⁺4 ⁺5 ⁺6 ⁺7 ⁺8 ⁺9 ⁺10

9. ⁻6 _____

10. ⁻1 _____

11. ⁺10 _____

12. ⁺5 _____

Problem Solving

Use the drawing of the New City Hotel to solve each problem.

13. A hotel elevator starts at the lobby. It goes up 4 floors and then down 5 floors. What floor is it on now?

14. A boy gets on the elevator at garage level ⁻2. He goes up 4 floors and gets off. What floor is he on?

15. A hotel guest gets on the elevator on the second floor and goes down 4 floors, then up 2 floors. What floor is the guest on?

16. The hotel manager gets on the elevator at the lobby. She goes up 2 floors, then down 4 floors. What floor is she on?

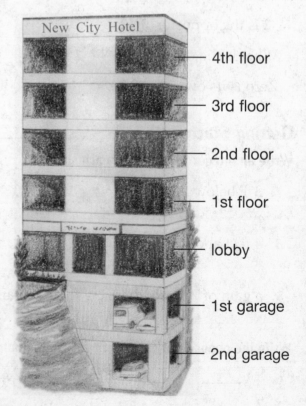

New City Hotel

— 4th floor

— 3rd floor

— 2nd floor

— 1st floor

— lobby

— 1st garage

— 2nd garage

Lesson 16-6 • Integers

Adding Integers

Alana enjoys rock climbing with safety equipment. On one climb, she slid 5 feet down the wall and then climbed 6 feet back up. How many feet in all did she lose or gain?

What integer shows how many feet Alana slid down the wall? _____

What integer shows how many feet Alana climbed up the wall? _____

Add the integers to find how many feet she lost or gained.

We use a number line to find ⁻5 + ⁺6.

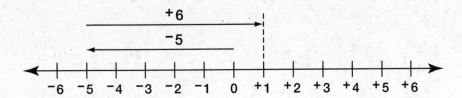

We start at 0 and move _____ units to the _____.

Next we move _____ units to the _____.

What number are we on? _____

Then ⁻5 + ⁺6 = _____.

Alana gained _____.

REMEMBER On the number line, we move to the left for a negative number. We move to the right for a positive number.

Getting Started

Use the number line to find each sum.

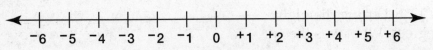

1. ⁺4 + ⁻6

2. ⁻1 + ⁻4

3. ⁻2 + ⁺4

4. ⁺2 + ⁺3

Practice

Add. Use the number line.

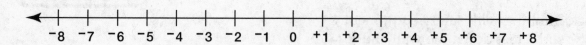

1. $^{+}5 + {}^{-}2$

2. $^{+}4 + {}^{-}3$

3. $^{-}5 + {}^{+}2$

4. $^{+}2 + {}^{-}4$

5. $^{-}3 + {}^{-}4$

6. $^{+}5 + {}^{-}8$

7. $^{-}5 + {}^{-}3$

8. $^{+}4 + {}^{-}5$

9. $^{+}3 + {}^{-}5$

10. $^{-}3 + {}^{-}1$

11. $^{-}6 + {}^{+}8$

12. $^{-}2 + {}^{-}3$

Copy and add. Use the number line. Drop the + sign for positive integers.

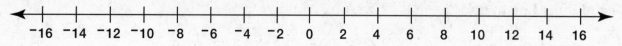

13. $10 + {}^{-}8$

14. $^{-}12 + 5$

15. $8 + 7$

16. $^{-}14 + 10$

17. $^{-}8 + {}^{-}8$

18. $^{+}6 + {}^{-}15$

19. $^{-}12 + {}^{-}4$

20. $^{-}8 + 12$

21. $18 + {}^{-}10$

22. $^{-}2 + {}^{-}12$

23. $14 + 4$

24. $^{-}12 + 6$

Problem Solving

Use integers to write an addition expression for each problem, then solve.

25. Mary had $15 in the bank. She deposited $25. Then she withdrew $12 for a new art set. How much money does she have left in the bank?

26. The temperature at sunset was 13°F. During the night, the temperature dropped 20 degrees. What was the temperature during the night?

Subtracting Integers

We can use a number line to show how subtracting
an integer is like adding the opposite integer.

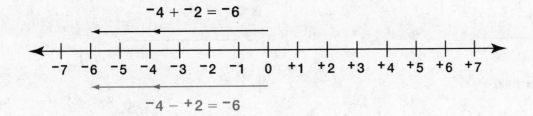

$$^-4 + \,^-2 = \,^-6$$

$$^-4 - \,^+2 = \,^-6$$

This shows the addition. $^-4 + \underline{\hspace{1cm}} = \,^-6$

This shows the subtraction. $^-4 - \underline{\hspace{1cm}} = \,^-6$

Subtracting $\underline{\hspace{1cm}}$ is just like adding $\underline{\hspace{1cm}}$.

REMEMBER To subtract an integer, add its opposite.

Change subtraction to addition.

$$^-4 - \,^+2 = \,^-4 + \,^-2 = \,^-6$$

Write the opposite.

Getting Started

Change each subtraction to an addition.

1. $^-4 - \,^+5 =$ _____

2. $^+7 - \,^+2 =$ _____

3. $^+9 - \,^-6 =$ _____

4. $^-8 - \,^-3 =$ _____

Subtract. Use the number line.

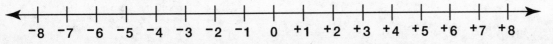

5. $^+6 - \,^-2$

6. $^-3 - \,^+3$

7. $^-5 - \,^-8$

8. $^+7 - \,^+9$

9. $^-8 - \,^-3$

10. $^+5 - \,^-3$

11. $^-6 - \,^+2$

12. $^+1 - \,^+7$

Practice

Change each subtraction to an addition.

1. $^-7 - {}^-5$ _____

2. $^+4 - {}^+6$ _____

3. $^-2 - {}^+9$ _____

4. $^+3 - {}^-7$ _____

5. $^+6 - {}^-2$ _____

6. $^-9 - {}^-5$ _____

Subtract. Use the number line.

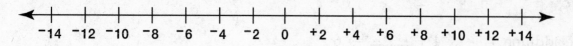

7. $^-2 - {}^-6$

8. $^+5 - {}^-3$

9. $^+5 - {}^+6$

10. $^-4 - {}^+3$

11. $^+6 - {}^-3$

12. $^-2 - {}^-8$

13. $^+5 - {}^+4$

14. $^+8 - {}^+5$

15. $^-9 + {}^+6$

16. $^+3 - {}^+10$

17. $^+7 - {}^-2$

18. $^-1 - {}^+7$

19. $^-8 - {}^-9$

20. $^+7 - {}^-3$

21. $^+8 - {}^+3$

22. $^-4 - {}^-4$

Problem Solving

Solve each problem.

23. Charley has $24 in his checking account. He tries to withdraw $31. Will the bank give him the money? What would be his new balance?

24. Mr. Brown is a baker. He starts the day with 14 pies. At the end of the day he has sold 35 pies. How many more pies did he have to make to be able to sell that many?

25. A scuba diver was 8 feet below the surface of the water. She went down another 5 feet. How far below the surface was she then?

Graphing Ordered Pairs

It's Algebra!

Ordered pairs are used to locate points on a grid. The pair (2, 4) names the point *A*.

We write: ***A*(2, 4)**.
What ordered pair names point *I*?

To find the ordered pair for point *I*, begin at the **origin** or 0. The first number tells how far to the right to go. The second number tells how far up the grid to go.

Point *I* is _____ to the right and _____ up.

The ordered pair for point *I* is _____.

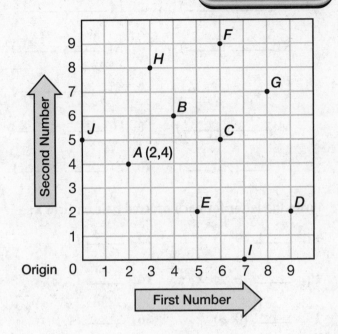

Getting Started

Write the ordered pair for each point. Use the grid above.

1. *B*(_____, _____)   **2.** *D*(_____, _____)   **3.** *G*(_____, _____)   **4.** *J*(_____, _____)

Write the letter for each ordered pair on the grid above.

5. _____ (6, 5)   **6.** _____ (6, 9)   **7.** _____ (5, 2)   **8.** _____ (3, 8)

Locate and label each point on Grid A.

9. *W*(5, 4)

10. *X*(4, 5)

11. *Y*(0, 3)

12. *Z*(7, 2)

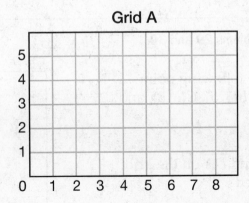

Grid A

Practice

Write the ordered pair for each point. Use Grid X.

1. C(_____ , _____) 2. E(_____ , _____)

3. K(_____ , _____) 4. X(_____ , _____)

5. F(_____ , _____) 6. A(_____ , _____)

7. M(_____ , _____) 8. H(_____ , _____)

9. D(_____ , _____) 10. Z(_____ , _____)

Write the letter for each ordered pair on Grid X.

11. _____ (9, 9)   12. _____ (3, 7)

13. _____ (6, 2)   14. _____ (3, 3)

15. _____ (0, 8)   16. _____ (4, 9)

17. _____ (8, 7)   18. _____ (9, 2)

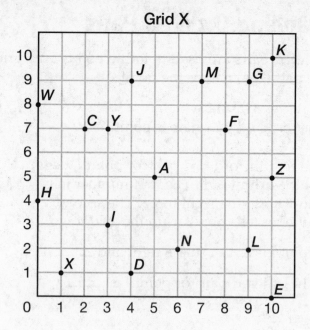

Grid X

Locate and label each point on Grid Y.

19. A(2, 7)   20. B(9, 6)

21. C(0, 5)   22. D(4, 4)

23. E(7, 4)   24. F(8, 2)

25. G(1, 8)   26. H(6, 0)

27. I(3, 3)   28. J(5, 1)

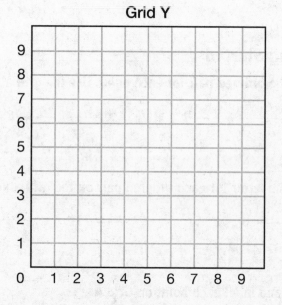

Grid Y

Problem Solving

Use Grid Z to complete Problems 29 and 30.

Grid Z

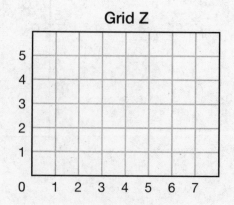

29. Locate and label the following points on the grid: A(2, 2), B(3, 5), C(6, 5), and D(7, 2).

30. Draw $\overline{AB}$, $\overline{BC}$, $\overline{CD}$, and $\overline{DA}$ on the grid. What figure is formed?

_____

Lesson 16-9 • Graphing Ordered Pairs

Name _____

Graphing a Rule

It's Algebra!

Alex collects comic books. He adds two books to his collection each week. The table shows how his collection grows.

x shows the number of comic books.

y shows the number of comic books plus two.

The table shows the relationship between pairs of numbers.

Complete the table to show *y* when Alex has 7 comic books.

What is *x*, if *y* is 15? _____

The rule for this table is add _____, or $y = x +$ _____.

x	y
1	3
3	5
5	7
7	

We can graph the rule by graphing the ordered pairs in the table. Then, connect the ordered pairs to form a line.

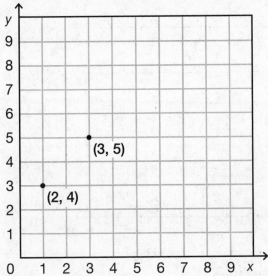

Getting Started

Use the rule to complete the table. Then, graph the rule.

1. $y = x - 2$

x	x − 2	y
2	2 − 2	0
4		2
6		4

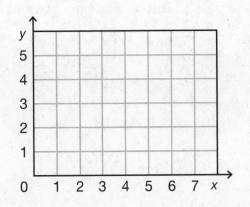

Practice

Follow the pattern to complete each table. Then, write the rule.

1.

x	y
1	7
2	8
3	9
4	
5	

rule: _____

2.

x	y
20	15
17	12
14	9
11	
8	

rule: _____

3.

x	y
1	12
5	16
7	18
9	
11	

rule: _____

Use the rule to complete the table. Then, graph the rule.

4. $y = x - 3$

x	x − 3	y
3		
5		
7		

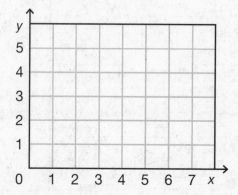

5. $y = 5 - x$

x	5 − x	y
5		
3		
1		
0		

Problem Solving

Make a table of values for the problem. Then, graph the values.

6. Michael has $10 in a savings account. He puts $5 into his savings account each week.

x	y
0	$10
1	

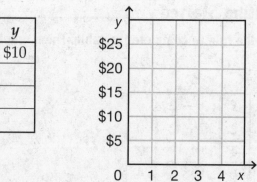

Name _____

Problem Solving: Review the Four-Step Plan

The four-step plan can help us to be better problem solvers. A review of this plan can remind us of ways to use it.

⭐ **SEE**

We state what we want to know, preferably in our own words. We state all the facts we know that will help us solve the problem.

⭐ **PLAN**

We think about the problem and the important facts and choose a plan to help us find a solution. Among the plans that will help us to solve a problem are:

Draw a picture or a diagram
Make a model with manipulatives or on paper
Act out the problem
Make a systematic listing or a table
Make a tally or graph
Look for a pattern
Determine missing or extra data
Collect needed data
Choose an operation
Write an equation
Use a formula
Guess, check, and revise
Work backward
Solve a simpler but related problem
Identify a subgoal
Restate the problem in our own words

Diagram? Pattern? Data? Formula?

⭐ **DO**

We carry out the plan and reach a solution to the problem.

⭐ **CHECK**

We check the problem for careless errors.
We see if the solution is reasonable.
We look for another way to solve the problem.

Apply

Solve each problem.

1. In a theater, the front row has 40 seats, with each successive row containing two more seats than the row in front of it. If the last row has 100 seats, how many rows are in the theater?

2. Fence posts are placed in a straight line 10 feet apart. How many posts are required to support 100 feet of fence?

3. A plane leaves Cleveland for Dallas at an average speed of 350 miles per hour. At the same time, a plane leaves Dallas, flying toward Cleveland at 300 miles per hour. When the planes pass, which one is closer to Cleveland?

4. Fran has 12 coins. Some are nickels, some are dimes, and some are quarters. How many of each coin does Fran have if the value of the coins totals $1.15?

5. A bag contains 4 red and 6 blue marbles. Without looking, you reach in and pick a marble, note the color, and return the marble to the bag. You do this 20 times. How many times can you expect to pick a red marble?

> ### Problem-Solving Strategy: Using the Four-Step Plan
> ★ **SEE** What do you need to find?
> ★ **PLAN** What do you need to do?
> ★ **DO** Follow the plan.
> ★ **CHECK** Does your answer make sense?

6. The cafeteria offers soup and sandwiches for lunch. You can have tomato, bean, or noodle soup with a ham, turkey, beef, or cheese sandwich. How many choices do you have if you already decided to take the bean soup?

7. The weather forecaster on television says there is a 40% chance of rain tomorrow. Is it more likely to rain or not rain? Explain how you decided.

8. There are 12 cows and geese on a farm. If there are twice as many cows as there are geese, what is the ratio of cow legs to goose legs?

Write an algebraic expression for each verbal expression.

1. a increased by 8

2. 10 less than n

Evaluate each algebraic expression for $x = 7$.

3. $x + 15$

4. $9x$

5. $84 \div x$

6. $31 - x$

Solve each equation.

7. $n + 8 = 25$

$n = $ _____

8. $19 = a - 5$

$a = $ _____

9. $114 + b = 143$

$b = $ _____

10. $7y = 49$

$y = $ _____

11. $\frac{n}{5} = 6$

$n = $ _____

12. $p \div 12 = 11$

$p = $ _____

Add or subtract. Use the number line.

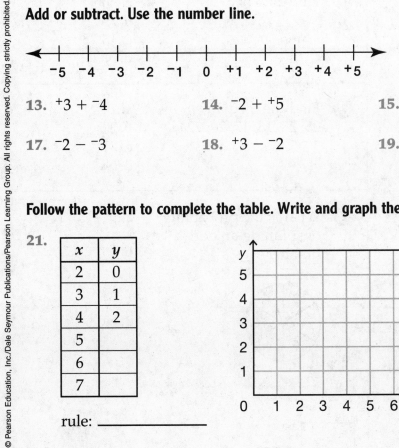

13. $^+3 + {}^-4$

14. $^-2 + {}^+5$

15. $^+1 + {}^-1$

16. $^-2 + {}^-3$

17. $^-2 - {}^-3$

18. $^+3 - {}^-2$

19. $^-3 - {}^+1$

20. $^+3 - {}^+1$

Follow the pattern to complete the table. Write and graph the rule.

21.

x	y
2	0
3	1
4	2
5	
6	
7	

rule: _____

Circle the letter of the correct answer.

1. $40.58
   ×   25

a. $1,014.50
b. $283.06
c. $10,145
d. NG

2.   4 ft 5 in.
   + 6 ft 8 in.

a. 11 ft 3 in.
b. 11 ft 2 in.
c. 11 ft 1 in.
d. NG

3. Simplify.
$\frac{58}{8}$

a. 7
b. $7\frac{1}{4}$
c. $7\frac{1}{8}$
d. NG

4. $\frac{1}{5}$
$+ \frac{2}{3}$

a. $\frac{3}{8}$
b. $\frac{3}{5}$
c. $\frac{13}{15}$
d. NG

5. $3\frac{3}{4}$
$- 2\frac{5}{8}$

a. $1\frac{1}{4}$
b. $1\frac{1}{8}$
c. $\frac{11}{8}$
d. NG

6. $\frac{5}{6} \times \frac{3}{8}$

a. $\frac{10}{8}$
b. $\frac{10}{24}$
c. $\frac{7}{48}$
d. NG

7. $1.235 + 2.04 + 0.5$

a. 37.75
b. 3.775
c. 1.424
d. NG

8. $2.5 \overline{)5.65}$

a. 0.226
b. 0.33
c. 2.26
d. NG

9. Find the missing number.
$\frac{n}{6} = \frac{18}{36}$

a. $n = 3$
b. $n = 12$
c. $n = 18$
d. NG

10. Find 20% of 375.

a. 300
b. 75
c. 18.75
d. NG

11. Find the median.
25, 23, 18, 17, 20, 22

a. 19
b. 20
c. 21
d. NG

12. What is the probability of spinning an odd number?

a. $\frac{1}{6}$
b. $\frac{2}{3}$
c. $\frac{1}{2}$
d. NG

☐ **score**

STOP

Glossary

A

acute angle an angle that measures less than 90° (p. 259)

addend a number that is added to another number (p. 1)

In 3 + 4 = 7, 3 and 4 are both addends.

algebraic expression a mathematical phrase that consists of variables, numbers, and operations (p. 345)

angle the figure formed by two rays with a common endpoint called the vertex (p. 259)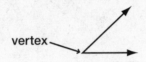

vertex

arc a part of the circumference of a circle (p. 265)

area the measure of a surface surrounded by a boundary (p. 119)

The shaded part of the square is its area.

Associative Property When the grouping of three or more addends or factors is changed, the sum or product remains the same. (pp. 3, 41)

(2 + 5) + 1 = 2 + (5 + 1)

or

(5 × 3) × 2 = 5 × (3 × 2)

average the number obtained by adding two or more quantities and dividing by the number of quantities added (pp. 85, 325)

B

bar graph a representation of numerical facts using lengths of bars to show information (p. 323)

base (of a geometric figure) a side of a plane figure or face of a solid figure (pp. 121, 287)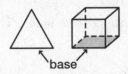

base

bisect to divide into two equal parts (p. 267)

C

centimeter (cm) a metric unit of length (p. 127)

100 centimeters = 1 meter

central angle an angle formed by the center and two radii of a circle (p. 265)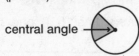

central angle

chord a line segment connecting two points on a circle (p. 265)

$\overline{AB}$ is a chord.

circle a plane figure bounded by a curved line made up of points all the same distance from the center (p. 265)

circle graph a representation of numerical facts using parts or sections of a circle to show information (p. 329)

circumference the distance around a circle (p. 265)

common factor a number that is a factor of two or more given numbers (p. 67)

Commutative Property The order of addends or factors does not change the sum or product. (pp. 3, 41)

5 + 7 = 7 + 5 or 3 × 4 = 4 × 3

composite number a whole number greater than 1 that has more than two factors (p. 69)

cone a solid figure with a circle for its base and a curved surface that forms a point (p. 287)

congruent a word that describes figures, sides, or angles having the same size and shape (p. 279)

cube a solid figure with six equal, square sides (p. 287)

customary units standard measures of length, weight, volume, and capacity (pp. 113, 115, 125)

Inches, miles, pounds, cubic feet, and ounces are examples of customary units.

cylinder a solid figure with two congruent circular bases and a curved rectangular region (p. 287)

D

data numerical information collected for a purpose (p. 321)

decimal a fractional part that uses place value and a decimal point to show tenths, hundredths, and so on (p. 209)

0.6 is the decimal equivalent for the fraction $\frac{3}{5}$.

denominator the number below the line in a fraction (p. 137)

In $\frac{3}{5}$, 5 is the denominator.

diagonal a segment that connects two vertices of a polygon but is not a side (p. 277)

diameter a chord passing through the center of a circle (p. 265)

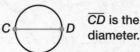

$\overline{CD}$ is the diameter.

difference the answer in a subtraction problem (p. 1)

digit any of the symbols used to write numbers; 0, 1, 2, 3, 4, 5, 6, 7, 8, and 9 (p. 7)

dividend the number that is being divided in a division problem (p. 71)

In $42 \div 7 = 6$, 42 is the dividend.

divisible A number is divisible by another number when the remainder is 0 after dividing. (p. 68)

divisor the number that is being divided into the dividend (p. 71)

In $42 \div 7 = 6$, 7 is the divisor.

E

edge a segment that is the side of a face on a solid figure (p. 287)

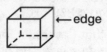

equilateral triangle a triangle with three equal sides (p. 273)

equivalent fractions fractions that name the same number (p. 139)

$\frac{3}{4}$ and $\frac{9}{12}$ are equivalent fractions.

evaluate to find the value of an expression (p. 347)

even number a whole number that is divisible by 2 (p. 44)

2, 4, 6, 8, 10, 12, . . . are even numbers.

expanded form a number written as the sum of its place values (p. 7)

426 is $400 + 20 + 6$ or $(4 \times 100) + (2 \times 10) + (6 \times 1)$.

exponent a raised number that tells how many times the base number is used as a factor (p. 70)

exponent
$4^3 = 4 \times 4 \times 4$

expression a mathematical sentence sometimes written with letters instead of numbers (p. 347)

$a + b = c$ is an expression.

F

face a plane figure making up part of a solid figure (p. 287)

factor a number to be multiplied (p. 41)

In $2 \times 3 = 6$, both 2 and 3 are factors.

factor tree a diagram used to show the prime factors of a number (p. 69)

formula a rule expressed using symbols (p. 203)

G

graphing drawing a picture of relationships among numbers and quantities (pp. 321–324, 327–332)

greater than a comparison of two numbers with the number of greater value written first (p. 9)

$10 > 5, \frac{7}{8} > \frac{3}{4}$

greatest common factor (GCF) the largest number that is a common factor of two or more numbers (p. 67)

$12 = 3 \times 4 \qquad 15 = 3 \times 5$

3 is the GCF of 12 and 15.

H

hexagon a plane figure with six straight sides and six angles (p. 277)

height (of a parallelogram) the shortest distance between the opposite sides (p. 121)

height (of a triangle) the shortest distance between a vertex and the opposite side or the line containing the opposite side (p. 121)

height (of a rectangular prism) a side of the prism (p. 123)

I

Identity Property Any number added to zero is that number; any number multiplied by one is that number. (pp. 3, 41)

$7 + 0 = 7$ or $7 \times 1 = 7$

improper fraction a fraction whose numerator is larger in value than the denominator (p. 151)

$\frac{6}{5}$ and $\frac{14}{3}$ are improper fractions.

integer a number such as $^-5$, 0, and $^+5$ (p. 355)

intersect to meet and cross over at a point (p. 263)

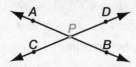

Line *AB* intersects line *CD* at point *P*.

inverse operations operations that undo each other (pp. 3, 63)

isosceles triangle a triangle with two equal sides (p. 273)

K

kilogram (kg) a metric unit of weight (p. 131)

1 kilogram = 1,000 grams

kilometer (km) a metric unit of length (p. 129)

1 kilometer = 1,000 meters

L

least common multiple (LCM) the smallest number that is a common multiple of two or more numbers (p. 43)

The LCM of 4 and 6 is 12.

less than a comparison of two numbers with the number of lesser value written first (p. 9)

$3 < 10, \frac{1}{8} < \frac{7}{8}$

line a set of points whose straight path extends indefinitely in opposite directions (p. 257)

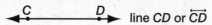

line *CD* or $\overleftrightarrow{CD}$

line graph a representation of numerical facts using points and lines on a grid to show information (p. 327)

line of symmetry a line that equally divides a figure to produce a mirror image (p. 281)

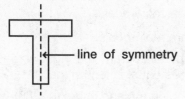

line of symmetry

line plot a graph that shows each item of information on a number line (p. 321)

line segment a part of a line having two endpoints (p. 257)

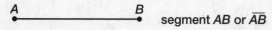

segment *AB* or $\overline{AB}$

liter (L) a basic metric unit of a liquid measure (p. 131)

1 liter = 1,000 milliliters

M

mean a number representing the average of a group of numbers (p. 325)

median the middle number in a series of numbers (p. 325)

$$5, 9, 17, 31, 50$$
$$\uparrow$$
median

meter (m) a basic metric unit of length (p. 129)

1 meter = 100 centimeters

metric units measures of length, weight, volume, and capacity based on the decimal system (pp. 127–132)

Meters, grams, and liters are basic metric units.

midpoint the point halfway between the endpoints of a line segment (p. 267)

milliliter (mL) a metric unit of liquid measure (p. 131)

1 milliliter = $\frac{1}{1000}$ liter

minuend a number or quantity from which another is subtracted (p. 1)

In $18 - 5 = 13$, 18 is the minuend.

mixed number a fractional number greater than 1 that is written as a whole number and a fraction (p. 147)

$5\frac{2}{3}$ is a mixed number.

mode the most frequent number in a set of data (p. 325)

multiple the product of any given number and a whole number (p. 43)

$10 \times 3 = 30, 10 \times 5 = 50$

30 and 50 are multiples of 10.

N

numerator the number above the line in a fraction (p. 137)

In $\frac{3}{5}$, 3 is the numerator.

O

obtuse angle an angle that measures between 90° and 180° (p. 259)

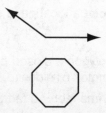

octagon a plane figure with eight sides and eight angles (p. 277)

odd number a whole number that is not divisible by 2 (p. 44)

3, 5, 7, 9, 11, 13, . . . are odd numbers.

opposites numbers that are the same distance away from zero on the number line (p. 355)

Order of Operations the order in which we do operations (p. 65)

Do the operations inside parentheses.

Multiply and divide in order from left to right.

Add and subtract in order from left to right.

ordered pair two numbers that define one point on a grid; the first number names the distance across, and the second names the distance up (p. 361)

origin the point on a grid represented by the ordered pair (0, 0) (p. 361)

P

parallel lines lines in the same plane that do not intersect (p. 263)

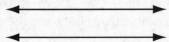

parallelogram a quadrilateral having two pairs of opposite, congruent, parallel sides (pp. 121, 275)

pentagon a plane figure with five straight sides and five angles (p. 277)

percent a word meaning "hundredths" (p. 303)

37 percent is written 37% and means 0.37 or $\frac{37}{100}$.

perimeter the distance around a shape that is the sum of the lengths of all of its sides (p. 117)

The perimeter of this rectangle is equal to 10 units.

$$1 \begin{array}{|c|} \hline 4 \\ \hline 4 \\ \end{array} 1$$

perpendicular lines lines that form right angles where they intersect (p. 263)

place value The value of a digit depends upon its position in a numeral. (p. 7)

plane a flat surface having infinite length and width (p. 257)

point a location in space (p. 257)

•B   point B

polygon a closed plane figure having three or more angles or sides (p. 277)

prime factor a factor that is a prime number (p. 69)

The prime factors for 60 are 2, 3, and 5.

prime number a counting number greater than 1 whose only factors are itself and 1 (p. 69)

$1 \times 17 = 17$ $1 \times 3 = 3$

17 and 3 are prime numbers.

probability a number that tells how likely it is that a certain event will happen (p. 333)

product the answer to a multiplication problem (p. 41)

product of primes the prime factors that equal a composite number when multiplied (p. 69)

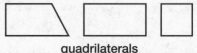

proportion an equation showing that two ratios are equal (p. 299)

If $\frac{a}{b} = \frac{c}{d}$, then $a \times d = b \times c$

Q

quadrilateral a plane figure with four straight lines and four angles (p. 275)

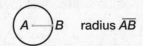

quadrilaterals

quotient the answer to a division problem (p. 71)

R

radius a segment whose endpoints are the center of the circle and a point on the circle (p. 265)

(A──B)   radius $\overline{AB}$

ratio a comparison of two quantities (p. 295)

The ratio of 3 to 4 can be written $\frac{3}{4}$.

ray a part of a line having one endpoint (p. 257)

E   F   ray EF or $\overrightarrow{EF}$

reciprocal When the product of two numbers is 1, they are called reciprocals of each other (p. 195)

$\frac{5}{8}$ and $\frac{8}{5}$ are reciprocals.

4 and $\frac{1}{4}$ are reciprocals.

rectangle a parallelogram with right angles and opposite sides equal in length (pp. 119, 275)

reflection flipping a plane figure (p. 283)

regular polygon a polygon with all sides of equal length and all angles of equal measure (p. 277)

remainder the number left over in a division problem (p. 71)

$$\begin{array}{r} 16 \text{ R4} \\ 6{\overline{\smash{\big)}\,100}} \\ \underline{-6} \\ 40 \\ \underline{-36} \\ 4 \end{array}$$

In the example above, 4 is the remainder.

rhombus a parallelogram with all sides congruent (p. 275)

 rhombus

right angle an angle that measures exactly 90° (p. 259)

In this square, all four angles are right angles.

 90° ← right angle

rotation turning a plane figure (p. 283)

rounding estimating a number's value by raising or lowering any of its place values (p. 13)

S

scale drawing a representation of an actual object using proportional measurements (p. 301)

scalene triangle a triangle with no sides the same length and no angles the same measure (p. 273)

semicircle a half circle (p. 277)

similar figures plane figures that have the same shape but not necessarily the same size or position (p. 285)

Figures *A* and *B* are similar.

simplest terms a fraction or mixed number whose numerator and denominator cannot be divided by any common factor other than 1 (p. 143)

simplest form   simplest form
↓   ↓
$$\frac{12}{36} = \frac{1}{3} \qquad \frac{34}{6} = 5\frac{4}{6} = 5\frac{2}{3}$$

simplify to rename a fraction in simplest terms (pp. 143, 149)

solid figure a figure that is in more than one plane (p. 287)

cube   pyramid   cylinder

solve to find the value of a variable in an equation (p. 349)

sphere a solid, round figure having a surface equally distant from its center at all points (p. 287)

square a rectangle with four sides equal in length (p. 275)

standard form a number written using the symbols 0 through 9 in place-value form (p. 7)

4,036 is in standard form.

statistics numerical facts selected and compiled to present information (p. 321)

stem-and-leaf plot a graph that groups together all data with the same number of tens (p. 331)

straight angle an angle that measures 180° (p. 261)

substitute to replace a variable with a number (p. 347)

subtrahend the number that is subtracted from the minuend (p. 1)

sum the answer to an addition problem (p. 1)

survey a way to collect data to answer a question. (p. 321)

symmetry A figure has symmetry if it can be folded along a line so that both parts match exactly. (p. 281)

T

tally marks used to count (p. 323)

terms the numerator and the denominator of a fraction (p. 137)

transformation sliding, flipping, or turning a plane figure (p. 283)

translation sliding a plane figure (p. 283)

trapezoid a quadrilateral having one pair of parallel sides (p. 275)

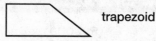 trapezoid

triangle a three-sided polygon (p. 273)

U

unit price the cost per unit of weight or volume (p. 155)

V

variable a letter used to stand for a number (p. 345)

vertex (pl. vertices) the point at which two sides of an angle, two sides of a plane figure, or three or more sides of a solid figure meet (pp. 259, 277, 287)

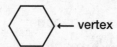 ← vertex

Volume the number of cubic units needed to fill a solid figure (p. 123)

Z

Zero Property of Multiplication If a factor is zero, the quotient will be zero. (p. 41)

TABLES OF MEASURES

Metric Measures

	Unit	Symbol	Relationship
Length	kilometer	km	1 km = 1,000 m
	meter	m	1 m = 100 cm
	centimeter	cm	1 cm = 10 mm
	millimeter	mm	
Mass	metric ton	t	1 t = 1,000 kg
	gram	g	1 g = 1,000 mg
	milligram	mg	
	kilogram	kg	1 kg = 1,000 g
Capacity	liter	L	1 L = 1,000 mL
	milliliter	mL	
Volume	cubic centimeters	cm³	1 cm³ = 1 mL = 1 g
Temperature	Celsius	°C	Water freezes at 0°C. Water boils at 100°C.

Time

Unit	Symbol	Relationship
second	s	
minute	min	1 min = 60 s
hour	h	1 h = 60 min
day	d	1 d = 24 h
week	wk	1 wk = 7 d
month	mo	1 mo = approximately 4 wk
year	yr	1 yr = 12 mo
		= 365 d
		= 366 d in a leap year
decade		10 yr
century		100 yr

Common Fraction/Decimal Equivalents

$\frac{1}{8} = 0.125$ $\qquad$ $\frac{3}{8} = 0.375$ $\qquad$ $\frac{5}{8} = 0.625$ $\qquad$ $\frac{1}{5} = 0.2$

$\frac{1}{4} = 0.25$ $\qquad$ $\frac{1}{2} = 0.5$ $\qquad$ $\frac{3}{4} = 0.75$ $\qquad$ $\frac{1}{10} = 0.1$

© Pearson Education, Inc./Dale Seymour Publications/Pearson Learning Group. All rights reserved. Copying strictly prohibited.

TABLES OF MEASURES

Customary Measures

	Unit	Symbol	Relationship
Length	inch	in.	
	foot	ft	1 ft = 12 in.
	yard	yd	1 yd = 3 ft
			= 36 in.
	mile	mi	1 mi = 5,280 ft
			= 1,760 yd
Weight	ounce	oz	
	pound	lb	16 oz = 1 lb
	ton	T	1 T = 2,000 lb
Liquid Measure	teaspoon	tsp	
	tablespoon	tbs	1 tbs = 3 tsp
	fluid ounce	fl oz	1 fl oz = 2 tbs
	cup	c	1 c = 8 fl oz
	pint	pt	1 pt = 2 c
			= 16 fl oz
	quart	qt	1 qt = 2 pt
			= 32 fl oz
	gallon	gal	1 gal = 4 qt
			= 8 pt
Dry Measure	pint	pt	
	quart	qt	1 qt = 2 pt
	peck	pk	1 pk = 8 qt
	bushel	bu	1 bu = 4 pk
Temperature	Fahrenheit	°F	Water freezes at 32°F.
			Water boils at 212°F.

Measurement Formula

	Figure	Formula	
Area	parallelogram	$A = b \times h$	Area = base × height
	rectangle	$A = l \times w$	Area = length × width
	triangle	$A = \frac{1}{2}b \times h$	Area = $\frac{1}{2}$base × height
Volume	rectangular prism	$V = l \times w \times h$	Volume = length × width × height

Index